ELIZABETHAN LIFE:

MORALS & THE CHURCH COURTS

ISBN No. 0 900360 41 0

To

the late HENRY HAMILTON GEPP and his son
THOMAS CHRISTOPHER GEPP, T.D., M.A.

Solicitors and Registrars of the Essex Archdeaconries

through whose goodwill the Essex Record Office has much benefited,
not least by the transfer of the Archidiaconal Records

Essex Record Office Publications No. 63

1 MODERN SEALS OF TWO OF THE THREE ESSEX ARCHDEACONRIES
depicted in Memorial Window to Mr. H. H. Gepp, the Registrar, 1971 (Chelmsford Cathedral).

ELIZABETHAN LIFE:

MORALS & THE CHURCH COURTS

Mainly from Essex Archidiaconal Records

F. G. EMMISON

Author of *Elizabethan Life: Disorder*

Chelmsford
Essex County Council
1973

Printed by

Benham and Company Limited, Colchester, Essex, England

Contents

ERRATUM
Introduction, page vii, line 2
for triology *read* trilogy

Introduction

It is probably desirable at the outset to repeat from *Elizabethan Life: Disorder* the broad aims of the intended triology: 'My commission from the Essex County Council, briefly, is to include as much information as possible from the original records . . . selecting what appears to be of value to the specialist and of interest to the general reader. . . . The volumes are therefore primarily source books. Owing to the immense number of documents' (or, in the present volume, entries), 'it was imperative to restrict editorial comment to a minimum. Only a fraction of the material has previously appeared in print, so that the reader is presented with a big corpus of new evidence.'[1] Volume II, like Volume I, I confess, has exceeded my allotted length, but so far my Authority has not decreed the penitential white sheet for me! Conclusions have again been restricted to relatively few passages; my terms of reference, in fact, preclude evaluation, which is left to scholars who are experts in their own fields. The essential aim has been to incorporate in the narrative account the original language wherever its intrinsic content or interest seems to call for it, while briefly dealing with or omitting 'common form' and repetitive material: generally, to prefer the record to a paraphrase.

The two surviving series of court books of the Archdeaconries of Essex and Colchester, in the Essex Record Office, which are nearly complete for the Elizabethan period except for the early years, contain approximately 100,000 entries. Even allowing for the fact that some entries of cases are repeated many times owing to parties' non-appearance, publication of any form of edited transcripts would have been out of question. Even an edition in calendar form would cost, at present levels alone, about £80,000. Fortunately, those who need a transcript or calendar of about the same period may study the content of court books for several other archdeaconries that have been printed, those edited by Professor Jenkins and Dr. Brinkworth having valuable introductions.[2] But each of these publica-

[1] *Elizabethan Life: Disorder* (1970), p. vii.

[2] R. E. B. Hodgkinson, 'Extracts from the Act Books of the Archdeacons of Nottingham' (*Trans. Thoroton Soc.*, xxxi, 1927); Claude Jenkins, 'The Act Book of the Archdeacon of Taunton, 1623–4' (*Som. Rec. Soc.*, xliii, 1928); F. G. Emmison, 'Abstract of the Act Book of the Archdeacon of Huntingdon's Court–Hertfordshire cases, 1590–2' (*Trans. East Herts. Archl. Soc.*, viii, 1928–33); E. R. C. Brinkworth, 'The Archdeacon's Court: Liber Actorum, 1584' (*Oxfordshire Rec. Soc.*, xxiii–iv, 1942–6); Brinkworth, *Shakespeare and the Bawdy Court of Stratford* [12 years between 1590 and 1625] (Phillimore, 1972); for the Henrician period, Alice M. Cooke, 'Act Book of the Ecclesiastical Court of Whalley [Lancs. and Cheshire], 1510–38' (*Chetham Soc.*, n.s., xliv, 1901). P. Hair (ed.), *Before the Bawdy Court: Selections from Church Court and other Records relating to the correction of moral offences in England, Scotland and New England, 1300–1800* (1972), which appeared while the present book was in the press, consists of extracts from printed sources.

tion, except that for Nottinghamshire, deals only with one or two volumes: the present account attempts, however inadequately, to cover the 58 Elizabethan volumes containing an average of 450 pages. In this connexion, Mrs. Owen recently observed, 'Since to some extent all ordinaries, whether episcopal or otherwise, performed similar functions, their records are, with some slight divergences of form and title, very like each other'.[1] The procedure in church courts (both consistory and archidiaconal) is set out in detail in several standard works.[2]

Such indication of the rich Essex material as was published earlier is virtually limited to a few articles in the *Essex Review* on penance, perambulations, apparitors, churchyard and seating disputes, and marriage causes, and to a brief general account.[3] The only other printed Essex material is in Archdeacon Hale's book, which for some mysterious reason is extremely rare.[4] This paucity of printed evidence is undoubtedly due to the obstacle of handwriting. Archdeacons' court books are among the most difficult archives to decipher (even plates 4 and 6 are relatively easy). Many of them reveal highly abbreviated Latin forms, and the writing is often atrocious because the record was usually made as each case proceeded and was sometimes so hastily scrawled as to be almost illegible to students unfamiliar with such act books. Two redeeming features, however, are that much of the language taken from the churchwardens' presentments is often entered in English and the deposition books are almost wholly in English.

Fortunately, specialist scholars and Essex students may now consult Dr. Anglin's thesis based on the court books of one archdeaconry – that of Essex.[5] Since its completion, Dr. Anglin has extended his research into the records of the Archdeaconry of Colchester, and he hopes to prepare a book covering both. This, like his thesis, will concentrate largely on the administrative machinery of the courts and on the clergy, especially their liturgical and ritual offences. In consequence, and because *Elizabethan Life* is concerned primarily with social and not institutional history, I have in general paid less attention to the aspects especially studied by Dr. Anglin.

The Archdeacon of Essex had jurisdiction over the deaneries of Barking, Ongar, Chafford, Barstable, Chelmsford, Dengie and Rochford (broadly,

[1] D. Owen, *The Records of the Established Church* (Brit. Rec. Ass., 1970), 12. See also E. R. C. Brinkworth, 'The Study and Use of Archdeacons' Court Records, 1556–1759' (*Trans. Roy. Hist. Soc.*, 4th ser., xxv (1943)) and the works cited in the preceding note.

[2] For example, H. Conset, *The Practice of the Spiritual Courts* (2nd. edn., 1700), T. Oughton, *Ordo Judiciorum* (2 vols. 1728–38), and H. C. Coote, *The Practice of the Ecclesiastical Courts* (1847).

[3] *Essex Review*, vols. xxxv, xlv–vi, xlviii–ix (1926–40); *V.C.H., Essex*, ii, 41–5.

[4] W. H. Hale, *A Series of Precedents and Proceedings extracted from the Act Books of the Ecclesiastical Courts in the Diocese of London* (1847). The *Bibliography* volume of *V.C.H., Essex* shows no copy in any Essex library; a photographic copy is now in the E.R.O. For an index of Essex parishes, see *Trans. E.A.S.*, xix, 308–10.

[5] J. Anglin, 'The Court of the Archdeacon of Essex, 1571–1609' (University of California Ph.D. thesis, 1965), a copy of which the author presented to the E.R.O.

central and S. Essex), except the peculiars and those parishes exclusively subject to the Commissary (or Deputy) of the Bishop of London 'in Essex and Hertfordshire'. (He sometimes exercised concurrent jurisdiction in 'archidiaconal' parishes, and for some of these he acquired exclusive jurisdiction in the Elizabethan period.) The Archdeacon of Colchester controlled the deaneries of Colchester, Tendring, Witham, Lexden, Sampford and Newport (N.E. and N.W., but not N., Essex), with the same exceptions. (See map inside back cover.) Two Essex parishes – Epping and Waltham Holy Cross – were subject to the Commissary of the Bishop 'in London, Middlesex and Barking'.[1]

There are *no* surviving Elizabethan records for the following jurisdictions (see map): (a) the Archdeacon of Middlesex (Essex and Hertfordshire division), whose area extended over the deaneries of Dunmow, Harlow and Hedingham (W. and N., but not N.W., Essex), and Braughing (E. Herts.), with similar exceptions; (b) (except for a single act book of 1561–2) the Commissary of the Bishop 'in Essex and Hertfordshire', whose exclusive territory comprised 26 scattered Essex parishes; (c) the peculiars of the deanery of Bocking (9 parishes in Essex and Suffolk), Writtle with Roxwell, and the Sokens (Kirby, Thorpe and Walton).[2]

Expressed in general terms, approximately one-third of the Essex parishes are therefore not represented in the present book. These parishes are also given in the Index of Places. Furthermore, the Bishop of London's Consistory court had concurrent jurisdiction with the Archdeacons' and the Commissary's courts over the whole diocese, except the peculiars.[3] Nevertheless in London, as in the extensive dioceses of Lincoln and Norwich, the archdeacons exercised considerable authority in matters delegated by the bishop, and in many respects their jurisdiction was almost co-ordinate with, rather than subordinate to, that of the bishop within their own territories. For some offences, especially recusancy, they also had concurrent jurisdiction with the justices of the peace in the court of Quarter Sessions, as already related in *Elizabethan Life: Disorder*.

It is important to note that the archidiaconal courts cited very few members of the gentry and upper class except in cases of subtraction of tithes, non-repair of chancels by lay rectors, non-attendance at church or communion (especially recusants), and testamentary and occasionally

[1] The relevant archives comprise act books, 1582–1603, and deposition books, 1562–1603 (in the Guildhall Library). These have not been examined by the writer.

[2] The jurisdictions and extant archidiaconal archives (including also wills and marriage licences) are given in Emmison, *Guide to the Essex Record Office* (revd. edn., 1969), 70–8. For other details, see *V.C.H.*, *Essex*, ii, 81–3; R. Newcourt, *Repertorium Ecclesiasticum Parochiale Londinense* (1710), ii, 1–2; and A. J. Camp, *Wills and their Whereabouts* (1963).

[3] The relevant Consistory court records comprise act books, 1558–1603, with gaps, and deposition books, 1566–1603, with gaps; some of the volumes are at present unfit for production (in the Greater London Record Office). They have only been briefly examined by the writer: depositions of Essex people number about 100, but the other books yield no Essex names. About 70 Essex wills (including clergy) are in *London Consistory Court Wills, 1492–1547* (ed. I. Darlington, *London Rec. Soc.*, iii, 1967).

other offences. Even so, gentry who were thus cited rarely appeared in person, but engaged court proctors. Persons of substance normally went before the consistory court, especially in contentious causes, and do not seem to have been bothered in *pro salute animæ* matters by any ecclesiastical court, except occasionally by the High Commission, at which they were also represented by proctors.

The following are the extant records which have been used:

Archdeacon of Essex
Act books: 1561–80 (very nearly complete), 1583–93, 1595–1603. (22 volumes, D/AEA 1A–22.)
Visitation books: 1565 (detailed), 1580–1603 (names of clergy, churchwardens, sidesmen and schoolteachers only). (3 vols., D/AEV 1–3.)
Deposition books: 1576–1603. (4 vols., D/AED 1–4.)
Excommunication book: 1590–1602. (D/AEM 3.)

Archdeacon of Colchester
Act books: 1569–1603 (very nearly complete). (24 vols., D/ACA 3–26.)
Deposition book: 1587–92 (decayed and almost illegible). (D/ACD 1.)
(Depositions, 1569–73, are at the end of the relevant act books.)

Commissary of the Bishop of London
Act book: 1561–2 (included in Wills register D/ABR 4).

Very few 'loose' papers have been preserved (see illustrations nos. 10–12).

There are also preserved Cause (i.e. suit) books for the archdeaconry of Essex, 1581–1603 (5 vols., D/AEC 1–5) and for the archdeaconry of Colchester, 1588–1603 (5 vols., D/ACC 2–6). Causes thus recorded do not appear generally in the Act books. (Early causes are in the Act books; the presumption is that the increasing volume of business prompted this division of court minutes.) They are mostly contentious suits relating to probate, tithes and defamation. These volumes are entirely in Latin, much condensed. Unlike the Act books, they wholly lack lively details. The entries are entirely procedural, recording the various stages or juridical acts in the suits, and the technicalities involved in these cases yield virtually nothing of interest to the social historian. The Cause books have not been studied by the writer, but as they record the stages in the case they would be useful to some students as quantitative evidence.

Nearly all sessions were held in parish churches. Typical itineraries of the court of the Archdeacon of Essex in two successive years were:

1563. 11 Oct., Barking; 12 Oct., Aveley; 13 Oct., High Ongar; 14 Oct., Great Baddow; 15 Oct., All Saints, Maldon; 16 Oct., Rayleigh; 3 Nov., Romford.

1564. 21 Feb., Barking; 22 Feb., Brentwood; 23 Feb., High Ongar; 24 Feb., Great Baddow; 25 Feb., All Saints, Maldon; 28 Feb., Rayleigh; 1 March, Romford.

All these were market-towns except Great Baddow, where the courts were held instead of in Chelmsford church, because the latter parish was subject to the Bishop of London's Commissary. On the other hand, although Romford was in the New College, Oxford, peculiar of Hornchurch and in the royal liberty of Havering, which comprised the parish of Hornchurch (including Romford and Havering) and was nominally exempt from the Archdeacon's jurisdiction, by long tradition he was given special leave to hold his sessions at Romford; and this was reaffirmed at the manor court of Havering in 1560.[1] The sessions of the Archdeacon of Colchester were held only at St. Peter's church, Colchester, and Kelvedon for one circuit and at Saffron Walden for the other.[2]

The business set out in the act books arose mostly from cases of 'correction' originating in the churchwardens' returns to the articles of enquiry delivered to them at the visitations. Presentments were submitted not only of provable facts but also on 'fame' (rumour), 'vehement suspicion', or merely 'suspicion'. The inherent weakness of proceedings based on such evidence will be amply illustrated. The next step was a citation to appear at court. When an apparitor was unable to serve it or the party could not be found, the judge issued a further citation to be served '*viis et modis*' (by any possible ways and means, such as affixing the document on his door or the church door). On attendance at court, the oath *ex officio* was administered, by which the accused was required to tell all he knew regarding the charge in response to a detailed inquisition. It was often complained that this oath presupposed the accused's guilt. Judgement might be postponed to the next session. If guilt was acknowledged, penance was assigned or an 'admonition' (warning) given, and perhaps also a fine by way of money to the 'poor men's box' in the parish church. Denial of the charge led to the defendant being allowed to purge himself with a given number of parishioners of the same sex; or, if a cleric, of neighbouring ministers. Failure to appear made him 'contumacious' and led either to immediate excommunication or to the deferment of penalty in the hope of his attendance. Owing to the intransigence of many who never appeared, their cases peter out after two or three sessions: a well-known feature of archidiaconal court records generally. Although 'no verdict' is occasionally mentioned in our account, tedious repetition of such a result is avoided.

Among the many striking features of archidiaconal court books is the wealth of direct or indirect oral evidence. Far from being confined to the depositions, some thousands of the routine entries recite the *ipsissima verba* used by defendants. Many churchwardens' presentments, too, give the

[1] Marjorie McIntosh, 'The Cooke Family of Gidea Hall' (Ph.D. thesis, Harvard Univ., 1967), 271; copy presented by author to E.R.O. In practice, the parish was under the Archdeacon's control.

[2] Details of the kind of business transacted at the visitations and synods, of the officials' and surrogates' duties, and of the circuits, places and frequency of sessions are fully discussed in Dr. Anglin's thesis.

phrases or epithets spoken by those charged with defamation of laymen or abuse of clerics. The court practice, in taking depositions, of demanding each party's age, places and periods of abode since birth affords valuable information, though meagre in actual quantity.[1]

No attempt has been made to analyse the slight degree of personal adjudication by each archdeacon.[2] Nearly all sessions were presided over by his deputy, known as the 'official', or by a local incumbent acting as the archdeacon's surrogate, such as William Harrison, vicar of Radwinter and author of *The Description of England* (1577). The archdeacons seem generally to have presided at the visitations and synods. When the official's office was vacant, a surrogate normally deputized.

Apart from the judge, the permanent officers were the registrar and probably a deputy registrar or scribe, together with several of the humble apparitors. In addition, each court had a few officers known as proctors, who represented parties by mandate or proxy letters.[3] Proctors were required in cases in which plenary, rather than summary, procedure was used. Most of these were 'instance causes' between parties, although occasionally 'promoted office' (criminal) cases would require plenary procedure and therefore proctors.[4]

Routine sessions of the courts, which, incidentally, had no headquarters, were usually held at three-weekly intervals. There were also, on the one hand, the archdeacons' annual visitation courts around Easter and synods about Michaelmas attended compulsorily by the clergy, churchwardens and sidesmen or 'questmen'; on the other, minor *ad hoc* sessions, sometimes held in an inn or the archdeacon's own residence,[5] to dispose of individual cases requiring urgent attention or for the parties' convenience. A record number of 46 sessions of various types were held in the archdeaconry of Essex in 1584. They were never in session during the Bishop's triennial visitations, when the jurisdiction was always inhibited by episcopal order. No sessions occurred during the vacations between the law-terms.

It is difficult to assess the integrity and the efficacy of the Church courts. In any case, their business was largely dependent on whether churchwardens were active, slack, or cautious in making presentments. It seems reasonable to assume that punishment by public penance in church or

[1] J. Cornwall, 'Evidence of Population Mobility in the Seventeenth Century' (*Bull. of Institute of Histl. Research*, xl, 143–52), based mainly on archidiaconal deposition books.

[2] The office of archdeacon during our period was held as follows: *Archdeacons of Essex*: Thomas Cole, 1559–71; John Walker, 1571–85; William Tabor, 1585–1603; Samuel Harsnett, 1603–9; *Archdeacons of Colchester*: John Pulleyne, 1559–65; John Calfhill, 1565–70; George Wythers, 1570–95; Thomas Withers, 1595–1617.

[3] Biographical details of the 'officials' of the archdeaconry of Essex with a full account of their activities and functions and those of the other officers are given by Dr. Anglin.

[4] For procedural details, see, for example, R. Peters, *Oculus Episcopi: Administration in the Archdeaconry of St. Albans, 1580–1625* (1963).

[5] 'White Hart', Colchester, 'Lion', Ardleigh, 'Bell', Walden, 'White Hart', Horndon-on-the-Hill, and 'Swan', Romford; also 'the house of the Archdeacon of Essex (*sic*) in the parish of St. Botolph', Colchester (John Walker), and 'the chamber of the Archdeacon of Essex', London.

market had some deterrent effect on the observers; on the other hand, the hardened or indifferent sinner might scoff at excommunication or penance, if he had not persuaded his friends to purge with him. The general impression is that, where there was co-operation between the court and the wardens, a restraining influence was probably felt; but in parishes with a licentious, indolent or ill-educated minister the spiritual standards may have been relatively lower; Goldhanger and Hadstock, among other villages, seem to fall into this category. But there is little doubt that the courts were influenced as much by the officials' avarice in collecting the maximum fees as by the need to save the defendants' souls; the former is apparent in the section on Contempt.

It had been the writer's hope to include in this second book on *Elizabethan Life* a separate part describing the Manor Courts. The Elizabethan court rolls, custumals and surveys of 74 Essex manors have in fact been written up. Its length, however, precludes publication in the present volume. Nor is it practicable, as each volume is restricted to about 350 pages, to deal with the completed chapters, based on the archidiaconal records, on 'Work and Play on Sundays' and 'Tithes and Perambulations'. They will therefore appear in the third book, together with a short section about the courts' testamentary business. As indicated in Volume I, the next will also incorporate much material from the 11,000 Elizabethan wills in the Essex Record Office. Volume III will also comprise a section about offences relating to Trade. With the addition of Manor Courts – the proceedings in which were largely based on the customs of each manor – the title will probably be: *Elizabethan Life: Home, Work and Customs*, publication being planned for late 1974. There remains one further and major omission from the present book – Witchcraft. The subject has been treated so expertly in Dr. Macfarlane's recent book, based on the exceptionally rich material in the Essex Quarter Sessions, Assize and Archdeacons' Court records,[1] that it would seem to be largely unnecessary and indeed somewhat impertinent on my part to duplicate or even to summarize the information. One aspect, however, that of 'cunning men' – white witches – deserves fuller description and will be considered for possible inclusion in the next volume.

In a book which tries to cope with such an immense amount of original material, it is desirable to tell the reader what sort of information is quoted and what is necessarily omitted. As already stated, an attempt has been made to include all cases of an interesting or unusual character; details are more specifically stated in the relevant sections and are also set out in the Note on Editorial Method (p. xvi). Where an entry is cited, the names of the persons mentioned and their abodes (parishes) are generally given, with the year. Some historians would hold that only the

[1] A. Macfarlane, *Witchcraft in Tudor and Stuart England* (1970).

subject matter is the real requisite, but the names of parishes are needed by local historians and the personal names by family historians, who nowadays delight in discovering the grave as well as the venial sins of their forefathers, well knowing that every family had its quota of misdoers. Even so, only a small fraction of such cases is represented in this book. A careful estimate by two Essex archivists of the number of personal names, discounting repetitions, in the Elizabethan archidiaconal books used in this volume is approximately 50,000! It is pointed out (p. 1) that over 15,000 were charged with immorality, but the vast majority of such entries are merely 'for incontinence', 'for a bastard child', or the like, without detail.

It was explained in *Elizabethan Life: Disorder* that the Essex Quarter Sessions records were among the most complete series in the country (those extant for other counties relate mainly to later years) and that no other Elizabethan Assize records had been previously used except for the subject of witchcraft. The thin field of published archdeacons' archives is matched by that of manorial records and wills. In this respect therefore *Elizabethan Life* goes part of the way in filling gaps in our knowledge of the social history of the ordinary people. It is to the gentry, merchants and yeomen that most archives relate. The affairs of the great majority of humbler folk are rarely, if at all, chronicled (apart from their being merely listed in parish registers, subsidy assessments and muster rolls), except in the records of the justices of the peace and assize and the manorial and archidiaconal courts: hence their peculiar value. The immense interest of archdeacons' records for the social historian has been emphasized by Professors A. G. Dickens and G. R. Elton and Dr. Christopher Hill in recent books.

Ingatestone Hall, December 1972 F.G.E.

Illustrations

ACKNOWLEDGEMENTS

I wish to express appreciation for the continued encouragement given by the Library and Records Committee of the Essex County Council, also by the Executive Committee of the Friends of Historic Essex which has again made a substantial contribution towards the Council's expenses. To my former colleagues, Mr. K. C. Newton, M.A., F.R.HIST.S., County Archivist, Miss N. R. Briggs, M.A., and Mr. A. Searle, B.A., and other members of the Essex Record Office, and to my wife, I am especially grateful for constant help during the preparation of the book; also again to my part-time secretary, Miss O. S. Hall, for typing, proof-reading and drafting the index of persons and places, and to Mr. A. Sorrell for drawing the dust-jacket. Assistance with various chapters is therein acknowledged, and I thank both Mrs. D. Owen, M.A., F.S.A., F.R.HIST.S., a leading authority on ecclesiastical records, and Dr. J. Anglin, whose thesis has also been frequently quoted, for advice on the Introduction. All the remaining faults are of course my responsibility. For allowing reproduction grateful thanks are expressed to the Wellcome Trustees (no. 2) and to the Provost and Churchwardens of Chelmsford Cathedral as well as to Mr. T. C. Gepp, M.A. (frontispiece).

NOTE ON EDITORIAL METHOD

All dates between 1 January and 24 March are expressed in modern style, which has also been adopted for the quotations and the names of parishes.

All cases quoted: usury; divorce; bigamy; incest; rape; venereal diseases; clerical immorality.

Nearly all cases quoted except those of a repetitive nature: all other sections except those given below.

Selection only: licensing of schoolmasters; conventicles; liturgical and ritual offences of the clergy.

Brief account only: recusancy.

Deferred for Volume III: work and play on Sundays and holy-days; tithes; perambulations; probate of wills.

Omitted: witchcraft (see p. xiii).

Editorial additions, e.g. christian names of many of the clergy, mostly taken from Newcourt's *Repertorium Ecclesiasticum Parochiale Londinense*, vol. ii (1710), and explanatory notes on rare or difficult words, are inserted in round brackets, as in the previous volume, to avoid disfiguring the page with square brackets.

References are not given, but year and parish facilitate the tracing in the original records of any of the 2,000–3,000 quoted entries; all references including folio nos., are, however, in the typescript copy deposited in the E.R.O.[1]

Abbreviations: Trans. E.A.S., Transactions of the Essex Archaeological Society; Ess. Rev., Essex Review; E.L.: Disorder: Elizabethan Life: Disorder (1970).

[1] Persons, especially those interested in a given parish, who are unable to decipher the handwriting of the original court books, may derive some help from the twelve large manuscript books compiled by that painstaking antiquary, Robert H. Browne, in 1903–19 (*D/AZ 1*). They cover the period 1540–1671, but he did not manage to deal with all the court books; of the 58 Elizabethan original volumes, his own books relate only to 35 (Archdeaconry of Essex 15, Colchester 20). They are somewhat incomplete transcripts, unindexed. While his copying of English entries was reasonably correct, his reading of Latin passages was often inaccurate; in general they must be used with extreme caution. (The present writer has amended a few of his books in red ink.) It is relatively easy to find entries for a desired parish because its name, as in the original, is usually written in the left-hand margin, and the finger can be quickly run down the pages of the transcripts. But if extracts are to be printed, it is imperative that they should be checked with the originals, the folio numbers of which are given in the transcript. A separate set of notes was made by Dr. Andrew Clark, a scholarly antiquary and rector of Great Leighs, in 1911–12 (*D/AZ 2*), in 28 small books for 1569–1640, but he used only 16 (Essex 9, Colchester 7) of the Elizabethan volumes. While his palaeography was excellent, his interest lay in ecclesiastical, not social, history, and his extracts are much briefer and more selective than Browne's.

1

Sexual Offences

Introductory

The fact that immorality cases are the largest category of offences determined the choice of subject for the opening chapter. Sexual aberration is also the commonest theme among the numerous defamation cases, some of which will be narrated later. But this massive evidence of illicit intercourse must not be construed to give a one-sided, unbalanced view of Elizabethan morals. Church courts were necessarily concerned with the affairs of the sinful minority. The rest of the adult population, in so far as they appear in our records, were charged with non-sexual offences; of these, many were devout Puritans or Roman Catholics whose consciences brought them before the courts for disobeying the ritual laws.

To tell the reader, however, at the outset that nearly 10,000 men and women were summoned on sexual charges by the Elizabethan Essex spiritual courts may tempt him in turn to indict the writer with exaggeration. Yet the figure would be over 15,000, had the archives of the Archdeaconries of Essex and Colchester been complete and had those for the remaining one-third of the county been preserved. Admittedly, the writer has made only random checks, but these have been fairly extensive, and the numbers show little variation in date or area. Another writer has compiled for a late Elizabethan year full analyses of Church court offences for 147 parishes in three counties:[1] compared with 247 parishes represented in the available Essex records. In his summary, sexual immorality accounts for 229 cases: equivalent to nearly 10,000 for the whole reign or over 27,000 for the 407 Essex parishes. The Elizabethan period covers roughly two generations, and using only our own lower estimate of over 15,000, it looks as though between 5,000 and 7,500 persons of each generation out of an estimated adult population of Essex of 35,000–40,000 were thus presented for immorality. Such are the unadorned, approximate statistics of the Elizabethan permissive society. But although the great majority of the presentments were based on indisputable evidence, the remainder were grounded on the less reliable testimony of 'fame' (rumour), 'vehement suspicion', or merely scandalous gossip.

[1] R. A. Marchant, *The Church under the Law: Justice, Administration and Discipline in the Diocese of York, 1560–1640* (1969), 219. My guess of 2,000 cases (*Elizabethan Life: Disorder*, 197), made before full study of the records, was therefore a clear underestimate.

From the vast number of Essex entries bearing on these human transgressions, only a minute fraction will be quoted, because 95 per cent are of a brief, routine nature. Even so, in every generation, the subject is a wide one, and sexual passions resulted in a variety of different offences being brought before the archidiaconal courts. We shall try to cite the more informative entries that fall under the general heading of 'incontinence' (the lawyers' term comprising both fornication and adultery), beginning with pre-nuptial intercourse resulting in 'bridal pregnancy'. Later sections will deal with prostitution, brothel-keeping and harbouring; bastardy; venereal diseases; incest; and other sexual offences.

Because the various sex charges were so commonplace in the archidiaconal courts, they were, by a natural corollary, known in vulgar parlance throughout England as the Bawdy Courts.

Bridal Pregnancy

Failing to exercise sexual patience in the short interval between espousal and marriage accounted for a very large number of couples being prosecuted for flouting the precepts of the Church and sentenced to perform penance in their parish church. We have adopted a recent writer's term, 'bridal pregnancy', for this offence. The spiritual courts dealt with thousands of women who showed physical sign of unchastity before marriage or gave birth soon afterwards. But the Essex act books, at any rate, afford only slight evidence of their being inflicted with the penitential white garb or the more humiliating forms of punishment reserved for those found guilty of fornication, adultery, bastardy, incest, or rape. While it would be an exaggeration to say that pre-marital intercourse was customary between many affianced persons or that some resorted to it as a test of fertility, it has recently been established by demographers that the practice was far from being rare.[1] Historians now accept that many Elizabethan parents and friends condoned it; the general impression is one of tolerance, and certainly not of severe censure except by the puritan and some other clergy and by the stricter members of the laity. Such leniency is readily explained. Betrothal was regarded as a contract not lightly to be entered into. The parties were deemed to be nearer the married state than in much later times. Breach of promise cases in the chapter on Marriage make this abundantly clear. But it is equally apparent in Essex and elsewhere that 'betrothal sometimes resulted from conception,

[1] Statistics of the incidence of pre-marital pregnancy, based on the pioneer research in the parish registers of Colyton in Devon, are given by P. Laslett, *The World We Have Lost* (1965), 139, and by E. A. Wrigley, 'Family Limitation in Pre-Industrial England' (*Econ. Hist. Rev.*, xix (1966), 88–109). The subject has also been studied by P. E. H. Hair, 'Bridal Pregnancy in Rural England in Earlier Centuries' (*Population Studies*, xx (1966), 233–43), and 'Bridal Pregnancy in Earlier Rural England Further Examined' (*Pop. St.*, xxiv (1970), 59–70).

rather than *vice versa*':[1] Shakespeare's marriage was probably an enforced one.

In extenuation of human passions it should be remembered that the average age of marriage was extremely high in comparison with that of the present generation: demographers have estimated that most brides wedded between 20 and 30, and most grooms between 25 and 30. Stated differently, there was a long span of about ten years, more or less, between puberty and marriage.

Presentments for pre-nuptial connexion or defendants' replies take such forms as: 'They long sithence hath been contracted in marriage, and intending marriage to be solemnized they kept company like man and wife'; 'He is lawfully asked in the church to the widow, and there he is conversant (i.e. associating familiarly) and thereby is suspected to live incontinently with her'; 'He and she are man and wife before God and lawfully contracted and the banns asked, and he doth intend to marry her out of hand'; 'They alleged that they were contracted to solemnize marriage', and after performing penance the man 'offered 13s. 4d. to the use of the poor, which the judge accepted'; 'They do accompany suspiciously and do ride together as man and wife, saying that they be sure (i.e. contracted) together before God, and yet will not be asked'; 'Lived suspiciously together a week before they were asked'; 'Being contracted together and could not conveniently be married'. With more excuse, a man presented for 'retaining a widow in his house', answered, 'They are contracted together, and she is so sick that he cannot procure matrimony to be solemnized'. Generally, and probably always, the court commanded parties presented for delayed nuptials to get married before a specified date or 'as quickly as possible,' so that the baby would be born in wedlock. John Mellor of Coggeshall, for instance, was ordered 'to marry her with such convenient speed as he can, and that on Sunday come sevennight before the churchwardens and others to the number of twelve before morning prayer in the church they shall acknowledge his fault with her' (1599).

In 1588 the bridal pregnancy of one of two 'Dutch' (i.e. Flemish) immigrants was dealt with in the normal way, and her lusty companion, John Mathewe of St. Nicholas, Colchester, was ordered to confess 'at the next Communion in the Dutch congregation in such manner as shall be assigned and set down in writing'. On the same day the St. Nicholas' wardens reported another member of the Flemish community, Joan Peanorthe, for incontinence that was not followed by marriage. Ten years earlier Francis Block of Colchester had been too ardent with Barbara Vanderheyden 'before she was divorced from Clare Vanderheyden', and was ordered to confess before the two town bailiffs, Nicholas Challoner, 'preacher', and four witnesses at the house of Mr. Robert Mott, one of the bailiffs.

[1] Hair, 'Bridal Pregnancy . . . Further Examined', 65.

Although when Thomas Harvell and Mary Mychell of Springfield were cited in 1600 he was able to claim that 'he was married on Monday last, the banns being lawfully published', yet the court decreed, 'In time of public morning prayer before Mr. (William) Daniell, parson there, and Mr. Massye, one of the churchwardens, and two other honest substantial men on Sunday next, they are to acknowledge they are heartily sorry'. Very occasionally hasty couples were enjoined to show their contrition at their wedding ceremony. In the same year John Munt and Grace Hubberd of Thorrington 'at the time of solemnization of matrimony shall in penitent manner in their ordinary attire acknowledge their fault'. Or it might be after the woman's delivery, as with John and Alice Cordall of Chingford in 1575; she had to confess before the congregation 'on the day of her purification' (churching), while he also had to pay 10s. to the poor.

A unique note made by the Court scribe in 1588 suggests that tongues had been wagging in two North Essex towns: 'Memorandum to cite the wife and maidens with child of Coggeshall and also such of (Earls) Colne which were with child before marriage, whereof several have notice.' An equally exceptional entry reveals that, when John and Susan Royse of Beaumont were presented by the wardens in the following year because 'they have been married but six weeks and she is now delivered of two children', the husband declared that 'they are none of his, and they did dwell before with one James Hunt of Moze', which by itself could not lay him open to a defamation suit.

Characteristic of the many obvious cases of pre-nuptial pregnancy are such phrases as: 'She being married at Midsummer last is delivered of child before her time'; 'His wife was brought abed somewhat before her time'; 'Having child by his wife 15 weeks after they were married'; 'Begetting of his wife with child 30 weeks before they were married'; and, as a probable illustration of poverty, 'He could not provide things for their marriage'. While Laslett has found in his Devon parish that 'more than half of the babies who arrived early had been conceived within the three months before the marriage ceremony and not earlier',[1] Hair states that 'substantial proportions of brides had conceived each month from nine months before marriage'.[2]

In 1591 Robert Gray of Coggeshall pleaded: 'He and his wife were contracted in the presence of their parents half a year before they were married in the face of the church. After the same contract their parents did vary in some points touching their marriage, the solemnization was deferred longer than they did expect, whereby they forgetting themselves had carnal knowledge whereby his wife was begotten with child, desiring the judge in justice to consider of his cause.' The decree: 'To acknowledge guilt before ten honest parishioners, viz. headboroughs.'

[1] Laslett, *The World We Have Lost*, 141.
[2] Hair, 'Bridal Pregnancy . . . Further Examined', 65.

Unusual circumstances were related to the court in 1592. James Burrowe, servant of Samuel Cromer of Mistley, admitted that 'he was found naked a-bed with Agnes Davye in her father-in-law's Snowden's house'; but he insisted that 'he went to bed to her with the knowledge and consent of Snowden and his wife, mother of Agnes, at what time he had the carnal knowledge of her body, her sister Alice Davye lying by them in the same bed; and he and Agnes are sure together in marriage and the banns asked between them.' Agnes was also cited, and even her sister, evidently to testify to her witnessing the act. William Snowden and his wife, too, were censured. With considerably less reason Cromer had to appear, but disclaimed any part in the matter and was discharged. The betrothed couple were enjoined to perform penance. Father-in-law at this time was sometimes used loosely for step-father. Similarly, Richard Shorten of Hatfield Peverel in 1600 'affirmed that he had been with Elizabeth Jennings before he was married, her mother lying in the same bed'; both her parents were also summoned. Thomas, the father, a tailor of the same parish, was reproved for working at his trade on the sabbath day: perhaps he was trying to earn extra money to buy the wedding gift. Like many other fathers, goodman Jennings might have found the advice of old William Cecil, Lord Burghley, very appropriate: 'Marry thy daughters in time, lest they marry themselves.'

Misbehaviour in 1592 resulted in a girl's sorrowful story. 'John Bailey would have married her, but his affairs hath caused him to go beyond the seas as a merchant to Constantinople in Turkey, whose return will not be until about Michaelmas next at the nearest, when he purposeth by the help of God to marry her.' The judge decided, 'Until which time is required a stay (i.e. postponement) as well for the punishment as for the marriage, and then they shall personally appear and take such order as by law is required'. Four years later there is an echo of the unsuccessful expedition to the West Indies, when a West Ham woman explained that 'there was a promise of marriage between her and one Richard Baker, who went in the voyage with Sir Francis Drake before they were married and begot her with child'. A similar tale, in the section, The Armada and Aftermath, of sudden call-up for Tilbury Camp just before the wedding, is interesting for the virtual recognition of the man's betrothed as 'his wife'.

At this point we may quote one of a number of charges, because they might otherwise be puzzling. Edmund Osborne of Manningtree-cum-Mistley was reported for 'committing adultery with Anne Shenne, which he hath confessed, and promised her marriage in the presence of the wardens' (1588). In our period 'adultery' (as in Matthew, v, 28) was sometimes used in a broad sense for unchastity and not exclusively to indicate that one or both were married.

Before dealing with sexual immorality generally, two further observations may be offered. The enormous number of reports of pre-marital relations that came before the courts probably represents only a proportion of couples who anticipated lawful union (and the same remark applies equally to those whose acts were not followed by marriage) because churchwardens, invested with authority for a single year, were in many cases loath to incriminate their fellow parishioners for fear of creating ill-will, and therefore turned a blind eye except to the more flagrant offenders. There is also the unknown number of concealed abortions and infanticides. As Wrigley remarks, 'The early hours of a child's life provide many occasions when it is easy to follow the maxim that "thou shalt not kill but needst not strive officiously to keep alive"';[1] though we learned in the previous volume a good deal about indictments for infanticide in England from the only accessible information – the Essex Assize files.[2]

Incontinence

The courts used the term 'incontinence' for both fornication and adultery, neither word being found, except rarely, in the act books. The vast proportion of presentments mention only the bare offence. We shall give only a representative selection of the more detailed entries in order to illustrate various aspects of this common failing in relation to Elizabethan society and the ways in which the courts dealt with it. It will be remembered that the gentry usually had the privilege of not being sued in the local courts, but rather in the consistory courts; the few references to the more substantial defendants will be quoted fully.

In the previous volume we stated, 'The county justices were indirectly involved with such behaviour (sexual immorality) in so far as their control of poor relief and victuallers brought to Quarter Sessions many cases of bastardy and a few charges of keeping brothels'. A few arrogant adulterers, however, came before them, and it is interesting to note that none of them was also prosecuted in the archdeacons' courts.[3]

By far the commonest charge was that the man, the woman, or both had been 'incontinent'; that there was suspected incontinence or a 'fame' (public rumour or report) of such misbehaviour; or it was expressed in more direct or disparaging terms, such as '*pro illicito coitu*', or that he, she or they were 'loose livers', 'light suspected infamous persons', 'had been naught together', or the like. Almost equal in number are the entries about women 'having a great belly', being '*gravida*', or 'pregnant'. Of these, somewhat less than half the cases lay against the male seducer, but it would be wrong to assume that the Church – or the people – showed a 'double attitude' in mainly persecuting members of the female sex. Occasionally the churchwardens were more explicit in accusing a woman of being a whore; and the graver charges, too, usually involved the male

[1] 'Family Limitation in Pre-Industrial England', 105. [2] *E.L.: Disorder*, 156–7.
[3] *Ibid.*, 197–200.

or female bawd giving her accommodation. If the regular prostitute or the unfortunate wench became pregnant, the man or woman in whose house she was likely to be or had been delivered was also cited to ensure that she would be punished or because she had departed without being handed over for punishment. But some had been promiscuous or merely ignorant and could not say who had victimized them. Two highly pregnant women with the inappropriate name of Godsafe were presented by the Blackmore wardens at the same session in 1597. Widow Godsafe did not know the tailor's name; but Alice Godsafe debited her shame to William Smith, who was accordingly cited as well.

The vast majority of the routine and brief presentments for suspected or actual immorality call for no comment; but an early case, among the acts written at the end of the visitation book for 1565, has a few unusual details. Anne Pease, a married woman of Danbury, was charged on suspicion of incontinence with 'one who is imprisoned at Colchester'. The judge asked 'whether she hath known the man that is in the gaol'. Her contention was that 'she hath been acquainted with him but with sight, and she never had to do with him nor none other but with her husband, and because of the voice of ill report John Choppell went with her to a Colchester person to clear her, and he took her on horseback to the gaol, and in no other way'. The verdict is not given.

As already stated, people of substance who sinned generally had the privilege of their cases being heard in the episcopal courts. Among the rare exceptions were two members of the Stanton family of West Ham. In 1598 Richard Stanton, gentleman, was presented by the wardens for 'vehement suspicion of incontinency with Jane Hawghton of London and divers others, as the fame goeth'. He made his will in 1600, mentioning only his two daughters. Perhaps he was the son of Robert, also of West Ham, who will appear in the Penance chapter for having impregnated another man's servant.

One of the earliest act books, in 1564, seems to reveal a determined campaign by the then churchwardens of Walthamstow. They reported for incontinence or suspected dalliance no less than eight women. Of these, three were servants and two were wives. One 'abutted' (rebutted) the charge; two were discharged; one had to purge by five women, but brought none and was ordered penance both in Walthamstow church and Barking market; and one had to 'stand at the church door all the service time in a white sheet, barefoot' (in February), 'with a white wand in her hand, and to desire all the people going into church to pray for her'.

Even after marriage couples were not entirely free from inquisitorial eyes. John Roote of Pontisbright 'liveth so ungodly with his wife that the neighbours are greatly offended' (1573). While the nature of the offence is not stated, it is known that the Church very occasionally reproved an over-lustful husband – the procreation of children being the main purpose of marriage in its eyes – and this may be one of these rare prosecutions. The presentment of John Best and his wife of Stock (1575), leading to a court order 'to behave themselves modestly', may also fall into this category.

Some prosecutions at the archdeacons' courts arose directly from the activities of the constables and watchmen, who produced suspicious evidence and sometimes unquestionable testimony of couples being taken *flagrante delicto*. Not a great deal is known about constables' power of privy search before the seventeenth century, and we have therefore quoted most of the incidents found in the Quarter Sessions[1] and archdeacons' archives. (Going outside our period, we may note that the puritan-minded vestrymen of Finchingfield were to decide in 1627 to supplement the constables' efforts with their own night-time search 'in the manner of a privy watch'.[2] Night searches were generally made by the watchmen and day searches by the constables, but a woman was found in the vicar of Kelvedon's chamber at 2 a.m. by 'watchman, constable and other honest men' in 1545:[3] Dogberry would have been in his element!)

The four earliest presentments occur in 1585–7. The first seems to show that a constable might even leave church to hunt out an absentee. Richard Dunsted of Hatfield Peverel was 'taken with Humphrey's wife, a sawyer, with his points untrussed and his hosen in his hands and his buttons unbuttoned in a backhouse or kitchen of her own, and thence brought to the church in the sermon time by Walter Hare constable of the same parish'. His face-saving repudiation ran, 'He liveth from his wife; as for the rest, he denies'. He was commanded to produce for purgation five neighbours, but neither he nor they attended, so he was excommunicated, after which his name disappears from the records. John Etonye of Easthorpe was 'found by the constables at Mott's house at Feering with Barrington's wife very unorderly, so much so that they would have set him in the stocks'; for which constables had authority. John Hunwick of Little Birch was charged, presumably on a constable's report, with 'keeping Barrington's wife Katherine and liveth very suspiciously with her, for they lay together at Mr. Green's at the New Inn, Chelmsford'. The three parishes are contiguous. Was Mistress Barrington a local prostitute? A Wivenhoe widow 'was taken by the constables at 11 o'clock in the night very suspiciously with a stranger who is now gone'; and a Hadleigh woman 'kept a man in her house one night, being commanded by the constables to depart, her husband not being at home'.

The next seven incidents all occurred in 1590–1600. Richard Potter, a widower of Great Coggeshall, and Audrey Underwood of Little Tey 'were found by the privy watch in the night time in the dark in one

[1] *E.L.: Disorder*, index *s.v.* 'search'.
[2] Emmison, *Early Essex Town Meetings* (1970), 111.
[3] J. E. Oxley, *The Reformation in Essex* (1965), 146.

chamber'. William Saulter of Witham 'was found and taken suspiciously with one Dorothy Prise by the watchmen at an unlawful time of the night'. A Colchester inhabitant was accused of 'retaining in his house upon a Sabbath day a man and a bad woman, and when the officers came to search the house he conveyed the parties on the backside' (i.e. let them escape from the rear of his house). Another quick get-away was related by Robert Hunt of Manningtree, who had 'received John Patterick of Beaumont and Elizabeth Sawcer of Colchester, lodging them in his bed, being strangers one from another, being taken by the watch; and Patterick fled out of the window'. A man named Thomas, a carpenter of Braxted, was incriminated for 'keeping company suspiciously with Dorothy wife of Thomas Danishe of Inworth, and have met divers time in private places, and the constables hath sought (i.e. searched) the house for him and hath been denied, and yet notwithstanding hath been found there'; the wife was also cited. Ursula, wife of Robert Hastler, of East Mersea, was 'taken very suspiciously in the night time in her bedchamber, her husband being not at home, with one John Stockley of Kelvedon, tailor, by one of the Queen's officers making a privy search in the night for a tailor which should have been a soldier, by the justice's warrant'; Stockley protested innocence and had to find four men to swear for him. Finally, there is the charge against Richard Wybeard of Sandon, 'taken in bed with widow Darbye by a private watch in the house of Thomas Thornton, whereby they are greatly suspected to have committed whoredom'; the widow was also accused, and Thornton, too, had to attend, but said he had let part of his house to the widow, and he was discharged.

It is impossible to tell from the next extracts whether a constable, watchman or private informer was the witness for the prosecution. Geoffrey Cole of Great Burstead, 'on Twelfthtide last, being abroad with others a-mumming and being late abroad about midnight, lying upon a bed in Sweting's house, Magdalen Wade was found sitting upon the bed, but no evil committed, as he saith' (1575); he was assigned purgation by five people: a pity that no details of the mumming are given. A Goldhanger wife was found with 'a beerbrewer's man of Maldon at the Bridge alone in the night time without candle, her husband being sent away to fit a lock' (1588). A Walthamstow woman was 'of incontinent life, having three strange men found in her house lodged in several beds, she being by the fire in her smock' (1591). A citation was issued against 'two parishioners of Earls Colne to be named by Mr. Addams (vicar), the man being accused that he did fight with him that he was found in bed with the woman by her husband, who ran after him with a naked sword' (1591). Sleeping around was thus a perilous exploit. Those who engaged in illicit relations after dark had to watch their own step as well as to listen for the watchmen's approaching step. But summary punishment was not confined to couples discovered in carnal affairs under a roof: a man and a maid, 'having been found in a pease field, he had been set in the stocks' (1595).

Instead of bringing the immoral offenders in the first place to the archidiaconal court, some constables and wardens hurried them before justices of the peace. As evidence of the overlapping jurisdiction of the secular and ecclesiastical officers, all such references in the archdeacons' archives have been noted, drawn mostly from the defendants' own statements in the Church courts. John George and Alice Mellowes of Bradwell-juxta-Mare produced 'letters of correction' under the hands of Mr. Edmund Pirton and Brian Darcy esquire, justices of peace, 'according to the book of the statute' (1585); so the judge decreed that further penalty was not required. Similarly, John Smith of Manningtree 'exhibited the order of his punishment or penance under the hands of Sir Thomas Lucas knight and Edward Grimstone esquire', J.P.s., and provided a certificate signed by four named parishioners (1590); after inspection, the judge discharged him. Thomas Gibbes of Hornchurch had been 'imprisoned by Lord Henry Grey of Pyrgo knight' (1589). Presented by the wardens and sidesmen of Barking 'on suspicion of evil life with Katherine (blank) his late woman servant and that he was drunk the same time' (1588), John Okeden's statement ran, 'Being overtaken with drink, he laid down in his clothes upon his bed; and being asleep she by the direction of one John Wainewright came and did lie on his bed by him to the intent that he should marry his maid, and they were found both together; yet by virtue of his oath he never had the knowledge of her body; and he was put in the stocks by the appointment of Mr. Fanshawe for the said offence and punished by the order of the justices of peace'. This was confirmed in court by Henry Spittle, one of the wardens, on which the judge discharged the defendant. William Stowers of Wakes Colne, charged with fornication with a woman who had since died, said that he had been punished and imprisoned but was instructed to prove his statement (1590). Accused of being 'found in a wood with the wife of Nicholas Geige of Stisted', Robert Wallys of Pattiswick stated (1593) that 'he was convented therefor before Sir Edmund Huddleston' (J.P.). William Harvye of Stanway 'had been punished severally as well by the justices as also by the judge of this court, viz. Mr. Ruste, and he thereupon took his oath and offered to make full proof', so he was dismissed (1599); Ruste, vicar of Felsted, was one of the Officials of the Archdeacon of Essex. The presentment of Thomas Carter of White Colne for lewdness with Mary Graunte of Earls Colne was made because 'she hath confessed before the justice' (1600).

It is hoped that a full evaluation of the evidence on the overlapping jurisdiction of the Archdeacons', Consistory and Commissary courts and those of Quarter Sessions, Assizes and Privy Council will be completed before long by Dr. Anglin (see pp. viii, 190–1).

In contrast to such action taken by secular officers, although hundreds of men and women were presented by the Church courts' own parochial informers in accordance with their oath of office and some were especially prone to sniff out any rumour, many churchwardens were themselves reprimanded for not denouncing their fellow parishioners. A solitary presentment of a man for living with another's wife, the former 'having had warning to the contrary by the churchwardens', shows that a few used their common sense or were backward in reporting their delinquent friends. Here are a few typical entries of wardens' negligence:

Little Thurrock. 'Suffering John Berd and widow Shoxborowe to keep house together unmarried and would not present them'; they replied that 'they never knew of any suspicious living' (1586).

Bobbingworth. 'Not presenting sundry faults according to their oath, one Hamon was incontinent before marriage'; answer: 'The matter was not known but sithence the last quarter' (1587).

Tolleshunt Major. 'Did not present William White who had begotten one Agnes Maning with child, as he hath confessed before the constable of St. Mary's Colchester' (1590); the judge instructed the wardens to show their presentment at the next session.

Earls Colne. 'Not presenting two harlots with child' (1599).

Bradwell-juxta-Coggeshall. 'Mr. Maxey's maid begotten with child by (blank); one Mr. Parker of Bradwell had a wench or his maid with child suspected, who is sent away. The wardens to be cited in not presenting these things' (1601).

Unmarried maidservants who got into trouble usually suffered, in addition to being assigned public penance in church, the penalty of dismissal. Turned out-of-doors by their master or dame, some deluded wenches also became liable to arrest under the vagrancy laws. An example in 1599 of such harsh treatment is seen in the case of Sarah Eyon of Great Burstead, 'late of Mountnessing, servant to Mr. Thomas Folkes in our parish, which have lived in whoredom with one Thomas Hopkins which was likewise servant to Mr. Folkes and is now gone out of the country, and they have not yet received punishment, saving only that Sarah was put out of service, and after by the warrant of a justice sent to Great Burstead as a vagrant, where she was born'.

Servants, male as well as female, had to be punished by the constables or by the Church court, and it was their masters' duty to see that they were presented and an offence to allow them to leave without punishment: more serious, to expedite their departure by secretly conveying them out of the parish. Employers, of course, were only too ready to hasten the exit of a maid who was pregnant or had recently been delivered of a bastard. The records testify to hundreds of such unlawful removals; and many more fled before being whipped, such as one wench who admitted that 'she went away from his service and was sithence at Ludham's of the Unicorn in Kelvedon' (1599). Similarly, Thomas Sayer of Frating, having in 1588 'suffered John Greenleaf, incontinent with Elizabeth his late servant, to depart unpunished', alleged that Greenleaf, 'by the way as he and the constable did go to the justice to have him punished, did run away, and one Webbe of Ardleigh and his wife, being Greenleaf's parents, know where he is at present'. When the wardens of Parson Harrison's parish in 1585 reported Beatrice Fordham, maidservant of John Copwith of Radwinter, adding 'Who is the father we know not', Beatrice 'was to be diligently searched for'; her master was also summoned for allowing her to leave.

Statements put forward by some men to exculpate themselves, if true, reveal that other wardens were responsible for officious or hasty action. We must again emphasize that the 'bawdy court' tempted malevolent persons to invent scandal, as in the case of Elizabeth Eaton of Prittlewell, who managed to persuade John Hastler, gentleman, to testify that Thomas Bumbey had maliciously spread a report of her incontinence (1592). We can also watch, for example, John Gowldringe the younger of Chigwell, refuting in 1590 a charge of 'haunting the house of Anne wife of Thomas Stondon'; he claimed that he was 'a poor labouring man and resorteth not unto the house but upon special and necessary occupations, as for to hedge, to ditch, to thresh and to do such other work or labour as Thomas Stondon doth hire him to do, and he desireth to be dismissed'; but three compurgators had to be found. Or Christopher Syday of Great Horkesley, who was alleged to have been involved in 1579 with one 'counted (accounted) a woman of light behaviour, and on a time about harvest last he going into an old house of hers for a bird nest to find a hawk, she was in the yard about the house unknown to him'; although he denied misbehaviour he was to be given 'correction'.

A somewhat incoherent account of disorder after a rural wedding is found under 1589. A Fairstead widow and a Sandon wife who

> went to Terling at the marriage of Sir Thomas Mildmay's daughter and were placed at Terling by John Adams and his wife at a friend of theirs to lie there all night, did depart in the evening with certain serving men strangers (being forbidden by the said Adams' wife, saying she was a widow), whereupon the serving men did beat Adams and kept them company all night in suspicious behaviour in a place unknown, not going home, the said Ballard's wife having a nurse child at home and nobody to look to it, and continued all that night in company of the said serving men; and the serving men the night following did report that these women of Fairstead near dwelling to Leighs were well occupied the night before by them upon a pair of stairs and elsewhere in the house; and this was reported in the house of goodman Myddleton in the presence of him, his wife and others, viz. in this want (i.e. way).

After this rigmarole nothing further appears. Persons charged with depravity often blamed the other party: self-justification would sound better in court than self-indulgence. So the plea of allurement was put forward by many defendants. There was not much to choose between the sexes in this way; tempters and temptresses were about equal in number. The first three cases among those we quote all belong to 1579. John Davies of Theydon Garnon asserted, 'She persuaded with him that she was a widow, which is most untrue; she is a married wife and her husband living, but otherwise he would have married her, and only by her enticements and provocations he committed the fact for which he is most heartily sorry'. Penance on Sunday and 5s. to the poor were ordered. The widow Dore of Cranham, suspected to be pregnant by Henry Packer, disavowed guilt and had to purge herself, but the man's version ran thus: 'A little after Easter, her husband being dead and she lying alone, she persuaded him to lie in her house, and the night she lay in one bed and he in another, and in the night she sithed (sighed) and he asked her what she ailed and she said that her feet were cold, and she willed him to come to her bed.' The inevitable followed; Packer declared his sorrow and penance was appointed. Jane Wright of Colne Engaine, who had borne a child of John Lawrence the elder of the same parish, told a bizarre story. 'Her master desired her on a certain night', so she declared, 'to hold his back which did ache, which she refusing was eftsoons required by her dame Joan Lawrence so to do, whereupon she lying upon the bed in her clothes holding his back a good time until she was a-cold was desired and enticed by him and his wife that night as at other times also to come in naked bed with them two, at what time he had carnal knowledge from time to time, her said dame lying in bed with him and warranting her that she should have no harm and that the other maids had used to do the like before'. Despite her plea she was sentenced, 'On Sunday next from the ringing of the first peal until they ring all unto morning prayer she shall stand in the church porch from the beginning unto the end in a sheet about her in the middle alley and confess her fault penitently after the end of the sermon, praying God and the congregation to forgive her'. Mostly, of course, they were simple acts of seduction.

There is also the extraordinary case in 1572 of mercenary craft employed against unsuspecting men by a husband in league with his wife – Thomas and Joan Nocke of East Hanningfield: a triple crime of extortion (or blackmail), adultery and keeping a phoney brothel. 'She doth lure men to her house, and when she hath them there, she doth entice them into her chamber, her husband lying in the chamber came down, putting them in fear of their lives, and agreed with them for malt or money, or what he could get; and namely they have used so Thomas Wardall and Thomas Gilder of Chelmsford.' Had the two undoubting Thomases not compared their experience of the hoax, this ancient ruse would probably have been pursued with much profit to the Nockes.

As would be expected, many of the multitudinous liaisons originated with masters who had abused their maidservants, while others arose from illicit amours between servants living under the same roof. Both remarks apply, on a graver level, to numerous bastardy charges. The Essex Archdeacon's act book for 1565–7 seems to have a plethora of such cases.

When Stephen Newton of Great Birch was accused in 1585 by his pregnant servant, the court directed her to 'be examined whether her master gave her money to go away and whether he laid money in a tumbrel or a cart, yea or no'. There was good reason; for in the form of words of her penance she had to confess having 'accused another at her master's procurement'. The Langham wardens in 1590 presented a pair thus: 'There is a glamer raised by Francis Duplack that John Warner her master hath committed fornication with her and begotten her as she saith with child.' (This is the sole occurrence of the obsolete word 'glamer', meaning scandal or public outcry, which has no etymological link with glamour.) In 1593 infamous intercourse was reported in Essex vernacular: 'George Sadler of Wix at the five-way leet said that John Wade and his man Richard Barker *alias* Smith did keep his maid to halves, meaning thereby that both had had the carnal knowledge of the body of Elizabeth Reynolds late servant of the said John.' (The meeting-place of four roads was often called the four wents or four-ways leet, though five is uncommon; but 'to halves' is a very rare phrase.)

In 1600 we find one of the infrequent cases which illumine, if faintly, a dark aspect of social history: the serving wench or her parents fearing to accuse her master's family. Stephen Riche, father of Joan Riche lately maidservant of Robert Baker of Little Bromley, 'suffered his daughter with child to depart unpunished'. When brought to court, the father claimed that 'she might be begotten with child by some of Baker's house (i.e. household) whom they durst not present'; adding, lamely, 'she was out of his governance'.

Millers, proverbially dishonest, were also sometimes dissolute with maidens sent by their customers. In 1590 John Wilson of West Mersea was 'alone in his mill, and the door being opened by such as came to the mill, Elizabeth Potter of Peldon was found with her placket down'. (Another rare word, meaning petticoat, first otherwise recorded fifteen years later in Shakespeare's *Troilus and Cressida*, II, iii, 22.) Henry Tailor of Great Bentley had to account (1591) 'for his misbehaviour unto maids when they come to his mill'. Another entry (1599) reads, 'Cite William Browne (son of Browne of Sible Hedingham), late of Wethersfield and now at Chalkney Mill in (Earls) Colne, miller – impregnated the daughter of (blank) Peryn of Codham Mill in Wethersfield'. Away from home (1572), Edward Man, the miller of Fingringhoe, seduced a wench 'in Salcott mill being then in the occupation of Robert Mavis her master'. But Thomas Raynes of All Saints, Maldon, was not to blame for his own maidservant's suspected misbehaviour with Thomas, a miller of the same parish (1595).

The sexes were reversed in employer–servant relations in two unproved cases. In 1583 Thomas Kempe of Romford was cited for 'suspicion of incontinence with Creamer's wife being his dame', Elizabeth Creamer also being cited in respect of 'her husband's servant'; both denied. And in 1592 an East Mersea servant reported that 'her dame did commit adultery or fornication with her man or servant who then dwelt with her, and thereupon hath grown a public fame within the parish that the premises are true'. In neither case can any subsequent proceedings be traced.

Having no spare bed was the defence, genuine or otherwise, of a number of men, each accused of having his maidservant to sleep in the same room. Although not customary, it was not uncommon in Elizabethan times for a servant to sleep on the floor 'at the bed's feet' of her master and dame. Many rooms were wretchedly small. Edward Glascocke of East Hanningfield, presented for 'lying himself, his wife and his maid together in one bed' (1587), contended that, 'about a year past, he being then a lone man, had but only two beds, and he had both a manservant and a maidservant; whereby he was driven to lodge his maid with his wife until he provided another bed'. After being admonished he was discharged. Henry Mannockes of High Ongar 'useth to lie with his maid in the chamber where he lieth himself, and thereby is suspected to live incontinently' (1587); and John Almond of Ardleigh was reported for a similar offence (1590).

Other cases revolved around the matter of bedchambers. In 1573 Thomas Gladwyn of Lexden, being asked 'what time Joan Earle widow came to his house, said that she came between 4 and 5 o'clock in the evening and tarried till 2 or 3 o'clock in the morning; and she lay in bed with his wife, he lying in the same chamber with his son; and about the said hour he brought her behind him on his horseback through the town of Colchester, and when he came to the town at Mother Spisealls corner there met him two of the watch and bade him stand till such time as they perceived who he was. And from thence he carried her to Bradfield-in-the-Manger in Suffolk, and there left her at one Mr. Egles. Also he denieth that he heard she was at that time towards any marriage with any other.'

In 1600 some searching questions were put to a Manningtree man named Edwards, viz. 'Whether he was at his parish church on Whitsun Sunday forenoon; whether he did not ride into Suffolk, for he was in his workday apparel, to serve the fair at Manningtree, whereby he was absent both forenoon and afternoon; whether he hath sent his wife commonly by the tide to Harwich market in the night season, his maid lying at his bed's feet in the chamber; and whether there hath not been a public fame that the witness of the parish have taken great offence thereat'.

Deep in this archival morass of alleged sin, the sociologist may enquire whether village talk or presentment tended to force some would-be bachelors to wed. There was an ample supply of maidservants, most of whom lived in. They were a major source of court cases. But some masters were incriminated only as a result of rumour. Peter Udall and widow

Cater, both of Prittlewell, were cited for incontinence because 'they have kept house together there two years, against the town's goodwill.' This was in 1600. Four years earlier he had apparently been suspected of attempted rape. Was he a slandered single man (the earliest Prittlewell register is lost) or a lecher with his maid or housekeeper? (see p. 46).

Summoned for suspicion of immorality with Joan wife of Arthur Wilson in 1588, Robert Mott of St. Runwald, Colchester, put in a long deposition:

> It chanced that on Sunday at night about seven weeks last past he happened to be at the Angel in Colchester, drinking with one Osborn's son, Joan Wilson, Maslin's wife, and Lawrence Browne until 12 o'clock; and so from thence went with the said company to Maslin's house and there continued about half an hour, and after they came to Wilson's for a quarter of an hour, and then the company departing he went to his father's house, and finding the doors shut, so that he could not go into bed, he went to Wilson's house thinking to lie with Putto, Wilson's wife's brother; and Putto being in bed, he went into Wilson's house in the Slaughter, and there was Wilson's wife, to whom he made request that he might lie with Putto her brother. Whilst he was in talking with his wife, Wilson came down in his shirt, bringing a candle, and thereupon he called up his folks and sent for Mr. Symnell and threatened to carry him before Mr. Bailiffs. But he said he did not commit any adultery or fornication, neither had he any such pretence.

Joan repeated much of the story, ending with 'because she was alone, her husband was in a rage, thereupon she sent for Mr. Symnell, who came in and pacified her husband', and she denied adultery. Both Mott and Joan were excommunicated, but only because they failed to reappear at later sessions. It looks as though the accused was the son of the bailiff who had had to arrange for the Dutch couple's penance in the same year.

The comment of John Wade of Coggeshall, charged with lechery (1591), that 'Mr. Newman hath sought my blood and seeketh it still', sounds harsh but rings true, as Lawrence Newman, the vicar, was one of the sternest of the Essex puritans. In contrast, another cleric, Richard Forthe, rector of Great Holland, took the trouble to journey to the court to vindicate a parishioner, Thomas Hilles, cited for suspected fornication with Joan Milles. 'The fame', he declared, 'grew of ill will and not otherwise'; and he secured the accused's acquittal (1589). John Kinge of Colne Engaine must have been notorious locally as a scheming adulterer. In 1590 he had to answer on two counts: 'Being in company, he did call up Miles Man being a-bed with his wife and sent him about his business and then went to bed with his wife; also he went to Colchester with William Clarke's wife to be bound in £6 to release him out of prison', and on the way twice took advantage of her.

Lack of maternal safeguards against youthful indiscretions led to at least two prosecutions. One woman 'suffered her daughter to be alone in the night season with one Lawrence Gillatt and others, and gave her leave to go with them to the dance' (1573); and another's daughter 'useth to lie two or three nights in Colchester in suspected places, and it cannot be done without her mother's leave' (1592). On the other hand, when charged with pre-nuptial unchastity, one man explained that 'his mother upon frowardness, being an old woman, after they were lawfully asked, would not suffer them to come into the house to be with her' (1601); they had to acknowledge their guilt before the minister and wardens.

References to what, in this context, might be termed the 'wages of sin', whether taken or rejected, show that payments in produce were about as common as rewards in cash. While unspecified 'money' is occasionally mentioned, several female defendants indulged in coarse comments about male meanness. Said one, 'He would have had his pleasure but he had not it, and would have given her a crown and it was but a penny'; another, 'He hath been seen to go into a widow's house on the backside suspiciously, and she said he was but a churl, for he would give her but 2d. a time'; and a third, 'Among other lewd and unseemly talk he said in effect that he would give her two groats to occupy her'. All three men affirmed their innocence and were either discharged or assigned purgation. A Kelvedon woman said that 'she was enticed to evil and he gave her 4d. and a purse'; both had to undergo public penance in church. In one instance the court was told (1562) that a man 'offered 6s. 8d. to his maid to have to do with her', but to her credit she refused the noble and reported her master, who had to do penance in a white sheet, bareheaded and barefooted, on market day at Aveley. Joan Barber of Ingatestone had to answer 'whether she had any gold given her by one (blank) to have to do with her' (1564).

Some women were proffered presents in kind: a petticoat cloth; a pair of gloves; or 'she hath abused her body with one Vale for two bushels of wheat' (1598, a famine time). In different circumstances the Fobbing wardens in 1598 presented a Corringham man and a Fobbing wife to whose house he had gone suspiciously and was reported to have given the husband 'his cloak and 16s. or 18s. beside to keep his counsel'. A most scandalous bargain was referred to in 1594. A maidservant alleged that her late master had offered her '40s. a year to serve him by day and 40s. to lie with him on nights'. A third party had regaled others with the story, getting himself involved in a defamation suit. The lengthy court proceedings following on his excommunication for non-attendance are related under that subject.

It is a pleasant change to discover some disclaiming imputed salacity on the ground of their having indulged in practical jokes. Gabriel Ingram of Great Holland had to explain, in 1599, why Joan wife of Richard Wynnyff of Beaumont and Isaac Turner were suspiciously in his house and Turner was found under a bed in Ingram's house in the night-time. Sheepishly, no doubt, Ingram was obliged to admit that 'he was asleep in his bed and knew nothing of the matter', and was discharged. Turner maintained that it was just a matter of 'mirth, he having been hired so to do by Gabriel's wife and one Swanson'; while Joan also said, 'The act whereby Turner was under his wife's bed was done in sport in harvest time'; and Katherine, Ingram's wife, confirmed the merry story. To boast of philandering exploits is a common weakness. The court books show how John Eckford junior of Canewdon, suspected with a maidservant, contended in 1575 that 'he did jest with his fellows that if he had lain with her he would again, but he never committed any evil fact with her'; on which the braggart had 'openly to confess that he had slandered himself and her and ask God's and her forgiveness and pay 2s. to the poor's box'. They also relate how Walter Willmott, likewise reported in 1597 for misbehaviour with Brecknock's wife, all of Hatfield Peverel, admitted that 'one William Hurlye, offering him two pots of beer to kiss her, he did go to her house about 2 o'clock, and upon that wager did kiss her'.

A sexual sidelight rarely noticed by other writers bears on the wearing of men's clothes by females of a lewd or lively disposition. A Littlebury woman 'did wear man's apparel disorderly in her master's house' (1585). The Great Chesterford wardens presented (1585): 'We did hear by voice of him that will justify (i.e. give evidence) that Hunt's wife, contrary to God's law, did put on man's apparel and went forth from one house to another so ungodly and shamefully, with other naughtiness of words.' The wife of Jacob Cornwall of Terling, charged with suspected unchastity with Thomas Burles, 'useth to wear young men's garters and said she would so to do till they came for them' (1592). Susan Bastwick, a wench of Stondon (1578), 'whilst she was in service with her father about Allhollantide (All Saints) last in a merriment came on horseback in a cloak disguised and demanded of him if he had any good ale, and sithence she went into Salcott (probably meaning Winstree) hundred to a sister of hers, and whilst she was there it was reported that she went away with child'. She denied the report, saying that it was most untrue. The judge advised her, that 'before she receive Communion she shall ask her father forgiveness'. One Sunday Joan Towler of Downham 'came into our church', so the wardens said, 'in man's attire in the service time' (1596). They did not add whether this phenomenon caused a disturbance. The final case is doubly interesting (1596): 'Cite the three daughters of Thomas Daye of Great Wenden and Joan daughter of (blank) butcher for going disguised a-mumming, and cite Thomas Daye for suffering them to go; cite the churchwardens to present them.' These spirited girls may be presumed to have acted shamefully by being 'disguised' (the usual term for mummery) in male attire.

We conclude the chapter with a short miscellany selected from the remaining thousands of cases, mostly of a regular nature, because of minor points of interest. Doubts about the matrimonial state gave rise to a few presentments such as those 'for incontinence with his pretended wife';

'keep company together as man and wife, but whether they be married we know not'; 'for suspicion that the woman whom he affirmeth to be his wife is not married'; or, more definitely, 'who is not his wife'. A couple were 'seen to stand close together against the butts, the woman's clothes above her middle, and they afterwards enquired for a hat band which was lost at that time, when the party that saw them said, "Did you tumble the maid so that you lost your hat band?"'. The man exclaimed, 'Why should I not do it as well as another? I was made fit for it!'; and he added facetiously, 'If she were with child I would keep it' (1593). 'Mott the molecatcher of Great Horkesley and the wife of Bartholomew Waters were found by her husband *in coitu*' (1593). A Great Chishall woman 'was seen in bed with a horse leech that used Mr. Cocks' house' (1588). When Richard Weston appeared in court for erring with Mr. Howsden's maid, it was stated that 'Weston's wife would have killed the wench with a spit' (1588). John Caine of West Ham was accused of immorality with the wife of Henry Battle of the same ,'being the gest wife' (a prostitute?) (1586). Eleanor Jellson, servant to Mr. George Colburne of Little Warley, received one Humphrey Fewwilliams (or Phewilliames) into her master's house (1579). Thomas Porter, miller of Witham, had to answer for suspected lewdness (1600). A woman affirmed that she was with child by Thomas Goodin, miller of (West or East) Tilbury windmill (1592). Another, that she 'hid him in the hay goffe' (1596): 'hay' does not mean drying grass, because a 'goaf' was a quantity of grain stacked in one hay, or bay, of a barn. Another, that Thomas Danishe, a pumpmaker of Stisted, had 'played the naught with her'. (1596). A little wharf, apparently unrecorded elsewhere, is referred to in the presentment of an Aveley man for 'incontinence at one Hooker's house hard at Lion Quay' (1579): probably at the point where the Mar Dyke runs into the Thames between the parishes of Aveley and West Thurrock.

Finally, a few brief extracts: 'by public fame a tempter and inveigler of honest maidens to commit fornication and filthiness'; keeping company with another man's wife, 'being forbidden her company before'; '(mis-) behaving himself with his selly (probably for "seely", innocent or defenceless) maidservant' (1599); 'they were seen together tumbling in a ditch, very unseemly'; 'she said that she was most part of the night talking at a stile with a young man whose name is unknown'; and the unique charge against a Grays Thurrock woman (who showed no racial discrimination) for having wanton fornication 'with a certain blackmore (*sic*) now dwelling in the town' (1592). Did 'one Palmer of West Ham, a gunpowder maker, for suspected incontinence' (1597), work at the Waltham Abbey Powder Mills? And if their transgressions were not seen or reported at the time, imminent appearance before the Heavenly Judge might lead, as in the case of one adulterer, to his 'confessing on his deathbed, viz. the very act itself', which brought the woman before the earthly judge.

Prostitution

While many churchwardens during the normal brief term of office were reluctant, despite their oath, to present some of their fellow parishioners for petty delinquencies, few were hesitant in reporting keepers of brothels and those who occasionally housed harlots. If this assumption is correct, the court books may provide a fairly accurate number of such 'bawdy houses' in the rural parishes, although this would probably not be true for the towns, in which the less notorious houses perhaps escaped their notice.

Prostitution, like bastardy, was an offence cognizable by both the secular and the spiritual courts, in each case, for different reasons. As we saw in the previous volume, licensed alehouse-keepers were charged not to engage in brothel business, and Quarter Sessions dealt with a number of offenders.[1]

The term bawd, in Elizabethan times, was applied in a general sense to a procurer or procuress, a brothel-keeper, or anyone engaged as a 'go-between' in such practices, whether male or female. A house of ill-fame was called a 'bawdy-house' or the like, whereas 'brothel' meant a prostitute until nearly the end of our period, when 'brothel-house' first appears, but this word was never used in the court records. The offence was usually 'hoistering', or 'houstering of bawdery'; very occasionally the registrar translated an oral or written vernacular presentment into the briefer *fovet lenocinium* ('procured').

Most of the cases have three common features: both husband and wife were charged; the presentment was based on a suspected offence; and while the prosecution was for 'common bawdery', 'keeping a house of bawdery', 'nourishing bawdery', or 'harbouring of harlots', often though not always only one inmate or frequenter was named.

Of paramount interest is the lurid light which the records cast on some of the Essex brothels. Let us take the earliest story, recounted in stark language. John Hall and his wife of Walthamstow were presented in 1564 as 'common hoisterers of bawdery in having a wench in their house'. Cited by the 'summoner' (generally called the apparitor), she exclaimed, 'The Archdeacon had nothing to do', and so 'they conveyed her away'. The record continues, 'One Bess and another wench were fetched out of the house by the watch, they being in company with Mr. Ferar's man, a stranger of London, and one John Martyn and Richard Machyn, by whom the watch was resisted and threatened to have daggers in them by Machyn. Hall reported that she would keep twenty-four hours though they were strong whores, and thence she is a scolder with a curate when he reproveth her or not she will say to the curate if he make water, "Take thy gear in thy hand and put it in thy mouth".' At the next session the Halls denied

[1] *E.L.: Disorder*, 203, etc.

the charge, were ordered to produce three compurgators, and duly came forward a month later with this number of men, 'who on the Holy Evangelist swore that they believe in their conscience that John Hall hath been no bawd nor never took in any to his house with child'. The court had no option but to 'restore' Hall (and presumably also his wife) to 'good fame'.

Nearness to the city accounts for many incriminating reports in the 1560s, especially from West Ham, Walthamstow and Barking. A man was prosecuted for 'harbouring of harlots for a privy gain'; and a wife as 'a keeper of common harlots and hath one now in her house which (i.e. who) is burned' (infected with venereal disease). In 1583 a woman who lived by 'Bow Bridge in West Ham' (the bridge leading into Middlesex) was 'suspected to keep a house of bawdery to the disquieting of all her neighbours', which she denied and was ordered to purge; and another of the same surname was reputed to live incontinently with 'Mr. Page, landlord of the house where she remaineth'. Next year Evance ap Rice and his wife of Stratford Langthorne in West Ham were presented for 'keeping of evil rule in their house and specially of bawdery, they keeping a victualling house, lodging strange men and women together in one chamber, and lodging strange men in his bed with him and his wife, he arising in the morning, letting them lie, as by the report of their neighbours'. Another West Ham man, John Warde, was detected in 1585 for 'bearing with his wife in her whoredom.' In 1595 two more of West Ham were charged: Ralph Willes, for 'keeping a whore in the Abbey Mill', and Thomas Ridley, for 'keeping an unmarried woman in his house', but he claimed that she was the wife of Thomas Edwards, 'now servant to my Lord Mounteagle' (not the fourth Baron Monteagle who received the warning of the Gunpowder Plot).

The most extraordinary presentment concerns a West Ham brothel in 1571. It contains two very rare words used in connexion with the prostitute's (or more likely the brothel-keeper's) equipment for welcoming 'guests' – an Elizabethan euphemism for customers. The woman was accused of being 'a maintainer' of two men's wives, who may be assumed to be the prostitutes in the house, and 'she had a glass like unto a pintle and a pair of ballocks for guests to drink in'. The archaic words signify penis and testicles. The procuress denied the charge, was ordered to produce three compurgatrices, who would testify that her oath of innocence was true. She managed to bring them at the next session, they assisted her in purging herself, so she was restored to good fame! The evidence suggests that this corner of Essex near the city may have ranked not far behind Southwark for the number of its brothels. But their proprietors, like Philip Henslowe, who owned several as well as managing the Rose and Swan play-houses on Bankside, might not be wholly disreputable.

Also of interest to sociologists is a case entered in the Colchester archdeacon's act book under 1596. A man named Robson *alias* Luter of

Kelvedon was prosecuted for 'harbouring of suspected persons of incontinent life in his house, viz. one Reynolds' wife for common adultery with divers, as the common fame goeth; she keepeth a 6d. ordinary, come that listeth'. Had the price been connected with Robson's house, it could have referred to that of a tavern meal.[1] But it is the woman's house and must be the prostitute's fee.

Some innkeepers or alehouse-keepers in the more rural parts were among the accused, such as one of Earls Colne for 'coming to church but once a month and doth keep a house very much suspected of bawdery', and another of Great Chesterford and his wife for 'receiving and housing suspected persons, his wife also suspected for her incontinent life' with three named parishioners. But there was no element of doubt in the presentment of a Frating man 'for houstering a whore, who had no habitation, in his house', or in that of a Canewdon man in whose house a woman 'hath been twice brought a-bed, and he is a maintainer of her evil', who ignored a citation and was in due course excommunicated. A Walden wife was charged in 1587 as a bawd, having 'offered to two other wives to come to play the harlot in his house' (another husband was also summoned).

The wardens of Parson Harrison's village of Radwinter in 1569 presented a man and a woman (not the man's wife) as 'suspected to maintain bawdery' – this during the period in which Harrison himself acted as judge when the sessions were held at Walden. Charles Bundocke of Downham in 1578 was 'suspected to be an evil and lewd provoker and procurer of women to lewdness and whoredom with him'. In 1585 widow Rame of Great Braxted kept a house of 'bawdry' and 'she was a bawd to Joan Rame her kinswoman', who was suspected to be pregnant by a Kelvedon man, also cited, 'for that he hath had his usual recourse thither and hath lodged there divers nights'. At Danbury in 1578 Francis Hickes and his wife were thought to be 'receivers of suspected persons into their house of incontinence', and at Great Birch in 1591 Katherine Tricker, widow, 'kept young folks as men and maids in her house in the night time suspiciously'; both women had recourse to purgation.

Sordid events were reported from Clavering in 1588. Joan Gwin was clearly the village prostitute, who had engaged '*in fornicariis amplixibus*' and 'hath had three bastards'. Her widowed mother, Eleanor Gwin, was also involved as 'bawd to her daughter and hath received and comforted her in her whoredom and she doth at this present'. Admitting that Joan 'by the appointment of the justices is now in her house and that she hath had a child by John Silling dwelling about Norwich', the judge warned her not to let her daughter depart unpunished 'out of the country' (neighbourhood). That was not all: Edward Wenham of Clavering,

[1] The *O.E.D.*'s earliest quotation in this sense is 1590; cf. 'The unwholsom ayre of an eight penny ordinarie' (1631) and '6d. ordinary supper' (1635).

'brother of the said Joan', probably meaning step-brother, 'was accessary to her whoredom in conveying and carrying her away to avoid punishment'. In the same year Edward Denham, aqua-vitae man (vendor of strong spirits) of Lawford, was up for bawdery in procuring a couple to commit fornication: perhaps the aphrodisiac qualities of his liquor helped in his nefarious activities. Another prosecution '*in causa lenocinii*' implicated a man who 'was a bawd to his own wife' and resulted in the couple having to undergo public penance 'barefooted and bareheaded tomorrow Tuesday in Rayleigh market'; and there is a second charge of a man who was 'a bawd to his wife'.

In 1589 'Mr. Golde, curate of Holy Trinity' in Colchester (Robert Goode was rector), was reprimanded for admitting a man and his wife to Communion, 'being suspected to keep suspected persons of bawdery'; and two years later the Trinity wardens presented a second couple for 'keeping harlots in their house' and a third for 'houstering naughty packs in their house in service time'. A naughty pack was a not uncommon term of abuse for anyone of low character.

A confused account with several obscure terms is found under 1592. Richard Underwood of Wakes Colne was summoned, suspected of having 'begotten Elizabeth Tyffin, the sister of the said Underwood's house' (*sic*), and his wife accused Elizabeth her sister and 'beat her out of doors, and Underwood then said he would put his wife out of doors'. Agnes wife of Richard Underwood was also condemned for immorality with three named parishioners. The entry continues, 'Elizabeth Tyffin did so accuse them, and Alcock' (one of the three) 'gave her cheese at hophouse to occupy her, and Wenden gave her money. They frequent Underwood's house daily to the great offence of the neighbours, being no victualling house.' It concludes, 'John Keble of Pontisbright saith that he would strip his house with bushes rather than suffer it to be a house of bawdery and hath forbidden them his house'. Does hophouse, apparently an unknown word, mean hop harvest?

Several other unsavoury characters may be briefly dismissed. Margaret Barnard of St. Giles and St. Botolph, Colchester, 'keepeth suspiciously three young women in her house' (1573); of John Dryver of Little Baddow, 'there goeth a common crime that he is an whore keeper' (1583); Mary, wife of Thomas Wilson, junior, of South Ockendon, 'a common scold and a railer of her neighbours and a filthy bawdy beast against her own mother' (1601); John Stebbing and his wife of Colne Engaine suspected to keep a house of bawdry' (1603). To complete the sinful record, seven other villages produced an alleged bawd for the court's consideration, nearly all of whom repudiated the charge: in two of the cases, 'a bawd to her own daughter'.

In these ways the churchwardens and the spiritual courts tried to wage war against the unholy trade. Their efforts were concentrated on the brothel-keepers rather than the strumpets and their customers. Relatively few presentments, in fact, lay against prostitutes, and some merely name the woman as *meretrix* and leave it at that. It is not always easy to see whether she was accused as a prostitute or as mother of one or more bastards. Typical charges ran, 'For a public fame of incontinence with four named townsmen', resulting in the woman and one of the men being excommunicated, while the others had to purge their denial (Barking, 1569); 'for a common harlot, who hath confessed she was pregnant' (Maldon, 1566); 'for playing the harlot and for having two or three children, being unmarried' (Walthamstow, 1580); 'for committing fornication with divers lewd persons, but none have their abiding in our parish' (Fordham, 1591). A prostitute who used an aphrodisiac powder is referred to in the chapter on Compurgation.

A Great Ilford pregnant prostitute who 'submitted herself to correction' in 1579 got this penance: 'On the day of her thanksgiving (i.e. churching), with a white wand, before the congregation, she shall penitently confess and give to the churchwardens 20s., to be distributed among the poor.' Her pecuniary punishment was an exceptionally high sum and must surely have borne some relation to her presumed financial circumstances rather than to her offence, which was common enough. Often churchwardens put in a wordy, composite indictment, and those of Stock in 1583 thus presented Barbara, wife of Christopher Driver: 'Suspected of living incontinently by common report with divers persons, as namely Anthony Errington deceased and one John Taillor, with others, and there go filthy speeches of her beastly behaviour, and it is noised that she hath had a bastard and never punished for it; also a maker of debate between neighbour and neighbour and a common scold and brawler'; all of which she denied. She produced three women and was then declared 'sufficiently purged'. The court ordered Driver and his wife to receive communion and to confess that they were in love and charity with all men. Errington was one of a poaching party which had carried off two stags from Crondon Park at Stock in the previous year.[1] On this occasion he was termed a gentleman, as also in his will, proved in that year.

Much is known about the seamy side of life in the cities of Elizabethan England, especially in the London stews on the south bank; but the reverse applies to the rest of the country. Because of this meagre evidence, we have therefore given all the Essex presentments, but it is probable that the borough records of Colchester, by far the biggest town (and a seaport) in Essex, would also disclose much about its brothels and prostitutes. A lively description of an incident at Mother Bowden's brothel in Chelmsford in 1567 was narrated in full in the previous volume.[2]

[1] *E.L.: Disorder*, 86, 240.
[2] *Ibid.*, 26.

Harbouring Unmarried Mothers

Passing from brothel-keepers to those who 'harboured', or gave accommodation, temporarily or otherwise, to harlots, vagrants or other women of doubtful repute, a few of the many reports will serve to illustrate this aspect. A Great Totham man 'received and kept secret a woman greatly suspected to be a harlot'; a married couple of West Ham 'received a woman which went by the highway and was delivered in their house'; a Colne Engaine man 'harboureth of vagrant persons and incontinent livers'. In 1575 'the ferryman of Rainham' (unnamed) was summoned to the court because 'he lodgeth a harlot who was there brought a-bed – she came out of Kent'. In the same year 'Master Cornelis and Evan his wife' of Barking were presented because 'they had harboured a harlot which came from Master Meeres a beer-brewer, and conveyed her away without punishment'; the man asserted that 'he received her by the commandment of the justices and discharged her by the same authority'; but he admitted she had not been punished. Unmarried mothers, as all mothers, had to give thanks to God for their delivery, and the charge against John Evans of Romford in 1580 for 'carrying away of a whore afore she was churched' exemplifies this. (See plate 14.)

One man maintained that he had lodged a pregnant woman 'named Emme Strong-in-the-arm by a warrant from the Masters of Bridewell'. Another stated that the harlot whom he had been charged with harbouring was 'now in Bridewell and punished for her naughty life'. Richard Radeley of Ramsden Bellhouse had cause for being angry with the wardens. Cited for harbouring a pregnant woman, he said that 'he received her by the consent, not only of the parishioners but by the letter of Mr. Archdeacon, because she was at his door sighing and almost lost for succour'.

The great majority concern unmarried mothers who had given birth in the defendants' houses; occasionally, however, the ill-fated women left before delivery. Typical phrases are:

> Hath a wench in his house with child and did not present it.
>
> A woman brought a-bed in his house and went away without punishment.
>
> Harboured an unmarried pregnant woman, now carted away by the justices.
>
> Having been commanded by the constable to have her forthwith coming after she was delivered, and when she was churched she was gone with her child, not known whither.

In 1564 an East Horndon man who had sheltered a pregnant girl, anticipating the Salvation Army's apt phrase by four centuries, pleaded that 'he took her in for God's sake', but was sentenced to public penance in the market and had to pay 2s. to the poor. Two years later the Archdeacon of Essex showed more sympathy in personally intervening. A certain Gabriel Galvano of Leyton had misbehaved with his maidservant, and both were summoned, together with 'Mistress Rooke, widow, of West Ham, because she keeps the said servant of Galvano in her house being pregnant'. Against the entry the scribe added a unique note, 'Mr. Cole will not have this cause called, for the said Rooke kept the said maid from drowning'. The good Samaritan, who had presumably saved the wretched would-be suicide, must be Agnes Rooke, the widow of Upton in West Ham whose will drawn up in 1572 is notable for its public and private charitable legacies. A less exalted person, many years later in 1600, showed similar mercy. 'For playing the whore' and getting pregnant, a woman of Collier Row in Romford was cited, also William Moundshawe of the same hamlet for harbouring her. 'Being constable', he told the court, 'he took her into his house in the way of charity till he could know Mr. Ramme's pleasure', a plea which was accepted. (Francis Ramme was clerk of the peace.) But when Robert Hardinge of Loughton was presented in 1564 because an unmarried girl 'went away from his house with child', he confessed that 'the wench went away unpunished, for that certain of the parish, viz. Mr. Stonard (John Stonard, J.P.) and others did examine her and they willed him to put her away, which he did'.

Sometimes the unmarried mother was relieved of a future burden, but her harbourer was still called to answer. A baby was born in the house of William Briant of Great Bromley and 'buried in the fields, but', reported the wardens, 'the mother, whose name we know not ne (i.e. nor) yet from whence she came, he suffered to depart unpunished, no knowledge being made of her deliverance, neither have given thanks before her departure; but we understand by your servant Croke that she was presented by the churchwardens of Beaumont by the name of Margaret Leach servant to George Cocke of Beaumont'. Briant was excommunicated.

Compassion for pregnant servants was indeed rare; even rarer when they gave birth to bastards. There was every reason for getting rid of them beforehand. Mr. William Barry of Walden had an extra excuse in 1585. A girl had been brought to serve him 'at Candlemas was twelvemonth, by Thomas Harrison of the same town, who gave his word that she was honest. But', said Master Barry, 'afterward she perceived she was with child and she accused one Robert French a scholar who boarded with him (Harrison?) to be the father of the child, and he delivered her to Harrison, who carried her away, whither he knoweth not.'

With the same last four words Thomas Prior of Romford ended his answer to the complaint in 1578 that 'he was consenting to the conveying away of John Cocke, his wife's son, who hath gotten two sundry woman with child and never punished for his fact, and the son is now escaped.' Prior 'was enjoined that he should do his best endeavour for the apprehension and punishment' of his step-son. One man asserted that 'she was somewhat of kin to his wife', adding that 'she came to his house where she remained about a sennight, and he perceiving her to be with child conveyed her away to London from whence she came, and riding with her towards London she stayed at West Thurrock, where not being well and near her time as it seemed by her he left her at the house of one Doe of Thurrock, where she was brought a-bed, but who is the father of the child he knoweth not nor where she is become'. Another was charged with 'receiving his son into his house and not bringing him to punishment'. Stealing back to the parents' home was the natural recourse of some unfortunate girls. But their shame could not always be concealed, for there might soon be a little burden on the poor rate. Sharp eyes saw to it that the wardens were obliged to present: 'She is with child and she is houstered in our parish by her father, as the fame goeth.' The Elizabethans seem to have been hard-hearted, but succeeding generations were equally so, and the unmarried mother received little consideration until the present century. Parents were thus liable to be censured for shielding their own children who had broken the seventh Commandment, but only three other presentments for not handing them over for the penalty have been noticed. In 1590 William Donkyn of Eastwood, confessing that he had 'harboured his daughter in his house, she being with child', told his story. 'She was begotten with child about Ashford in Kent where she was in service and came to his house about the middle of October last, and when she had been there three days he was admonished to put her away by the constable because she was suspected to be with child, and so he put her away incontinently, not suspecting her then that she was with child. She returned into Kent where she hath received punishment.' He was discharged. A cleric, apparently the curate, offended in 1595. William Vixar of Fyfield, let his own daughter 'go away unpunished'. His plea was that she departed without his knowledge, but he was enjoined to confess in church that 'he had offended God and the congregation in harbouring his daughter'. There was also the case of Ralph Cox of Dedham in 1599, who had not brought his daughter, delivered of a bastard three or four years past, 'to punishment, which was concealed by Mr. Dr. Chapman and the churchwardens'. (Edmund Chapman, the puritan lecturer at Dedham, would not have been expected to overlook any bastardy offence.)

Roger Thompson of Hornchurch, in 1579, was haled before the court because 'he hath a young woman in his house, being great with child, who is not known whether she be married or not'. Irritated by the citation, he said, 'She is the wife of William Thompson his kinsman, who was married sithence Michaelmas last but he is now in the North country and is not able to keep house as yet, and for kindred sake, considering their poverty, he suffereth them to remain in his house until she is delivered'. Nevertheless he was ordered to bring her after childbirth to receive punishment for her guilt before marriage. But soon afterwards her husband appeared and brought a certificate from John Horsefale, rector of St. Peter, Paul's

Wharf (London), of the marriage there, whereon the judge dismissed the case.

An extraordinary presentment came from Great Horkesley in 1600:

> Judith Hasellastanke, dwelling a year with Mr. Bownd parson (John Bound, rector), suspected to be with child, was sent away by night with Dick Beckwell then his servant and now dwelling in Colne and John Morcott now sexton, and afterwards he sent hue and cry after his maid, saying that she had stolen silver spoons and money. She was carried to Billericay or to Horndon-on-the-Hill, and being there delivered of child two persons were bound for the discharge of the parish there by the hands of Mr. Bownd, as is thought, and after that she was carried to Bungay in Suffolk by the said Morcott, as is thought.

Typical of other incidents is that of Joan Moreton of Little Baddow, charged with being pregnant by her fellow servant in their master's house, who said that Leonard Jaques was the father but had fled. The judge imposed the usual penance and also ordered 'Mr. Blake', presumably the master, to be cited. There are in fact many entries such as 'The fame goeth that she is with child by one who is fled that should have married her'.

It is refreshing to find some presentments the responses to five of which refer to more distant matters and incidentally to several persons of renown. In January 1586 Elizabeth Vaughan *alias* Jones was reported to be pregnant in Edward Vaughan's home at Barking and suspected to be unmarried. There appeared on her behalf James Vaughan, gentleman, who stated that she was married when he was present, two years ago, in 'Develinge', to one Robert Jones of St. Katherine's, London, 'who is now in Flanders serving under Mr. Philip Sydney in her Majesty's affairs'. The judge discharged the woman because Vaughan was 'reputed to be an honest gentleman, as by a letter sent from Mr. (blank) appeareth'.

Three years later the court also dismissed George Syday and his wife, of Bradwell(-juxta-Mare), in whose house 'a stranger, not known whether she is married, was brought a-bed'. The man deposed that Mistress Elizabeth Smith *alias* Foskue came by way of travelling to London to meet with her husband Mr. John Smith, hoping of his return, who went over with Sir Francis Drake as a Captain, as it is credibly reported and known, but he was drowned in the voyage'. Smith was only one of 8,000 of the 15,000 who died in the unsuccessful expedition of Sir John Norris and Drake to the coast of Spain. Is it a mere coincidence that two women bearing these names turn up in the next decade married to men who had crossed the high seas? In 1596 the Walthamstow wardens reported Robert Pery for 'lodging one Elizabeth Vaughan' who gave birth in his house, but he alleged that 'she is married to Mr. Morris Owen who is now gone with my Lord of Essex'. (Robert Devereux, Earl of Essex, unlike Drake, achieved a notable victory at Cadiz.) The same parish in 1598 accused Henry Hester, who explained how, 'at the request of one of his friends, he received Elizabeth wife of Henry Smith who went the voyage of my Lord of Essex'. Drake's name has also occurred earlier. In 1591 the Walthamstow officers named Robert White for harbouring his servant Bridget Smith and her bastard child. Bridget, they said, had 'nominated one Thomas Chapman, late servant to Mr. Rowe, to be the father', and added that Chapman 'lieth in Sir Francis Drake's house at Dowgate at surgery' (under surgical treatment). Ordered to produce Bridget, they claimed having sought her in vain and were discharged. As a tailpiece, Hugh ap Harris of Mountnessing in 1574 had harboured a woman 'great with child in his house', married to a sailor 'beyond the seas'.

When John Atkynson of Barking was accused in 1587 of 'having a suspected woman brought abed in his house and gone away unpunished', he explained that she was 'one Elizabeth Willson, the lawful wife of Christopher Willson, one of her Majesty's Chamber, which said Elizabeth by reason of acquaintance came to his house by chance, and was churched there, and then went away, and Christopher Willson brought in a certificate of his marriage which was solemnized at the Savoy (chapel)'. He was discharged.

An apparently unique charge of harbouring of a different nature, preferred against a gentleman, is found in 1591: 'Mr. William Hollingsworth of Stondon Massey, for keeping the wife of one Mr. Ryvet in his house, contrary to the articles of the laws of this realm.' Mistress Ryvet of Stondon was also presented for 'living suspiciously from her husband'. Hollingsworth was the Crown lessee of Stondon Place. Two years afterwards he assigned his lease to William Byrd, the composer, for £300, who in 1595 secured a further lease from the Crown for the lives of his three children successively.[1] Was Hollingsworth's lodger the wife of a member of the Ryvet yeoman family of Thorpe?

Not unnaturally, some persons accused of harbouring women claimed that they were genuine lodgers. In 1584 the West Ham wardens reported Christopher Smyth for receiving a woman called Mary Udall with a child on Christmas Day, who stayed 'with a man lying in the house, and the band and hat of the man was found in her chamber suspiciously'; Smyth had also taken in a pregnant woman 'on the morrow after New Year's Day, who remained there about six days until such time as the constable brought him before the justices and banished the town of the woman and laid Smyth by the feet'. To this dual charge his reply was that 'he keepeth a victualling house and lodged the parties as passengers and not otherwise, and he was punished by sitting in the stocks'; the judge dismissed him. Rainham ferry appears again in 1597, when John Bateman, accused because of a child born under his roof, explained that 'he keepeth a victualling house beside the ferry, and she came late one evening as a guest and she was delivered the next day'. (He probably ran both ferry and inn.) A Barking wife, similarly presented, was able to convince

[1] *V.C.H.*, *Essex*, iv, 243.

the judge that she had taken in a woman 'as a guest and upon necessity, she keeping a victualling house', but she had to pay 5s. to the poor. A fellow townsman in like circumstances named the man who brought an unmarried woman and the child's father; the latter had agreed to pay him 2s. 8d. a week. A married couple of Ardleigh admitted having had 20 marks from a man, presumably the bastard's father, for the lodging of a woman from Lincolnshire. The parishioners of Theydon Garnon, on behalf of one in whose house a single woman had been delivered, certified his being a very poor man: 'She was a walking woman and came into his house by chance, he not consenting.'

Before being acquitted in 1591 Edward Benbrick of West Ham said:

> He entertained one Martha Tompson late the wife of Phoenix Tompson of Rochford deceased about Christmas, being great with child, begotten by her husband who left her as he thinketh, and at the request of John Johnson of Bow his own aunt's wife's brother. Which Martha came to him as a guest in that he keepeth a victualling house, and she came very bare and was very near her delivery of child, only upon compassion that he bare to the state of the poor woman. He requested this respondent to receive her until she were delivered of child. Upon promise made by her that she would content him for his house room, viz. 6d. every week, which in part before her departure she did satisfy, he received her, having first a certificate from the parish of Rochford that she was a married woman. There she continued for the space of eight weeks, in which time she was delivered of child, and is departed away with her said child whither he knoweth not, after she had given thanks for her delivery and the child there christened.

A different category comprises charges which were rebutted for the simple reason that the pregnant women had been taken in on the orders of the parish constables or a justice of the peace. These cases, where genuine, seem to imply some wardens' singularly inept officiousness. A Cranham man claimed that 'the constable willed him to receive her'. Of the five further instances of justices' orders, an East Ham man, presented for harbouring a harlot, answered that 'he was directed by Mr. Seisley' (of Barking), a justice of the peace, to take in the woman, who 'declared to him that she had a husband who was gone to Flushing' and that the J.P. had guaranteed to 'hold him harmless against the ecclesiastical laws'.

The eternal vigilance against the entry of unaccompanied pregnant women is also illustrated by the deposition of Thomas Strayte (whose abode is not given) in 1584, explaining (and getting release) how

> he was requested by John Argent his dear friend of Purleigh to let the wife of his friend sojourn at his house for a season; but, being loath so to do without the consent of the chief of the parish, Argent offered a bond of £100 to discharge him and the parishioners from any charge or trouble touching the woman with the child she went withal, which the deponent was content to receive her. He does not know if she returned. She was the wife of Thomas Daws who she said dwelt at the Forest Side (probably Waltham Forest) and durst not be seen for debt. The deponent said he had been punished and in part paid by Argent 6s. 8d. a week for her board, but she is honest. The minister of East Mersea would not christen the child until the second sabbath day after the birth. The woman hath appeared and submitted to order of law, and the deponent taketh himself discharged.

Bastardy

We have already remarked that bastardy cases came before Quarter Sessions when the matter of providing for the offspring had to be adjudicated. Other aspects of bastardy were touched upon in the previous volume under the headings of infanticide, immorality and alehouses (the conditions of some victuallers' recognizances embraced a clause against lodging women about to give birth to bastards).[1] The archdeacons' courts received innumerable presentments about bastardy as a sexual offence.

The subject will be dealt with in the next volume as part of the wider question of poverty and vagrancy. The chapter will include examples of the detailed depositions taken by J.P.s from unmarried mothers and of midwives and neighbours present at the birth, passed to the County Bench for their consideration of the often highly complicated problem of determining paternity. This was usually followed by a maintenance order on the father or on both parents and a sentence. The records of punishment for either or both parties reveal a good deal of variety, but generally involved phrases such as 'to be tied (together) to a cart's tail, stripped naked from the waist upwards, drawn twice through the parish, and whipped with (twenty) stripes by the constables', or 'to be set in the stocks from 8 a.m. till 8 p.m.'.

Venereal Diseases

The Essex archdeacons' court books have yielded some fragmentary but valuable information about the incidence of venereal diseases in Elizabethan times.[2] Before quoting the entries, it is desirable to refer briefly to the medical authorities. Several standard works have asserted that there is a paucity of British writings on the subject before the end of the sixteenth century. While this is true so far as competent accounts are concerned, William Clowes being the first English venereologist (1575), Dr. M. A. Waugh notes five earlier writers between 1546 and 1563 who made some reference to the matter; but, as he remarks, this printed material is remarkably small in comparison with the number of continental works.[3] There is virtually no authoritative modern history of venereal diseases in England.

Whereas gonorrhœa is of very early origin, there seems no doubt that syphilis was a new disease brought from the New World to Europe on the return of Columbus and his sailors. Appearing in Portugal in 1493 and in

[1] *E.L.: Disorder*, 143, 157, 197–8, 203.

[2] By the kind invitation of Dr. F. N. L. Poynter, Director of the Wellcome Institute of History of Medicine, London, I contributed a paper based on this section at a seminar at the Institute in 1971, following a paper on 'Venereal Diseases in Sixteenth Century England' by Dr. M. A. Waugh, since published in *Medical History*, vol. 17 (1973), 191–8. I wish to thank Dr. Waugh and other venereologists for their advice at the seminar.

[3] See n. 2.

England by the next decade, it became known as *morbus gallicus*, or the French (or Spanish) pox. The term *lues venerea*, or venereal disease, was first used by a French writer in 1527, but 'the separate pathologies of syphilis and gonorrhœa had not been formulated, being considered part of the same disease' until much later.[1] In 1503 Henry VII's wife had a young servant for whom 20s. was paid to 'a surgeon which healed him of the French pox',[2] but Henry VIII's 'bad leg', which was treated in 1527 by Thomas Vicary, a royal serjeant-surgeon, may perhaps have been due not to venereal disease as has so often been categorically stated but to a bad varicose ulcer. (Vicary also treated Sir William Petre for his frequent attacks of the stone and Petre was probably the last patient before his death.[3])

In 1506 steps were taken to suppress the ancient brothels in Southwark (wooden buildings with river-stairs, a little above London Bridge), which were under the jurisdiction of the Bishop of Winchester! Action had resulted almost certainly from the rapid spread of syphilis. St. Bartholomew's Hospital soon became three-quarters occupied by syphilitic victims. 'It happeneth very seldom', wrote Clowes, the erudite surgeon at that hospital, 'but that among every twenty diseased persons taken in, fifteen of them have the pocks'.[4] He claimed that over a thousand patients suffering with syphilis had been cured by himself and three others in five years. The treatment given was by mercurial inunctions or a decoction of guaicum (a resinous drug prepared from the tree of that name, plate 2), and later by fumigation. Shakespeare's (sweating) 'tubs and baths' (*Timon of Athens*, IV, iii, 86) refers to the latter form of treatment.

The prosecutions recorded in the Essex court books, however, relate almost wholly to gonorrhœa, except perhaps the single case of 'pocks'. Andrew Boord in his popular *Breviary of Helth* (1547) was the first medical writer to mention gonorrhœa as well as syphilis. 'If a man be burnt with an harlot', he declared, 'and do meddle with another woman within a day, he shall burn the woman.' Shakespeare was one of the very few literary writers who adopted the verb: 'Light wenches will burn, come not near her' (*Comedy of Errors*, IV, iii, 58). The earliest mention of burning apparently occurs in Guy de Chauliac's *Chirurgia magna*[5], (1363) which has a section on 'heating and filthiness' of the penis 'for lying with a unclean woman'.

Dealing with the Essex material, apart from the single cases referring to the 'pocks' and a woman 'greatly diseased', all the entries use the term 'burned'. Of these, two mention surgeons and a third reference to a brothel

[1] Waugh, see p. 31, n. 2.
[2] *Privy Purse Expenses of Elizabeth of York*, ed. Nicolas (1830), 104.
[3] Emmison, *Tudor Secretary*, 253–4.
[4] Quoted by Dr. Waugh.
[5] Translated by Mrs. Margaret Ogden (Early English Text Soc., no. 265, 1971).

2 TREATING VENEREAL DISEASE

Essex archives have unique material (pp. 31–6). A rare engraving, entitled *Hyacum et Lues Venerea*, by Philip Galle (1537–1612) after Jan Stradanus (1523–1605), Antwerp, from *Nova Reperta*, by Jan van der Street, Antwerp (1600?). A patient drinks a decoction of guiacum bark, which is being cut up, weighed and cooked: a treatment, brought from the New World, that had become popular. (By courtesy of The Wellcome Trustees.)

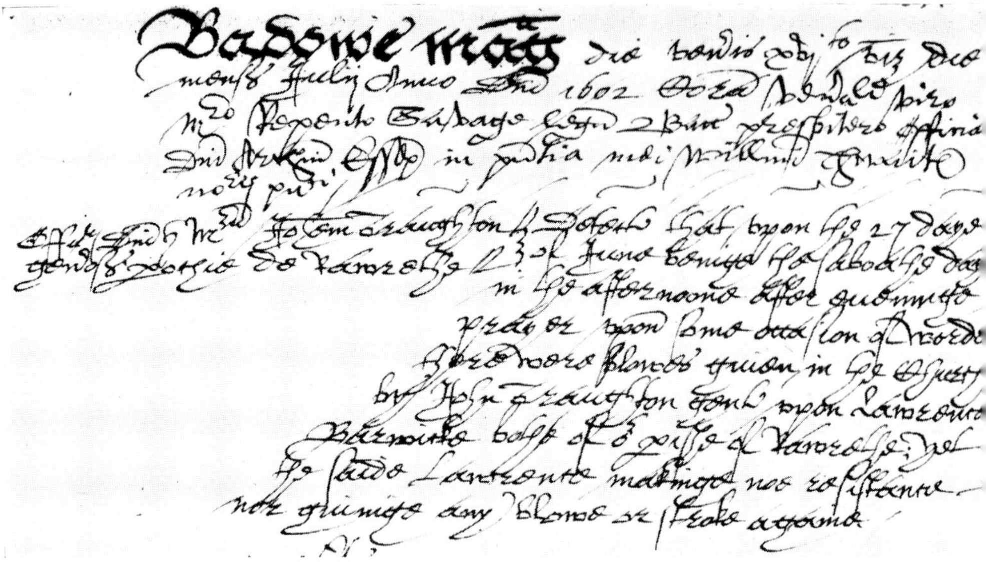

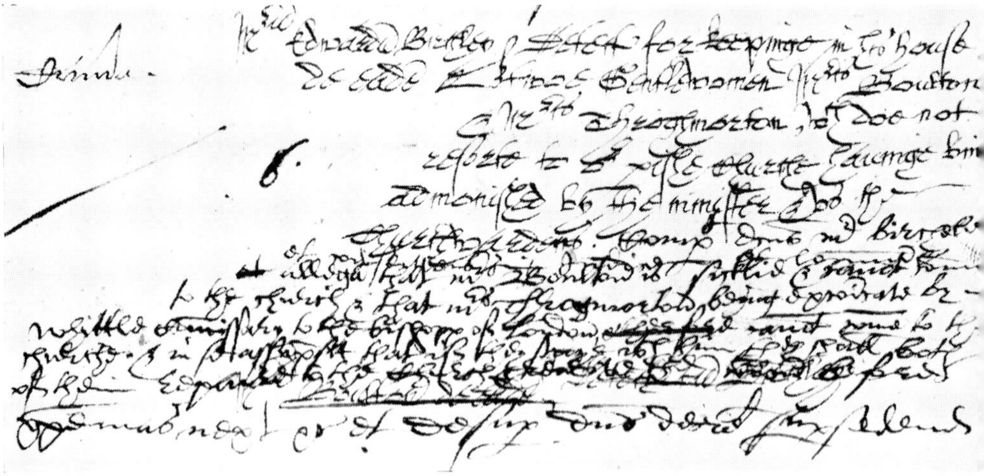

3, 4 GENTRY AMONG THE ACCUSED

The bishops' consistory courts heard most of the cases affecting the upper classes, but a few offences were cognizable by the archdeacons' courts.

3 (upper)
John Traughton, gentleman, assaults Lawrence Barwicke in Rawreth church, 1602. Usually spelt Troughton, his recent pirateering exploits may explain his short temper (p. 116).

4 (lower)
Harbouring two Catholic gentlewomen brings Mr. Birchley to court, 1600. Mistress Throgmorton is one of the recusants paying regularly the £20 a month fine for absence from church (pp. 93–4).

'surgeon' concerns that of the 'greatly diseased' woman who was 'in great danger of death'.

The entries will be related under the following headings: (a) men charged with burning women (3); (b) women charged with burning men (6); (c) men and (d) women presented because they were infected (7 and 8); (e) both parties charged, or sex not stated (2); (f) unusual cases (4); and (g) cases referring to surgeons (3). Analysing the extracts differently and equating group (d) as males who had infected females and (c) as females who had infected males, also adding three for each sex from (f) and (g), we have the following totals:

Men who had infected women	14	
Women do.	16	
Sex uncertain	2	... Total 32

It is noteworthy, however, that four charges were apparently malicious and seven were only suspect though one was highly so. No similar amount of material bearing on the disease seems to have been discovered in any other local records of our period.[1]

Group (a) comprises a West Ham man, 'reported by a common fame (i.e. rumour) that he hath burnt her', who denied the charge and had to purge himself with five honest neighbours (1579), and Thomas Robertes of Great Burstead, accused on like grounds 'to have burnt his wife', penalty being reserved (1588). A third charge lay against John Drywood of Hornchurch, who found it wise to engage counsel on his behalf after being presented by the wardens (1587). Thomas Moore, a notary public, having shown his proxy letters, first sought Drywood's absolution from excommunication through his earlier non-appearance, which was granted. He then alleged that his client was not obliged by law to purge on account of the woman's malicious accusation that he had burnt her, stressing that there was in fact no suspicion of his behaviour and that on her own confession she was a common harlot, whereas he had led a laudable life in the parish. Drywood's discharge was thus secured. The woman also was charged with immorality.

In group (b) four of the cases occur early. A woman sued another for 'calling her whore which burnt men'; the accused confessed that 'she called her so, for that she counselled her husband to misuse her' (1564). The unnamed wife of the vicar of North Shoebury (Robert Hawks) was presented 'because she did burn William Steven of North Shoebury half a year past'; Steven also had to answer for incontinence with her (1566). John Harrison of Thorpe in the parish of Southchurch, summoned at the same session for adultery with Younge's wife of Great Wakering, refused to answer the citation 'because Southchurch is a peculiar of Canterbury and outside the jurisdiction' (of the Archdeacon of Essex),

[1] There is a single mention of 'burn' in this sense in E. R. Brinkworth (*The Archdeacon's Court, 1584*, Oxfordshire Rec. Soc., xxiii, 1942).

which was true (1566). Then followed an indictment against Younge and his wife 'because he played the pimp (*fovet lenocinium*) for her and she burned her husband'. The registrar added his own comment, 'Presented through malice at the petition of Mr. Harrison'. The fourth entry is among the acts for two sessions in 1566 which are written at the end of the visitation book for that year. John Crushe of Margaretting, having denied that 'he rode with a harlot up to London where she burned him', had been assigned to purge with three neighbours, defaulted by attending again alone, when penance was enjoined, 'viz. at Chelmsford tomorrow in the market-place, with a white sheet on his back and likewise in Margaretting church at Communion time'. Far from being abashed, he exclaimed 'in the presence of the whole court that Mr. Archdeacon will discharge some for the like matters of whoredom and others he will punish extremely, and as he favoureth so he judgeth the party'.

The charge against Joan Nele of Great Oakley was that 'she lived incontinently with Robert Barnes, now of St. Osyth, and there was a talk given out first by William Ailward that she had burnt him and that she hath been very familiar and merry in his company' (1580). John Sell of Walden and Ann Hopwood *alias* Sell were accused of 'living asunder scandalously, and she is suspected of incontinent living and had a child before marriage' (1587). They both appeared, when he said that she was 'an upright and honest woman and she did never burn him, neither had he at any time any evil suspicion touching any incontinent living of her'.

Category (c) begins with Simon Wall of Ingatestone, who was reported 'to have lived in fornication and to have been burnt' (1587). Three brief entries run: 'He was burnt in adultery – she is in Chelmsford at the Blue Boar' (1588); 'He was burnt *ex meretricio concubitu*' (1588); and '*per quam est combustus*' (1597). These are the only occasions on which the scribe resorted to Latin in connexion with the disease. The presentment of an (unnamed) ostler at the 'Crown' in Romford for 'being burnt by a harlot' (1580) is linked with that of the brothel-keeper who acted as a 'surgeon' (below). John Rudd of Rickling, 'as the crime goeth, hath been burned with an harlot, but by whom we know not, neither whether it be so or not we know not, but as the fame goeth' (1585); his will is dated 1596. Richard Beere of Great Sampford was 'burnt by incontinent living and receiving into his house a light woman' (1594).

The earliest case in category (d) lay against a Walthamstow woman, 'taken in adultery with a man at Ware (Hertfordshire) who did burn her' (1569). 'Fame of incontinence, by reason whereof she was burnt', was denied by a woman of St. Nicholas, Colchester, who (in law, at any rate) cleared herself with three compurgatrices and was restored to good fame (1577). Joan Gallowaie of Havering 'in the extremity of sickness' (childbirth), named no less than five men, 'but she did falsely accuse them all' except for one who 'did burn her very pitifully'; she was ordered penance on Sunday next in Romford chapel (1578). Another woman 'was burnt, by her own confession' (1599). Not so, however, with the wife of John Neppe of Coggeshall, who was cited 'upon a crime to be so common that she is burnt, but by whom we (i.e. the churchwardens) know not'; a marginal note indicates, 'She is at St. Giles in Colchester' (1600). A Canewdon woman was 'burned by a butcher which did lie in her house, as the report doth go' (1602). The wardens of Layer-de-la-Haye presented that 'there is a brinde (burned) woman in the house of Mr. Teye suspected of incontinent life' (1589); perhaps a reference to William Tey of Layer-de-la-Haye Hall, whose house had suffered a mass attack two years earlier.[1] George Witham and his wife of Chipping Ongar were accused of 'keeping ill rule, and being a bawd to his wife, and John Salinge did carnally know her, and she was burnt' (1570); purgation followed on his denial.

There were two cases in which both parties were presented. A Romford couple had to answer the presentment that 'he hath burnt his wife or his wife burnt him, and that she for her part is vehemently suspected of incontinence' (1580). John Pyke of Kelvedon blamed Joan Johnson, 'he being provoked by her procurement' to commit fornication, but the woman pleaded not guilty and purged herself with six other women (1574); the scribe jotted down, 'Brent' (burnt).

Coming to the entries which have unusual features, a West Ham woman named Standeley kept a brothel which included an infected prostitute (1563), but no proceedings against either women were recorded. A somewhat ambiguous presentment concerned William Chapman of Witham, who 'married a wife from Chelmsford who did burn him, and then William Shether, Robert Allen and Nicholas Lowe did separate them asunder and took bands (bonds) that they should not challenge (claim) marriage one of another, and caused the woman's goods to be taken away from Chapman' (1597). Such separation by laymen, even if they were churchwardens, would appear to have been *ultra vires*. Ultimate tragedy had occurred when a Feering wife was accused of 'committing fornication with Enoch Greve, who drowned himself, being so burned that he could not abide the pains' (1590); the coroner's inquest unfortunately is not preserved in the Assize records. The sole reference to 'pox' (syphilis) as well as to doubly passing on the disease is found in the case against the wife of Andrew Knightbridge of Rayleigh, 'suspected of adultery with one Edward Leggatt of Hockley, who hath given her the pocks, and so she had given them to her husband' (1596).

Special interest attaches to two surgeons and a woman euphemistically so termed. Another Rayleigh man, suspected of incontinence, explained how, at the earnest request of the woman, 'who was greatly diseased, he

[1] *E.L. Disorder*, 121; but Morant, *History of Essex*, i, 412, gives Thomas Tey as lord of the manor.

carried her behind him upon his horse to Chelmsford to Mr. Dr. Cotten, a physician, for his help and counsel in her disease; and she contented him for his pains therefor; where she was very sick, Mistress Rowland then being in company with her; and he brought her home again, she being in great danger of death; and otherwise denied the charge' (1585). (A 'Dr. Cotton the physician' was one of the many London and Essex doctors who attended Sir William Petre several times during his long bout of illness in 1559–61.)[1] John Grieve senior of Coggeshall was presented because 'he is a surgeon and useth to heal those that be burned with committing fornication' (1588). The third case was brought against Agnes Newman, widow, of Romford (also a woman in her brothel), for 'keeping a harlot in her house, and being a common surgeon to common strumpets and such as be burnt, and keeping their counsel' (1580); the ostler already mentioned was one of the victims.

It is noticeable that there is no reference to the disease having proved fatal, except indirectly in the suicide case; that, too, has the only mention of pain, except perhaps for the 'very pitifully' entry (a word then having the opposite meanings of arousing pity, or despicable). The record book of a St. Botolph-without-Aldgate, London, parish clerk gives syphilis as the probable cause of twelve deaths in 1585–99.[2]

Incest

Sexual intercourse between persons related either by kinship or by affinity (i.e. blood or marriage) was prohibited by the Church, but it was not a secular crime. Man and wife being 'one flesh', the very early Christian teachers had exaggerated relationship by affinity into equal importance with consanguinity. In the Elizabethan period the prohibited degrees of marriage were supposed to be known by those who could read the 'Table of Kindred and Affinity' at the end of the Second Prayer Book. In the eyes of the Church, cohabitation by relations, as it presumed intercourse, was also regarded as incest. (Etymologically, incest merely meant 'unchaste', from Latin *incestus*.) Some of the cases that follow involved marriage, but the majority did not.

In a pioneer local study, based on the records of the two Essex archdeaconries, Dr. Macfarlane recently came to some important conclusions with regard to the attitude of the ordinary people to incest.[3] Contrary to the general view, 'the element of horror so often described by anthropologists' (and accepted by historians) 'appears to have been completely

[1] Emmison, *Tudor Secretary*, 249 n. For other provincial doctors, see R. S. Roberts, 'The Personnel and Practice of Medicine in Tudor and Stuart England' (*Medical History*, vi, 363–82).

[2] T. R. Forbes, *Chronicle from Aldgate* (Yale Univ., 1971), 101–6.

[3] A. D. J. Macfarlane, unpublished University of London M.Phil. thesis, 1968, 'The Regulation of Marital and Sexual Relationships in Seventeenth Century England, with special reference to the County of Essex' (the author presented a copy to the E.R.O.).

absent in Tudor and Stuart England'; and he adds that 'incestuous marriages met with little disapproval'.[1] He also gained a clear impression that 'the dreaded and horrific sexual offence was not incest', but, if anything, 'buggery, that is homosexuality and bestiality'.[2] On the controversial religious problem of marriages of cousins, he reminds us that, while 'canon law forbade the marriage of both first and second cousins, the civil law allowed the marriage of first cousins', though the Anglican Church deemed it 'not advisable'. Of such unions, we quote, with permission, his further discovery: 'No trace has been found of the argument that incest would lead to the birth of unhealthy children, or childlessness or failure to produce male heirs.'[3] It is interesting to note that the word 'incest' is restricted in the records chiefly to closely-related persons, most of the remaining charges being more in the nature of ordinary incontinence; the present writer, too, has found only a single instance of the offence being deemed a revolting one, apart from the man who lay with his old mother.

Two definite charges of incest in the first degree are recorded, both with daughters and both in the 1590s. Of these, a Great Birch man named Godward confessed to intercourse on one occasion with Margaret Godward and was sentenced 'to kneel upon his bare knees from the second peal to evening prayer till the second lesson be done and to do penance in Colchester market'. There were also four cases of suspected incest with daughters. A parishioner of St. Leonard, Colchester, named Dowdale, had been 'taken by the constables for vehement suspicion of incontinence with Patience, his own daughter who is 22 years of age, now married by licence from the Commissary of Essex to one Osias Johnson'. (The will, dated 1593, of his father, also Osias, described him as a clothier of Kelvedon.) In 1576 the tightly-knit little island community on Foulness was embroiled in recrimination. Robert Withers, John Demyn, George Cooke and William Man were presented for 'uttering slanderous words against John Challice in saying that he had a child by his own daughter'. At the same session Robert Withers, this time 'of Great Sutton' (i.e. living in the detached part of Sutton parish in the island), was presented because he 'raised a bruit', indicating evidently that he had initiated the defamation. But there was a separate charge against Challice on the same day: 'He persuaded John his daughter to burden Charles Withers to be the father of her child and she should not accuse William Sellendine to be the father, who in very deed was the father.' This Challice denied; but instead of having to purge he was discharged: a very unusual decision of the court, which must have been convinced that he was the victim of the islanders' malice. It was in 1596 that abhorrence was expressed against William Foster, presented by the Barking wardens 'upon the suspicion of a most shameful incest with his own daughter; the ground on which suspicion we

[1] A. D. J. Macfarlane, unpublished University of London M.Phil. thesis, 1968, 16–17.
[2] *Ibid.*, 18. [3] *Ibid.*, 52.

build not only upon common report but upon the assertion of honest women who have had the examination of the young wench'. Foster was assigned to purge, following his disavowal.

Four mother–son cases are found. Two women were presented, one for 'lying in bed with her son, being 20 years old, every night'. The other was not only accused of 'incestuous life with her son, he lying in bed with her, being 17 or 18 years of age', but also of suspicion of witchcraft, in which the woman, Agnes Billinge of South Ockendon, defaulted in her compurgation by producing no witnesses to her oath of innocence. Edward Pexwele of Dedham admitted only that 'he lay in a loft in the bed of his mother divers nights, his baking being at an end and having none other shift of beds' (1593). Edward Saunders of Great Stambridge had 'often lain with his own mother, an old woman, to the great offence of many' (1601); she also was charged. It will be seen that there is little or no evidence of incest having been committed in these instances.

A case of suspected incest between a married woman and her brother in 1590 reads, 'Against Mary Rambe of Great Waltham there goeth a common crime that she lieth with her own brother'. John Rambe, cited at the same session for 'having put away his wife', alleged: 'She being very willing to go to her father's for a space, one night between 10 and 12 o'clock he went to his wife's father's house, and his wife arose from the bed where she lay and lighted a candle and went up into the loft where her father lay in the bed and her brother in another, and her said brother's bed was turned down on the one side as though one had come out late there hence; and while he was talking she took her hose from under her said brother's bed, which was a great suspicion that he should think that she lay there before, but further proof he hath not.' There was clearly disharmony between Mary Rambe's family and John, as he was summoned again a few months later for not living with his wife, when his answer was that 'he is not agreed with his father-in-law, but his father-in-law doth mistrust him and beat him, and he offereth himself to live quietly with his wife but George Quilter and his wife and Humphrey Sweeting and his wife do repugn (i.e. oppose) him in this his purpose'. The Ram(b)es of Great Waltham seem to have been unlucky in their matrimonial affairs, as will be seen in the section on Betrothal. Joan Christmas of Manningtree was presented by the wardens in 1571 because she 'lay with her brother'. Pleading guilty, she was assigned 'to confess her sin before the congregation'. In 1585 Edward Wickes of Greenstead(-juxta-Ongar) had been 'taken in committing whoredom with Elizabeth Dunckhorne his sister', and she was likewise accused. Neither surname occurs in the parish register. A graver affair, of which no other facts are given, is learned from the court's rebuking John Mulberrye and John Butler, wardens of Mile End, Colchester, in 1601, 'for not presenting an incest committed between Edmund Cooke and Rose Payse which did begat two sisters with child'.

Uncle–niece liaisons were dealt with on three occasions. For the second time within eight years Great Birch had an incest case. 'Joan Peverell hath done her penance, but the same doth no ways satisfy the parish because they (the wardens) verily think her fault to be incestuous by her own uncle Henry Bridgman of Much Birch' (1599). Appearing, he successfully claimed that he 'hath been called before Mr. Commissary and there hath made his canonical and lawful purgation before him as appeareth by certain letters testimonial and showed at the last court, and therefore he ought not to be called again by new presentment'. Richard Austen of Little Oakley was reported for 'incontinent living with Judith Shynne, his maidservant and kinswoman (*cognate*)', actually his brother's daughter (1576). His penance: 'Walk through Colchester market in a white sheet, bare-headed and bare-footed, a white rod in his hand, and so stand openly in the place appointed for an hour's space, likewise in church next Sunday and on the second Saturday following in Colchester market.' His niece was given an identical sentence. The third case resulted in judicial separation. In 1564 Nicholas Weaver *alias* Allsaundre of Barking was incriminated for incest with Dorothy Alesaunder, 'his brother's daughter', to which he confessed. An even stiffer punishment involved sessions 'tomorrow Tuesday in Romford market, also on Wednesday in Romford, in Brentwood market on Thursday, then similarly on Saturday in Barking market, and in Barking church on Sunday'. The court received on the same day the petition of Frances Davye his wife (evidently her maiden name) for divorce and separation *a thoro et mensa*. 'Whereon the judge, having God before his eyes, pronounced the sentence and decreed that she shall have the one half of the goods that be his.' The certificate of the husband's penance was duly entered in the act book.

There is also an ambiguous case, brought in 1577 against George Thorogood of Hornchurch, who had 'incestuously disordered himself with his near kinswoman, viz. her father was his grandfather, Alice Male being sometimes in house with him'. The defendant put the blame on her 'wicked and lewd enticement', declaring, 'She came into his bed and by that means she was brought abed, but the child was not his as he believeth, for that she committed the said fact before with others as she hath confessed'. He added, 'She and he were brothers' children', which of course substituted a first-cousin (cousin-german) relationship. Whichever was true, the judge accepted the confession and directed him to do penance in church during the reading of the gospel. (See p. 288.)

In 1583 gossip led to Henry Lewter of Woodford and Ann Haines of West Ham being charged on 'suspicion to live incontinently, he lying at her house at certain inconvenient times'. Both gave an explicit statement that they were 'near of kin together, being sisters' children cousin germains'. Luter confessed that, 'upon occasion of hurt that he had of one of his legs by a fall, he came to his cousin's house where he remained about six days for that it was near his surgeon who dwelt in Whitechapel'. Ann added that he was 'a suitor to her in the way of marriage and by that means he repaired to her house, and she not yielding to his suit hath discharged herself of him'. The judge, however, decided that the presentment was insufficient and the rumour unproved and he dismissed the case until further proof should be submitted.

Specific indictments for cousin marriages were brought against Andrew Fuller of Dedham, who 'committed incest with Katherine Cock his cousin german and hath begotten her with child' (1589), and against Lancelot Mundaye of Berechurch, who 'married Margery Fenner, they being sisters' children' (1601). In the latter case the court learned that they had gone to Wivenhoe, and at the next session they were ordered to 'acknowledge their guilt in open church'. As already pointed out, these first-cousin charges are puzzling, because, although disallowed by the Catholic Church, they were not prohibited in the Levitical degrees nor by the Act of 32 Henry VIII, c. 38 (1540).

Charges of incest owing to affinity are almost the same in number as those for consanguinity. Four concerned men's relations with their step-daughters. William Skott of Barking had 'gotten his wife's daughter with child' (1575), which he denied and was assigned to compurgation with eight neighbours. John Guyan of Coggeshall, probably one of the family of clothiers, confessed to incest (1576), which resulted in a two-hour public appearance in Colchester market and in church on Easter Day 'at morning prayer, standing forth before the congregation'. A Mistley man named Bennett was accused (1590) of keeping 'suspicious company with Bayning's wife, with whom he lodged, Mrs. Bayning is Bennett's wife's own daughter'. The fourth prosecution is more detailed. William Harvye of Stanway impregnated Margery Carver, 'his wife's daughter, in adultery'. The man appeared and stated that he had already been punished for the offence by the order of Sir Thomas Lucas knight and Mr. (George) Southerton esquire, J.P.s, both by imprisonment in the county gaol at Colchester and 'by whipping at a cart's tail in and through the town of Colchester as by his stocking in Stanway churchyard during all morning prayer the last sabbath day'. Despite his claim, the judge ordered him to make public confession in Stanway church 'in his usual apparel having a white wand in his hand, kneeling and speaking such words of his penance as shall be delivered to him in writing by the authority of this court', also to pay 3s. 4d. to the wardens for the poor.

Although having been 'found in bed with his daughter-in-law Mary Bundocke, as his own brother hath affirmed in Braintree market before sufficient witnesses', John Catraule of Black Notley denied the charge and had to purge (1588). A woman was reported for having committed incest with her father-in-law and was excommunicated for non-appearance

(1591); the presentment of an unmarried mother led to the citation of her brother-in-law (1588); another woman married 'her (unnamed) sister's husband' (1600); a man was 'incontinent with his wife's sister' (1579); and another was suspected 'to live incestuously with his mother-in-law' (1594).

Incest with her brother-in-law as well as with another man figured in the charge against Margaret Manister, *alias* Giver, of Woodham Ferrers, in 1572. The jade 'lay in bed with one John Gyver being her husband's brother night by night, sometimes in his clothes and sometimes in his shirt, and one Thomas Browne did lie with her for the space of one week, and then she lay in a chamber severally with herself, and then the said Browne broke through the solar boards to her, but she called for no rescue and drank saven, and that night she fell sick and so was the whole week after. And the time the said Browne did lie with her she sent her children and household to the solar to lie, and they lay both in the parlour beneath.' This solitary reference to saven is of interest. It was a drug prepared from the dried tops of a small evergreen bush of that name, strongly poisonous, and accordingly was used as a common means of procuring abortion. At the next session Margaret's husband attended and 'sought the royal indulgence to be granted to her and the benefit of the same Parliament'; it was granted and the woman was discharged. This degree of affinity ('a man may not marry his brother's wife') was of course the vital issue in Henry VIII's divorce of Catherine of Aragon, as she had previously wedded Arthur, his deceased elder brother. There would have been no 'Elizabethan Life' without the decision that his marriage had been illegal, enabling him to be united with Anne Boleyn, who gave birth to Elizabeth. (The 'royal indulgence' refers to one of Elizabeth's general pardons.)

Suspected bastardy rather than incest brought David Bigg of Dedham to court in 1591 to answer the presentment for 'suspicion of incontinence with his wife's sister in his house, whereby she had a child which she confessed before Mr. Forthe a justice in Suffolk; Bigg being called in question before Mr. Grimston a justice in this shire was bound by him as reputed father to keep the child or bring in the true father'.

Four cases, including three marriages, of incest with a deceased wife's sister have been noted. In the earliest case (1572) it was the father who was first cited. Thomas Whitt of St. Peter, Maldon, said that 'he had given his consent to Nicholas Stephen to marry his daughter, being married to another of his daughters before'. He undertook to bring her to court, under penalty of the law. In the meantime she produced offspring of the unlawful marriage. Her punishment was 'to stand in the parish church of All Saints in a white sheet over her uppermost garments, the which sheet cover her whole body, all the service time, penitently before the congregation there assembled, and to give to the poor people of Maldon 40s. and the poor scholars of the University either Oxford or Cambridge 20s', a heavy fine which suggests that she had money of her own. The Rawreth wardens presented 'Lancelot Wade of Rawreth and Joan Wright of Rayleigh his pretended wife', because 'he hath begotten her with child, his late wife's sister' (1575). They both attended and confessed that they were married in Widford church last Easter. It was adjudged that 'hereafter they do not cohabit and keep company together under pain of the law' and that they perform penance in Rayleigh church on Trinity Sunday. When Richard Mott of Virley was charged (1590), he stated that 'about 16 years ago he married Margaret Graunte, with whom he continued for 5 years and she being dead, he about 20 (*sic*) years past married Elizabeth Graunte her sister, by whom he had divers children.' A victim of the foul slander (1591), John Whitbread of White Notley had to answer concerning 'a child by his deceased sister(-in-law) Mary Evered, which fame being raised by relation of light persons, in our consciences we think it to be untrue'. The churchwardens had carried out their duty of presenting village gossip, and the court wisely ignored it. John, described as 'of Writtle, gentleman', was the third son of Thomas Whitbread of White Notley, gentleman; Mary his sister had married Richard Everard of Black Notley.[1] The Whitbreads farmed White Notley Hall. It was not until three centuries later, and then only after many abortive bills, that Parliament passed the Deceased Wife's Sister Marriage Act (1907).

The last two lines in the Prayer Book table prohibited marriage with the offspring of a spouse's brother or sister. It is represented by six charges. Edward Chamberlyn and his wife in 1578 'had married within the degrees, viz. his wife's brother's daughter'. This he admitted, but claimed that they had been lawfully licensed to wed by the bishop's chancellor; the judge, however, prohibited him for consorting in future with his 'pretended' wife. The court lost no time in prosecuting Edward Asheton and his wife, of Hornchurch, in 1587, only one month after their wedding. He produced the archbishop's licence for his marriage with Agnes, daughter of John Stephen, late of Hornchurch, who he declared was 'sister's daughter to Joan Lyncoln his first wife, the which degree is without the compass of the table of degrees, and he solemnized the marriage in Brentwood chapel by John Knighton the minister of Brentwood by virtue of the licence'. The entry ends with an abbreviated note in Latin to the effect that they were discharged until it should be otherwise decided by law. In 1589 John Killingmarshe and Mary Harris of Rayleigh were both summoned. She had promised him marriage but was not contracted 'and understandeth that she can not lawfully marry with him for that she was his last wife's sister's daughter and therefore within the degrees of marriage'. The man confirmed, and the judge commanded them not to consort. In the following year John Ball and his wife, of Little Horkesley, had to answer

[1] Herald's *Visitation of Essex, 1612* (Harl. Soc., xiii (1878), 320).

because he had 'married with his wife's sister's daughter contrary to the laws of this realm'. On stating that he had already been cited by the Commissary court, he was 'dismissed from further vexation', the usual phrase in case of such a defence. The wardens of Chingford presented John Cordell junior and Joan Askewe as 'incestuous persons, for she is his brother's daughter by the mother's side, and he had a child by her'. The case was first entered in May 1602; Cordell's failure to attend led to his excommunication; the entry was repeated until several months after the Queen's death, when it was dropped. The recalcitrant John was probably connected with the well-established Cordell yeoman family of Cheshunt, a few miles away in Hertfordshire.

The sixth case came from Tendring in 1584. If we understand it rightly, the much reduced 'sin' of marriage of the fourth degree was further 'halved'. But the court was relentless, despite the fact that the co-defendant, Mary Rivet, *alias* Cressye, who 'believed herself to be of the parish of Tendring', had wedded John Rivet about twenty-five years ago! She was interrogated and deposed: 'John Rivet and John Cressye's mother were brothers and sisters by the half blood, viz. they had both one mother but two fathers.' The final phrase seems to imply that the mother of John Rivet and John Cressye's mother had married twice, so that John Cressye's mother was half-sister to Rivet. Doubtless advised by friendly villagers, Mary submitted to the court's jurisdiction, but said that 'she referreth herself to the laws'. On this minimal breach the Church's fulmination runs: 'They were enjoined not henceforth to cohabit or treat each other with marital affection in any way, under penalty of law. They shall both resort to the parish church of Tendring and stand near the chancel door, their faces turned towards the people, from the first lesson of morning prayer until the sermon or homily be preached or read, and they shall kneel down and penitently confess their fault in committing of incest and both declare their sorrowfulness and shall ask God's and the congregation's forgiveness and promise never hereafter by God's assistance to offend in the like.' This decree was made at the second hearing of the case, held in the 'Hart Chamber in the White Hart' at Colchester: apparently a private session before the Archdeacon personally. But the man did not turn up on either occasion.

A unique case is found in 1584, though without the relationship being given. The humanitarian way in which an incestuous lunatic was dealt with may be without precedent in Elizabethan Church court records. Anthony Walker of Burnham confessed to unlawful intercourse with Margaret Younge and submitted himself to the court's correction, on which the judge (the Archdeacon's Official) ordered penance. But in the afternoon of the same day, the Official received a letter from the Archdeacon himself, as a result of which the following decree was written in the act book:

> Anthony Walker was greatly distressed in mind, and desperately minded by reason of his lunacy, and being required to deal gently and easily with him, for fear he should desperately cast away himself, as it was credibly informed and certified; and also perceiving the great perplexity and desperate behaviour of the same Walker in Court, and for the avoiding of further extremity of some desperate attempt that he would use towards himself, willed the same Walker to serve God and to take good instructions of Leper the minister as also other good preachers thereby for his amendment of life; and upon the Sunday next after Easter, if there be a communion, or some other Sunday before the next court, if there be a communion in Burnham church, there penitently and openly before the congregation, meekly kneeling upon his knees, confessing his lewd and abominable fact of incest and fornication by him committed with Margaret Younge, according to his own confession, in manner and form as it shall be directed to the minister in writing.

The judge decided that penance be deferred until the court was informed 'that his fit of lunacy had left him'. (William) Leper was curate to Peter Lewes, soon to be known as one of the violently quarrelsome clerics.[1]

There are three other charges in which the relationship was omitted. In 1589 Daniel Spencer of Wix was accused because 'he was godfather to his own child, he and his wife at that time standing excommunicated for incest and for marrying within the degrees of kindred prohibited'; but he claimed that 'his wife is lately dead and that he hath been punished for his incestuous marriage by the judge as Commissary to my Lord Bishop of London'. In the following year Peter Salmon of Tolleshunt Bushes (Knights) was presented by the wardens of 'committing of incest with his kinswoman Mary Browne', she also being reported; and in 1601, when William and Rebecca Markes 'singlewoman' of Wix were reported, the man because he had had intercourse with Rebecca 'his kinswoman, as the public fame goes', he repudiated the rumour.[2]

Other Sexual Offences

Indictments for rape or attempted rape had to be tried before the Assize judges. Somewhat unexpectedly, the Assize records for Essex yield very few charges.[3] In contrast, twenty-three cases came up at the archdeacons' courts, of which seventeen were for attempted rape; of the latter, two were brought against a rector and a curate, as narrated under Clergy.

John Gouldthwaite of Kelvedon was presented by the wardens of Rivenhall in 1590 because 'he hath committed fornication with one Joan Summerson of our parish, as she hath confessed before the justice and the constable, vehemently against her will'. He challenged the charge and was assigned to purge with six persons, three of each parish. The entry

[1] *E.L.: Disorder*, 112, 144.

[2] A charge of incest, on which a true bill was returned but no sentence recorded, heard at the Middlesex Sessions, is apparently unique in Elizabethan secular court records (*Middlesex County Records*, i, 152).

[3] *E.L.: Disorder*, 196–7.

continues: 'It appears to the judge that he is bounden to appear before the justices for a rape.' At the next Church court he announced that he had been 'called before the justices of Assize and was cleared of the matter, and he never committed fornication nor did he attempt the same'. This is borne out by the gaol calendar of persons awaiting trial at the Midsummer Assize, his name appearing among those 'discharged because no wrong was found against them'. But a month later the act book reads: 'We present once again John Gouldthwaite' for further suspected misbehaviour with Joan Summerson, 'and the matter is very offensive to the parishioners.' This time there was no hint of rape. (In the previous year he had been one of the victims of a bogus clerk of the market for defective weights.)[1]

Also in 1590 Joan Somers of Downham (despite the similarity in name with the previous case, there is no connexion) declared that, 'upon a certain working day, happening about Christmas last, she being in a plough field serving of her dame's cattle, Rice Evans came unto her and told her that she might now cry her heart out before anybody could hear her cry, and so indeed as she saith he did violently abuse her body and committed fornication with her'. But, strangely enough, the presentment lay against her – for fornication – and this was her defence. The entry is left unfinished. In another case six years earlier, John Robinson of Dovercourt, butcher, was accused of adultery with Jasper Cole's wife, also because he 'did strive with one Harvy's wife who was with child, which child was thus destroyed, as she said before divers of our parish'. Surprisingly again, no further record of this thwarted lecher is found; instead of which we learn that Jasper Cole disturbed the church when his wife 'should have done penance'. In 1596 William Cofield of Stanway, having to answer for suspected incontinence with Rose Durrell of the same, alleged that he, 'being convented for a rape committed with her, had his trial for the same at the last Assizes at Brentwood and was thereof quit'; but there is hiatus in the Assize files between March 1595 and June 1596.

Not unnaturally, as in all generations, there were some borderline or unproven charges. Katherine, wife of John Lee of Aveley, 'taken in bed committing adultery with Robert Wrignelles, a waterman of Purfleet' (in West Thurrock), claimed that 'he provoked her, partly by force'; but she (not he) was ordered full penance (1585). Leonard Whitfield of Little Baddow was accused by his maidservant because, on her refusing to go to bed with him when his wife was away, she ran downstairs pursued by him and locked herself in a milk house; he admitted being 'ill minded', but all he said was that 'she were better to lie with him than alone' (1583). Likewise Harvey's wife asserted that 'she was driven' by Richard Keble of East Mersea 'to shut the door against him for that he could have had to do with her'; to which Keble protested that it was 'vague and uncertain'. The

[1] *E. L.: Disorder*

judge, 'having considered the contents of the presentment', discharged him (1592). Two entries in 1602 record how one woman 'hath commonly reported that sundry times he hath attempted her to be incontinent with him, but she affirmeth that she so resisted him that he prevailed not', the case being dismissed; and another said that a man 'did attempt her chastity and would have been naught with her', but her story was at once discounted when a third party testified that she had slept with two young men. Rebutting the presentment of 'vehement suspicion that he offered after a violent and shameful manner to dishonest Agnes Warren in the house of her husband', Peter Udall of West Ham purged with four neighbours. There are a few other vague charges with imputation of violence brought by women, most of whom used the customary 'would a had to do with her'.

It was imperative in rape prosecutions in the civil courts to take the alleged victim's deposition; but virtually none for our period has been preserved. The archidiaconal archives have one concerning two servants in Mr. Brockett's house at Willingale (Nicholas Brocket, lord of the manor of Willingale Doe). Pestered to become betrothed, the maid eventually agreed, provided that her father consented. Still importunate, the man feigned illness, sending a fellow servant to summon her to his bedside, where again he sought her promise. On her refusal, 'by strength he strived with her, but she withstood him' (1590). So again it was only a case of attempted deflowering.

The small number of prosecutions for alleged violent assaults on virgins' chastity or wives' virtue as compared with the ubiquitous evidence of premarital or illicit intercourse is somewhat unexpected. Perhaps females' fear of court proceedings induced inaction until pregnancy was realized, when it was probably too late to accuse the assailant except under the ordinary bastardy machinery.

What is now known as indecent assault was a term that had not been coined in Elizabethan times, but at least one relevant item has been noted. In 1579 Thomas Newman of Hatfield Peverel had to answer because 'he hath used unseemly behaviour and gestures in uncomely manner with one Clement Harris, kissing and otherwise uncomely behaving himself towards her'. Of course he denied 'doing any further thing with her' beyond 'casting her down and kissing her in harvest time in one Durrifall's field; and for the fault he did submit himself and asked God presently forgiveness, and so the judge dismissed him'.

John Harris of Layer Breton 'behaved himself very disorderly by putting forth his privities' (1581). His defence, genuine or ingenuous: 'Upon occasion of losing 6d., he did untruss his points and let down his hose to show that he had it not.' (Points were tagged laces that tied the hose to the doublet.) He was ordered to confess his disorderly behaviour 'before Mr. (Peter) Hawkes (rector) and three or four others of the same parish'. William Overed of Ashdon, 'being a man appointed to keep the church clean', was presented by the wardens because on 24 March 'he did go into the chapel and there pissed' (1587). Alleging that he went 'into the chapel to make water upon his hands, being sore' (a well-known supposed remedy), he was ordered to acknowledge his guilt in church on the following Sunday. Richard Walker *alias* Pigeon 'did set his windows open and was abusing of prick' (1588). Having confessed, he was enjoined a similar penance. The wife of Thomas Evered of Ardleigh was accused (1589) as 'a scold amongst her neighbours, and for that she did openly make water in a glass before men and in their sight, and then threw her own water out and filled it with drink, and then drunk to the said men'. We are not vouchsafed the court sequel. The Earls Colne wardens presented Henry Abbott junior, who 'in his drunkenness said that his privities or prick was longer by four inches than one Clerke there' – his drinking companion' (1590): the theme of a later generation's lewd limerick. His unconvincing defence was that he 'never knew or heard the detection was true'; so the judge ordered the wardens to cite Clerke at the next session to give his own testimony, not recorded.

A few presentments for other sexual offences are recorded in the court books of the Archdeaconry of Colchester. While the sins of Adam and Eve, Onan, the men of Sodom and the daughters of Lot were not uncommonly mentioned by early monastic writers, specific records referring to charges of gross indecency and homosexuality are believed to be very rare before the seventeenth century, and cases of public exposure seem to be virtually unknown before this offence became cognizable in the secular courts. The entries which have been found are therefore of some interest to criminologists.

Mr. Cooke, schoolmaster of Great Tey, was presented on a serious charge, presumably paederasty. 'He is a man', the wardens reported, 'of beastly behaviour amongst his scholars, and teacheth them all manner of bawdry' (1594). Cited to attend the next session, he failed to appear, and there is no further entry of this case.

2

Other Personal Offences

Defamation and Discord

Strangely, enough, Defamation was not one of the Seven Deadly Sins, though often begotten of Envy and Ire. Defamation in the ecclesiastical courts was the counterpart of slander in the secular courts. The former term was used primarily by the Church lawyers, but the parties generally referred to slander. In his article on Defamation, Burn discussed at great length the criteria that determined which court should properly have jurisdiction in such causes. Only if slanderous speech bore on the moral character of the plaintiff could the Church courts prosecute; though it was asserted, but not always maintained, that they had cognizance in all causes where a minister was defamed. If the slander included 'spiritual mixed with temporal words', the action lay in the civil courts; but calling a man 'bastard' was a secular offence as it 'tended to a temporal disinheritance'. There were other curious distinctions. To designate a woman 'bawd' rendered the speaker liable to citation by the Church; to declare that a man or woman kept a bawdy house, however, was a lay offence. In Tudor and Stuart times the commonest abusive epithet was 'knave', originally not a word of reproach but merely signifying a male servant. Slanderers of course had a rich store of stronger vulgarities at their disposal; but only if these imputed vice, such as 'whoremaster', did an action for defamation come before the spiritual courts.[1] Such, at any rate, was the law as explained by Burn. But the archdeacons' records make it abundantly clear that the appellation 'knave', qualified in any way, amounted to defamation and the case was appropriated.

In the age when Shakespeare has shown that rude attributes were bandied about almost indiscriminately, it is surprising that so many who thus voiced their feelings were presented for defamation: a term which in later times postulated graver denigration of character than some of the commonplace Elizabethan invective. Defamation accounts for at least six hundred cases in the two Archdeacons' courts: a very much larger number than the indictments for slander at Quarter Sessions and Assizes.[2]

A large proportion of the charges were of course in the nature of abuse rather than defamation. Of the latter, it will be perfectly obvious that

[1] R. Burn, *Ecclesiastical Law* (edn. of 1773), i, 476–84.
[2] *E.L.: Disorder*, 66–79.

5 BLACK CHAPEL, GREAT WALTHAM

The fifteenth-century chapel-of-ease at North End, four miles from the parish church (p. 86). The adjoining priest's house, not seen, is on the left of the chapel. (Essex Record Office.)

[illegible] Robert Withers [illegible] non frequentant [illegible] et in parochia de [illegible] in foulnes [illegible] parochia de Sutton magna [illegible]

[illegible] foulnes [illegible]

6 FOULNESS FORMULA

Foulness formerly 'belonged' to five mainland parishes, but, although it acquired its own parish church *circa* 1545, the other parishes still asserted claims. Robert Withers, one of eight islanders charged with not going to Sutton church, defends himself in language worthy of a lawyer: 'They are of the parish of Sutton but not in the parish of Sutton but of Foulness.' The Court decides on a compromise (p. 91).

[illegible] Henricum [illegible] detected for that they were contracted together and afterward [illegible] et Johannam Brewer de [illegible] the said Henrie sould the said Joane unto Edward Croxen for xs. and for that the [illegible] not paid the said Henrie did forbid the ba[illegible] [illegible] Edwardum [illegible]

7 SALE OF HIS BETROTHED

Henry Marshall and Joan Brewer, being 'contracted together', he sells her to Edward Croxen for 10s.; because it is not paid he forbids the banns. His defence: she had 'promised matrimony but he hath no proof'; she denies (p. 144).

much arose from the ubiquitous welter of parochial gossip and intrigue. Many of the presentments were framed only in general terms, such as using opprobrious or indecent words, or calling another a common slanderer, notorious slanderer, common railer and slanderer of honest men, slanderer of neighbours, backbiter and slanderer, scandalous among her neighbours, or busy with her tongue. Of specific speech against women, the commonest disparaging word was whore, occasionally varied with arrant (or errant) whore, privy whore, Bridewell whore, or whore and witch. Not infrequently two women confronted each other with the same term, or such mutual recrimination led to 'harlot' being countered by 'witch'. In such matters the judge usually demanded that they should 'reconcile themselves'.

Often, however, the verbal obscenities were recorded in full. 'Thou art an whore', a Woodham Ferrers woman spat at another, 'and it was an whore's touch to have a whoremace knave to hold thy head, and thy deeds will prove thee whore'; but she admitted in court that 'she knoweth none other but that she' (i.e. the slandered party) 'is an honest woman' and craved her forgiveness. A Great Oakley man 'slanderously infamed' a widow, 'calling her whore, arrant whore and ridden whore, who hath been of good name and fame heretofore with us' (the churchwardens); he was cited at the same session for having refused to pay the parish clerk's wages for two and three-quarter years. Even more to the point is the slander thrown at a maidservant by a man who not only called her a whore but bade her 'to keep her tail'. A Cressing tailor's colourful epithet for a neighbour's wife was 'butter-mouthed whore'. An Ingrave villager went farther in crediting another tailor with having three such women, naming the houses where they lived. The Great Sampford wardens reported an embittered villager who 'used railing speeches against some of his honest neighbours, calling them dogs, sly whelps, and they might have barked before they bit'. In contrast to whore, bitch was sparingly applied, though the combination of bitch and witch, referring to an old woman, was irresistible to at least one man; 'most falsely', the presentment added, 'so as he could not with a good cause receive the Holy Communion'. A malicious declaration that a parishioner had 'a strange woman with child being not his wife' elicited the wardens' comment, 'which we believe in our consciences not true'. A West Mersea man, thinking that four women had called him 'dog', said openly that they were all bitches; openly, therefore, in church he had to withdraw his words.

Other Elizabethans' aural endurance of oral injury saved the courts fortunately from being overwhelmed by thousands of calumny cases.

In all generations tales of sexual immorality have spread like wildfire among small communities, or have been spitefully invented in the sure knowledge that they would soon circulate. So it was that wilful defamation was alleged by many for this and other offences. It must often have been touch-and-go whether the slanderer or the slandered party was to be prosecuted. Rejected lovers provide an example of each: one man tried to debase the woman in the eyes of his rival and was promptly charged; but another woman, similarly reviled, asserted that she was in court 'only by evil report' of a man 'who was once a suitor unto her by way of marriage, and in that she liked not him he did maliciously slander her, and he himself bade one of the sidemen to present her'. When Margaret, wife of Henry Gravenor of Dedham, was charged in 1600 with 'vehement suspicion of incontinence' with Robert Glover of Dedham, her husband declared that she was a woman of good fame and was the victim of false rumour amplified by malevolent and hostile parishioners, so she had the opportunity of purging with five neighbours.

But on another occasion the husband had to defend himself against his wife's recriminations. Under their oath of office churchwardens of course had little option but to present people whose reputation had been assailed. There is little doubt, however, that a few officers were too ready to accept idle talk. In this case, like so many others, they had to report the story going around the village. Thus John Lewis of Chigwell found himself presented in 1590 for 'haunting suspiciously Elizabeth the wife of William Dalian'. The resulting proceedings fill a whole page of the act book. 'He hath in no way', he claimed, 'deserved to be suspected of evil behaviour', contending instead that 'his wife by too much jealousy hath raised a slander and given it forth to his great discredit and grief and contrary to any truth'. Admitting that it was offensive to her that he 'doth sometimes resort unto the house of William Dalian, who was his servant by the space of two years', he offered to enter into a bond never to keep company with the woman again and to submit to the court's discretion. The judge decided to accept the proposal. Lewis was enjoined to bind himself accordingly in the sum of £20 to the archdeacon; also next Sunday after evening prayer 'to come up into the chancel and there before the minister and wardens acknowledge his sorrow'. The money penalty seems to be unreasonably stiff: it was equal to the value of, say, several horses. By his will, proved in 1604, he termed himself a tanner and he provided generously for the poor of Chigwell. He apparently forgave his jealous wife, Bridget, who was his residuary legatee and sole executrix, but he gave to Dorothy, wife of William Willford of St. Martin's near Aldersgate, 'a legacy which I promised her, namely £20'. No relationship is mentioned; was she a former lover? But he could not have had a more respectable overseer of his will: Samuel Harsnett, the vicar, later to become Archdeacon, also Archbishop of York – the founder of Chigwell School.

It is ironical that the plethora of pettifogging persecutions for loose living which earned the 'Bawdy Court' its colloquial name was swollen by so many charges based on unreliable if not mendacious scandalmongering. Very occasionally, it is true, churchwardens tried to perform a dual duty – presenting but exculpating at the same time, as those of Canewdon did in John Capperton's case; 'which crime', they explained, 'was first raised by John Wood of the same parish, who is of no credit'. Some victims, like John King of Colne Engaine in 1589, countered such testimony with vigour. 'He was not presented by all the churchwardens', he declared, 'but by one of them upon ill will by the instigation of one Joan wife of Henry Smithe, being his notable and notorious enemy, and upon her slanderous report; for the which he attempted law against her in this court in a cause of slander, and did pain her to be excommunicated in not appearing to answer the same suit'. The judge, carefully weighing the circumstances, discharged him. In a case concerning two Stanford-le-Hope women in 1567, the plaintiff was ordered to pay 53s. 4d. taxed costs. She appeared, paid this sum, and penitently declared, 'Whereas goodwife Gillman said, "Fie, fie on your honesty", I do here recant and deny the same to be false and untrue and knowing none otherwise by you but that you are and always have been an honest woman, and therefore I ask you forgiveness for such evil and slanderous sayings and reports'. Such a formal recantation is very rarely met with in the records.

In the previous year an aggravated case involved first a layman and then the Archdeacon of Essex himself. William Clarcke, described as a minstrel, and William Charles, *alias* Carles, both of the parish of Hornchurch, were prosecuted by Hugh Wylcockes for saying that he was 'a basket butcher and he should flea a cow in the wood with Alison's wife, meaning that he should have his pleasure of her'. It was proper that a criminal charge should precisely interpret any colloquialism (metaphorical flea-removal from the female form will shortly be referred to in a similar context), but the exact meaning of 'basket butcher' is not clear. Both having protested their innocence, Clarcke 'publicly accused Mr. Thomas Cole in the parish of Keldon in English, viz. that such a religion he careth not for, and for railing words he in the presence of divers men said that Mr. Cole was a knave'. Archdeacon Cole was being addressed perhaps as rector of High Ongar and Stanford Rivers, which lie close to Kelvedon Hatch.

William Carr of Ingatestone was maligned in 1593. The court learned that 'there is no fame' of his incontinence with a woman, 'saving that Thomas Sweeting, his apprentice, by the provocation of one George Dowsett, did report that he was naught with her, and being before Mr. Mildmay, justice of the peace, he did revoke his speeches'. In 1590, challenging the wardens' presentment that John Dynes, tailor, had been unchaste with her, Thomasine Stookes of Cressing said, 'There is a rumour raised by divers of that parish which owe me malice, and I am of good opinion and credit amongst my neighbours'. So a commission was given to Henry Crane, rector of Rivenhall, and Henry Robinson, rector of Fairstead, to arrange for her purgation with four persons.

A double presentment, also in 1590, illustrates the behaviour of a slut that was paralleled in many villages: James Dowtye of Kelvedon, accused through Dionise Crackbone declaring how he had slept all night with Joan Shawe, which he denied and managed to get a full discharge; and (blank) Barrett of Ulting, prosecuted because 'the fame goeth that he hath lain with Dionise Crackbone, she and Joan Shawe falling out, and in their anger railed one with the other and said likewise that Dowtye had lain with Joan Shawe'.

The courts dealt with many other curious accusations, of which only a few can be selected. From Pontisbright (the parish now called Chapel) in 1583 Thomas Baker senior brought a case against a man named Crowche, who had related how Baker 'reported and affirmed that Mistress Turner whilst she dwelt at Thomas Boteslye played the whore with my Lord of Oxford's men, that Mistress Beriffe had played the whore with that short-legged knave Lawrence her man, and that Mistress Hawkin had played the whore with Browninge a physician late of Peldon'. Crowche's answer was that Baker was 'not thereby defamed, for he spake the words in deed, and Baker is the same Crowche his father (i.e. Crowche's father-in-law), for Crowche married with the daughter of Baker, which is yet alive'. (The will of a James Browninge of Peldon, proved in 1591, does not term him a physician.) In the same year a Wimbish woman, 'going from church on a Sunday in Stourbridge Fair, John Wright met with her and took her by the arm and offered to kiss etc. (*sic*); and she answered that she was not for him and told him afterward that there was a speech abroad the parish that he was his father's gelding'. This she later repudiated, explaining that another woman mainly 'worked the rumour', so the latter was charged with defamation. Also in 1583 a Romford slanderess told another woman that her husband lived incontinently with a third woman who 'got her living with the swell of her brows', a novel way of describing a prostitute. A Burnham woman was grossly insulted in 1566 by a neighbour who 'asked her if she had not need of a tarse' (penis). The sentence: 'To stand in Maldon market-place on Saturday in a white sheet and a white rod in his hand, confessing that he hath evil used his tongue filthily, which he should have used otherwise to God's glory.' In 1593 a Ramsey woman, answering a charge of slander in 'reporting herself to have been incontinent with John Mayers, now sayeth that it is not so, but that she was counselled to say so by Mr. (Thomas) Sayer, parson of Wrabness', who was then cited to explain: yet another summons for this licentious scoundrel, whose name will recur more than once.

Showing handwriting and spelling much less professional than his successors, the deputy registrar or clerk of the Archdeacon of Essex at the court held in Romford chapel in February 1566 scribbled at top speed his record of the suit brought by John Clarke, *alias* Syms, on his wife's behalf against Alice Lewes of Woodford for defamation. He punctuated the man's statement with a few easy Latin phrases. Here is the strange result, which calls for literal quotation:

> Dicta Alicia dixit in presentia of Lielis [*sic*, for Lewes] wyeffe and Howchinsons wyeffe that Syms wyeffe shollde be suspiciuslie in a chamber with a straynge man et similiter in presentia uxoris Howchinson dixit that as Mr. Roger and Mr. Hearne weare a howntinge they shollde saye to a neybour of the same towen who it was she cowllde not tell was bydden by them to take in a lewed wooman that they shollde see doinge incontynentlye together and she tellynge the tale beffor Howchinesons wyeffe axed her who that shoolde be and she verryeffied and saied by our lordes hartte it was Syms wyff.

While the previous volume gave the reader the actual words of several highly obscene rhymes, including the long Chelmsford ballads, he is not vouchsafed any new verses from the act books. Richard Waters' wife of Stapleford Abbots in 1601 'slandered her neighbours by a rhyme made of John Cloves' maid'; and Thomas Ellys of Boreham in 1597 'reported a rhyme upon the names of sundry men and women in our parish, but will not be knowledge made of it nor of whom he had it', although he added in court that there was 'a rhyme of the girl of the sideman', on which he was cautioned and discharged.[1] That is all specifically about scurrilous versifiers, and their actual doggerel is not recorded; but a third case tells us more about the origin of the three verses already in print,[2] of which the first runs:

> Here dwelleth an arrant bichant whore,
> Such one as deserves the cart.
> Her name is Margaret Townsend now.
> The horn shows her desert.

The present writer had added that 'its author is probably revealed in the roll for the following Hilary (Quarter) Sessions, 1584, when Stephen Bull of West Ham was bailed by two fellow parishioners and a Writtle man at the suit of Nicholas Townsend's wife'. We now find in the archdeacon's act book the presentment of Margaret Townsend, 'suspected to be an evil woman of living by reason of letters set upon her door, willing her to amend her evil life'. The accused declared that Bull had 'confessed before Sir Thomas Lodge the justice that he made one of them, whereupon he is bound to appear at the Assizes, which bill was set up upon spite for that she rebuked him for that he caused her husband to keep his and other lewd company and spend that he had'; and she maintained that she lived virtuously. The judge dismissed her 'until sufficient evidence be forthcoming': a rare instance of purgation not being demanded because the prosecution had fallen flat. Bull's name is found only once in the Assize files – among the prisoners in the county gaol in 1587. Although a number of City merchants were building new houses in West Ham, it is

[1] Could he be the 'Father Ellys', a Chelmsford barber, who figures slightly in the indictment against Thomas Chitham of Boreham for writing the ballad in 1600 (*E.L.: Disorder*, 72, 75)? Mr. A. M. C. Field kindly pointed out that it should have been printed in *4* stanzas of *6* lines each (cf. p.74); stanza 1,1.3, ends 'then', and 2, 1.1, 'flood'. [2] *Ibid.*, 68.

evident from what was said under Prostitution that the area near Bow Bridge had a number of undesirable characters, to which may now be added others, including Stephen Bull. At the previous session Edward Lum of that parish had been detected for keeping ill rule in his house in harbouring Margery, his wife's sister, suspected of evil and incontinent life with Bull; to which Lum replied that Margery Fenton, his wife's sister, was kept as a servant; but she denied the charge and had to purge.

One of the more virulent ways of slandering a husband was to call him a cuckold. The emblem ascribed to cuckolds by ancient custom was a pair of horns. When Arthur Dixson sued Ellen Cordie in 1574 for defamation, she confessed to having 'willed him to take a saw and to saw off his horns, which she meant thereby that his wife was not an honest woman'. More humilating than oral innuendo was the adorning of the door or fence of a cuckold's house. Next year the court dealt more firmly with another defamer, Joan Cooper of Great Burstead, whose charge was that of slandering her neighbour by 'hanging a horn on her neighbour's pale'. Was she one of the most brazen-faced Essex hussies? The act book actually notes that 'she brought in a horn' into the court. If importunate allies had emboldened her to act the buffoon, her lame reply was that 'she did hang it up upon Parker's pale, but upon no evil intent'. Affronted or amused, the shrewd judge gave her condign penance: 'On Sunday next she shall openly confess that she was sorry for slander of her neighbour, she there having the horn hanging on her sleeves'. Where did Edward Edwardes and Richard Lambert, of Helions Bumpstead, presented in 1585, perpetrate their prank? They were charged on suspicion that 'they set up horns in John Boyton's stool', which could mean either his church seat or his close-stool (privy), perhaps in an outhouse. Four years later, as will be related, a cleric was the unfortunate victim of horns nailed on his door. The final illustration is a similar one. In 1595 Henry Barwick of Great Tey had to answer a multiple presentment for not attending church, sowing discord among his neighbours, frequenting the alehouse, and setging up a pair of horns at William Welles' door. In the previous volume we narrated the much more detailed account of how two Burnham householders' doors, likewise marked with horn 'ensigns' by a local gang at night, afforded morning mirth to a jeering crowd, and how obscene doggerel and ballads often designated cuckolds.[1] Thus, in Elizabethan Essex, unfaithful wives' affairs gave rise to horseplay, and court archives reveal the close link between morals and customs.

In an obscure statement about several Cranham persons, Thomas Braine, the curate, said in 1579 that 'about a sennight past he heard Henry Packer affirm that he had slandered the widow Doore in saying that he had abused her body, and for so reporting he had 20s. given him,

[1] *E.L.: Disorder*, 69, 72, 108.

and also the same Packer offered to lay 10s. that he should do no more or other penance; and further that William Vear doth retain Packer with meat and drink and money, as is reported'. Was Vear a homosexual? The widow had to find two Cranham compurgators and two of the 'next parish'; having failed to do so, she was awarded penance for suspected living with Packer. In the following year Packer was detected 'for keeping Joan Huntley unmarried, being with child', but was discharged because he said on oath that 'the constables willed him to receive her'.

As a result of gossip by a cleric's wife, Humphrey Kenwelmarsh of Woodham Ferrers was presented in 1575 as a slanderer of his neighbours. 'There was controversy between him and Mr. Norden their minister'; he had spread a tale of how Mistress Norden declared that 'John Stelliman's wife was Elizabeth Saunders' woman and Wheeler's wife was Henry Saunders' woman'. The judge ordered him to justify his defamatory remarks. He did not appear again and was excommunicated. Norden was evidently the curate, as the rectory was held by Nicholas Johnson from 1568 to 1611.

'Detected for uttering most vile words which are not for to be used' introduced a defamation case against three West Ham wives in 1590: 'Agnes Brathwayte reporteth that Elizabeth wife of Nicholas Boswell played the naughty pack for a wallet, and the wife of George Clark likewise played the naughty pack with three quissions (cushions) under her for a shoulder of mutton, and thereupon Boswell's wife arrested Brathwait to the Counter (prison) in London'. Examination merely produced statements about 'whore' being shouted at each other.

It looks as though a Stanford-le-Hope man named Rattle (perhaps a son of Thomas Rattle of that parish, whose will was proved in 1579) was a man of low morals and little credit. John Slayterford had to answer in 1584 for 'reporting to sundry of the town that Rattle was with Margery Daye in the fields suspiciously and in an inconvenient place', but was immediately discharged. The case was followed by a similar slander charge against John's wife, Frisewith, for saying that 'there was one that could have pulled Rattle from under a coverlet from Wright's wife'; and she, too, was dismissed. Nor was Margery Daye any better, as we shall see shortly in the Waples case.

Inevitably there were instances of grave slander by which a woman tried to father her bastard on an innocent man. In 1599 'Mr. Henry Amcotts of Cranham' (apparently the testator whose will was proved in 1607) was victimized by his maid; and in 1576 four men of Foulness defamed another islander by imputing his having committed incest with his daughter, who accused another, as related under incest.

Three deposition books for the Archdeaconry of Essex covering 1576–92 add a little to our knowledge of the less presentable side of Elizabethan life, especially the defamation causes. A few of these have been selected.

A case in 1581 was supported by the depositions of five witnesses on behalf of John Clement, who had been slandered by Edward Maggett; all belonged to Doddinghurst. The act book for 1580–3 is lost, so that the deposition book is the only record. This was what two of them said: the others' statements were similar. George Marden, who had lived there since birth, aged 61, deposed that 'Thomas Taylford, John Harding and Richard Witham one day between Whitsuntide and Midummer last, in Richard Marden's house in Doddinghurst, being daysmen or arbitrators chosen by both parties, who were both present, touching a controversy between them by reason of slanderous words spoken by Maggett, they long debated the matter but could make no final end. But they brought it to pass that if Maggett would give Clement 12d. and discharge the (expenses of the) court they would agree for Clement's part, but the daysmen for Maggett denied (i.e. refused) it.' Later, however, Thomas Taylford 'willed him to make an end, and Maggett said to Clement, "If I cannot prove that you offered a woman a groat to have been naught with her and if I cannot prove by William Hope and Richard Reynolds the constables that you had two harlots in your house locked in your house, and when the constables came to search for them according to their office you locked the same harlots up in a chamber whereby the constables could not have seen them, and you did give the constables a pot of beer and sent them away without doing their office, I will pay your charges, and if I do prove it you shall pay my charges", to which Clement agreed.' The deponent 'had heard that Clement did present himself into the court to clear himself of the slander first raised by one Reve and then Maggett, but he never heard that he was presented by the sworn men, neither yet excommunicated to his knowledge.' Maggett proved obstinate and was prosecuted three years later for contempt.

John Hardinge, husbandman, who had lived there for about 16 years and before that in the parish of South Weald, aged 40, had known Clement and Maggett for about 10 years. 'One day a little before harvest Maggett came to his house, and before Mr. West, curate of Doddinghurst, falling in talk with the deponent, Maggett declared he heard Reve confess in Moss's house that Clement kept two women suspected of incontinency in his house, and that the constables had been there and could not find them, but in the end they found them there and willed this deponent to tell Clement. Accordingly, Hardinge next morning willed Clement to clear himself, or otherwise he would present him at the next Court, he this deponent being then a sworn man; and thereupon had just occasion to tell him of it for the safeguard of his oath. Within a while after, he heard that Clement had entered a suit against Maggett for slander.'

Disparagement of Dr. John Walker, Archdeacon of Essex, was incidental to a dissolute defamer of another man's wife in 1584. This was revealed in depositions of two witnesses in a case against Thomas Waples. Robert

Dethicke, gentleman, of Stanford-le-Hope, where he had lived for 11 years, and before that at Cheston (?county), aged 22, had known the parties for about 11 years. 'About six weeks ago on a Sunday in the forenoon, John Sammes talking with Thomas in the churchyard suddenly requested this deponent to rehearse those words which he had spoken of Day's wife (for a suit should have been commenced by her against Sammes for rehearing of those words, if he could not prove them to be spoken by Waples), and then in this deponent's presence Waples rehearsed the words, viz. that he could never be rid of Day's wife before he had his pleasure of her. He believeth that Waples spoke those slanderous words only for the defaming of her good name and fame amongst her neighbours, being esteemed since of worse credit than before. Waples was a man who had sustained much punishment for abusing himself in word and deed, being whipped at a cart's arse (i.e. tail) for his offences, and gotten a woman with child in Stanford-le-Hope, doing penance for the same openly in the church. He heard it credibly reported by his master, Mr. Edward Riche esquire, that Waples should (i.e. did) say that he neither cared for Dr. Walker nor never a Walker in England.

The deposition of John Sammes, labourer, of the same parish, where he had lived for about 10 years, and before that at Corringham, aged 38, runs as follows. 'About 10 or 11 weeks ago Eme Cockes his mother going to Waples' house by chance, as she told him, heard Waples report to her that he could never be quit or rid of Margery Daie before he had his pleasure of her. Thereupon Sammes told goodman Rattle what speeches Waples had uttered, which Rattle told to Daie's wife, and thereupon Sammes was fetched by Mr. Rich's warrant, justice of peace, to answer at the suit of Daie's wife, whereby he was constrained to look if he could get Waples to confess the said words before witnesses or else to stand to the order of the law. It chanced that, about six or seven weeks ago on Sunday morning after service was ended, Waples and he met in the churchyard, and Waples asking him why he slandered him with goodman Daie this deponent answering that he had not slandered him otherwise than he had told his mother, which was that he could not be rid of Daie's wife before he had his pleasure of her'. On which Sammes called Dethicke, as already narrated. Sammes also 'believeth that there is some malice or rancour depending betwixt Waples and Daie's wife, but she hath borne a good name before this present. Waples was such a person that he hath committed many heinous offences, namely, he got a maid with child about five years ago, and besides was whipped at a cart's arse by the justices' appointment for other offences, and he is one whom there is no credit to be given to his word, and is reported and taken to be a very naughty man of his living.' Rattle's reported relations with Day's wife in the same year have already been noted. Stanford must have been a hotbed of slander.

The suit brought by John Shouncke against Henry Willet in 1585 yields a valuable comment on perjury committed by some compurgators, as often occurred. William Syssell of the parish of Hornchurch, where he had lived for about three years and before that at Wiggington in Yorkshire, aged about 60, had known the parties for about 16 years. 'About half a year ago on a Sunday he, Jeffery Woodcroft, Henry Willet, John Shouncke, William Nicholson and his wife, and Richard Tyler, being all drinking together in Nicholson's house, after they had made an end of their drinking, Kathering Towison came to him and asked when she should break the matter to Shouncke concerning the slander which was raised against her by Shouncke, as she affirmed, the deponent willed her to break it then and told her there was no better time. She asked Shouncke how it chanced he had raised such a slander of her (which was that she was taken in bed with a man); he answered that there was no honest man there would say so that he had raised such a slander. Then Katherine asked Willet whether it be so or no, who said that Shouncke did say so. Willet and Shouncke falling at great words together, Willet saying, "Who would trust thee, for thou forswore thyself and all the compurgators in the compurgation, and that I will prove".' William Nicholson of the same parish, where he had dwelt about 20 years and before that at Frissenton in the parish of 'Arladon' (Arlecdon) in Cumberland, aged about 40 years, said that, 'all drinking and making merry among themselves', the encounter between Katherine Towison and Shouncke, as related, took place in his house in Havering, she being his servant. The slander, according to his deposition, was that 'she was taken in bed with her master, and thereupon she was turned forth of her service'. Jeffery Woodcroft, weaver, of the same parish, where he had dwelt for six years, before that at Blackmore about nine years, and before that at Stondon, aged 29, said that 'Shouncke and Willet falling forth insomuch that they were almost going by the ear together, Willet uttering the slanderous words as to Shouncke being forsworn, Shouncke requested all the parties named to bear witness'.

The oblique obscenities of George Larder, with the further use of the flea figure of speech suggesting that it was a common local epithet for a lecher, led to his being sued by Thomas Griffen. Richard Bone, husbandman, of Upminster, where he had dwelt about five years, before that at Great Stambridge about five years, and before that at Stoke Nayland in Suffolk, aged 42, deposed: 'Upon a time happening a little before Whitsuntide last, he with divers others was drinking in one Palmer's house in Upminster, when he and Larder were talking pleasantly together, Larder said that Griffen could take a flea off Nicholas Herd's wife's belly when he listed, and that Griffen had the use of her body as commonly as either Larder or this deponent had with their wives, and that Griffen and Boyland would occupy their wives for them.' John Swetinge, tailor, of Upminster, where he had dwelt for about 30 years and before that at Hornchurch, aged 48, declared that they were drinking, as related, 'when one of the company said to goodman Larder, "Let us go home", whereunto Larder said, "No, we need not to go home, for Griffen and Boyland will occupy our wives for us"'. In answer to one of the interrogatories, Swetinge admitted that nine years ago he 'was set in Upminster stocks for keeping counsel of one that stole a goose'. George Mawle, husbandman, of Upminster, where he had lived about twelve weeks and before that at Hornchurch, aged 22, stated that 'in haytime last he was the household servant of George Larder, and sundry times heard Larder, upon malice as it seemed, say that Griffen could take a flea off Heard's wife's belly as often as he list, which speeches he used sometimes at supper as in other places in his presence and that of Larder's wife and his daughter'. Larder, an Upminster husbandman, was apparently an inveterate partridge poacher.[1]

When John Worme of Blackmore prosecuted a parishioner for defamation in 1586, the court heard some striking, if salacious, speech. In his suit against Helen Rand, here is the statement of Joan, widow of Nicholas Wolberd of Barking, formerly of Blackmore for about 16 years, born at Fyfield, aged about 27. 'In haytime last being a little after midsummer she and her late husband and Helen Rand and her husband were at making hay in a mead of Mr. Smythe of Blackmore called Holmes Mead, at which time William Boxer, officer under the Archdeacon of Essex for Chelmsford hundred (i.e. an apparitor), came into the mead to cite Helen to appear before the Archdeacon or his Official for certain abuses, as he said; which Helen in the presence of herself (Joan) and her late husband, Boxer and Helen's husband, declared to Boxer at the serving of the citation, that John Worme would have been naught with her and would have laid her down upon a bed in her own house and before she could get rid of him she was fain to promise him the use of her body the next night. Worme did say unto Helen, when he would have had his pleasure on her, that he could make as good a cunt of a lath and two coney skins as his wife had.'

In the same year a thin cottage wall and a neighbour's clamorous taunts heard through it resulted in a defamation suit. Thomas Boulter, tailor, of Romford, where he had dwelt since infancy, aged 60, deposed: 'One afternoon a little before Easter Margery Oliver was drying and smoothing clothes in his house, upon licence given to her for the good neighbourhood of her father and mother, and in talking to his wife while she (Margery) was swathing the clothes, suddenly Elizabeth Stevens his next neighbour fell in railing and miscalling Margery with a loud voice, she being on the other side of the wall in her own house, saying, "Thou art a Bridewell bird and hast had a child, and thou art a whore and an arrant whore, and I will prove thee one and stir in it an thou darest".

[1] *E.L.: Disorder*, 250.

He knoweth her speech very perfectly, because she has been his next neighbour these seven years.' And Agnes his wife, who had lived at Romford for 26 years, formerly at Maidstone in Kent, aged 40, said much the same. The use of the archaic 'an' (*if* thou darest) late in the century is the only instance noted in the act books.

A deposition in the suit brought in 1591 by John Coxe against Geoffrey Luckin shows a somewhat different aspect. Hugh Bailey, of the sign of the Cock in Romford, where he had dwelt since birth, aged 53, said that he and Thomas Haines were churchwardens of the liberty of Hornchurch. About Michaelmas last, in his house and in the presence of himself and others, Luckin 'demanded certain questions touching the presenting of Coxe of Collier Row, and asked whether Coxe did not make any complaint to them that he (Luckin) should be suspected of incontinency with Convers wife of Collier Row'. Bailey contended that Coxe had made no such complaint to either of the wardens. 'On which Luckin said, "Howsoever it is, I cannot live in quiet with my wife, for when I am from home then Coxe is at my house with my wife, and when I am at home my wife will be at Coxe's house", to the end that they should make presentment of the matter that due correction might be extended as their fault deserved'.

Statements of two North Weald Bassett men reveal a well-meaning but unfortunate attempt of the curate to effect a reconciliation between a parishioner and his mother-in-law. The first witness was Nicholas Stephen, weaver, of North Weald Bassett, where he had dwelt for one year, before that at Canfield for 20 weeks, and before that at Sawbridgeworth in Hertfordshire, born at Fyfield, about 30. On 12 December 1589 'Mr. Bradley the minister, John Cooper, Edward Poole, himself and Robert Spranger being at the vicarage, Mr. Bradley and Poole using some persuasion to Spranger to become friends with his mother-in-law (mother of Thomas Fuller), between whom were some contentions, Spranger, being somewhat importunate, and thereupon Mr. Bradley said that if he were vicar he would make them friends or else they should drive him out or he would drive them out of the parish. Then Spranger said, "You are always harping at me, but you will not see the whorish crime that there is in the house", at which Mr. Bradley willed this deponent, Poole and Cooper to bear witness to these words. Spanger named nobody nor any man's house but the deponent thinketh that he meant the house of Henry Fuller, father of Thomas. Being demanded by this deponent what he should bear witness to, Mr. Bradley said, "That Robert Spranger saith that Thomas Fuller lieth night by night with his cousin Agnes Grave".' Edward Poole, one of the churchwardens of North Weald Bassett, where he had lived for eight years, before that at Bobbingworth six years, before that at Willingale, before that at Ingatestone about six years, and before that at Bobbingworth, said that the incident occurred on a Sunday after evening prayer, that the mother-in-law's name was Katherine Fuller, that he himself 'was loth to move' Spranger to become friends with her because 'he had many times before requested him thereto and would not be persuaded, yet upon the often and earnest entreaty of Mr. Bradley he entreated him again to be at unity with his mother-in-law'. Spranger told Mr. Bradley that 'he was grieved and could not find in his heart to be friends with her', adding the words above including 'harping at me' and 'whorish crime', and otherwise confirming Spranger's deposition; but he 'denied that Thomas Fuller went night by night, as Mr. Bradley did unjustly allege'.

Alleged slander involved the vicar of Rainham and two well-known local families in 1600. Joan wife of Laurence Lommes of Rainham husbandman, where she had lived for 20 months, before that at Stifford for three years, at Aveley 12 years, born at Redlington in Rutland, aged about 56, deposed that one Sunday before Palm Sunday last in the afternoon after evening prayer, she being sick, Mr. Buck came into her house and sat down on a stool in the hall, the wife of William Grene sister to John Frith being there; and suddenly Mr. Buck seeing her said, 'Goodwife Grene, you have a jolly boily knave to your brother goodman Frith to maintain all the rogues and knaves and whores and thieves and a murderer against me'. Whereupon she answered him, 'God forbid it should be so, I have known him an honest man', being there present Laurence and Frith's wife and no more. Laurence Lommes of Rainham, where he had lived for ten years, born at Howgate in Leicestershire, aged about 40 (*sic.*), said that on a Sunday before Easter last when one Joan Hatter a maid of the parish was buried after evening prayer, Mr. Buck the vicar, going towards his lodging which was beyond his house, told him that he was hardly used by his (i.e. Lommes') wife, whereupon he answered that he was sorry she should do so, and so went forward towards his house where his wife stood in the door; and when Mr. Buck came he said, 'You have lost your evensong', whereunto she answered, 'I am an old woman, you must bear with me'. And after that Mr. Buck at their desire went into the hall and sat down upon a little table, and after other speeches said he was sorry that Frith had put goodman Harte out of his farm being an honest man and set in a thief. And then speaking to Grene's wife sister to Frith, 'That boily knave thy brother beareth or maintaineth with all the whores and knaves in the town against me'. John Quick of Aveley labourer, who had lived there for 20 years, born at Romford, aged about 30, added nothing fresh, and repeated 'and a murderer'. While 'jolly' was a mild expletive, the exact meaning of 'boily' is not apparent. The Assize files are somewhat incomplete at this date, so that the hypothetical murder cannot be traced, but they reveal that, eight years later, Frith was the victim of highway robbery, losing his gold ring, sword, doublet, jerkin and 14s. cash, two of his six assailants being hanged. (For goodman Harte's wife, see p. 224.)

From defamation of one or two individuals, or by a Colne Engaine man, who in addition to being excommunicate for fornication a long time was 'a most filthy slanderer of divers of his honest neighbours', we pass to those who cast abuse on their fellow parishioners generally, though mostly on the women. A Rochford man 'reported that there is but six honest women in Rochford' (1591); but the neighbouring market-town of Rayleigh could not even boast of that number in the eyes of another man who declared, 'There are not five honest women in all town' (1587). (An honest woman in Elizabethan times implied one of virtuous character.) A Woodham Ferrers man said, 'There is as many whores as poor in the parish' (1575); he submitted himself to correction, so the judge ordered him to confess in church. A Rainham married couple, however, who 'made a filthy crime (report) of the most part of the inhabitants' (1584), at first refused to undergo penance, were pronounced contumacious and excommunicated, but later appeared and sought absolution. A third market-town, Witham, was past redemption according to one accused of 'defaming the honest women of the town, saying that there is not one amongst them of honest conversation' (1592). Another village was no better: 'There is none in Stondon (Massey) but cuckolds and cuckold-makers' (1584). For this remark John Searle, a parishioner, was a 'slanderer of his neighbours'. Refuting the charge, he stated that 'William Ingold of Stondon reporteth that he heard Mr. Borne affirm' how he (Searle) had thus defamed the parish; but John Rogers confirmed his hearing it when working with Searle. Borne, or Bourne, is a rare Essex surname; is he the 'Mr. Eborne' who himself was cuckolded five years later when curate of West Ham?

At any rate, words too foul to be repeated in the West Ham wardens' view (1590) had come from the tongue of Cecily, widow of William Bentley, who seems to have thought she could get a free drink by solacing the curate. Her alleged offence was 'reporting that there be none but cuckolds in Stratford Langthorne, with other slanderous speeches which are not to be rehearsed'. On appearance she declared that 'all she said unto a certain widow that was her neighbour, unto whom the beer brewer's clerk of Stratford bare good will as it was thought, was these words following in jest and not otherwise, viz. "Where is the cuckoldlike clerk, for I want beer?", and no other words'. The judge ordered her to purge herself with six neighbours. We have already noticed in the Prostitution chapter that Stratford had a nest of brothels.

A West Mersea man (not the fellow who slandered four women in 1577) expressed himself in pejorative, if somewhat enigmatical, language (1588), 'using of opprobrious words against the honest women of West Mersea, saying that they were two teams of sluts, naming twelve in a team; and further said that there were women that were hackney horses to ride by the tymes sides'. 'Tyme' is apparently an archaic form of 'team';

Thamesside seems less likely in connexion with Mersea, though 'hackneys' (prostitutes) flourished near the riverside.

The clergy's calling laid them especially open to criticism or calumny for any moral lapse or suspected lapse. Conversely, puritan-minded ministers' ritual deviations or castigating sermons led to their being slandered or reviled. So many cases of each kind of detraction came before the courts that two later sections will be devoted to them.

Although not maligned to the same extent as many of the clergy, some churchwardens and a few questmen (sidesmen) received their share of disparagement. Much of this was earned through performing their obligation to present backsliders.

An indictment in 1572 lay against John Gray and Peter Gray of Wivenhoe, who 'being reproved for not coming to church reviled the churchwardens, calling them knaves and churls'. They were commanded to confess before the congregation and to reconcile themselves with the wardens. Twelve years later their successors were also 'misused' by a man who 'bade a turd in the teeths', a nasty and not infrequent contemporary phrase.[1] An Upminster woman, the wife of John Stinte, had stood excommunicate for two or three years. She was charged afresh in 1596 with 'scolding with the churchwardens and railing with them because they have made presentment of her for her filthy behaviour and bad dealing'. In 1587 John King of Colne Engaine, accused of 'houstering' (harbouring) two incontinent persons, 'did swear by God's blood that he would spend twenty nobles upon the churchwardens for presenting him and bade a pox on them', and he 'misused one of them in doing his duty, calling him hollow-hearted knave and threatened to meet him'. (A noble was worth 6s. 8d.)

A woman called her churchwardens 'knaves in doing their office', adding that 'they were officers for a dog' (church dogwhippers?); others were merely accorded the term knave, or they 'were gotten into a knave's office'. 'Railing on the churchwardens doing their office' and 'abusing the churchwardens with beastly speeches on being reproved' are not uncommon entries. One warden was called 'liar'; a second, 'whoremaster'; a third, 'busy merchant' (fellow). Several pairs were 'jackanapes'; one pair was addressed as 'mad fools'. The Witham wardens of 1595 were 'patch panels and pillards'. A rector had been earlier 'a mender of saddles and panels', p. 209. A patch-panel is defined in the *Oxford Dictionary* as 'one who patches panels, an abusive appellation'; and a pillard as a plunderer or robber. An irate Elmstead woman who had been reported for incontinence in 1591 'miscalled the churchwarden and wished when he died he might die like a devil and his tongue might hang out one foot long as black as a coal'. Some Essex folk revealed an imaginative turn of speech.

[1] Cf. 'Turd i' your teeth' (Ben Jonson, *Bartholomew Fair* (1614), I, iv).

A Stanford Rivers man slandered a warden because 'divers persons in their parish' had been cited: perhaps he had been a little too officious. Stephen Hograve of Abberton, denounced in 1584 as 'a disquieter of his neighbours, living very contentiously', told one warden that 'none of them in that office but were forsworn' (perjured), to which both officers added piously, 'to no small grief unto our minds'. Reported in 1592 for 'using the churchwardens very unreverently in speeches', Thomas Hills of Little Leighs sent his wife Joan to the court, where, she alleged, 'He used some words to the churchwardens who russed her husband against the wall, being a lame man'; 'russed' is apparently Essex dialect for 'rush', to drag or push forcibly.

More picturesque language resulted from a double presentment made against John Culpack of St. Nicholas, Colchester, who had no compunction in reviling the officers generally (1591). 'He did abuse one of the churchwardens and one of the sidemen and one of the constables because, finding him not at church, we came home to him and told him that we were sorry to find him in such fault; presently he burst forth in words and said that we came to assault him and said that we had blackbirds in our breasts but it would not prevail against us.' The second count was for 'most shamefully abusing the churchwardens on Our Lady Day', saying that 'the court was well occupied to make such lord's officers as we were and that the churchwarden was a blasphemous knave'.

Instances of sidesmen who were abused are found in citations against a Grays Thurrock woman for 'brawling and railing against the questman, calling him knave, thief and rascal' (1596), and against Richard Turner of Manningtree for 'often absenting himself from church and calling the questman Jonas Hedge fool and dolt for going to his house to warn his maidservant to the church, asking him why did did so' (1600).

There was of course often little distinction between defamation and discord: many defendants had to anwer for both. While probably few towns and villages were free from at least one 'common slanderer' (and some were infested with several), it was no doubt equally true of the 'common sower of discord among neighbours' and the 'common scold'.

The qualitites of scolds, according to the lexicographers, are a propensity to ribald or abusive speech, brawling (noisy quarrelling), or both. Alternatively they were called unquiet (or disquiet), or quarrelsome. 'Unquiet' had much the same meaning as quarrelsome, as, for example, in 1561, when two Havering women were 'very unquiet with their neighbours' and each had to pay 2d. to the poor. Other common phrases were 'she causeth strife' between man and wife; 'a breeder of strife'; 'a setter of discord through her evil tongue'; 'a troublesome person amongst her neighbours by her unquietness of tongue'; 'abused her tongue'; 'a malicious, contentious and uncharitable woman'. Of double charges we find:

'a sower of discord between her neighbours and a carrier of tales between party and party'; 'a notorious common scold and makebate between her neighbours' (i.e. mischief-maker); 'uncharitable scolding with her neighbours and a blasphemer of the Word of God'; 'suspected to live incontinently and to be busy with her tongue and unquiet'.

Most of these trouble-makers either denied having emitted such oral blasts or ignored summons. To make their purgation the courts usually demanded seven or even eight neighbours, probably to try to ensure that it failed and penance followed, though some reprobates remained excommunicate for long periods. A few pestiferous females appeared more than once. Clemence, wife of William Bird of Ingatestone, presented in 1600 as 'a very troublesome woman and a scolder among her neighbours', had the task of disproving her guilt by a certificate from 'Mr. (Anthony) Brasier (rector) and three worthy parishioners'. But she was up again on a precisely similar charge a few months later, when she was excommunicated. Or, in the other archdeaconry, there was Marian Roberts, reported in 1593 by the Moze wardens as 'a disordered person, who being cleared in the spiritual court of her disordered life cometh into our town (i.e. village) and goeth from house to house railing and slandering and setting disorder between neighbour and neighbour'.

The wife of James Tomlinson, one of the wardens of Holy Trinity, Colchester, was 'a disquieter of her honest neighbours in her speech unreverently, and did break the glass windows down of Thomas Ennes, and did call his wife tinker's bitch' (1558). Family disharmony existed at High Ongar. William Staine 'misused his wife with stripes contrary to all order and reason, with great controversy betwixt her husband and her' (1588); and Richard Staine senior and junior were summoned as sowers of discord between the couple. Giles Hales and Andrey Howell of Great Waltham both acknowledged that 'there hath been brawls amongst them'; the man added that 'he, sorting (agreeing) to meet her, demanded why she did belie (slander) her, and called her the devil's dungcart' (1578). He had to confess in church and give 12d. to the poor men's box; she, to purge with three neighbours.

A Blackmore wife was cited as a common scold and for calling another a whore; a widow of St. Botolph, Colchester, presented as a scold, 'railed unfit for any Christians'; another parishioner, previously reported as a common scold, 'doth no whit amend her of that, but hath scolded and fought with her neighbour, being an old man in his own yard'. Exceptionally, one woman 'scolded upon her own mother'. But a Romford 'scold and sower of discord', according to her own statement, had merely stood up for her husband: 'he being abused in words by the goodwife Grafton, she did somewhat unadvisedly use undecent words'.

Sometimes, of course, the husband was the sole victim of the scold. In 1579 John Fynch of Feering 'useth to lodge and harbour Christopher

Russell's wife without his consent, counselling and aiding her by all means to be disobedient to her husband, by reason whereof he cannot rule his wife as a man should'. Fynch was peremptorily told to clear her out of his house. In 1587 Mistress Adams of Colne Engaine was 'a cumbrous (troublesome) woman with her tongue to her husband'; and in the next year 'the wife of Banks the smith and his daughter (the wife of Harryes)' were accused of 'fighting with and beating their husbands', all being Kelvedon folk.

After hearing counter-charges, 'She called him knave and he called her drab', the judge demanded 'the one to ask the other forgiveness'. A Danbury wife, presented as a common sower of discord, was absolved on the rector's petition on her behalf. Occasionally a married couple were jointly dubbed as 'scolders and brawlers against their honest neighbours', or even 'common scolders by day and night'.

The male scolder was a rarer phenomenon: men's language was stronger than mere scolding. Only three are on record as such: one, 'a common scolder, a railer, and a very busybody'; another, 'a railer, scolder and a busybody'. The third, John Wall of Rainham, was accused jointly with his wife in 1567 of 'scolding, victualling in service time, drunkenness the woman, incontinence before marriage, and lodging men and women together not married, and that was on Saturday last'.

The defence of Stephen Vincent of Hockley, who had slandered another's wife in 1601, declaring that 'by her evil tongue he hath lost a horse, sheep and cattle to the value of twenty marks', was that 'he did speak such like words in choler'. This sort of defamation almost amounted to an accusation of witchcraft, which was in fact imputed in a multiple charge in 1601 against David Tarver of Great Oakley for 'being a most troublesome, disquiet and slanderous fellow among his honest neighbours, for calling the wife of James Bean witch, and for brawling with Philippa the wife of Robert Palmer'. Many of the prosecutions with witchcraft were of course a specially hostile kind of defamation.

Some churchwardens' multiple presentments undoubtedly pinpoint the worthless and the ne'er-do-wells whose delinquencies could not be concisely expressed in one or two counts. One such miscreant was Miles Gurnell of Wivenhoe, reported in 1588 for 'vehement suspicion of incontinent life with a woman that was brought to the town and keepeth her in his house; a drunkard, a brawler, a railer, and a common sower of discord'; neither he nor the woman had received communion for a whole year. She was also by way of being an unlawful schoolteacher, as related under Licences. Another noxious man was Richard Fuller of Langford, who directed his energies towards vituperation of the Church and its functionaries. Not only in 1591 did he abuse the minister, as noted under the Clergy, but 'he misused the churchwardens in railing on them and calling them very knaves and trim mates; he railed on the ecclesiastical jurisdiction and on the ecclesiastical courts, calling the courts bawdy courts and courts appointed altogether for money; he was a common swearer; he refuseth to pay 4d. towards the charges laid out about the church and expenses laid out by the churchwardens; and he stealeth, and was excommunicated, but refuseth to be absolved'. 'Trim' was meant ironically, like our use of 'fine'. The verdict is not given. At the same session the court learned that George Haven of Black Notley 'liveth disorderly, repairing very seldom to church; liveth or rather lurketh in our parish, his wife dwelling at Coggeshall; and useth unfit contemptuous speeches to our minister, being in the churchyard, our minister without' (i.e. outside).

The misdemeanours of Roger Cowper, one of the Goldhanger wardens in 1591, are set out in eight separate presentments, the key words being:

Slandering Mr. Knight, parson and preacher.
Slandering John Coker, sexton of Goldhanger.
Slandering William Godfrey's wife of Goldhanger.
Brawling and railing of divers of his honest neighbours.
Drunkard.
A letter and hinderer of them that would hear the Word of God preached, and being rebuked he answered contemptously, 'I care not for the Word of God'.
Swearing and blaspheming of the name of God in his common talk, and being reproved he answered 'I will swear again and again', and so he did.

As for drunkenness, he alleged that he had already been cited in the Commissary's court; all the rest he disclaimed. His wife was also prosecuted for slandering Godfrey's wife; and there followed slander charges against other parishioners. Goldhanger was evidently seething with discord.

The bridge, too, between vilification and violence was a short one. In 1579 the wardens denounced Robert Kynge and Alice his wife of High Laver because they 'live very unquietly together, to the evil example and disquiet of the neighbours'. Alice declared that 'Thomas Allett of the parish gave her counsel that she should forsake her husband's company, and her husband went about to kill and she liveth in fear of her life, and she hath showed herself ever since very stubbornly through her husband's froward dealings'. The judge accepted her statement but ordered her 'on Sunday come sennight in the church to openly submit herself to her husband and to ask his forgiveness and to promise amendment'. When goodman Alborough and his wife of Danbury were charged in 1566 with disturbing their neighbours, the man stated that 'his wife does not wish to come to his bed, wherefor he took water and threw it on her head'. But she retorted that he 'had oftentimes been abroad a-nights and days, spending away his thrift (i.e. substance), and when he cometh home he doth abuse her and beateth her'. He had said that very day that 'if she would tell anything against him to the judge he would keep her with stealth; and whereas he hath given her meat and drink he will give her water and bread'. On her oath she declared that 'he did put a knife to her throat and a halter about her neck'. Strangely enough, no further proceedings are entered; perhaps the judge thought the court's time should not be wasted by such futile bickerings. In 1585 John Warde of Fobbing 'abused Susan Tramells in pulling her forth of her bed and did beat her unreverently'. But it was a man's retaliation in 1593, when the wardens reported 'William Hylls of Sandon as a very lewd and uncharitable man with his wife and hath used her most ungodly, not only by refusing her company but also by beating her most cruelly without any pity or compassion'. To this his answer was, 'Upon occasion that his wife had beated and misused his sister and some fatherless children he had in his house, he gave her eight strokes with a wand, for the which he is sorry for now'; and he was given penance by acknowledging his guilt before the minister and wardens. In any case, wife-beaters could always claim that they were following the advice of the old couplet:

A woman, a dog, and a walnut tree,
The more you beat 'em, the better they be.

A rather vague presentment was made against John Dines of Cressing in 1588: 'He and his sister Agnes did misuse John Dynes his brother and would a-murdered him for that she liveth there single and he keepeth her in a barn.' Typical of many minor assaults was the charge in 1588 against Judith, wife of John Carpenter, who confessed that she 'called Morris's wife whore in words and did fight and beat her and did throw a pair of shears in her back'.

Drunkenness and Swearing

William Harrison, writing in his north Essex vicarage, fulminated against excessive drinking. 'Certes,' he declaimed, 'I know some ale-knights so much addicted thereunto that they will not cease from morrow until even to visit the same, cleansing house after house, till they defile themselves and either fall quite under the board, or else, not daring to stir from their stools, sit pinking (i.e. blinking) with their narrow eyes as half-sleeping, till the fume of their adversary be digested, that he may go to it afresh.'[1] Drunkenness was an offence dealt with by both the secular and the spiritual courts: by Quarter Sessions, because it led to breaches of the peace;[2] by the Archdeacons' Courts, because of its moral degradation.

The archives of the two Essex church courts disclose about two hundred presentments for drunkenness. An equally frequent charge was that of drinking ale, without necessarily being inebriate, during service time on a Sunday or a holy-day, and was an aggravated form of the second most common offence – absence from church. Regarded as a distinct transgression from drunkenness, it also included the alehouse-keeper serving drink

[1] Harrison, *Description of England* (2nd. edn., 1587), ed. G. Edelen (Cornell Univ. Press, U.S.A., 1968), 139. [2] *E.L. Disorder*, 202–17.

at such times. Here we are concerned only with public drunkenness, though a few offences occurred on holy-days. But we must not assume that the Church looked upon alehouses as nurseries of debauchery. It was convivial drinking to excess that earned spiritual censure, because it loosened the tongue and lessened sexual restraint.

'Was drunk', 'a common drunkard', 'a notorious drunkard', 'he drinketh till he be drunken', or 'all overcome with drink of Christmas Eve'; such were the brief presentments which brought many men (but no women) before the courts. Some offenders risked prosecution only if they were unruly. Then the charge was more specific: 'drunkenness and ribaldry'; 'a common drunkard, blasphemer and swearer'; 'a common blasphemer of the name of God, a drunkard and a ribald'; 'a drunkard and a railer of his neighbours in his drunkenness'; 'on market day he was much distempered with drinking'. A Barking inebriate, 'being rebuked by the churchwardens, answered that he must be drunk four days in the week', which, not surprisingly, he later denied. The Rayleigh wardens in 1601 reported of one townsman that he was 'a common drunkard and a railer and chider, to the great grief of the ungodly and great danger of his soul', language suggestive of puritan leanings. Compare the opinion expressed by the same parish to Quarter Sessions five years earlier: 'There is in Rayleigh ten victuallers and alehousekeepers, whereof we think that five of them would serve'.[1] Slander or abuse was so often the concomitant of drunkenness that the courts dealt with them as joint charges. The reply of Nicholas Nosewell of Prittlewell in 1586, when accused as 'a drunkard and a railer of his neighbours in his drunkenness', that 'sometimes he hath been overseen in drink and then hath used some hard speeches towards them', was as honest as could be expected. Even some churchwardens, too fond of the ale pots, had to answer, like Roger Cowper of Goldhanger. A few of the clergy with time on their hands found it hard to learn, as we shall see later and as Shakespeare was to say, 'Every inordinate cup is unblessed, and the ingredient is a devil'. Often two or more venial sins are combined in a single presentment – for example, that against Anthony Locker of St. Giles, Colchester (1593), for 'not receiving holy communion since our Lady Day last and cometh little to church, and on 23rd of May he was led home by his wife, supposed to be drunken because he fell down by the way like a log'.

Thomas Fletcher, another Barking man, was 'very often drunk, and upon a Monday in the afternoon after Easter in the Bull at Barking among others was notoriously drunken', but he managed to purge his offence. One drunkard 'would have killed his wife, had she not been saved' by two villagers; and another in his drunkenness 'would have killed his bullocks, and because his wife denied him he had like to have broken her neck': thus, at any rate, the wardens of two parishes opined. A crude entry tells

[1] *E.L. Disorder*, 204.

of one who was 'so drunken that he was not able to stand upon his legs and did force his wife to go to bed'; on being reproved he had declared that he would rather be drunken every day than be sober. 'So drunken', in fact, introduced more than one presentment: 'that he lost his hose and shoes'; 'that he fell off his horse'; 'that he could not go in the streets but fell quarrelling'. A Lawford man was 'so foully drunken on Whitsun Wednesday in so much as he was not able to get home but lay in the fields by the way'; and another of the same parish was 'so drunken on New Year's Day that he was not able to go of his own legs and so was led home'.

The wardens of Colne Engaine felt obliged in 1603 to deal with the drinking prowess of William George, who, 'being strong to drink, delighteth to beguile others with drink'. Mr. John Bramston, notary public, appeared as his proctor and challenged the charge, from which George managed to purge himself. A Terling churchwarden's account of a drunkard in 1599 left little to the imagination: 'On the Sunday at night after Trinity Sunday and the Monday morning he did bepiss his bed and bewray his apparel, and not able to stand he was laid upon a bed and then led home.' The most interesting case reveals some irreverent drinking rites. This is what the Corringham wardens wrote in 1598:

> One John Smith of this parish, Richard Cottes of Orsett and George Landish of Barking, after great abuse in drinking, did at their parting take with them into the field at the town's end, where they meant to part, four or six pots of beer, and there setting them down did kneel upon their bare knees, humbly kneeling down and kissing the pots and drinking one to another, prayed for the health of all true and faithful drunkards, especially for Mr. Andrew Browghton, as they said, the maintainer and upholder of all true and faithful drunkards; and having done kissed each other, and for a memory of their worthy act did every man make his mark upon an ashen tree that stood there.

A clear instance of the old adage, *In vino unanimitas*! The judge ordered them to acknowledge their guilt before the minister and wardens of their respective parishes.

Almost as vivid is a description of buffoonish impersonation. The charge was laid against John Badcocke of Rayleigh in 1589:

> He, with others more (sitting upon their alebench and greatly abusing themselves at one Mother Larkinge's house), took upon him and was called by the name of Mr. Parson, another taking upon him and was called by the name of churchwarden, another by the name of a sworn man, another by the name of the honest men of the parish, and another by the name of an apparitor whose name was Thomas England; thus sitting, abusing themselves like drunken sots.

He explained that they 'being merry had some merry talk, but not in any disordered manner or in any manner of ways overcome with drink, nor did use some like speech as is here objected against him, for the which he is heartily sorry for his part if any have taken any offence'. Penance before the wardens and six parishioners was the mild punishment for their besotted indulgence in onomastic fun, if not onanistic sin.

A variety of other excuses, seldom resourceful, was offered by defendants. One 'had been drinking but was not thereby distempered, only he was ill stomached'; another, who 'hath a lightness in his head and hath that impediment that a small quantity of drink overcomes him', was enjoined by the judge to be a total abstainer. A Barking alehouse-keeper who kept disorder 'by drinking and swilling' replied that he drunk 'but of his own drink'. In 1600 Richard Newton, innkeeper of the 'Cock' at Coggeshall, accused by the wardens of 'disorder by sundry persons whose names they do not know', explained that it occurred when he was away from home 'and by such as his wife could not rule', and he was acquitted. Next year four men of the same town, who had not satisfied the strongly puritan congregation for their 'faults of drunkenness', alleged that they 'did drink upon thirst only three pots of beer in the house of Somersham of Much Tey and that there was no drunkenness amongst them', a statement which was accepted. A Tollesbury man's defence on being charged because he was 'overcome with drink' was that, 'having wrought in the highway, he was whitt (hot?) and did drink very much'. One market day a Lawford man was 'much distempered with drinking and drunken that he had lost his maund' (basket); he was ordered to perform penance in church. A Colchester man confessed that he had 'offended in that vice of drunkenness, for which he submitteth himself to the correction of the judge'. Such an outright admission was rare, although a few did so reluctantly in naïve terms, such as: 'He was somewhat charged with drunk but not drunk', which resulted in the judge's equally ingenuous injunction, 'He shall not hereafter use any such drunkenness'. In two further cases a man was ordered to 'abstain from overcharging himself with drink' or to 'abstain from strong drink and wine'.

Thus, so far, the treatment accorded to drunkards has seemed fairly lenient. But this was not always so. In five cases the offender was sentenced not only to public penance in his church but also to exhibit into the bargain a tankard, a quart pot, an empty cup, or three empty pots, in front of him, or, to one victim's extreme chagrin, to distribute a barrel of beer to the poor! Details of these humilating punishments, which may perhaps have served as a future deterrent to the drunkard but certainly afforded mirth to the less pious members of the congregation, will be found in the chapter on Penance.

Often associated with drunkenness, slander or scolding was the common tendency to swearing. Churchwardens and questmen were enjoined to present all who offended their brethren in this way. Over one hundred men and a few women are found to have been cited as 'a common swearer', or 'a grievous swearer', varied sometimes by 'a common swearer and liar', 'an abominable swearer and a common drunkard', or 'utters divers great oaths'. St. Botolph's, Colchester, seems to have appointed an unsuitable parish servant: 'Our sexton', the wardens reported in 1584, 'is a railer, a blasphemer, a swearer and a slanderer, and suspected of drunkenness.'

Blasphemy was a rarer and graver offence than ordinary cursing, though some churchwardens were rather vague about the difference or inclined to combine them in their presentments. They used such graphic phrases as 'a common swearer and blasphemer of God's holy name and a filthy talker', 'a blasphemer and swearer of sedition and a liar', or 'a common blasphemer of the name of God and a forswearer (i.e. perjurer) of himself in his common dealing with men'; or they included blasphemy with other moral lapses, as of one for speaking 'ribald words, blaspheming the name of God, and keeping undecent company' with another man's wife. Charles Payne of Buttsbury had clearly earned disfavour in 1593: 'He liveth very disorderly, neither frequents his parish church, neither in any order amongst his neighbours, but will most unreverently blaspheme the name of God by cursing and swearing even at his own mother'. He was given penance and instructed to ask her forgiveness.

'A great blasphemer of God by horrible and abominable oaths' and 'a scoffer of the Word of God' are typical of other blasphemy charges. It was laid against two Rayleigh men in 1575. One of them stated: 'In talk among others, he said there is divers that do not pass by the Word of God a whore's turd, which words were lewdly uttered by him'; for which heinous blasphemy he submitted to sentence and was ordered to 'show himself sorrowful next Sunday, desiring God and all whom he offended to forgive him'. At Little Ilford, so it was alleged in 1569, an Anglican went much too far in expressing his anti-Catholic feeling, 'Our Lady is no better than his black bitch'; but the judge found that the accusation was not true and 'dismissed him from further vexation'. On the other hand, William Dowtie of Moreton, two years later, said, 'There is no harm in swearing by the mass', and was ordered to confess that 'he did amiss and to request the whole parish to take example by him'. To another offender the court somewhat optimistically enjoined a sweeping future prohibition, 'so that he sweareth not by God, the Prince, his neighbour or himself'. But what is the explanation of the lively simile used in 1580 by a Stock parishioner who was presented for 'liking (likening) the Trinity to a foot ball play'?

Blasphemy was a form of profanity, which also embraced irreverent or impious acts. Profane conduct was seldom presented; a few charges of this nature appear in the 'irreverence' section of our account of Church Disturbances, which also gives other cases of blasphemy.

Clerical drunkards and swearers, of whom there were many, with a few blasphemers and profaners, are dealt with under the Clergy.

Usury

The medieval Church had set its face sternly against usury, that is, money given for the *use* of money lent (the word 'interest', the rate per cent, did not appear until about 1575). The exigencies of trade, however, finally forced Parliament to breach the canon law, and by the Act of 37 Henry VIII, c. 9 (1545), usury was punishable only if more than 10 per cent was taken. The statute was repealed in 1552, but re-enacted with the same allowable maximum rate by 13 Eliz., c. 8 (1571); bonds providing for a higher rate would be void. Despite the need for reasonable interest, the ancient prejudice was deep-rooted, and the Act was passed only after a prolonged struggle against popular as well as clerical opposition.

The earliest Essex prosecution, in 1578, lay against Mark Simpson, rector of Pitsea, 'suspected to be a usurer'. He admitted having 'lent out a little money, and had 2s. in the £, after the rate of 10 in the 100; but he did not urge the same, but only the parties themselves, whom he lent the money to, did of their own good will give him after the same rate; but under compulsion, he did urge the same'. Although not convicted as a usurer, his action was regarded as unclerical and the judge decreed that, in part penance, 'he shall openly read the 15th psalm, acknowledge his guilt, and give 5s. to the use of the collectors (for the poor)'.

In 1588 Percy Harris of Elmstead was reported by the wardens as 'an usurer, viz, for taking of one Rushemer 4s. in the pound and the shoeing of a gelding'. He confessed to receiving 4s. interest for a year and a half and the shoe of a gelding worth, as he thought, 12d. The money and his shilling valuation, too, brought his rate to 16⅔ per cent per annum. The judge ordered him to return the 4s. before the next court and to certify his having done so by the minister and wardens. But it is not clear why Thomas Parish of Berden was adjudged guilty 'for lending his money at usury' in 1580 to John Corbett of Newport and Simon White of Birchanger '£10 after the rate of 2s. of the pound for one year', for the court bade him pay 2s. 6d. for the use of the poor of Berden. He had charged only the legalized maximum rate of 10 per cent. When William Young of Great Bentley was accused in 1593 of 'letting of his money out to usury', he answered that the loan of £6 13s. 4d. had been made 'after 2s. in the pound'; again, avarice but not usury under the statute. In 1584 John Poole of Fyfield denied the 'common fame of letting forth money to usury', insisting that 'he hath lent money for love, but not much money, and hath taken under 2s. in the pound'. His four compurgators affirmed the truth of his oath.

A charge of usury could also be brought for an excessive levy in kind. The two cases in this category concern payment of grain. In 1581 Reginald Hedge of Ramsey lent 2s. to Simon Cawston and received a peck of barley in usury for the loan. Hedge declared that Cawston offered him a peck but he did not take it. But (blank) Taylor of Bunge Row in Great Braxted was presented in 1597 for 'notable usury in taking 4½ bushels of barley for the loan of £5'. The five remaining charges, which were dismissed, were for 'suspicion', 'vehement suspicion', 'fame', or 'common speech' of usury. Of these, two lay against a widow and Thomas Banckes of West Ham, gentleman, who was alleged to 'live partly by the use of his money in usury; she had to purge, but he was discharged.

The somewhat ambiguous Essex evidence allows no definite conclusion to be drawn; so we must await the publication of other Elizabethan Church court records.[1] Harrison personally did not denounce usury, noting it as one of the social factors condemned by 'old men yet dwelling in the village where I remain' (Radwinter). Usury, he remarked, was 'now perfectly practised almost by every Christian and so commonly that he is accounted but for a fool that doth lend his money for nothing'; after which he expatiated, as he often liked to do, on Roman parallels.[2]

[1] Episcopal visitation articles that referred to usury specifically quoted the Act of 1571 and the 10 per cent maximum, e.g. those of Bishop Bancroft, 1601 (W. P. M. Kennedy, *Elizabethan Episcopal Administration* (1924), iii, 348). Two Elizabethan indictments for usury were heard by the Middlesex justices: against a London merchant-tailor for taking £100 for the loan of £500 and the 'broker' who arranged it, and against a gentleman who drove a bargain for a loan of £10 at an excessive rate (*Middlesex County Records*, i, 93, 189).

[2] Harrison, *op. cit.*, 202–3.

3

Religious Offences

Absence from Church

With the reissue in 1559 of Edward VI's Act of Uniformity (1549), by which the use of the Book of Prayer, in slightly revised form, became obligatory again, Elizabeth's first Parliament decreed compulsory church attendance for everybody above fourteen on all Sundays and holy-days. This was to be enforced 'upon pain of punishment by the censures of the Church, and every person so offending shall forfeit for every such offence twelve pence, to be levied by the churchwardens to the use of the poor'.

Ante-dating returns about non-attendance in the Archdeaconry of Essex visitation book for 1565 are four books for 1561–2: three for the archdeaconry and one for the Commissary of the Bishop of London. The first three have presentments of seventy individuals for not going to church or not receiving communion or for both offences; the other book has none.[1] In the meantime vigorous steps had been taken by the bishop and the archdeacons to pursue the search for offenders by means of the churchwardens' presentments, and the results are disclosed in the visitation book, as noted in a later chapter. Thereafter throughout the reign, and increasingly in the later years, the presentments name several thousands of individuals for not attending their parish church.

From time to time the wardens of many parishes put in lists of ten or more names: thirteen delinquents, for example, at Horndon(-on-the-Hill) in 1592; eleven at Walden in 1594; and at Black Notley 'a great many of the parishioners upon the sabbath days absent from evening prayer, and the churchwardens and questmen sometimes themselves and not presented', resulting in an order to cite the wardens. This was not the only occasion when officers were in disgrace. In 1590 Thomas Manne, one of the White Colne sidesmen, was reproved by the wardens because of frequent absence. But none of the lists is as long as those of parishioners who did not receive Holy Communion, as we shall see shortly.

Failure to report persons not attending or not communicating was undoubtedly due in the first place to some wardens' laziness in rounding up adults not seen to be present. In a few parishes non-attendance may perhaps be associated with the indolent or disreputable character of the

[1] 'Enforcement even of this basic requirement (i.e. attendance) remained patchy throughout the 1560s' (G. R. Elton, *The Tudor Constitution: Documents and Commentary* (1960), 410).

minister. In others, the reported absentees were those who were puritan-inclined and went to conventicles or to neighbouring churches where they were assured of 'godly preachers'; at the other extreme there were always the scattered groups of Catholic recusants, referred to later. Finally, there were those who frequented alehouses or were working at their trade or craft when they should have been at church, and will be dealt with in the next volume (*Home, Work and Customs*).

Of those who sought spiritual guidance in another parish church, we may quote, for example: John Baite of East Tilbury 'goeth to West Tilbury to hear the Word preached' (1586); 'To cite the parishioners of Littlebury which goeth to Great Chesterford and to cite the churchwardens to present their names' (1595). Of more importance are two special concessions granted by the Archdeaconry of Essex court. Six Shopland men, together with the wife and maidservant of two of them, cited for absence, were 'licensed, two of them, only when there is no sermon at Shopland church, to go elsewhere where there is a sermon, and not all of them to be absent from their parish all upon one day, and the other four to be at their parish church during all the sermon time and the reading of the homily when there is no sermon, under penalty of the law.' This was in 1587, and next year an equal number of Canewdon men sought similar leave for not attending their own church except on one Sunday in each month.

Among the six transgressions for which Robert Hamond of Bobinger (Bobbingworth) had to answer in 1586 were: 'He said some of the parish were devils'; that 'it were as good (to) steal a horse as to play of lawful game on the sabbath day'; and that 'he useth unlawful conventicles and often absenteth himself from his parish church and will not pay his forfeitures for his absence'. To the last he replied that, 'Where there is no sermon he goeth to other churches where the Word is preached, and therefore he will not pay'.

Lawrence Newman, the moderate puritan vicar of Coggeshall and a leading member of the Dedham 'classis', attracted six (named) Feering men in 1583; they were absent from their own church, 'knowing that there should be a preaching at Coggeshall'. Next year Thomas Maggett of Doddinghurst 'useth to go to Mr. Wyersdale and Mr. Reddereg to hear them preach when their own minister doth either preach or expound the scriptures at their own parish.' (Mark Wiersdale and Thomas Redrick were both leading puritans and among the signatories to the petition of the same year (p. 192): vicars of All Saints, Maldon, and of Hutton respectively.) In 1585 John Keale of Woodham Ferrers 'frequenteth Danbury where he heareth the Word preached', and was ordered, like most of the others, to attend his own church. Of some significance is the statement put in by Richard Yawlinge of Woodham Mortimer in the previous year on being charged with six weeks' absence: 'He saith he will not come to church unless there be a sermon preached, for the public service read in the church is no service unless there be a sermon.' In court he added: 'He dwelleth in a house builded on a common which is not certainly known whether it be in Woodham or Hazeleigh parish, and he goeth to such church where there be a sermon, and he is not so well edified by service as by sermon.' He had to confess his fault in church. In similar strain Robert Winche of North Ockendon in 1599 'refuseth to come to common prayer unless there be a sermon'.

Unusual circumstances were referred to by Edward Fage, gentleman, of Doddinghurst, when he was detected in 1583 for absence on Whitsunday and the next Sunday: 'Mr. Cotesford the minister (Samuel, the curate), being requested to follow the Prayer Book, preached against him, whereupon being not in charity he went to Stondon those days.' The curate was in trouble at the same time for not wearing the surplice.

Another interesting and indeed unique statement is that made by William Sorrell of Great Bardfield (1599), on being reported by the wardens for absence one Sunday. 'Within the time of their presentment', he alleged, 'there was not above 20 or 40 people at church, he being present, being 200 of houseling people in the parish' (i.e. communicants, or those of age to receive the 'housel' or Eucharist).

The scribes rarely noted the amount of the statutory fine to be paid, and there is even less evidence in the court books of actual receipt of the money. Among the few entries found is that concerning (blank) Brett and Thomas Moore of Ramsden (*sic*) for default on four Sundays in 1567, when each was directed to pay 4s. The act book of the Essex archdeaconry for 1565–6, as well as those of earlier date, reveals that the usual court 'fine' was not always the statutory 12d. but was sometimes as low as 2d., perhaps on account of poverty. Some absentees were also assigned public penance in church on the following Sunday.

Non-payment of fines is recorded sporadically. By far the largest sum overdue was owed in 1580 by a Radwinter man, William Sexton, who had been absent from Harrison's church for three-quarters of a year. The judge ordered him to pay 40s. to the wardens for the use of the poor, 'besides his penance'. (Harrison had ceased to preside at the Walden court sessions in 1576.) In 1591 Richard Fuller of Langford had 'not paid for his absence from his parish church while he was with us for ten Sundays, 10s. according to the statute'. A more complicated prosecution originated in the Lawford wardens' report that John Cooper and his wife had been absent from 3 October 1597 to 20 March 1598, 'being 18 sabbath days, whereupon they want 12d. for every sabbath day'. Appearing, Cooper explained that 'being sued for tithes before Dr. Stanhope (Edward Stanhope, Bishop Aylmer's Vicar-General), he hath stood excommunicate since, and being lame he could not go to London to procure his absolution';

a reasonable statement, as no excommunicated person might enter a church. Yet the judge ordered him to pay up and to frequent his church and his wife to acknowledge her fault before the congregation.

An exceptional decree was made in 1580. William Boyton, a Walden scrivener, had to pay 20d. (not 20s., but why not a multiple of 1s.?) for 'absence from the church on Sundays and holy-days', and was also given a special direction: 'He shall at every Spiritual Court in the round of the Archdeacon of Colchester in the town of Walden personally appear and then deliver into the same court one instruction or lesson for reforming of his own manners learned out of our instruction from the last court proceedings.' No doubt his recalcitrant attitude justified this appropriate punishment for an educated offender. He would seem to be identical with a testator with that name, then living at Helions Humpstead, whose will is dated 1596.

Apart from these cases, there are less than a dozen concerning non-payment of 12d. for a single lost attendance. A few who had refused to pay their 'forfeitures' of 12d. were haled before the court, some of whom certified that they had done so on being cited.

Only two references have been noticed to churchwardens' default in collecting the shilling fines. In 1576 those of East Hanningfield of the previous year were censured for having 'gathered no money of such persons as were found absent from the church'; and six years later those of St. Martin, Colchester, 'never went about to take the forfeiture of 12d.' No Elizabethan fee-books have been preserved, and it is difficult therefore to say, from the evidence of the act books, whether collection was strictly supervised by the courts.[1]

As is well known, the Act of 1581 imposed the extremely harsh fine of £20 a month on Catholic recusants who failed to attend church, but this statute was not enforceable by the Church courts and its effect is a matter outside the scope of this book, apart from a brief reference in the following section on Recusancy. A single echo comes from the court book of the Archdeacon of Essex in 1591. 'Mr. Gage and his wife of Leyton' had been presented, but his servant appeared in his stead, stating that he was indicted to pay £20 a month as a recusant, and the servant produced a tally from the Exchequer. Quarter Sessions had a concurrent jurisdiction in the matter of recusancy (but not the fines), and the rolls contain long lists of Catholics who refused to attend service or to receive communion. Ordinary absentees rarely appear in the justices' records and then only because of other offences. For example, in 1599 the Barstable hundred jury presented John Burrowes of Great Burstead because he was 'a misordered fellow and cometh not to church and a common drunkard and a blasphemer'.

[1] Kennedy (*op. cit.*), vol. 1, cci, convinced that the 12d. fines 'were consistently enforced'.

Compulsory church-going embraced a long list of holy-days, now almost forgotten among Anglicans although the catalogue is still given in the Prayer Book: nineteen saints' days, and in addition the Circumcision, the Epiphany, the Annunciation of the B.V.M. and her Purification, the Ascension, and Christmas; also Mondays and Tuesdays in Easter and Whitsun weeks. To the Elizabethans they meant rest from work, but many self-employed artisans could ill afford the idle time and those engaged in agriculture and millers were frequently tempted to beat the elements. Presentments for non-attendance were often for 'Sundays and holy-days' without naming which saints, but some were for specified days. An illustration is seen in the charge against John Sooton of Beeleigh Mill (in Maldon), for absence on Whit Monday in 1595, which he challenged, producing a letter from the minister and wardens that he was at church in the forenoon before the second lesson. The Act of Uniformity also enjoined all members of the congregation 'then and there to abide' for the entire service and sermon. Late arrival or early departure was an offence, and some delinquents created minor disturbances by so doing, instances of which we shall mention later. The prize presentment surely goes to John Lawrence of Peldon in 1597, 'for going out of church before the sermon ended to charm a thorn out of a maid's leg'. This he denied, saying that 'he was sent for by goodwife Westbrowne of Abberton to do the matter he is accused of', so he was given the chance of purging with four friends. Elizabeth Westbrowne, duly cited at the next session, brought along Abraham Foaks, who vouched for her 'very good name', adding that she was 'good to the poor'.

Ordinary sabbath-breach cases will be in the next book (p. xvi). Men with the soundest defence were those whose absence was occasioned by 'official' duties for the State or for keeping the Queen's peace. Richard Chadwicke of Leyton said 'he was a warden in the Tower where he receiveth the Communion and repaireth to church' (1580). Richard Heyward of Earls Colne, who asserted that 'he was hired upon a commission to gather petre for the Prince', had to prove his claim by four witnesses and to give 12d. to the poor (1578); and Anthony Parker of Little Sampford, 'a saltpetre man whereby in the service of the Prince he is busied in Hertfordshire', declared that 'when at Sampford he useth the church' (1587). Saltpetre was the chief constituent in the manufacture of gunpowder, and authorized collectors had arbitrary power to enter dovecotes. The prohibition of export of corn during the famine years at the end of the century is reflected in the case of John Bush of Salcott, who affirmed his being 'a searcher of ships for transporting of corn from Colchester' (1597).

Two constables were among the accused. Romball Taylor of Stock told the court that 'by reason of his office he hath sometimes been absent', but nevertheless had to pay as much as 2s. 6d. to the use of the poor

(1579); and William Rich of Elmstead explained how, 'being charged by Sir Thomas Lucas, Mr. Grimston and Mr. Pyrton (J.P.s) by their warrant to bring a soldier before them to serve the Queen and being about the apprehension of the same, did leave the prayers', on which he was ordered to prove his statement and was later absolved (1596).

Manning two of the three ferries over the Crouch estuary was claimed to be a seven-day job by the ferry-keepers when cited for absence from church. The passages over the creek were from Creeksea, just above Burnham, across to Wallasea Island for Canewdon; from North to South Fambridge; and from Woodham Ferrers across to Hullbridge for Rayleigh. Fambridge and Hullbridge are eponymous names commemorating lost bridges (the latter finally collapsed in Elizabeth's time).

John Richmond of North Fambridge had to answer two counts in 1576: 'He refuseth to pay 2s. 10d. that he was sessed to the reparations of the church and he hath been absent ten Sundays the last year.' Promising to pay, he stated that 'he hath been very often away from church by reason he keepeth the ferry and must always be ready at the waterside'. This the judge approved, with a direction to pay the rate arrears and an extra 3s. 4d. for the poor.

In 1579 William Hicklett of Canewdon said that 'he keepeth the ferry', but he admitted absence on three Sundays 'when he might have been at church'. The judge ordered him to give 12d. to the poor and to acknowledge his guilt in church. Next year it was the turn of Nicholas Perrin of South Fambridge, who made a similar statement.

In 1579 Richmond's deposition was much longer:

> He hath been about four times at his parish church sithence midsummer last, also four times at Hazeleigh and twice at Woodham Mortimer (*sic*) upon occasions. He keepeth a ferry, the common passage into Rochford hundred, whereby he is bound to ward by day and watch by night to receive and transport all lawful passengers passing out and into the same hundred at all times. His boat is to be guided by three at the least and sometimes with four. The benefit of that ferry being insufficient to keep continual stipendiaries for that purpose, he is driven to intend (*sic*) there upon himself, so that urgent necessity enforceth his absence, by reason wherefore he desireth to be dismissed.

He was ordered to purge himself with three neighbours. Excommunicated for non-appearance, he attended a little later and was absolved from the sentence. This time his statement included a broad hint about the importance of maintaining the ferry on Sundays in case of an emergency. 'The ferry is the Queen's Majesty's open and common way for all passengers, as well on her Majesty's special affairs as other her Majesty's subjects, to pass to and from the towns in Rochford hundred.' He repeated, 'Thereunto he is tied and abound and the benefit of the ferry is not sufficient to maintain a servant, deputy or substitute', but he claimed, 'Sometimes he repaireth to his parish church to hear divine service as the necessity of the place and room will suffer him'. The court, being informed of the truth by Mr. Hixson, curate of North Fambridge, Thomas Duplett and

Geoffrey Wale, his neighbours, dismissed him on his paying 2s. 6d. to the poor for his negligence and exhorted him to be at church 'as often as he could'.

Having been absent in 1587 on three Sundays (and not paying 11s. 3d. for the repair of the church), the response of John 'Richman' senior was a brief re-statement of his obligation to be in 'continual residence in readiness', on which he was commanded in future to frequent his church unless there was urgent business to the contrary. Not surprisingly, no further complaints were made in the perilous times which immediately followed. Twelve years later the Fambridge crossing figured in a romantic episode.[1]

When John Hyckes of Leyton pleaded in 1580 that he 'was not absent but upon special occasions of business, viz. when in the country travelling to get his living', he was acquitted 'by reason of poverty and on the testimonial of certain neighbours' provided that he produced his minister's certificate of attendance when at home. One of three absentees from Rayleigh church in 1588 said that he was 'a musician and goeth oftentimes to weddings', but was told to find six neighbours to confirm this. In 1575 Edward Lea *alias* Singleton of West Ham asserted that, 'being a tanner, he doth work far from home, sometimes in Kent as in other far places, but when he is at home he repaireth to his church', and he was acquitted.

Exemption was sought by eight defendants on account of their serving well-known magnates or other substantial persons. Michael Lylle of Fryerning pleaded, 'I am Sir William Petre's man and cannot come, and I am a smith', but was ordered to give 4d. to the poor and to do penance in church (1564). George Collard of Walthamstow said briefly, 'I am with my Lord of Bedford' (1567). Philip Scotte of Stock 'hath frequented West Hanningfield church because he was servant with his master Mr. Clovell' (Eustace Clovile, J.P., of Clovile Hall in West Hanningfield), and was ordered to purge with three neighbours, a seemingly illogical sentence. John Vale, of St. Mary Magdalen, Colchester, was 'attending upon his master Sir Thomas Lucas, whose household servant he is, at the public service' (1581). William Cock of Little Warley fared better on stating that 'sometime he went to West Horndon to service and to Sir John Petre's to dinner, for he works there commonly', and he was discharged (1591). Thomas Dybble, of Trinity parish, Colchester, was 'attendant upon Mistress Awdley at Berechurch and in Norfolk where he doth attend the church' (1596). Discharge was also given, despite 'great negligence in coming to church', to John Coleman of Bradwell-juxta-Mare because owing to 'attendance on my Lord Bishop of Chichester, Almoner to her Majesty, he is forced sometime to be from home' (1597), and to William Greene of Tollesbury, 'doing service to his lord and master the Lord

[1] *E.L.: Disorder*, 186–7.

Thomas Howard' (1599). In 1587 the wardens of East Tilbury presented Mary Skott, gentlewoman, in the house of Thomas Hamans of that parish; but it was Hamans who appeared in court, explaining, 'The cause why she came to this respondent's house is that she is landlady and (he) is bound by his lease to keep her and her train two times in the year and a dozen horse, otherwise he doth harbour her in his house'.

Attending fairs instead of church figures now and again in the act books, and all the cases are quoted. Four men were prosecuted, all in the 1590s, for carrying their wares to or from the important Stourbridge Fair, because it involved labour on the sabbath; and in 1587 a pale-maker named Draper of Stanway admitted that 'he was absent a fortnight, being at Stourbridge Fair', but asserted that 'he was at Chesterton church' (near Cambridge). In the same year several men of Ugley 'lost divine service and were at Thremhall Fair on St. James's Day'. This fair, held at Thremhall Green, on the boundary of Stansted Mountfitchet and Hatfield Broad Oak, seems to have had a riotous reputation.[1] In 1584 Robert Harr, of Great Tey, 'being interrogated how often he had been at his parish church since Shrovetide, replied that he hath been but thrice, but hath been at other churches, and that he was at Maldon Fair one day'.

An accusation by the wardens of Coggeshall in 1590 against Samuel Robinson for absence on a Sunday, 'being Witham fair day', led to his averring that 'he was Witham church both morning and evening prayer, confessing that he showed his shoes the same day in the fair to be sold'. Strangely enough, the court apparitor for once testified on behalf of a defendant – that 'he saw him at Witham church at evening prayer'. Despite this, Robinson had to prove it; duly producing a certificate under the hands of several parishioners, he was discharged. Next year a man named Wright and his wife of Inworth 'resorted to Tiptree Fair and Witham Fair, being on the sabbath days'; four more Inworth men and their wives were at Tiptree Fair on Sunday, 25 July 1595; John Guyon and Ambrose Till, the Coggeshall wardens, were instructed to report 'what persons of Great and Little Coggeshall were at Tiptree Fair on the same day'; and in 1597 a woman of Chipping Hill in Witham 'lost morning and evening prayer on the sabbath day being St. James the Evangelist in going to Tiptree Fair'.

Of course fairs drew parishioners from prayers. They were breaks in the dull routine of their lives, all the more so as most sports and games were banned. And if some fairs fell on Sundays or holy-days, the Church knew well that many fairs originated in people gathering together on the feast day of the dedication of the church. Ingatestone fair, held on St. Edmund's Day, is an example. (The word itself is of pagan origin, from Latin *feria*, fair.) In fact, some were held in ancient times in the churchyard,

[1] *E.L.: Disorder*, 2, 67, 112, 291.

until God's acre was declared out of bounds by an Act of 13 Edward I. Most market towns and some villages by old custom had one or two fairs each year, and a large number were held on saints' days or even on Sundays. In Parson Harrison's list of fairs all over England, at least ten fell on a sabbath day and many more on festivals of the pre-Reformation Church, the chief of which were retained under the Religious Settlement of 1559.[1] But the majority of the fairs had become 'paltry, little else bought or sold in them more than good drink, pies, and some peddlery trash; wherefore', Harrison declaimed, 'it were no loss if divers of them were abolished'. The worst feature was that they tended 'to the corruption of youth, who (all other business set apart) must needs repair unto them, whereby they often spend not only the weekdays but also the Lord's Sabbath in great vanity and riot'.[2] Suppression of disorderly fairs was sought by the more sober-minded parishes in petitions to Quarter Sessions or on the justices' own initiative.[3] On three occasions juries for several hundreds in Essex presented fairs held on Sundays – doubtless through puritan influence. In 1578 the Dunmow and Uttlesford hundredal jury did so: 'One fair commonly kept at Little Dunmow upon the Sunday, contrary to the laws of God and the laws of this realm, the Sunday after Our Lady Day in harvest; my Lord of Sussex. Also a fair kept at Thaxted upon the Sunday in like disorder, on Sunday before Whitsuntide; Thomas Saward, bailiff of the manor.' Neither lords of these manors would have been pleased with the presentment, for fairs were a source of income from fees for booths. Similarly the County Bench was informed in 1580 of 'a fair kept on Sunday being the first day of May here in Chelmsford', and in 1584 'Brentwood fair was kept on the Sabbath day'. After a fifteen-year interval, the grand jury in 1599 presented, 'There was a fair kept at Earls Colne on 25th day of March (Lady Day), upon the Sabbath day, contrary to the statute, and a fair kept at Hadstock on the 17th day of June being the Sabbath day'. No Sessions order books of the period have survived, so we do not know what steps, if any, the justices took. The reader may see for himself how far Harrison's dates for these fairs coincide with surviving fairs; Brentwood and Earls Colne are not mentioned by him. The actual law governing fairs is not quite clear: it seems that the real prohibition applied only to hours of public worship. 'But', as the worthy Harrison often wrote, 'to my purpose, from whence I have now digressed'.

Two curious pleas were advanced by Thomas Poplit of Rochford – that 'he was outlawed at the suit of Mr. Harris of Woodham Mortimer, and his wife is franzy (i.e. insane), and neither do absent themselves upon any contempt'; he was discharged. An entirely different reason – the fear of incarceration following arrest for debt – was submitted by about twenty absentees, who, as some were obliged to say, 'dare not go abroad', i.e.

[1] Harrison, *op. cit.*, 392–7 [2] *Ibid.*, 392. [3] *E.L.: Disorder*, index *s.v.* 'fairs'.

leave their houses, or 'so much indebted'. When Mr. Fitche of Great Leighs was summoned, William Curtis, his domestic servant, appeared and explained that he 'is indebted to sundry persons and is afraid of arrest' (1587); John Callis of Stanway attended, saying that he 'is indebted and dare not come' (1597); John Anderkin of West Hanningfield 'feared an arrest by Nicholas of Chelmsford' (1587); William Finshe of Chigwell 'is indebted and executors are forth against him' (1587); and Thomas Crachrodd of Great Tey 'durst not come for that he is greatly indebted' (1593). Failure to pay up after forfeiting a recognizance or bond was another form of debt, hence John Smith of (West) Bergholt 'durst not come to church for fear of arrest, being a surety for another' (1601). In all such cases the judge's sentence was predetermined, but it had little effect, as excommunication deprived men of their religious, though not their civil, benefits. Cited in 1575, Robert Ruddie of Hornchurch sent word that he could not attend because 'he was arrested by a bailey' (bailiff), but, somewhat illogically it would seem, was ordered to purge himself with two neighbours. The circumstances attending the remaining presentments were similar.

The law, ironically, was also broken by those engaged in lawsuits necessitating their presence in the royal courts in London. John Grene of Dedham, 'negligent in coming to church', explained in 1580 that 'by reason of certain suits and executions against him by Mr. Hubberd of Suffolk he did absent himself and not for any contempt', and he was told to give 2s. 6d. to the poor. Another example is that of Thomas Shelley of Loughton, who in 1587 'hath been absent about nine or ten weeks, having stood before the Bishop of London for a suit depending there'. A few other unusual excuses were offered, such as that of a Rayleigh man who 'had a horse sick of the stavers (staggers) and brought a bottle (pottle, equivalent to half a gallon) of hay with him'. But the most curious presentment lay in 1585 against Stephen Bruges of Little Totham, who had 'been away twenty Sundays and more but run shacking about we know not whither, very ungodly, and will not obey good orders'. (Shacking, or roving about idly, is a dialect word that has been rarely, if ever, recorded before the latter part of the next century.)

The courts considered that living a long way from their parish churches was not always excusable, despite the rigours and sometimes the dangers of travel along miry roads subject to sudden flooding and the hazards of crossing unsafe bridges or deep fords. In the previous volume we saw how the very frequent presentments of bridges left no doubt as to the perilous condition of many of them.[1]

The first case is exceptional in its being linked with work, which could hardly be a proper excuse unless he was a living-in servant. At any rate,

[1] *E.L.: Disorder*, 19–26.

John Blacke of Leigh was ordered to prove that 'he doth work with Mr. Thomas Church of Runwell Hall about six miles from the parish' (1580). Thomas Rame of Theydon Garnon, merely offering the fact that he had a farm at Little Dunmow (about 20 miles away), 'where he is most resident', was peremptorily commanded to conform (1574). Richard Harris, of More Hall in Rainham, after eight weeks' absence, gave this reason: 'Part of his ground lieth in Aveley parish and his house standeth ¼ mile from Aveley church and 2 miles from Rainham, wherefore he repaireth most commonly to Aveley church, but payeth all duties and receiveth Communion at Rainham' (1574). The judge told him to receive the Eucharist in Rainham church before St. Blase's day (3 February).

Thomas Awdly, stating that 'Stanway church is two long miles distant from his house', was warned 'to frequent his parish church more diligently' (1580). Thomas Adams of Aveley claimed that he was 'a lighterman and employed many times upon the Thames for the carriage of ordnance and other things abroad' (i.e. some distance away, perhaps to Tilbury blockhouse), 'and when he is at home he goeth to Wennington church, being hard by his house, and Aveley church is a mile and a half from him'. Despite his 'humble petition', his attendance at Aveley was demanded. William Marler senior, of Kelvedon, explaining how he 'dwelleth far from his parish church and near to Bradwell church and Coggeshall church, to which churches in foul weather he doth repair', got a similar direction (1592). In his will, proved in 1602, in which he describes himself as 'gentleman', he refers to his 'capital tenement called Marlers' and desired to be buried 'in the chapel where my seats are, in the church of Kelvedon'. The answers of Robert Howland and Richard Went, both of Widdington, who 'dwelling far from church, do come seldom to their parish to hear divine service', are not recorded (1578); but Stephen Rich of Great Bardfield, having been summoned, Edward Rich attended to point out that his father was 'a very aged man and a very dim sight and lame, and he dwelleth from his own parish church two miles and near to Little Bardfield church by ½ mile', asking leave for him to receive communion there (1598). This was granted 'during winter, except at the festivals of Easter, the Nativity of St. John the Baptist and St. Michael and other Sundays on which he could conveniently go to his parish church'.

John Saunders of Faulkbourne, reported because 'he and his household do somewhat absent themselves', replied, 'He dwelleth far from his parish church and near to Witham church, whereby in the short days he hath absented himself from his own parish church'; an excuse that might have been justified in a remote moorland parish but hardly in his flat neighbourhood (1590); nor was the statement of a man named Cowel of Great Tey that 'his wife was lame, 60 years of age, and he lived a long way from church' convincing (1588). Three Inworth men each declared that 'he was willing and diligent to come, yet upon the day, by reason of the tediousness (i.e. wearisomeness) of the weather he was absent' (1590). Three of Nazeing put in different excuses: Peter Tyson, 'by occasion of some necessity of his daughters'; John Reynolds, 'by reason of foul weather'; and Robert Camp, 'by reason of sickness and weather' (1597).

Because North End lay four miles from the church of the very extensive parish of Great Waltham, an inhabitant of that hamlet thought he was safe from detection. Richard Cowland, 'under the colour of a chapel which is at the North End neither resorteth to the said chapel nor to his parish church', alleged that he went to the chapel, and was ordered 'to repair once a month to his parish church' (1603). This refers to Black Chapel, the picturesque timber-framed, roughcast little edifice with its wooden turret and attached chaplain's cottage, built probably late in the fifteenth century as a chapel of ease for North Enders (see plate 5). (The accounts of the Black Chapel Trust, from 1685, are now preserved in the Essex Record Office.) It is one of the few remaining old Essex chapels. A generation earlier William Badcock of the same parish had claimed by his servant that he 'was aged and lame and dwelleth a mile or more from the church and did forbear until he was better able to come' (1579), to which the reaction was, 'Pay 3s. 4d. to the poor men's box.'

When Robert Sparrow and his wife and four servants of Childerditch were accused of being 'very negligent in coming to church' (1599), his contemptuous rejoinder, 'They dwell nearer divers other parish churches than their own', earned the expected order. The courts also had to deal with the problem of detached parts of parishes, of which there were many in Essex, though some were small in area and contained no dwellings. Thomas Crowe and George Hulke of Fobbing each declared that he was 'dwelling seven miles from the church and hath been oftentimes when he can conveniently come' (1586). The parish had three detached parts, all marshland and not distant, two apparently uninhabited. In the other lay Borley House, adjoining Holehaven Creek, not more than two miles from the church along a track by a small farm or cottage called Oozedam but probably seven miles round by water, which may have been easier. It looks as though these two buildings were their homes. Likewise William Sache of Tollesbury stated, 'He dwelleth three miles from the church and goeth to Tolleshunt Bushes (now Tolleshunt Knights) church' (1599). Tollesbury had only one detached part, a tiny area almost equidistant from the two churches but just to the west of Salcott and Virley churches. If his home was there, why did he not attend one of them?

The problem of church attendance by the inhabitants of the adjacent islands of Foulness and Wallasea – a cartographical jigsaw of detached parts of mainland parishes – was a special one. The cases are of considerable interest and will be described in a following section.

Presentment of absentees was thoroughgoing and incessant. Pleas of illness were rarely successful if of a temporary nature. While some gave only brief answers such as 'sick, very old and poor', 'extremely sick and lame a long time', 'hath been bedridden a long time', or 'could not come without danger to her body', a few gave the nature of their ailment. Richard Thaire of Great Baddow, 'absent from church forty-three times in twelve months', said that 'he is troubled with the stone', and he was discharged on paying 2s. to the poor (1587). A Stanway man named Godfrey, who 'was bursten (ruptured) and kept his bed and went not abroad and could not go to church and made show of such weakness and infirmity', was ordered to appear in court and to acknowledge his guilt in the meantime in church (1597). Hugh Gill of Little Baddow, 'very negligent', answered, 'By reason he hath been visited by the hand of God with great pain in one of his knees, he could not stir for the past eight or nine weeks, and also for that he hath been in suit of law and hath been very much from home he could not come to divine service' (1587): a somewhat contradictory statement from an allegedly arthritic victim. Another man sent word that 'he is so impotent, loathsome and lame as he is not able to come to the court' (1589). The case of a woman whose husband said that she had been 'so sick for two years past that she could not go' was dismissed. Walter Lovell and his wife of Great Baddow submitted a double plea: 'He attendeth partly upon my Lord Chamberlain and partly on other necessary business in London, where he orderly resorteth to church; and his wife dwelleth far from her parish church and is of loneliness sick and is a lone woman in his house, but absenteth not for any contempt' (1590); neither was excused. More than one explained that 'his negligence happened because of a sore upon his face', 'he had a sore mouth', 'eyes sore', or the like. The plea of a malingerer that 'sometimes in the afternoon, by reason of an infirmity in his head, he hath been absent', led to the decree, 'He shall come out of his pew and ask God forgiveness for his fault'. A sham ailment was perhaps submitted by Robert Fokes of Layer Breton, whose answer to the charge (1584) of being 'much absent and he gathered acorns on a Sabbath day' was 'his infirmity, viz. the flux' (probably dysentery).

Neither did the Church give old folks much relief, not even at eighty, which was regarded as an advanced age in Tudor times. There was no automatic age exemption. The age of five persons presented for absence has been found, three of whom had in fact reached eighty and the others were allegedly nonagenarians. Our period is too early for resort to baptism registers for checking. John Fordham senior, one of four absentees at Little Chishall in 1588, explained, 'He is aged 80 or near thereabouts and dwelleth near Great Chishall church, and although a mile from his own church whereby through his weakness he goeth to Great Chishall church he promiseth hereafter every second Sunday to repair to morning and evening prayer'. Anne Wilson of Weeley in 1591 stated that her absence was 'not contempt, but her age, weakness and sickness, above the age of four score'. In the previous year the wardens of Wakes Colne had reported Mr. Thomas Stutvilde and Mary his wife. The husband appeared and made this statement: 'He for his own part, being but of late come to that parish sithence Michaelmas last, at sundry times hath repaired to the church there, although a mile distant; and his wife is of the age of 80, blind and sickly, whereby she is not able to go to her parish church, but refuseth not the same upon any contempt'. Dismissing the charge, the judge nevertheless decreed, 'He and his wife, so near as they can, shall duly repair to the parish church there'. The fourth citation was that of a nonagenarian of Leigh. His wife attended, saying that he was 'a very old man and so impotent and lame that he is not able to go so far up the hill to the church, being of the age of lxxxx or very near' (1578). The road from the riverside to the church is certainly one of the stiffest, though short, climbs in Essex. The last concerned a dual charge against an even older person. The scribe wrote her age clearly, and again we quote the figures as written. The Colne Engaine wardens reported in 1580 that Joan Lawrence 'hath been negligent in resorting to her parish church, and as the common crime goeth she was bawd to her husband in being privy to her husband's lying with Jane Wright'. (He must have been many years junior to the old procuress!) Her excuse: 'By reason of the impotency of her age, being as she said of the age of lxxxxj years and her house distant from the church three quarters of a mile and a very foul way'. She managed to produce three compurgatrices to endorse her plea of innocence. Whether old or infirm in 1602, (blank) Hellam senior of Stanford Rivers 'cometh not to our church (or as we believe unto any other) throughout the whole year, neither did he receive the Communion the last Easter, but he allegeth decrepity; albeit we are fully certified that he can both work and wander to the market, which is of greater distance from his dwelling house than the church'!

Occasionally other defendants stressed the need to care for infants or for aged or bedridden parents, such as a woman who could not attend because of sickness of her child for the past six weeks or another who was at home looking after two young children. Richard Silverstone of Mistley with Manningtree said that he was 'in suit of law for land in Suffolk and his wife hath divers young children and no maidservant', but both were ordered penance in church (1590). Richard Browne of Mile End, Colchester, explained that he was a cattle-drover (and therefore often away from home) and his wife 'hath four small children, so small as she, having no servant, may not depart from home to church for fear if hurt happen' (1587). A Farnham man affirmed that he had 'carried children nursed to London and he heard service at Aldersgate church' in London. William Foxe of Springfield stated that 'his wife is lame and sick and hath no servant, and he is glad (*sic*) to abide at home and look to her' (1592). Margaret, wife of John Claydon of Ashdon, senior, pleaded: 'not wilfully nor negligently but sometimes by reason of her own sickness and sometimes by reason of the weakness of her mother, an old blind woman, who in duty she hath been enforced to attend upon and comfort', but she was enjoined to frequent her church (1584).

In contrast to these proceedings against senile people there is virtual silence about those who had reached the age of compulsory attendance. In fact, only two references to children, both aged fifteen, have been found in the whole period. It would seem therefore that parents' vigilance – if only to avoid the shilling fine – was extremely thorough, as was that of ministers in seeing that they were catechized.

Thus, many absentees submitted their various excuses of office, service, debt, distance, sickness, age, and so forth. Some of course had little or no excuse. John Daynes of Rayleigh frankly admitted that 'he was at a bride-ale at South Benfleet and sometimes with his friends, but not upon contempt' (1585), and was ordered to acknowledge before the minister; also four South Weald men, that 'upon necessity they are sometimes invited to their friends, as to a bride-ale, and sometimes to dinner, and sometimes are visited with sickness' (1590). There is a small miscellany of the lazy sort: John Hoskynne of Beauchamp Roothing 'absenteth himself on Sunday before Whit Sunday, loitering at home in his bed' (1576); William Farrar of Rayleigh, 'at breakfast being Sunday in time of divine service' (1585); 'did lose his service both forenoon and afternoon, and having no let (excuse) but sleep'; 'spendeth the sabbath day idly and is scant never at church'; 'at evening prayer time standing and walking in the market at Walden'. Another lame answer was made by George Cole of Rainham, who, 'being in the house of William Owers in time of divine service and was there taken by the constable', said that 'he came for a clean band (neckband), and so to have gone to the church, and the constable came'. William Luce, a Manningtree man who had 'spent the time of evening prayer in a boat', had to produce from his wallet 12d. for the poor.

The bounden duty of churchwardens and questmen (sidesmen), enforced by their oath of office to report absentees, subjected them to abuse, scorn and slanderous remarks, some of which led to the defendants being charged with defamation. The unpaid officers could not be expected to tolerate the sort of derision shown by Thomas Hoppwood of South Fambridge, who 'before this time hath been presented for absenting himself, and it appeareth was lightly passed over, for at his return from the court, in reviling and scoffing manner, said the churchwardens were fools for their pains to present him, and still refuseth to come to his parish church; but what the cause is we refer the consideration as also his former use to the discretion of your court'. An insolent, but terser, retort from one absentee reads: 'I keep my church well enough.' Other examples of the treatment received by the parish officers are given in the chapter on Defamation.

A churchwarden himself, William Graves of West Hanningfield, was doubly indicted in 1587 for 'being negligent in coming to church and sleeping in service time'. Quite exceptionally, Edward Dillick of Dedham, when reported for similar negligence, alleged that 'he being out of apparel was ashamed to go to church' and was told to prove it. Assuming that he was abjectly poor, why is his the sole case? The date is 1597, within the period of acute distress.

Among the commonplaces of life is shaving. Much is known of the toothdrawing and other services of barber-surgeons, but very little of their main work. We therefore go outside our period to quote a rare sidelight. The Colchester archdeaconry book in 1543, recording a Colchester man's absence from church both on 'high Sundays' and holy-days, gives the wardens' comment: 'He is lurking at home and every body that will go to him to be shaven he is ready to shave them, and doth shave them upon such days as though they were his common working days. We marvel thereat.'

A unique document is preserved in the file for the summer Assizes, 1594. It is attested by Thomas Fell, vicar, James Champneye and Thomas Hawse, churchwardens, Thomas Hammon, constable, and Isaac Geslyng, one of the petty constables, all of East Tilbury.

> Forasmuch as Mr. Thomas Cranmer esquire hath required at our hands the intimating and true certifying of his repair and his wife's repair with his family unto Divine Service and receiving of the Holy Communion at such time and he and his family be there resident; that so thereby he might satisfy some persons of great account to us not named; pleaseth it therefore to be advertized that Mr. Cranmer and his wife and family be not always couchant and abiding at his mansion place in the parish, but at such time as he maketh abode there both he and his family do frequent Divine Service at the parish church and also both he and his family received the Holy Communion at the parish church the week before the Nativity of Christ last past.

The Islands of Foulness and Wallasea

The peculiar parochial circumstances affecting the inhabitants of these two islands resulted in some interesting presentments. Horace Round drew attention to the subject in his masterly introduction to the Essex Domesday, which recorded how many of the pastures for great numbers of sheep that belonged to inland manors lay in the Thames and Crouch estuary marshes; in one case (Little Warley), as much as ten miles away on the mainland opposite Canvey island, and in another (Prittlewell), eight miles distant at the west end of Canvey.[1] These marshes later became detached parts of the inland parishes. Wallasea island consisted of eight

[1] *V.C.H. Essex*, i, 369–71 (with maps).

detached portions of five parishes. The marshlands of Foulness belonged to the parishes of Rochford, Sutton, Little Wakering, Shopland, Eastwood and Little Stambridge, but no map showing these areas has been preserved for this island. For the ease of the Foulness inhabitants, a chantry chapel was founded in 1386, and the chaplain was authorized to administer the sacraments to them. Later, at the dissolution of the chantries, the chapel became a parish church and rectors were thereafter instituted.[1] But, although the chaplains, and later the rectors, were entitled to the tithes of the islanders, the archdeacon's books reveal more than one attempt by the mainland parishes to enforce church attendance.

The first complaints in 1576 obliged some Foulness islanders to journey twenty miles to the court held in Great Baddow church. Presentment had been preferred against Robert Withers and his wife of 'Rugwood in Foulness' because 'they have not frequented their church (i.e. Sutton) and do not receive Communion for one year and more'. Appearing in court, he claimed that 'they are of the parish of Sutton but not in the parish of Sutton but of Foulness, where they do repair to divine service orderly and so have done time out of mind of memory of man, and all the tenants heretofore were allowed to repair to Foulness by lawful composition made by the Bishops (*sic*) of Canterbury and London and not at any time to come to their parish church.' (He was correctly versed, the original endowment charter of the chantry being in the name of the archbishop, with the bishop's consent.) There follow identical presentments against Robert Crippes of 'New Marsh' in Foulness and his maidservant, Robert Michell and his wife and Robert Lorkinne and his wife, all 'dwelling in Foulness in the parish of Sutton'. A reasonable compromise was made by the judge at the next session: that all the named islanders should 'repair three several Sundays every year' to their parish church of Sutton and also 'receive in the next communion there' before Michaelmas. Shortly afterwards, Withers and the others 'of the parish of Great Sutton and also Andrew Brodewater,[2] rector of the parish church of Foulness', were cited. They were enjoined to certify that they had received communion in Sutton church, and Brodewater had to attend the court 'to put forward his own interest'. He duly showed his letters of institution by Edmund (Grindal), Bishop of London. Depite adjournments they failed to attend and were all pronounced contumacious. This prosecution then seems to have lapsed. (See plate 6.)

Three years afterwards, in 1579, the same four men, but not their wives nor the maidservant, were again reported for not attending Sutton church. Again, too, they referred to the ancient document 'made and

[1] Newcourt, *Repertorium* (1710), ii, 271–2. For the island generally, see J. R. Smith, *Foulness: A History* (E.R.O. Publns., 1970), which has a reconstruction map of the medieval parish boundaries in Foulness; the author has since found that the earliest known date of the foundation of the chapel is 1283.

[2] Newcourt, *op. cit.*, ii, 274, gives Christopher Broadwater, apparently a misreading.

produced' (so they had managed to get a copy, doubtless translated from the Latin); and their presence at the next session was ordered, with the same result, followed by excommunication. At the following court, however, Crippes appeared, begged the benefit of absolution from the decree, paid his fee, and it was granted. The judge then decided, 'For that he can show no lawful cause wherefore he should not repair to the parish church of Sutton, he being within Foulness, he shall acknowledge his said parish church of Sutton once every year, viz. between the Fridays of St. Anne and St. Thomas the Apostle, in the future, according to the composition, and to receive the communion there if there be then a communion administered'. A similar instruction was given in the next year to Withers and Michell.

No more is gathered until 1599, when John Saunder and his wife, of 'Great Borwood', and Richard Man of 'Little Borwood in Foulness in the parish of Shopland', were charged by the wardens of Shopland with 'not receiving communion in our parish church where they are to show their obedience every year at Easter.'[1]

Wallasea island was specifically considered by the court in 1593, when the Hockley wardens tracked down Edward Crispe, 'dwelling in Walletts'. Their statement ran: 'He is reported to be of the parish of Hockley, and hath used (as we are informed) aforetime to pay his offering for himself and his wife to our minister at Easter; he neither the last Easter paid his offering nor since that time hath been at our church.' Unlike the Foulness men, he yielded at once and promised to attend and to pay, and was discharged. In actual fact, he may have lived not on the island but in the detached part of Hockley (seven miles away) on the opposite bank of the fleet separating Wallasea from the mainland.

In the remaining cause it may be assumed that the absentee's home was in the detached part of Eastwood lying in Wallasea island. In 1580 Thomas Bradock of Eastwood said in his defence that 'he dwelleth five or six miles away and frequenteth Paglesham church'. Six years later he was again summoned, when he estimated his distance at four miles, and he was directed to attend his own parish church of Eastwood.

The exact duties of the inhabitants of the two islands thus seem to have remained somewhat anomalous. Their ancient permission to avail themselves of the services of the chantry priest was in fact only allowed as an expedient, because, as Morant puts it, 'by reason of the swelling of the water, they could not always resort to the proper parish churches'. The great sea surge of 1953 and others before it in fairly recent years are a reminder of the inhabitants' periodic submission to the elements.[2] They led a strange and somewhat isolated life.

[1] *V.C.H. Essex*, i, 371 (see map opposite p. 369).
[2] Hilda Grieve, *The Great Tide* (Essex County Council, 1959).

Recusancy

Recusancy, or, more strictly, Popish Recusancy, in Elizabethan Essex is a very well-documented subject of which only the briefest account will be given. The reason is twofold: a good deal of the material on Essex recusancy has already been published, and it has been thoroughly exploited in an academic thesis.[1] Several lists of recusants for the whole county were printed many years ago by the Catholic Record Society; among them, the 60 Essex names in the diocesan returns of 1577,[2] another national list compiled in 1588,[3] the earliest Recusant Roll of 1593,[4] as well as shorter contributions about Essex recusants. Numerous articles on Elizabethan (and later) recusants have been published by the Essex Recusant Society.[5] These include extracts from the Quarter Sessions Rolls, from 1573, relating to the few Catholics in trouble before the Act of 23 Eliz., c. 1 (1581), which raised the 12d. penalty under the Act of Uniformity of 1559 for church absentees to the crushing sum of £20 a month and was of course directed primarily against Catholics. Thereafter long and fairly regular lists of names appear in the Sessions Rolls from 1581 and in the Assize Files from 1588. The list of 1586 has been transcribed in full.[6] Annual lists of recusants, with the fines paid into Exchequer, have also been published for 1588–1603.[7] Of more importance are the articles scattered through the 14 volumes at present issued. They deal in detail with some of the outstanding Essex Catholic families and with special aspects of recusancy in the county, making available relevant material in the State Papers and Public Records as well as in the Quarter Sessions and Archdeacons' records. Among the major contributions are those on 'The Religious Beliefs of the Petre Family under Elizabeth', the composer 'William Byrd and his Family at Stondon Massey', and the attitude of the Crown and the county justices towards these and other influential families or distinguished Catholics who received a strong measure of protection. A few of them appeared in our previous volume as defendants to separate charges of sedition, such as Thomas Hale of Walthamstow.[8]

Other notable Essex recusants occurring in the records of the secular and spiritual courts were Thomas More of Leyton (grandson of the Lord Chancellor), Monouxes of Walthamstow, Waldegraves of Borley and Navestock, Wisemans of Wimbish and Great Canfield, Lady Throckmorton of West Ham, Mistress Katherine Audley of Berechurch (niece of another Chancellor), George Gascoigne of Walthamstow, Mannocks of Little Oakley, Southcotes of Witham, Whites of Hutton, Wrights of South Weald, Pascalls of Great Baddow, Atslowes of Downham, Scotts of Chigwell, and Tyrells of several parishes. There were others, in some ways just

[1] M. O'Dwyer, 'Catholic Recusants in Essex, *c.*1580–*c.*1600' (London Univ. M.A. thesis, 1960).
[2] Cath. Rec. Soc. *Publns.*, xxii, 48–51. [3] *Ibid.*, xxii, 120–9. [4] *Ibid.*, xviii, 119–20.
[5] *The Essex Recusant*, i–xiv (1959–, in progress). [6] *Ess. Rec.*, i, 75–7. [7] *Ibid.*, i, 53–61.
[8] *E.L.: Disorder*, 39–62.

as interesting, as Lady Winifred Barrington, whose second husband, Thomas Barrington, was an equally staunch Puritan; or Rooke Green of Great Sampford, whose stubbornness led the Privy Council to instruct William Harrison, vicar of Radwinter, and John Lawson, vicar of Walden, to confer with him 'to bring him to conformity in religion': to no avail, so he was confined to Colchester Castle gaol.[1]

Two hearings at a session of the Archdeacon of Essex in 1591 will be quoted because they illustrate different kinds of special pleas submitted by acknowledged recusants. Thomas More admitted his absence both from communion and from service 'of long time; and allegeth that he hath been imprisoned in divers places, for his conscience would not permit him' to attend; 'and doth now remain her Majesty's prisoner, and goeth abroad, being bound to answer when the Council shall call for him; and therefore ought not to be further any ways molested, as appeareth by a warrant' from the Council. He also explained that his goods and lands had been seized by the Crown; and 'he therefore requireth to be dismissed'. On behalf of Margery Lady Throgmorton (see plate 4), Richard Swarton acknowledged that the presentment was true; 'but allegeth that his mistress hath a sufficient warrant to dispense, both for herself and for her whole household servants, that they shall not be troubled by the Ordinary or any other; but only to be at the Council's commandment, whensoever they shall be called'. The Privy Council had given similar bail to go 'abroad' (i.e. at large), subject to return to prison within ten days' warning, to Thomas Hale, their neighbour.[2]

Much research in the Public Records has recently been done on the controversial question of the extent to which the £20 monthly fines were actually collected.[3] Some, now termed 'church papists', nominally conformed by going to ordinary service while absenting themselves from communion. Special studies have also been made of recusancy in two other counties;[4] and for those interested in the contrasts between the two religious parties on opposite sides of the Anglicans' *via media* there is an invaluable work dealing with our period.[5]

Twenty years ago two loose papers were found in much later Sessions records. One, now assigned to Epiphany Sessions, 1588, poses a puzzle. It is a letter from John Aylmer, Bishop of London, addressed to the Sheriff and Justices of Essex and dated 30 December 1587. If, as he declared, the Church Court 'officers' (the Officials or the Registrars?) suppressed the names of certain recusants, how were the county justices able to notify the Bishop? The reader may be able to solve the problem:

[1] Harrison, *op. cit.*, 25, n. 20. [2] *E.L.: Disorder*, 61.

[3] See articles in *Ess. Rec.*; for other counties, see P. McGrath, *Papists and Puritans under Elizabeth I* (1967), and the invaluable introduction by Dom H. Bowler to *Recusant Roll No. 2, 1593–94* (Cath. Rec. Soc., vol. 57, 1965).

[4] H. Aveling, *Northern Catholics: The Catholic Recusants*, (1966) and H. R. Wark, *Elizabethan Recusancy in Cheshire* (Chetham Soc., 1971); also A. L. Rowse, *Tudor Cornwall* (1941), 342–79.

[5] P. McGrath, *op. cit.*; also W. R. Trimble, *Catholic Laity in Elizabethan England* (1964).

> Whereas not long since I have been given to understand from some of you that sundry persons in several parishes within the County of Essex have been presented unto my Archdeacons' officers for recusancy, of purpose that their recusancy might have been certified by me to you: and that notwithstanding by my said Archdeacons' officers that the persons presented have been omitted out of my certificate and so have escaped unpunished; these are therefore to pray and require you by your letters to advertise me particularly of the names of all such persons as have been so presented and not certified, and in what parishes they were so presented, and when and how often, and with the several names of those churchwardens who did so present them. And that you also cause them who made these presentments to come to me or to my Chancellor to verify that they did so present and to declare unto whom such presentments have been delivered; so as it may be known by whose default such presentments have been withdrawn or concealed, that the parties therein offending may be proceeded against according to justice. For as I would not any ways be a maintainer of such vile disorders, so will I God willing see the offenders herein severely punished, to the example of the Country.

The other undated paper, possibly of the same year, provides a contrast and a rare example of a conforming recusant. It is signed by Aylmer and Thomas Dove, vicar of Walden ('curate' is used in the wider sense of having the cure of the parish):

> Whereas one Jeffery Thorowgood of the parish of Walden was presented for a recusant and indicted the last Quarter Sessions for not coming to church to hear divine service there; these may be to certify unto you that he cometh very orderly to church and hath received the holy sacrament by the hands of Mr. Dove, curate of the same town, wherefore we request you that no process be awarded out against him.

Did the profligate rector of Downham provide one well-known recusant with an excuse for not receiving communion at his parish church? The facts are gathered from two documents preserved in the Quarter Sessions roll for Easter Sessions, 1582. One is a letter from Archdeacon Walker, writing from his 'house at Paul's churchyard', to Thomas Roberts, rector of Ramsden Crays, authorizing him to administer the sacrament to Sir Henry Tyrell, because he had requested the Archdeacon 'to appoint some honest man' to do so owing to 'Mr. Drywood and he being at some variance'. Dated two days later is the certificate of Tyrell's having taken communion that day 'in his oratory place at his mansion house called Fremingnalls in the parish of Downham upon Easter even, in the presence of all whose names are underneath written, being communicants with Sir Henry'. The signatories are headed by Thomas Tyrell, his brother, and followed by Mistress Avice Daniell, five others, presumably household servants, and the rector. Fremnalls manor house was demolished a few years ago when Hanningfield reservoir was constructed; it was not Sir Henry's only residence, and he was described as of East Horndon a few months earlier (Heron Hall in that parish being his usual home), when he was one of the few listed recusants for whom the grand jury found 'No true bill'. The Tyrells, like the Petres, were too influential a family to prosecute. William Drywood, rector of Downham, had been indicted at

Quarter Sessions in 1579 and 1580 for barratry and gaming as well as for calling his flock 'notorious liars and drunken thieves'.[1]

Some of the more substantial recusants will also be found in the chapter on Licences in connexion with charges for employing unlicensed private tutors for their children.

Akin to recusancy was the illegal use of papistical objects. The visitation book for the Archdeacon of Essex, 1565, discloses virtually no 'superstitious' relics: what were used secretly by faithful Catholics was another matter. A few months before, Andrew Glascock of Stanford Rivers (a Catholic stronghold) had not only 'refused to say his belief' but had also 'burned tapers', for which he had to perform penance and contribute 12d. to the poor. Two lay offenders appeared before the Colchester judge many years later. One was Thomas Baker of Kelvedon, who, immediately after his abnormal and successful compurgation related under that subject, had to defend himself in 1583 on a charge of 'keeping idols and images'. To that he replied, 'Idols, images and the cross were in his house, whereof some, he knew, were defaced, viz. the cross, other the more which he saith he did not know of'. Such ambiguity brought forth the peremptory command that 'those undefaced be defaced before Mr. Monke and Mr. Wilton' – two of the ministers who had just cleared him of being a common slanderer. In the following year (1584) George Clark of Great Oakley was detected by the wardens for 'having a mass book in his house'. In 1578 Thomas Brayne, curate of Cranham, was 'suspected of papistry, and he allowed the pictures of certain saints, also he doth preach, being unlicensed and also of small learning'. His answer was that 'he doth expound upon the Gospels and Epistles, and otherwise denies, saving that he did see certain images and pictures, but otherwise he did not regard them'. The judge accepted his statement, admonishing him not to expound in future.

The first Essex victim of prosecution under Elizabeth was Sir Thomas Wharton. In 1561, three months before she visited his house, New Hall, Boreham, on royal progress, it was raided by John de Vere, Earl of Oxford and Lord Lieutenant, where he found many 'instruments of superstition'. Wharton and Sir Edward Waldegrave were committed to the Tower for having mass said in their houses.[2] Wharton was apparently freed, but Waldegrave died there within a few months. After the Act of 27 Eliz., c.2 (1585), Catholic homes were searched for priests' hiding-holes,[3] but the act books provide no new evidence about them.

[1] *E.L.: Disorder*, 145, 219. [2] *Ess. Rev.*, xvii, 57–66, 121–32.

[3] For the full story of the capture at Widow Wiseman's house, Broadoaks, Wimbish, in 1598, see *Ess. Rev.*, xxvii, 22–34; for a brief note about hiding-holes at Ingatestone Hall, see *Tudor Secretary*, 292; for an account of the trial of John Payne, priest there, see *E.L.: Disorder*, 50–2.

Conventicles

We have referred to the fact that some wardens presented fairly long lists of absentees. The problem is often to distinguish the devout Catholics and Puritans from the ordinary defaulters. We know, however, that some were the 'godly' (i.e. Puritans) who were attracted to unorthodox services, sermons and preachings by dissenting ministers. Although we have only dealt briefly later on with those whose tenets brought them into conflict with the Church, we must quote the words of several lay and clerical defendants because of the insight they afford about these illegal conventicles. The prosecutions are all found between 1582 and 1584. They are the counterpart of the Catholics' secret masses.

Helen Colman and Dorothy Fenning of Ramsey each had to explain the circumstances in which 'upon Midsummer day last, being Sunday, she with others was in a wood in the parish, where they heard one William Collett expound or make an exposition upon the third of St. John's Gospel'. The first woman said:

> She was in the wood that day about 4 o'clock in the afternoon, going thither with Fenning's wife, her fellow Dorothy, and Ancheras Wallis to carry meat thither for Collett's dinner, where they found him having in his company Edward Durifall, Gallowaie's wife, and others whom she knew not, to the number as she believeth of a dozen, where they had roast beef and a goose; and after they had eaten, Collett read certain words out of a book standing on a ladder, and after he had read he cast away his book, but other exposition she heard none.

Dorothy Fenning's deposition was very similar, and they both added that 'there was a hollow stub growing and divers stubs of trees whereon was moss laid for seats, and the ground trodden bare with much treading'. The court then heard the 'personal answers of Edward Durrifall of Ramsey to the articles against him' to this effect:

> Upon Midsummer day at afternoon, having slept, his mother-in-law, Richard Gallowaie's wife, and his wife her daughter, desirous to walk, they thought it good to walk to the wood where William Collett the servant of Mr. Lucas was keeping hawks, which Collett the same day had desired this respondent to come to him into the wood to make good cheer; whereupon going thither they found him there with divers others, viz. Dorothy Jennings and Mr. Lucas' maids and Wallis' wife and other company of children, who were eating with Collett a goose and a piece of beef which was roasted in the wood, which Collett, sitting as they found him at meat, did read somewhat out of the Third of the Gospel of St. John but made no exposition; and soon after he departed again with his wife and mother-in-law, leaving Collett reading. Howbeit, he said that there is a bruit raised up that Collett did preach, but he saw it not, and he was never there before.

It matters little that the judge's sentence, if any, is not recorded, but the humble gospellers' midsummer meeting in the depths of the big wood alongside the Stour estuary invites comparison with the famous woodcut depicting the Queen's luxurious hunting picnic, which had appeared seven years earlier in Turberville's *Noble Arte of Venerie*.

The other cases came mostly before the Archdeaconry of Essex court and describe the more normal domestic conventicle, with or without a minister being present. That troublesome pedagogue, John Leche, was referred to by Thomas Legatt of Hornchurch, gentleman, when he stated that Leche catechized and preached in his (Leche's) house in that parish and that he was one of his hearers. Ralph Stephen of Great Wakering was cited because 'he useth private conventicles in private places, others not being of the family'. Denying the charge generally, he admitted: 'On the Lord's days after the service ended, being in the church, he doth meet with his neighbours and sing psalms and confer upon the parcel of Scripture together that they have that day, sometimes meeting at one neighbour's house and sometimes at another's that are well given, after which ended they sing a psalm, which meeting is only on the Lord's day or holy day.'

In one of the many charges which the rector of East Hanningfield had to answer (or sometimes ignored and was automatically excommunicated), Matthew Daile and Audrey his wife, two of his flock, were first directed to explain their 'using secret conventicles contrary to the Queen's Majesty's laws, in resorting to Mr. Seredge, parson of East Hanningfield his house with divers others'. It reads much like that of the previous defendant: 'After the psalm ended, Mr. Seredge useth to pray, which order of exercise he useth to use sometimes more sometimes less, which he taketh should not be a conventicle.' But the rector completely denied the charge, and he was able to produce as supporters Charles Chadwicke, curate of Danbury, Richard Black, curate of Rayleigh, Thomas Lorkin, rector of Little Waltham, and Derickus Helden, rector of Little Stambridge, ministers mostly well known for their puritan leanings. On oath Seredge affirmed: 'He hath not at any time had or used any private conventicles in his house contrary to law, saving that sundry times divers of his honest and well disposed parishioners and sometimes others of other parishes upon the Lord's days after evening prayer ended meet together in his house and sing psalms and use prayer and not otherwise, which is not against the law; and if he hath offended in the premises he referreth himself to the correction of his Ordinary.'

There were 'night conventicles', for example, at Strethall on the Cambridgeshire boundary, and at Aythorpe Roothing, some parishioners combining 'profitable lessons' with supper invitations. Of more importance were the frequent weekday conventicles ministered to by George Gifford, vicar of All Saints, Maldon (see below).

Finally, there is the double charge against William Pond of Langdon Hills: 'He made a conventicle in his house and had divers there at it, Mr. Redderiche vicar of Hutton being there and preached both Monday and Tuesday. Also he refuseth to kneel at the Communion and at the Confession, but most commonly leaneth his back to a pew.' Pond admitted, 'Sometimes he hath stood at the pew when others hath kneeled, but he hath not refused to kneel, and sometimes he hath sat with his hat on his head in the time of service, but not in contempt; otherwise he denies'. The vicar himself was summoned for 'preaching in William Pond his house Monday and Tuesday'. This he denied, 'saving that upon a certain working day, happening about Michaelmas last past, the day he perfectly remembereth not, he dined at Pond's house amongst divers others whose names he remembereth not, at what time he read a lesson and answered to a question and not otherwise'.

Something in the nature of a conventicle seems to be implied in the presentment against William Walker of Cold Norton in 1583 for 'using unlawful reading and catechizing in his house by one Faunce of Maldon and John Gardiner of Heybridge'; but Walker claimed that it was 'in his own house and with his own family only' and that Faunce was a member of his family.[1]

Unlike the answers of some of the protestant martyrs under Mary's regime, there is an element of equivocation in these Elizabethan dissenters' replies in the 1580s. They knew that their statements would not lead them to the stake; they gave disarming answers in the hope that they would be allowed to sing more psalms and say more prayers; they were not subjected to imprisonment as the congregationalists like Bunyan were to be a century later. A relatively tolerant attitude – to Puritan nonconformists – still prevailed in this decade, but the previous decade had seen the Government clamp down on the Catholics. Near the end of the reign the act books for the first time mention Brownists – followers of Robert Browne, regarded as the founder of congregationalism. But only two of these separatists are found, both in 1601–2: Edmund Bridge of St. Peter, Maldon, 'vehemently suspected to be a Brownist', also presented for absence from communion for the past year at All Saints' church (the two parishes were united); and (blank) Perryman of Great Birch 'is a Brownist and doth recite'; no later proceedings against them are recorded. The Act of 35 Eliz., c.1 (1593), was the culminating measure against nonconformists and sectaries, but it seems to have left relatively little mark in the Essex Church court archives.

Absence and Rejection from Communion

The statutory duty of church attendance included receiving the sacrament on days when Holy Communion was administered – usually Easter, Whitsun and Christmas – notice of which had to be given on the previous Sunday. Absence from communion, however, was a separate offence. Every parishioner was required to partake of the Lord's Supper at least three times a year, and the minister had to exhibit to the courts the names

[1] For some further details of conventicles in Essex and other counties, drawn from the archidiaconal and other records, see P. Collinson, *The Elizabethan Puritan Movement* (1967), 372–82.

of those who were not present at Easter. After dealing with absence, we shall describe cases of rejection by ministers of intending communicants and of refusal by parishioners to receive from their minister.

About 70 absentees were reported in 1561–2 to the Archdeacon of Essex. A considerably higher number of defaulters were named at his Visitation of 1565, and five parishes where many had not received did not furnish a figure. The result may be illustrated by the presentments in the following year by the wardens of Bradwell-juxta-Mare: John Broke of New Hall (*Nova haula*), Thomas Bradocke, three men named Thimble, and their wives had not received; but Richard Brice, the curate, appeared and certified that all ten defendants had done so at Easter. As with failure to attend divine service, in nearly every case the court ordered the defendant to receive the sacrament 'at the next communion' and to send in a certificate to that effect (plate 10). No certificates of course were submitted by the more obstinate recusants, and in the following paragraph virtually no attempt has been made to indicate whether some of the groups were probably made up of Catholic absentees. Other groups may have included persons who were drawn to neighbouring parishes by puritan preachers or even to the sort of conventicles of which a few were reported to the courts, as already noticed. Of the former, here is another presentment. In 1584 Thomas Wittam of Steeple and his wife 'received at Mundon or elsewhere the Word was preached, and he cometh not to Steeple because the Word is not preached'; to which charge his defence was that 'he is not in the parish of Steeple but in Stansgate': a flimsy excuse because it was never a parish, and, although the few inhabitants of Stansgate were in medieval times allowed to 'go to the conventual church there, as to their parish church',[1] the Priory had been dissolved as far back as 1525.

From 1569 onwards the archives for both archdeaconries are available. While most parishes reported each year only a single person, a husband and wife, or a few individuals, marked absenteeism was disclosed in about a dozen towns and villages. A group was reported at Horndon-on-the-Hill, where eight men had 'not received the Eucharist' in 1576. This is an isolated case, and no other parish presented more than a few persons until the 1590s, except Blackmore, from which 16 were notified in 1585. In 1590 the Ramsey wardens were instructed 'to declare names of such as have not received, there are a great many'; those of Peldon likewise, but the second clause is not repeated; and those of Great Bentley, 'to exhibit a bill of all those that have not received thrice this last year'; no such lists are given for any of these parishes subsequently. Also in 1590 ten Walthamstow persons were presented, eight being members of the recusant Hale family.[2] Next year the Leyton wardens reported 14 parishioners, including Henry Vanwilder and five other Vanwilders, whose names are also entered under several later sessions, after which they vanish. Later in the

[1] Newcourt, *op. cit.*, ii, 558. [2] *E.L.: Disorder*, 59–61.

year ten Rochford men were accused, who put in the extraordinary answer that 'their wives lay in at Easter, which was the cause of their not receiving'! As many as 27 parishioners of Inworth were charged in 1592 with not receiving at Easter; a few appeared after being cited, but one of them said, 'He asked me frivolous questions, as what should become of their bodies when they were in the grave and whether all the world should be saved'. From Elmstead a total of 46 names were listed in 1593; husbands and their wives formed the majority, and a few domestic servants were included with their masters; the scribe added, 'Mem. to send out the suspension of the minister' (see below). At the same session 40 Peldon villagers were cited, but the circumstances were exceptional in so far as the reason was 'through the sickness of their minister': a somewhat illogical prosecution; puzzling, too, as the rector, William Tey, was himself also accused at the same time for not wearing the surplice and not saying the litany, the epistles and the gospels. Next month nearly all the Peldon and Elmstead defendants attended and had to pay the court fees; after which neither of the groups appeared again, and it may be assumed that there was little or no further cause for complaint. In 1599, however, Reginald Metcalfe, rector of Elmstead, was presented for 'refusing to give the wardens the names of such of his parishioners as have not received the Holy Communion', to which he replied that 'he gave a note of the names' and was discharged.

In 1594 seven Great Wenden parishioners were in trouble, and in the next year the Walden wardens put in 33 names (all men); one was 'absolved', the rest cited. Apart from three incontinence cases, the entire business of this session was devoted to presentments for the same offence from other parishes: supposedly the result of pressure imposed on the clergy and the wardens at the preceding visitation. In the following month twelve more Walden parishioners were charged, and a few from other parishes, including four from Elmdon, and Edward Newport, gentleman, of Manuden and his servant. No further absentees were summoned until the next year, when the regular list of excommunicated persons included nine Walden and three Elmdon persons. Again, in 1597, 28 men, and in 1598, 16 men and two women, mostly fresh names in each year, were given in the Walden presentments. A Coggeshall list of names in 1597 has no less than 36, mostly married couples. Seven Strethall men were named in 1599. Thereafter no long lists are seen.

A solitary presentment in 1590 will serve to correct any impression of general absenteeism given by this series of extracts. Thomas Smythe of Barking, presented for not receiving at Easter, merely answered, 'There was such a multitude': probably no exaggeration and a reminder of the crowds that must have filled the churches of such populous parishes at the obligatory Easter Eucharist.

But long lists and statistics are somewhat meaningless, except to the local historian, without detailed analysis of the probable reason for the defaults, which we have not attempted to compile. Absentees from communion, as from service, fall into the same disparate groups of Catholics and Puritans on the one hand and the irreligious on the other, such as Isaac Lock of Wivenhoe, reported for a year's absence, 'besides he is a great swearer'. Salvation of the soul drew many communicants away from wholly conforming ministers to the anti-ceremonialists, but few of these laymen prejudiced their 'godly' pastors by admitting why they failed to receive in their own parishes. Only one, in fact, specified his conscientious objection. In 1584 William Walker of Cold Norton (who had been accused in the previous year for a conventicle) was presented for 'going to Mr. Gifford of Maldon to receive the communion without his minister's licence'. He partly temporized by asserting that he 'received in his own parish as orderly and as often as any of the parishioners do, and also received with Mr. Gifford, vicar of Maldon, which he lawfully may do, as he heareth'. Henry Cannon, another Cold Norton man, was cited for the same offence. Both were told to conform. Gifford had recently been instituted to the living of All Saints and was also the town preacher. Devout puritan, he was soon to be one of the thorns in the archdeacon's flesh.[1]

Unlike absentees from divine service, there was, however, no statutory fine for not receiving the sacrament, nor, as in the case of some offences, was a payment into the poor's box ordered. Excommunication was the only penalty open to the Church courts, even in the case of persons like William Hancock, servant with John King of Colne Engaine, or (blank) Silvester, *alias* Clarcke, of Woodford, who had not communicated for three and two years respectively. But the very first recorded offenders, John Bastwicke and his wife of Romford, were discharged in 1561 provided that, in addition to receiving communion, they gave 'to four poor people their dinners and give them 2d. apiece'. Provision of meals is never found subsequently as an appropriate punishment for any offence.

Fewer excuses were offered than those put in for absence from church. Thomas Hotspur of Little Baddow confessed that he had been 'but once last year, for that at the Communion times he had other affairs' (1575). When 'Mr. Weston Browne and Chace his servant' were challenged, the former declared, 'I am a serving man and attendant always in London, and there received'; to which is added, 'The like for Chace' (1571). William Wood of Rainham was 'a household servant with Mr. Weston, high sheriff, etc.' (1600). In addition to a few pleas of illness, there is one of mental illness. Thomas Lawrence of St. James, Colchester, having been presented, his brother William came to explain: 'He is unfit to receive because he is a lunatic and as it were insensible without reason' (1590). Of three Feering absentees, Thomas Selfscale had in the meantime passed beyond the court's jurisdiction, the registrar noting, 'He is hanged'

[1] *E.L.: Disorder*, 52, 265.

(1600). The Assize file has the indictments of Thomas and of John Selfscale of Little Dunmow, labourers, for stealing a cow. John was found guilty, read his 'neck verse' (labourers seldom managed to claim benefit of clergy), and was branded; Thomas confessed.[1] The prosecuting witness was Thomas Farrer, who was rector either of St. James, Colchester, or of Langham.[2]

Absence from communion was one of the few offences for which the gentry were not exempt from summons to the archidiaconal courts. Of five Romford men reported in 1585, Thomas Turke, gentleman, alleged on his appearance that 'he was a prisoner in the Marshalsea at Easter last, where he received', and the judge ordered him to receive before St. Bartholomew's Day. Although holding the office of chief constable of the Queen's liberty of Havering-atte-Bower, he had been the leader of a small gang who committed three highway robberies, collecting £27 16s. in all; but he managed to secure his release by the general royal pardon of the following year.[3] Also in 1585 the court cited John Pilborow, whose answer was that 'he received not at Hatfield Peverel these two years but received at my Lord of Sussex's house' (New Hall, Boreham) 'at Easter was twelvemonth and at Terling at Easter last'. He brought a testimonial to that effect and was also directed to receive again – in his case, twice before Easter. This enables us to identify the John Pylborowe of Hatfield Peverel, who had been charged in 1572 with abducting a young female ward, with 'Mr. Pilburrow, servant of the Earl of Sussex', who occurs incidentally in a disseisin case in 1585.[4]

One of the little-known facets of Elizabethan life is the relative frequency with which a minister 'repelled' an intending communicant from receiving the sacrament. At least twenty-four cases involving about 50 persons have been noted in the Essex act books. The Prayer Book rubric for the administration of the Lord's Supper is quite specific in its instructions to the 'curate' (i.e. the minister) regarding his duty to reject two kinds of persons – every 'open and notorious evil liver, so that the congregation by him is offended or have done any wrong to his neighbour by word or deed', and 'those betwixt whom the minister perceiveth malice and hatred to reign'. With anyone of the first sort, the cleric was to 'advertize him in any wise not to presume to come to the Lord's Table until he have openly declared himself to have truly repented and amended his former wicked life, that the congregation may be thereby satisfied, which afore were offended; and that he have recompensed the parties whom he hath done wrong unto, or at least declare himself to be in full purpose so to do'. Contentious neighbours had to reconcile themselves before receiving and promise to live in charity. If only one of the parties at variance forgave the other, the

[1] P.R.O., Assizes 35, 42T33. [2] Newcourt, *op. cit.*, ii, 169, 365.
[3] *E.L.: Disorder*, 274. [4] *Ibid.*, 125, 195.

minister 'ought to admit the penitent person, and not him that is obstinate'.

Before quoting examples of ministers' refusal to administer, we may note an unusual presentment illustrating how the Lord's Supper occasionally engendered strong feelings among the irreligious. Charged with not receiving for a whole year in 1581, George Allison of Coggeshall gave as his reason, 'One Mary Webb lately received in contempt of the minister, and he had been as good to have received a dog to the Communion; and said further in derision that it was a worthy Communion he warranted in respect of Mary Webb's receiving'.

The earliest example noticed concerned John Goose of East Tilbury, who alleged that 'he was ready to receive and was put back by the vicar' (1574). He was enjoined to substantiate this by witnesses and in the meantime to receive. Gilbert Anond, vicar of Boreham, rejected William Pooles and John Haywood in 1575 and the wife of Edward Staine ten years later, 'upon a common crime (rumour), as the minister saith'. At the same session in 1585 another Boreham man, Robert Gibbins, was prosecuted for 'abusing the minister in words, for the which he was put back from the Communion for that he would not reconcile himself'; the court commanded him to do so, 'and if he hath offended the minister either in word or deed he shall ask his forgiveness'. Occasionally a defendant protested that no reason was given for refusal, as with Robert Kinge of Great Stambridge, who was rejected by 'Mr. (Thomas) Barwicke, the parson, the cause he knoweth not'.

John Devenish and his wife, who were among the 27 Inworth persons cited in 1592, said that Mr. (Ralph) Wharton, the rector, had twice repelled them. An unusual reason for refusing was given by Thomas Houghton, curate of Theydon Mount, in 1584, when one communicant failed to produce his marriage certificate. Extreme action was resorted to in 1591 by Mr. (Brian) Atkinson, the dissolute rector of Wivenhoe. He was cited to explain why 'he would not admit one Thomas Bettes who was absolved in this Court, and so repelled him from the Communion and commanded the constable to carry him out of the church'. But it was the puritan ministers who were more inclined to refuse the Lord's Supper to those whom they deemed to be unworthy.

In 1589 four parishioners of Goldhanger were involved in disputes with one or other of two ministers, but mainly with the vicar, John Knight. John Tiler was presented by the wardens because 'for some controversy he did not receive Holy Communion at Easter and thereupon the minister did repel him from the same'. He declared that 'he was in perfect charity and tendered himself to Mr. Horner, late curate of Goldhanger, and affirming that he was not in charity with Mr. Knight, vicar there, he did repel him from the Communion, and that Mr. Horner is now departed'. Tiler added, 'There is no vicar at Goldhanger nor service said', and he 'wished the Court to provide a minister for Goldhanger'. John Wade claimed that, 'being in charity, he did orderly tender himself to Mr. Horner and he refused to admit him without cause'. It was Mr. Knight who refused John Heveningham, because 'he had slandered him (the vicar), which he doth deny'. The vicar had also rejected Edward Selrowe, 'who tendered himself two times'. Judging from these entries and from other offences, the state of religion in Goldhanger must have been fairly low.

It is not surprising to find the name of that uncompromising puritan, George Gifford, among the rejecting clerics. Seven of his parishioners did not receive in 1583. One, Robert Lune, stated: 'He offered himself three sundry times to Mr. Gyfford, the vicar, who refused to admit him for that he said he heard a crime of suspicion of incontinence between him and Mary West, which crime he confesseth'. Another puritan, William Seredge, rector of East Hanningfield, was cited several times in the 1580s for turning away parishioners. One occasion, when he repelled as many as 19, must have been a memorable event in the spiritual life of his parish. As Dr. Collinson remarks, 'He probably reserved the sacraments for the godly faction with whom he kept "secret conventicles and meetings" on Sunday evenings'.[1] His outstanding nonconformity is referred to later. Appearing in response to one citation, Seredge said, 'He could not suffer Richard Browne nor his wife, William Totnam, Agnes Clarke and Robert Totnam, for that they did stand excommunicate; also he rejected Richard Turke for he could not say his belief (the Creed) nor the Ten Commandments'. The court ordered that 'they be restored to the church when they can say their belief and show their diligence in the same'. A third puritan minister is found to have turned away a man in 1595: Thomas Greye of Coggeshall 'tendered himself dutifully and orderly, but Mr. Newman his minister did refuse him through private grudges between them'.

Christopher Parker of Little Waltham maintained that he 'offered himself, but Mr. Lorkin (Thomas Lorkin, rector), without just cause hath objected'; also that 'his mother, being a very old woman, hath not received'. The judge asked Mr. (George) Parnell, vicar of the adjoining parish of Broomfield, to administer to them 'with a competent number in Mother Parker's house'. Roger Goodwin, curate of Layer-de-la-Haye, justified his forbidding Lucy Clover in 1588 because Richard Choppin, another parishioner, declared that 'she had misused him, in coming from the church, by calling him "hornesby" and other slanderous speeches'. Lucy may have coined the epithet – evidently another variant of the 'horn' group, indicating a cuckold.

In 1590 Nicholas Foote of East Horndon said that 'he was repelled at Easter Week Low Sunday because he had called the minister "False prophet", which he alleged was never so spoken'. John Odell, one of nine Ashdon non-communicants, had offered himself at Christmas 1588,

[1] P. Collinson, *The Elizabethan Puritan Movement*, 349.

'but his pastor would not permit him because at the Assizes holden at Chelmsford on 14th July he wilfully did take a false oath, to the great offence of the congregation, until he had acknowledged his fault with repentance to the satisfaction of the congregation'; he was excommunicated. The Midsummer Assize file has no mention of him. Four years later the quarrelsome vicar of Ugley[1] received one of his several citations. John Waylett asserted that 'he was repelled by Mr. Darloe, he tendering himself'. The vicar was enjoined to show why he refused, and Waylett was given leave to receive from the rector of the adjacent parish of Quendon. Darloe had also repulsed Thomas Savell and his wife, but 'they are gone to Harlow', a few miles away. George Darloe resigned in the following year.

Denial of the sacrament did not entitle communicants to the return of their offerings. Illogical as this may have seemed to the contributor, they were a lawful source of the minister's income, loss of which was not justified because of the spiritual shortcomings of any of his flock.

In 1595 as many as 15 Langford men and women were turned away. Among them, the wife of John Sibthorp declared that 'her husband having paid their offering to Mr. Grayseborow, the curate, he receiving the money yet expelled them, whereupon she said that he might send them away like fools, having received their money'. The court ordered them to be reconciled. When Hamo Carter was summoned, also in 1595, he gave this answer: 'On Good Friday last he came to Mr. (Robert) Hunter their parson of East Horndon and gave him 6d. for his own offering and for his wife and Faith Burre his maidservant, and told Mr. Hunter that they did mean to receive the Holy Communion on the next morrow; and Mr. Hunter answered him that his wife and his maid should receive, but he would not receive him; and then he said, "The 2d. which I have paid you I pray you give me again", and Mr. Hunter said, "No, I may take my offerings though you do not receive".' A similar complaint arose in 1599. Presented for not receiving and for interrupting the minister at the communion, Thomas Harwood of Little Bardfield protested that 'the minister did repel him, whereupon he said, "I pray you give me my money again"'. In both instances, the court assigned the men to receive. John Akerson and his wife of Kelvedon tendered themselves in 1601 to Mr. (Thomas) Simpson and 'paid him their dues'.

A different refusal is recorded in 1591. 'Mr. (Roger) Weston (vicar) affirmed that the domestic servant of William Hoye of Wormingford is a very simple wench and without taste or knowledge of religion and not to be admitted to the Holy Communion'; yet on the same day Alice his wife and Martha his daughter were presented for not receiving, and Hoye appeared, certifying that both had communicated, and the case was dismissed.

[1] *E.L.: Disorder*, 167.

Although rejection of a communicant by the minister is almost unheard of in the present century, it was the subject of a prosecution under the Clergy Discipline Act, 1963, at the Gloucester consistory court in 1969. The rector had been in conflict with the squire and other parishioners. His activities having attracted much attention, some press reporters attended his church one Sunday morning. Unable to go to the normal communion service in his own parish, because of his journalistic duties, one of them attended, but was repelled by the rector, seemingly because he was a reporter.

On a number of occasions the reverse obtained, the communicant refusing to accept from his minister. At the session held in Barking church on 18 September 1564 'Mr. Haddon' of Barking declared that 'the priest had great pocks, whereat he refused to receive Communion, but instead to receive it with another'. Unreasonably, he got a dusty answer and a fine: 'to pay 2s. 6d. this day sevennight.' The next entry shows that 'Mr. Burre and his wife of Barking' had not attended service on Sunday before Easter nor received at Easter, their justification being that 'the plague was then in Barking town'. The judge ordered Burre to pay 12d. to the poor, to confess his transgression, and to receive within a fortnight. The Burres were recusants. (The epidemic of 1563–4 was severe in many parts of England, a thousand dying weekly in London.) Henry Filoll and Mary his wife of Aveley objected in 1602 'because Mr. (Thomas) Austen their vicar hath the piles in the highest degree etc. (*sic*) and they doubt (i.e. dread) infection, and therefore desire that they may receive the Communion at the hands of some other minister there'. Again the court showed no sympathy, and the couple were instructed to receive at the vicar's hands. John Luson of Greenstead-juxta-Colchester in 1581 refused to receive from the unnamed minister 'because he handleth the bread unreverently with filthy hands'.

In 1566 Christopher Dryver of Stock excused himself and his wife on the ground that 'they were not in peace because the rector of Stock is a drunkard', but they were both assigned penance and had to give 6d. to the poor. The Stock manor court rolls show that the rector, Oliver Clayton, and Driver were often at loggerheads with each other.[1] Clayton, who was also a farmer, committed various minor offences in that capacity, and the Drivers were an unsavoury couple.

William Pinder, Clayton's successor, was on even worse terms with his parishioners. Three men and the wives of six other men complained to the court in 1587. Charles Whiskard (a miller) and William Newman, 'in the name of the rest, affirmed that there were disagreements between them and Mr. Pynder, the rector, when they received the Eucharist; and they earnestly begged that they should be assigned to receive in some other

[1] F. W. Austen, *Rectors of Two Parishes* (1943), 53–5.

parish, with some sufficient minister'. Apart from the vague hint, in the licentious libel ascribing cuckoldry to many Stock husbands including Whiskard, that the latter was a papist,[1] none of the nine named plaintiffs appear in recusant lists. The judge's decision ran: 'In consequence, Mr. Official, for certain reasons by which he was moved, assigned all to receive in the parish churches of West Hanningfield or Buttsbury or in either of them, and enjoined the rectors there to receive them.' Strangely enough, however, the incumbent of Buttsbury (a perpetual curacy) seems to have been Lewis Madocke (also rector of Fryerning), to whom the libel attributed Catholic leanings. In the previous month Pinder had been presented as a non-resident (he was also rector of Mottisfont, Hants.) and for 'leaving his church unserved divers times since Hallowtide'; and three months afterwards for 'not saying service on Wednesdays and Fridays'. His reply was that he was engaged in lawsuits in London, and that 'divers times none came to the church, and the service was omitted'; on which the judge commanded him to be present at the public prayers, under penalty of the law. The chapter on Contempt of Court shows how he insulted the Archdeacon himself in 1590.[2]

Randall Hawle and his wife of Romford abstained in 1583 owing to 'discord between him and Mr. Atkins the curate, and at Easter last he could not receive for that his house was infected with the sickness'. (London had had another visitation of the plague in 1580–2.) The Wicken Bonhunt wardens reported in 1583 that 'all received Communion saving Ann Bradbury', who alleged that 'there is a controversy between her and Mr. (William) Swynho, parson there, and that he hath very greatly misused her so that she cannot with a quiet conscience receive the Communion'. Three years afterwards Mr. John Botfishe and Petronilla Botfishe of Tendring said that they were 'wrongfully set down', in her case 'through the uncharitable behaviour of John Richardes, curate there, saying that she was arraigned at the bar and was burnt in the hand, and of his wife calling her "Drab, jill and rogue", so that she could not find in her conscience to receive'. Despite being branded as a felon, Petronilla's name is not found in the Assizes or Quarter Sessions records. In 1591 Wilfred Luthey told the court that the reason for his not receiving was lawsuits between him and John Spenser, the vicar, both in the Queen's Bench and the Commissary Court of Essex. The judge was probably aware of this as he gave a moderate admonition, to 'use the best means he can that unity and concord may be between them' and to receive in his church before Michaelmas. Spenser seems to have been of unsound mind or in his dotage, according to other evidence.[3]

Discord between laymen was also a not infrequent reason for their not

[1] *E.L.: Disorder*, 69–70. [2] For Pinder, see Austen, *op. cit.*, 74–94.

[3] *E.L.: Disorder*, 59, which describes Wilfred Lutie as a gentleman; the act book, by a clerical slip, gives *Winyfridum*.

receiving. Nicholas Simon of Blackmore would not communicate because 'he was at controversy with one Reve of the Bridge insomuch as he sought means to kill him' (1588). Such an accusation naturally resulted in a court demand 'to prove the truth of the premises and to receive Communion and to confess to be in love and charity with all men'. Richard Reve was also charged because of a 'fame that he and others in contempt of the judge in the name of a citation, having a ballet, did cite the miller of Stock to appear before the Commissary of Essex the next court after'; he declared that 'he was in company as it is objected, but he himself was not to blame'. Stock was a hotbed of 'ballets' (scurrilous ballads).[1] William Robinson, servant of John Amie of Hutton, did not receive 'because of some jar between him and his master' (1598). 'Because of quarrels between them' or 'they are at variance with one another' are phrases used by other absentees.

It would not be surprising if widow Painter of Romford, who had 'never received Communion', had also been indicted as a witch, for her statement ran, 'Always when she is exhorted thereunto, she will find herself aggrieved with one thing or another, and that there is a thing speaketh within her and telleth her what she should do'. Perhaps the court, in ordering her to receive, adjudged her as slightly demented. An aggravated offence was reported from Dedham in 1582. Rose Barton had not received for seven years, because 'one Bettes' wife hath called her "Whore, thief and murderer"'. The judge followed the usual practice in enjoining reconciliation with her accuser, to receive, and 'to acknowledge her guilty negligence'.

'Mr. William Pennett of Ardleigh', presented by the wardens in 1589, gave a long-winded answer: 'Divers suits and troubles have been maliciously by sundry of his illwillers and enemies commenced against him without cause, and thereby being troubled in conscience and finding himself unfit to receive he durst not proceed the last Easter time, not of any contempt or misliking; whereupon he humbly desires the judge to forbear and give him some reasonable time to receive after those suits were ended, protesting that he would be ready to receive so soon as he could find in his heart and conscience to receive.'

Other untoward and even profane incidents attending the administration of the Lord's Supper are narrated under Churchwardens.

Before leaving the clergy's part in the sacrament, we should remember that it was also their duty to instruct the youth of the parish and to see that they could recite the Lord's Prayer, the Ten Commandments, the Creed, and the Catechism; and they were authorized to deny the Eucharist to persons who were unable to do so. That such rejection took place is evidenced by several entries, such as those of a woman (1588) 'because she cannot say the Lord's Prayer nor the Ten Commandments'

[1] *E.L.: Disorder*, 68–70.

and of George Reignolds, his wife and another woman of Theydon Garnon (1587), who had offered themselves, but 'Mr. Jeye', apparently the curate, 'rejected them for that they could not say the Catechism set forth by Mr. Nowells' (Alexander Nowell, Dean of St. Paul's).

Heresy

'It is impossible', wrote Burn, 'to set down all the particular errors which may properly be called heretical, concerning which there are and always have been so many intricate disputes.' As regards sentencing any person accused of heresy, he added, 'No spiritual judge, who is not a bishop, hath this power'.[1]

Three peripheral cases, however, have been found in which the Essex archdeaconry court passed judgement. In 1583, Dr. Bingham, the Official, received a detection against Richard Baker and his wife of Romford for 'using of their talk something savouring of false doctrine; and she something of witchery'. The man declared that 'he never read the Scriptures, and Christ's Godhead was given him of the Father; only that Christ said, "My Father is greater than my father"; and being demanded whether a Jew or Christian is best, he answered that it made no matter whether he were a Jew or Christian, seeing that he do well'. Baker was directed to undergo penance. Richard Plate, a Romford weaver, in the same year was presented for 'false opinions – the Son to be less than the Father and can do nothing without the Father give him leave.' In a remarkable series of objections to purgation, described later, the court took its own action in 1587 against Augustine Draper of Leigh on the grounds that 'the common report (is) that he doth not acknowledge the immortality of the soul; and by his own speeches he hath affirmed the same'. The judge ordered him to 'have conference with Mr. Beriman, Mr. Negus and Mr. Dent sundry times in meeting in Leigh church whereby he may be fully persuaded of the immortality of the soul, and to certify under their hands of his full persuasion at the next (court); and likewise (it was reported that he said) that 'there is no transubstantiation in the sacrament, and God hath his lawful ministers and they ought not to have any salary or stipend, but to live of the altar'. The witnesses against Draper were Thomas Puplet, Robert Binger and John Carnell. John Berryman, William Negus and Arthur Dent were rectors of the neighbouring parishes of Rochford, Leigh and South Shoebury: not all of the same leaning, the first being one of the 'unpreaching ministers', the others puritans, and Dent was to become a prominent divine. Five years earlier, Dent had been engaged by Richard Lord Rich, the leading Essex puritan, to deliver a sermon at Rochford Hall, one of the Rich's two residences. Not having arrived, one

[1] Burn, *op. cit.*, 589, 591.

Robert Wright preached instead, calling the local clerics 'a pack of dumb dogs'. This led to a petition to Cecil from six of them, including Berryman and Dent. About this date, an amusing anecdote tells how Dent castigaged a Cambridge scholar who had preached at South Shoebury on the Fair-day a sermon too learned for the bucolic parishioners. 'Next time you come to my parish', said Dent, 'bring shovels and spades, and plain truths.' In 1601 his *Plaine Mans Pathway to Heaven* was printed. Forty-one editions had been published by 1831. Written in rustic dialogue, Bunyan's *Life and Death of Mr. Badman* was closely modelled upon it.[1]

Church and Churchyard Disturbances

By Tudor legislation the Assize judges could impose severe penalties on persons who interrupted or stopped any minister saying prayer or administering communion. Under the Act of 2 & 3 Edward VI, c.1 (1548), a convicted person was to be fined £10 for the first offence and £20 for the second; the Act of Uniformity (1559) increased them to 100 and 400 marks respectively, and the third offence carried forfeiture of all goods and life imprisonment. The concurrent jurisdiction of the ecclesiastical judges to censure or punish such persons was preserved, but if punishment was inflicted the Assize justices could not sentence for the same offence, and *vice versa*.

The Church's attitude was reasserted by the Queen's Injunctions of 1559. No one 'without a just and urgent cause shall use any walking in the church, nor shall depart out of the church; and all ringing and knolling of bells shall be utterly forborn', except one bell immediately before the sermon (Injunction no. 18). Disturbing, mocking, or jesting at the minister was prohibited (no. 36). The laity were expressly charged to treat their ministers 'charitably and reverently', and not to 'contemn or abuse' them (no. 28). The general Visitation articles of enquiry, also issued in 1559, affirmed these provisions, emphasizing among other items the need to enquire 'whether any have used to commune, jangle and talk' in service time.

The Act of 1 Mary, session 2, c.3 (1554), had provided that any person who 'shall maliciously or contemptuously molest, let, disturb, vex, or trouble a minister while preaching or celebrating the Mass or other such divine service' was to be committed to gaol for three months and afterwards to Quarter Sessions, 'there to be discharged if repentant, otherwise to be returned to gaol until penitent'; and it was held, after Elizabeth's accession, that 'other such divine service' covered the Common Prayer. Again, the ecclesiastical courts' powers were in no way abrogated.

[1] *Ess. Rev.*, lvii, 196–200. The writer added: 'Many thousands of copies have been sold, but outside the dozen or so large libraries not a copy can be found; it seems to have been thumbed away by sheer hard wear'; there is now a copy of the 1704 edition in the E.R.O.

Violent disorders in church or churchyard were dealt with by 5 Edward VI, c.4 (1551); because these offences were cognizable in the Church courts before the statute, their co-ordinate jurisdiction was maintained. It begins, 'Forasmuch as of late divers and many outragious and barbarous behaviours and acts have been used and committed by divers ungodly and irreligious persons, by quarrelling, brawling, fraying and fighting openly in churches and churchyards'. Preambles to statutes are not necessarily accurate statements, and the strong terms of this opening clause have been deemed suspect by at least one historian. The Essex archives furnish perhaps the fullest extant evidence for the whole country, and it is significant that both the secular and the spiritual court records amply confirm the truth of this preamble.

By section 1, the punishment of an offender convicted on the testimony of two witnesses was 'suspension, that is to say, if he be a layman, *ab ingressu ecclesiæ*, and, if he be a clerk, from the ministration of his office for so long time as the ordinary shall by his discretion think meet and convenient, according to his fault'. The next section imposed on anyone who 'shall smite or lay violent hands upon any other, either in any church or church-yard', the grave sentence of major excommunication involving exclusion from 'the fellowship and company of Christ's congregation'. Section 3 empowered both justices of assize and of the peace in cases of assault, or merely drawing a weapon, in church or churchyard, to order one of the offender's ears to be cut off; this was additional to excommunication by the Church court.

The most outstanding fact is the extraordinary number and variety of disturbances and quarrels which took place, especially during or immediately after divine service. Month after month the courts dealt with cases of layman insulting or assaulting layman or churchwarden; layman disturbing, mocking, slandering, or even striking cleric; occasionally, too, cleric abusing or attacking layman; or, twice, cleric quarrelling with cleric. Many of these squabbles, of course, arose from the large and partly irreligious congregations present owing to compulsory attendance. On the other hand, a few of the troubles arose from differences of opinion in an age when liturgical aspects of the services were vital questions with some of the earnest laymen. The Elizabethan words for these quarrels were brawling, railing, or, occasionally, brabbling. Typical of a number of brief and uninformative presentments were those against parishioners who 'made a brawl in the church' or were 'common brawlers in the time of divine service', but generally the court insisted on being given details.

While low academic or moral qualities of some clerics led to their receiving vehement complaints from their flocks, puritan ministers' protracted sermons in other places tried the patience of the less devout and the youth.

In many congregations, too, there were the irreverent, the coarse and the foul-mouthed, whose impulsive acts or sayings, especially if levelled against their ministers, could not always be overlooked when the churchwardens made their quarterly presentments. Justifiably or not and for different reasons, strong anti-clerical feelings were voiced in some parishes both by religious- and irreligious-minded people.

Disturbances of one kind or another in Essex churches and churchyards seem to have been even more numerous than in other parts of England. Essex people of course had always been prone to radical and anti-clerical demonstrations, and in Tudor and Stuart times puritan sympathies were particularly strong. But, conversely, it may also be assumed that anti-protestant feelings in the Catholic North gave rise to many similar outbreaks. At any rate, it is an important but little known aspect of Elizabethan life that demands fairly full documentation.

Disputes about pews – a burning question to the socially conscious members of the congregation – were of a somewhat different character and will be described in the next section.

Apart from the fact that the act books often fail to give the sentences, such as are recorded for misbehaviour in church or churchyard were by no means uniform. 'Suspended from ingress to the church according to the Statute' is certainly noted in a dozen instances, but some violent combatants were assigned only the usual form of penance by confession; this seems to have been ordered in place of, not in addition to, being debarred from church services. Occasionally quarrelsome members of the congregation had to give one or more shillings to the poor men's box as well as to undergo penance. Those found guilty of irreverent conduct were not suspended, but were assigned penance. The same remark applies to others who indulged, without serious disturbance, in slanderous remarks in church. A few offenders who acknowledged their guilt in court were discharged without punishment.

A full account of the church and churchyard disputes and affrays, found in the Assize and Quarter Sessions records, was compiled for the previous volume.[1] We shall now look at the disorderly scenes displayed on the other side of the archival diptych and drawn from the archdeacons' registers. Of all the many defendants, only four came before both the secular and the spiritual benches: Martin Clipsam of Stanford-le-Hope, John Goldringe of Langdon Hills, and Patrick Ferne of Sandon, all rectors, and John Troughton, a former ship's captain.

Despite the Protestant swingback there is only a solitary note of a church disturbance in the early act books. Richard Everard of Great Waltham, doubtless the owner of Langleys, was charged in 1563 with 'troubling Mr. Holland at his sermon time'. He failed to appear, was excommunicated with penalty reserved, but later discharged because 'Mr. Holland hath

[1] *E.L.: Disorder*, 66, 121, 159, 189–94, 213.

not prosecuted his cause'. At the same session Matthew (blank), curate there, was also accused of the same offence. Attending and being asked 'who rung the bell, he said that he knoweth not'. Apart from interfering with the preacher, the offenders seem to have been among the many who were averse to giving up the old custom of Hallowmas bell-ringing, described in the next section. The victim was probably John Holland (father of Philemon, the translator), who became rector of Great Dunmow in the following year.

Even allowing for the fact that both Sessions and Archidiaconal records are slightly incomplete in Elizabeth's first decade, neither of the courts record many charges until well into the 1570s. One or two explanations could be advanced, but they would only be hypothetical.

The disorders usually arose out of rude or slanderous remarks. On May Day 1582 William Townes 'with a high and lewd (*sic*) voice quarrelled and brawled with John Rolfe, contrary to the statute made in the time of King Edward VI, in Wix church after morning prayer, to the disturbance of the congregation'. Fourteen years later William Chesshier was presented for 'swearing, banning (i.e. cursing) and railing' in the same church, 'calling Thomas Stowe rascally knave, tinkerly knave, and boy', to which the wardens added, 'Oftentimes he is a common swearer and blasphemer of the name of God'. In 1598 John Joice of Great Chesterford, charged with 'brawling and railing with Thomas Reynolds the elder most ungodly in the church', answered that the other fellow 'called him thief and villain and a false knave'.

The Queen's Day, or Coronation Day (so-called, but in fact 17 November, the day of her accession), when the nation was supposed to count its blessings in having Elizabeth on the throne, often chanced to be too rowdily celebrated, especially in the queen's ageing years. On 'Coronation Day' two Rayleigh men 'fought with boys and struck them in the church' (1589); a St. Peter's, Colchester, man fought in Holy Trinity church and drew blood (1597); while three named men 'and others' of Trinity parish 'quarrelled and fought in the church of All Saints on the Coronation Eve at night insomuch that there was blood shed' (1591). In another Coronation Day prank (1588), Richard Norton of Colne Engaine, churchwarden, blamed because he 'struck a boy in the church', explained: 'A poor boy of the parish called John Spurgin of the age of 16 or 17 did shut him and others out of the church whereby they could not ring as they ought to do, and thereupon for his sauciness therein he gave him but one little box of the ear.'

These were minor squabbles in comparison with the violent row between Martin Clipsam, rector of Stanford-le-Hope, and Tristram Blaby, a preacher, the story of which was narrated at length.[1] The congregation was divided into opposing factions supporting the rival clerics. When the

[1] *E.L.: Disorder*, 189–92.

rector was cited by the Church court, he attended and 'begged to be released', alleging that 'the matter he was suspected of, viz. brawling and using unseemly speeches in the church and churchyard, is now depending before the Judges of Assize and not yet determined'. This was granted, but William Partridge, who had led the anti-rector party, was also cited to 'reply to certain articles concerning the controversy', and he, too, stated that 'he standeth bound by Mr. Archdeacon at the next Quarter Sessions'. The Queen's judges must have been irritated with this violent factional dispute leading to assault, but their verdict is not recorded.

In 1577 Thomas Smith, gentleman, of Blackmore (who was lord of manor of Blackmore Priory) 'with others openly in service time in the church made a brawl to the disquieting of the parson and the people gathered together, being then going to service'. He said, 'By the means of others giving him occasion, there was high words'. The judge accepted the confession. In later years he was involved in more serious controversy with the villagers.

Presentments for physical assault in church, though not necessarily during service-time, were made against William Style of Mountnessing for striking Thomas Mathewe in Woodham Ferrers church (1577), John Jellibrond of Hadstock for striking and 'breaking a boy's head, but not of malice', he claimed (1598), and against a Stanford Rivers man who 'brawled, chided, smote and laid violent hands on another' (1602); two Greak Wakering wives fought, and had to confess in church and each give 12d. to the poor; two Wivenhoe men fought with their stools (1599); and Thomas Beale, a servant of Mr. Rochester of Great Oakley, fought in the tower (1601).

A grave charge was preferred in 1596 by Rebecca, wife of Nicholas Lyttlebury of Great Bromley, who declared that 'her daughter was like to be stifled in a ditch by James Lyttlebury, servant to William Clerk, and thereupon some words in the church, but no brawling or brabbling sort'. She was assigned to prove her allegation by the minister and three parishioners, but there the record ends. John Upcher of Fordham, prosecuted for 'some brawling speeches against Thomas Milbye in the church' in 1593, asserted that 'he was provoked by Milbye reviling him and calling him hedge creeper'. In 1597 Philip Norden, of Mile End, Colchester, was 'drunken and disorderly in time of divine service' and was also an adept at 'alluring and kissing of married women'; denying all this, he had to find four neighbours to purge him. His will, proved in 1618, shows him to be a tile-maker. Accusing Grace Payne in Fairstead church of theft one day in 1600, Elizabeth Belsted of Terling 'did charge her with felony and did challenge that she had a pair of gloves, an apron and a handkerchief in a brabbling manner'.

Perhaps the most intriguing incident, though tantalizingly obscure, was that which caused the wardens of Great Tey in 1600 to present Henry

Hasellwood of Coggeshall: 'He and divers companions misdemeaned themselves in our church in sermon and service time that day that one of them was killed, being the second Sunday after Trinity'. The accused's statement ran, 'He went and sat among the maids, and he did go up a ladder as to make a sermon-time'. On his oath he denied 'knowing the names of any unsorth fellows in that lewdness or rashness'. ('Unsorth' seems to mean disorderly, according to Halliwell's *Dictionary*; it is not recorded in the *Oxford Dictionary*.) He was ordered to confess his guilt next Sunday in church. Nothing is seen about a murder or accident in the secular courts' archives. Next year Hasellwood was in court again, this time for 'staying in the churchyard in sermon time and casting stones upon the leads, to the great disturbance of the whole congregation'. His version was that 'he was at Mr. (Thomas) Stowghton's sermon two hours and a half, and being urged to exonerate nature was compelled to go out of the church, and not upon any contempt'.

There were disturbing scenes at St. Giles, Colchester, in 1600, apparently because Frances, wife of Marcel Goodwin, was an unsavoury character. She and her daughter were in their own pew when William Rogers 'came and with vehemence bade them come out', exclaiming, 'I will pull you out'; and after service in the churchyard he called the wife 'Gossip, housewife, flurt and Jill', and said that he would pull the gown off her back. In court Frances admitted that she retorted by calling him Jack, and Rogers was debarred from the church. Next year the wife of William Pydd of the same parish was cited for calling Frances, somewhat inaptly for a woman, 'Butcher, cur, butcher's dog, and crockback'.

It is interesting to find in 1597 an incidental reference to a 'parish notice'. Nicholas Wright of West Mersea, brought to court, said, 'Being constable and surveyor, he gave warning to the parish to come to amend the highways upon a certain day, whereof Richard Foakes and James Donnyng now deceased did laugh him to scorn, whereupon he did ask them what they meant thereby and he wished the churchwardens to present the same'; instead of which the wardens presented Wright, their version being that he 'brawled in the church after evening prayer'.

Slander and assault in Great Bentley church in 1601 obliged the wardens to report how 'Mr. Fison complained that Robert Wigge came into the church, calling him knave, rascal, runabout and drudge, thrusting him from him with violence against the ends of the stools, and dared him to go out, so that he, going out to the north porch door, Wigge struck his hat off his head'.

A disorderly incident in 1602 involved a character whose activities were more useful to England in distant parts than in parochial affairs. The Rawreth wardens submitted: 'On 27 June being the sabbath day in the afternoon after evening prayer, upon some occasion of words, there were blows given in the church by John Traughton gentleman upon

Lawrence Barwicke, both of our parish, yet the said Lawrence making no resistance nor giving any blow or stroke again' (plate 3). In 1600 Captain Troughton had been appointed commander of the *Lioness* on a voyage into the Mediterranean to suppress English pirates. In later life, this sea-dog became a member of the first Lord Petre's household at Thorndon Hall. The case is remarkable, too, because the jury of Chelmsford hundred independently presented Troughton for fighting in the church, striking the collector for the poor with a 'walking stick'.[1] He was also reported to the archdeacon's court later in the year for not receiving communion.

Unseemly demeanour during Divine Service produced parallel prosecutions in connexion with the Eucharist. Article 6 of the 'Advertisements' issued by Archbishop Parker in 1566 ordered that 'All communicants do receive kneeling'. Complaints against those who disobeyed led to a few being rejected from receiving. Of Robert Smythe of Great Sampford it was presented, 'There is a public rumour that he, out of order and contrary to the Book of Common Prayer, did receive the Communion sitting' (1584). Two Great Burstead men, John Turnar and Augustine Wattes, were charged (1583) with obstinately refusing to kneel. Both replied that 'they thought Christ ministered it sitting, but, sithence being better instructed, they hath received it kneeling'. When Helen Somner of Little Laver only sat, Reginald her husband attended, explaining, 'She was great with child and received sitting for ease and not upon contempt' (1587). The judge might have censured the wardens for making such a frivolous charge, had it not been for the fact that the Somners were suspected dissenters.

The parish officers were sometimes involved in quarrels in God's House. Three incidents in 1590–1 may be quoted. The same Robert Wigge 'brawled and scolded with the churchwardens, calling one of them a rogue'. The Wivenhoe wardens reported a man for 'falling out with us and most shamefully hath used us in speeches not decent for men in our place, viz. knaves, slaves, busy knaves and pickthankly knaves'. (A pickthank was a tale-bearer, especially a court informer.) Of Roger Stephen and his wife of Frating it was alleged in 1590 that 'she is a very contentious woman among her neighbours, and she and her husband did abuse and brabble with John Baker constable openly in the church at morning prayer, using many slanderous words, amongst which Roger said that the constable (doing his duty about her Majesty's affairs) had made his warrant himself'. Suspension from access to their church was their punishment.

In 1578 a parishioner of St. Leonard, Colchester, 'brawled in the church and called Mr. Turner, the high constable, knave, etc.'; and in 1593, Edward Reade, a warden of Earls Colne, abused Edward Potter, a constable, in the chancel.

[1] *E.L.: Disorder*, 185; his mural monument is in Ingatestone church (*ibid.*, plate 17).

Irreverent conduct in church was a not infrequent charge, but whether vulgar action or deliberate dissent on liturgical grounds is not always clear. A presentment from Coggeshall, a parish well known for nonconformity, is possibly indicative of this attitude. In 1586 three youths each 'being by our minister willed to rehearse the commandments at the time of catechizing at evening prayer, did not only refuse to answer but sat unreverently with his hat on his head, to the evil example of all the rest of that sort'. In 1600 two Coggeshall boys 'sat unreverently with their hats on their heads in time of divine service, contrary to the 13th Article'; and another Coggeshall man was reported for the same offence in 1602. The shortcomings of the wardens and questmen of South Benfleet in 1590 led to a reprimand for failing to provide a communion table and a chest and to present a couple for incontinence, one of whom should also have been reported for 'usually sitting down upon his tail or clapping his hat upon his head in gospel time'.

The Elizabethan Church commanded all to bow at Jesus' name, but two South Benfleet men and their wives, who in 1587 'contemptuously refused to make reverence at the name of Jesus', are the only persons thus charged.

Girls were occasionally reproached for giggling, such as two Walden young women 'who would not be ruled in the church by the churchwardens'. But 'one that laugheth and giggleth in service time' belonged to the other sex and was also accused as 'a common swearer and blasphemer of the name of God'. There is also the unusual presentment of an Earls Colne man in 1587 for 'contemptuous behaviour in church and for swearing by St. Anne and St. Lucy'.

The Turpin tribe of Great Sampford (probably ancestors of Dick the highwayman of Hempstead) were often in trouble with the authorities. William Turpin was presented in 1596 for 'his unreverent behaviour in sermon time'. Like Dick, he vanished, temporarily at any rate.

The long sermons, such as the two-and-a-half-hours' infliction by the Coggeshall vicar, of course tempted some boys to misbehave, and the wardens used several oblique phrases, such as 'being evil occupied in service time'. While 'playing upon his instrument', a now obsolete euphemism for a male organ, probably implies masturbation rather than musical exercise, there is no ambiguity about the Feering wardens' charge in 1602 against one 'for profaning of the sabbath day in playing upon his easement alias instrument in times of divine service'.[1] A few years earlier, another youth, unwilling to join the congregation, 'stood in the street and threw stones which fell on the church of St. Peter, Maldon, and broke the tiles'. Bored or boisterous, Dorothy Richmond at Great Holland church 'thrust a pin in Edy Alefounder's buttocks in divine service', which not unnaturally caused 'disquietness' (1593); and at Marks Tey two youths 'whirled up of hats in service time' (1595).

[1] Cf. A. L. Rowse, *Elizabethan Renaissance*, 149.

In 1602 Samuel Squire of Pattiswick was presented for 'late coming to church and for laughing when the minister readeth the Litany'; to which he said, 'It was by sight of Sir Edmund's fooling in the church': a human touch in reference to Sir Edmund Huddleston, an active J.P., whose Pattiswick Park was a favourite haunt of poachers.[1] Squire being questioned by the court, the scribe jotted down in the margin, 'He did mend his countenance from laughing' – the Elizabethan equivalent of trying to keep a straight face. Complete congregational calm, in fact, must have been a rare phenomenon: even if the quiet was not broken, for instance, at Great Oakley by three 'common talkers in the time of divine service' or elsewhere by men who 'talked very loud and contentiously', there might be, as we have seen, disturbance from noisy drinkers and dancers in a neighbouring alehouse.

The irreverence of many was of a more passive nature. Some dozed off quietly and briefly unobserved, but the stentorian slumberers who 'sleep offensively' could not be ignored, nor could those who 'continually sleep in time of divine service'. A few said they were 'very sorry', when haled before the court. What William Graves, churchwarden of East Hanningfield, said, when he himself was reported in 1587 for sleeping during service, is not on record. Four men slept in Heydon church in 1597, but the record for somnolence goes to Ramsey. Was it a very sultry Sunday or a very long sermon? At any rate, in July of the same year 'There were eighteen that slept in the church, and some of them being told thereof by the churchwardens did defy them and bade them to do what they could'. Perhaps it was some would-be sleepers during sermons at Bardfield Saling who objected to John Reynolds' wife in 1585: 'She readeth so loud upon her book that the people cannot understand'; in any case, she had to acknowledge her offence next Sunday.

When a boy was presented because he 'writeth scoffing and uncomely rhymes in the church', regaling his pals no doubt with whispered recitals, his father, John Boyden, decided to attend the court, undertaking to thrash his son (*ad puniendum suum filium verberibus*) in the presence of the wardens and the parishioners in church on the following Sunday.

It was also an offence to quit the service before the end or to arrive late. 'Going forth of the church the last Sunday when Mr. Griffin went to the sermon', as well as being 'a contentious person, a common quarreller with his servants, and very negligent in coming to the service', were the charges brought against William Poyner of Upminster (1588), whose reply was that 'he had occasion to go to a wedding two miles off and should have come late if he had stayed till the sermon ended'. (Richard Griffin was curate at the adjoining parish of South Ockendon, and had been licensed to preach shortly before this date.) A double transgression was committed by a Black Notley man named Harolde through 'irreverently coming into Fairstead

[1] *E.L.: Disorder*, 241.

church in sermon time and departing again immediately, notwithstanding the parson willed him to stay' (1593). From Hadstock the wardens reported one 'negligent coming to church', neither will he continue when he is there, but goeth out many times to the evil example of others, and when talked to maketh light of it' (1587). Another, 'very negligent in coming and when he cometh behaves himself very irreverently', had to pay 2s. to the poor. William Fuller of Elmstead was cited, having been 'admonished by Mr. Metcalf (the vicar) for his negligence and contempt divers sabbath and holy days, as also departing out of church in service time, and for not kneeling down at the Litany and other prayers, for sleeping and other irreverent behaviour' (1591). His specious response was that 'he kneeleth upon one knee at the Litany and denieth the rest of the article'. Another man who 'cometh ordinarily after the sermon begun and seldom tarrieth till the end' showed somewhat exceptional contempt; and there are several other reports of those who 'would not tarry to the end of the sermon.' The watchfulness of the officers for any who might 'slip away' before the end of the service (as some servants did and were presented for this trifling offence) raises the question, How did members of the congregation, especially elderly men, relieve their bladders when the sermon seemed to be interminable? Presumably their temporary absence in the churchyard was overlooked, provided that they returned. If they did not come back, then presentment followed, as in the case of Richard Dryver of Strethall in 1599, who explained that 'he tarried in church till 12 o'clock at noon and being troubled with the strangury he was driven to depart, being thereof then grived and he did not depart in any discontented manner'. Strangury[1] was certainly a painful urinary complaint arising from 'the stone', an ailment with which Secretary Petre was often troubled.

For a very different reason Robert Westley of Hempstead was presented, also in 1599, for 'calling the singing of the psalms bellowing'; whether musical or liturgical critic he was sentenced 'next sabbath day in morning prayer to step out of his pew and acknowledge his fault'.

Many a fracas occurred when the congregation made their exit into the churchyard. 'Railing' or 'buffeting each other' there was a very common delinquency; less often, scuffles took place in the church porch. A few charged with 'some words of choler which they were sorry for' made up their petty squabbles; but others, such as Robert Wakelinge and Nicholas Twyne, two of Harrison's flock at Radwinter, refused in 1586 to attend court and were excommunicated. A Fairstead man who 'would not surcease brawling, notwithstanding being admonished' by the wardens, maintained that the other party 'called him knave and Jack twenty times', but was suspended; and 'irreverent speeches not to be named' were

[1] Emmison, *Tudor Secretary*, 250.

shouted in another 'chiding and brawling' incident. Blood was shed in All Saints' churchyard, Maldon, and 'slitgut knave' used by one party in a brawling match.

The Aveley wardens reported in somewhat fulsome language in 1574 that a parishioner 'did smite and give another a box on the ear to the great disquietness of their neighbours'; but the Tollesbury wardens took a more cautious view in presenting a quarrel at Christmas 1584, 'for how or wherefore we know not, some affirm that it was in the churchyard and others that it was not, and that it was not above a box of the ears or two at the most'. (The editors of the *Oxford Dictionary* did not find this homely phrase before 1601.[1]) Of two Rayleigh men who 'broke the Queen's peace in the churchyard', one admitted that 'he gave a blow on the ear, for that the other spurned him on the shin'; he was ordered to pay 12d. to the poor and do penance. During a dispute in Shenfield churchyard, the victim, struck on the ear, 'offered to strike with his knife'. Two men were having an altercation in Kelvedon churchyard in 1594 when one shouted, 'Jack, and bade a turd in his teeth', an unpleasant Elizabethan expression that we have already come across. Next year John Waylett of Ugley 'exclaimed to Robert Meade, church clerk, that he was a pickthank knave to say that his boy did wrestle in the churchyard in time of divine service'; but Waylett averred that Meade had 'urged him thereto'. Brabbling in the churchyard and calling another 'dolt, ass, fool and knave' was partially admitted by a Weeley man, but his version of the words was 'fool, ass and coxcomb'. In Earls Colne churchyard John Reynolds, a butcher, struck Thomas Allen and drew blood in 1582; and eleven years later in the same place Edward Potter, who had insulted one of the constables in the chancel, used similar language a fortnight afterwards and 'made a great brawl and did term divers persons of great credit to be knaves'. Appearing, he stated that he had already been punished for his double offence 'by the justices' order'. Bloodshed was only just avoided at Colne Engaine in 1595, when Amos Manship 'brabbled and quarrelled at the church door in sermon time with three men, and in the quarrel his wife did draw her knife in the churchyard, as she hath confessed'.

In 1597 'Umpton, gentleman, of Tolleshunt Major (probably John Unton, gentleman, whose will was made in 1609) was cited. He alleged that John Lowe and John White quarrelled, 'whereupon he, being constable and charged by the minister to go into the churchyard and to see the peace kept, came to them chiding and did charge them to keep the peace, whereupon Lowe did see White's mouth to bleed as strucken by Lowe and called him liar'. John Trappes, one of two Paglesham men who spat in each other's faces, excused his behaviour by saying, 'Some words passed between them but not in such sort as it is presented, as he was in his

[1] But it occurs in the same year, 1584, in the Oxfordshire act book (Brinkworth, *Oxfordshire Rec. Soc.*, xxxiii, 89).

shop adjoining to the churchyard, for which they are both heartily sorry'. When two Woodham Ferrers men were charged with fighting in the churchyard, one said that the other 'did take and gryve (i.e. hurt) him, and he to defend himself did strike again'. The churchyard of Finchingfield was the scene of a fight 'on 17 November being Coronation Day', 1587, resulting in a Great Bardfield man being presented; and that of Kelvedon in 1595, when another housewife 'drew her knife, as she hath confessed'. Assault at Stock in 1600 was described at some length. 'We present and complain', the wardens wrote, 'that there was a great and insolent misorder committed in our parish, as we are informed, viz. there was a battery in our churchyard between Christopher Parnell and Pierce Skott, the fray being begun by Parnell. He said that, upon certain speeches given, Skott did offer to strike at him with a cudgel which he had in his hand, and Parnell did bear off with his arm and struck up Skott's heels.' A cudgel was used in several other churchyard brawls, of which no details are offered.

Two Aveley wives named Lane and Thomeson were presented in 1564 because, 'being at variance before their coming to the communion, they in the receiving of the communion fell out one with the other; and the cause was about a nurse child which Lane's wife had of one of London, viz., that she had but small keeping both of wood and coal and little suck for both children, and told the mother that the child died of the bleach'. The judge 'in the people's presence in court ordered them to ask the one the other forgiveness and to give to the poor 2d.' (The *Oxford Dictionary*'s definition with earliest quotation for 'bleach' is 'a disease of the skin' (1601), apparently affecting infants.) A generation later another Aveley wife was a mistress of poisonous speech. In 1602 Elizabeth, wife of Richard Langlye, was accused of 'railing against sundry of her neighbours and upon our vicar (Thomas Austen), and on 24th June she railed on goodman Leverett our churchwarden immediately after prayer in the open street before many there assembled, calling him whoremaster knave, old knave, old swagbag, and that the judge of the court should ask (as she then exclaimed) if there was not an honester man to be chosen churchwarden, with other bad speeches; she railed also upon one Harry Rooke, calling him villain, thief, lepland, and that he had provided a saddle for others to ride in it'. (The meaning of 'lepland' has not been traced in this or other variant spellings.)

Not all such disorders took place before or after service. Churchyards were common meeting-places for settling all kinds of parochial and personal affairs, and as nowadays public footpaths ran through many of them. Some of the assaults were probably little more than the horseplay of lively youths. 'It was in sporting and playing and wrestling together sore against his will' in the churchyard was the plea put forward after a broken arm was reported in 1579 by the wardens of Norton Mandeville, the population of which was so small that it rarely occurs. The wardens of Little Laver, another tiny parish, seldom had anything to present, but when they brought William Aylett for 'breaking the head of Young's son', he said, 'Seeing Young's son fighting with another boy and thinking to have parted them, he did strike Young's son by chance and broke his head with the key of the church door'.

Accused of striking another in Loughton churchyard, the defendant said that 'in jest and sport and not upon any choler or anger he did trip up his heels as he was sitting upon the church rails'. He had to acknowledge 'before Mr. (Richard) Fydlinge the parson and to pay 12d. to the poor'. The prosecution of Michael Hardman of Margaretting, who 'brawled and fought in the churchyard of Ingatestone on the fair day' in 1590, is paralleled by that about trading in the same ground in the previous year, seen in the manor rolls. Also in 1590 John Stephens of Terling struck Edward Abdale, standing in the churchyard; '*ab ingressu ecclesiæ*' was decreed, but he 'humbly begged benefit of release because he is churchwarden', which was granted.

When Richard Mathew of Chigwell was indicted in 1576 of striking one Purcas, his reply was worthy of a defending attorney. 'Angry words passed between them,' he declared, 'but were done near the churchyard wall in the street and not in the churchyard, viz. upon the groundsel of the church gate.'

The longest account describes 'brawling, falling out and fighting' in belfry, porch and churchyard of All Saints, Colchester, for which John Gwye of St. Runwald was presented in 1592. According to his deposition:

> Peter Smith did quarrel with him and said he was a proud scurf, asking him if he would not ring, whereto Gwye said that he was a paltring saddler to call him proud, for he did wear nothing of his, whereupon Smith did give Gwye a box of the ear; Robert Pickas, his fellow, taking his part, Smith did strike at him, and Caser the sexton, being by, desired Smith to be quiet, saying that he was a drunken fellow. Peter Jenkyn of St. Botolph's, glover, did brabble with Smith and Pickas and took part with Gwye and one Robert Appleton being the master of Middle Mill and his servant now dwelling with Isaac Duk of Lexden, who took this examinate's part and (that of) the said Pickas and brought them out of the church. Smith followed him and made his nose bleed in the church porch and the churchyard. There were part taking and falling out by all persons then present, but who more this examinate now remembreth not. This was at 12 of the clock in night upon the Queen's eve.

Against the name of Pickas, also presented, '*Similiter in omnibus*' was entered. All credit to the court scribe, who managed to take down this involved deposition straight into his register with only two minor alterations. Our final extract has provided two more rarely recorded words of oral abuse. Elizabethan idiom was rich in the choice it offered for counter epithets: 'scurvy' was common enough, but the noun almost unknown as such; paltring, or worthless, was a fine retort.

This is far from being a full account of disturbances in God's Acre. It was the scene, too, of unruly and sometimes violent football and other games and occasionally of festive dancing, as already noticed. Assaults and other disturbances in church and churchyard were also within the county justices' purview as breaches of the peace; and some extraordinary scenes were narrated in the previous volume.

So much for disturbances between laymen or against the officers, but not primarily directed against the ministers. Animosity towards the clergy, on personal or religious grounds, gave rise to discordant voices and other kinds of disturbances in church and churchyard. The massive abuse or slander to which these and other clerics were subjected in incidents apparently unconnected with services is related in another chapter. While some devout ministers drew the right response from their flocks, the attitude of the majority was probably not unlike that described at the end of our period: 'For my parishioners, they are a kind of people that love a pot of ale better than a pulpit, and a corn-rick better than a church-door, who, coming to divine service more for fashion than devotion, are contented after a little capping and kneeling, coughing and spitting, to help me to sing out a psalm, and sleep at the second lesson.'[1]

A woman disturbed an unnamed minister of Great Wakering (1574); another interrupted the vicar of Great Burstead, also unnamed (John Okeley?), on Easter Monday when he was celebrating communion (1575); yet another (an excommunicated woman) disturbed the minister of Wix as he was coming into church (1588); a man and a woman railed on Robert Hunter, rector of East Horndon, in the church (1575); a man misused the minister of Great Tey (1589); Robert Derington, *alias* Pecke, reviled Joseph Burton, vicar of Walthamstow (1580). Exceptionally, John Drywood agitated the minister of Eastwood in service-time by bringing his bows and arrows into church, and was ordered to pay 3s. to the use of the poor (1587); if he had wanted to be ready for after-service practice at the butts, he may not have felt so willing next year to defend his Queen at Tilbury Camp nearby.

John Umfrey of Shenfield disquieted the parson in service-time in 1574. He produced four parishioners, who said that he was innocent, 'saving he confesseth that a bailiff served a writ upon Easter Day on Mr. Done (Thomas Dunne) the parson, which writ was taken out at the suit of this respondent. (Arrest in church was forbidden by law.) In 1581 William Turner of Earls Colne was 'a brawler, quarreller and contentious person for that he spoke to Mr. Vicar, being in the pulpit calling a woman out to do her penance, and told him that he was out of his text and it was no part of his service touching the contention'. Three years later John Kenton hindered communion in Langdon Hills church by 'his much brabbling'; and the same evening he 'railed and brawled, for the minister told him that he might as well kneel at the reading of the confession of

[1] Nicholas Breton, *A Merrie Dialogue*, quoted by J. Hurstfield and Alan G. R. Smith (eds.), *Elizabethan People: State and Society* (1972), 136.

their sins as others, and it is thought that he hath setters on' (a setter-on was an instigator).

There were violent scenes in Burnham church in 1586 and 1587. The wardens and two other men were presented 'for not suffering their minister to preach, but contemptuously withheld him forth from the pulpit last November'. Was this the disreputable Peter Lewes, the vicar?[1] If so, they may have been justified, but the judge decreed that 'they shall hereafter use their minister well and charitably'. The 1587 incident is mentioned later. In that year four Beauchamp Roothing men were reprimanded for 'breaking into Abbess Roothing church and bringing in Mr. Ward, an unlicensed preacher being suspended, to preach'. The door being shut, they entered 'at a certain way, not to the intent to let Mr. Ward into the church but only to hear the service'. Churchwardens were involved (apparently with some justification as will be seen later) in a somewhat similar incident in Holy Trinity church, Colchester, in 1590. Cited 'for keeping and shutting the church door against the minister and would not suffer him to say service', they were peremptorily ordered to deliver the door-key to Mr. Good, their parson. In the previous year one of the wardens of St. James in the same town, 'not knowing Mr. Miller to be licensed, took the book away from him in service time'. (The clergy list for the parish is deficient at this period.)

An unusual charge was brought by a warden against Mr. Southcote, gentleman, of Little Totham in 1599, 'for disturbing the minister of our parish and would not let him say any service, being Christmas Day'. Southcote's answer was that 'he went into the chancel owing to the door being locked before Mr. Knight of purpose, and being denied to sit there by Mr. Knight he did sit in the minister's seat'. The judge commanded him to acknowledge his fault openly in church next Sunday upon his knees. (Lawrence Knight was rector of Goldhanger-with-Little Totham, the latter being only a chapel to the mother church, but it is not clear to which building this incident relates.)

Excommunicated persons were debarred from the spiritual benefit of church services and the sacraments. Jeremy Burton of Elmstead had received such a punishment in 1590 for various offences but turned up in church afterwards. 'Being commanded by Mr. (Reginald) Metcalfe, the vicar, in the evening prayer to depart the church for that Mr. Commissary signified unto me and a churchwarden that he stood excommunicated', so the vicar stated, 'he not only reproached and interrupted me, but also even in the time of divine service stirred up such disturbance through his intemperate and reproachful words that the whole parish was disquieted and some departed their way.'

Unwillingness to attend church is exemplified by the blasphemous retort of John Goffe at Ramsey in 1595: 'Being in the churchyard with

[1] *E.L.: Disorder*, 112, 144.

other company a little before service began, the minister beginning service and said the Lord's Prayer, he in contempt of the minister and the service openly said, "Our Father which art in Heaven, by God, we must go into the church", with other suffing speeches.' (The meaning of the penultimate word has not been found.)

Among the many clerics who were publicly reviled during service, several were addressed as 'knave', and that is all the wardens reported. In 1596 Stephen Riche of Great Bromley 'railed, chided and brawled in a most odious manner' with John Heckford the curate, 'being ready to go to morning prayer', and a short time afterwards called him 'knave and perjured knave'. In 1599 Peter Webbe of St. Botolph, Colchester, was reported 'for abusing Mr. (William) Reade, minister and parson of St. Trinity, calling him "Knave Reade" in despite, and five times thou'd him'. (To address a cleric or other superior by 'Thou' was insulting.) A Terling wife one Sunday in 1596 at the communion table 'called our minister wrangler and prater'. At Kelvedon in the same year 'Mr. Richard Walker, an excommunicated person, used contemptuous words in the church to Mr. (Thomas) Simpson minister on Sunday was sennight, saying that he put him in the Court and he was in fault and it cost him 4s.' In 1598 William Nashe, a warden of Arkesden, 'did brabble and rail in the church against Mr. Brownrigg minister there (John Brownridge, vicar), viz. that it was a shame that he did him open wrong and open injury, in great anger and fury, and called him churl'. (Nash's will, proved in 1610, shows that he lived at Rockells, a small manor-house in the parish.) Coarse language was also used at Hempstead in the following year. Robert Askewe was charged that 'when the minister reproveth generally the congregation, he useth unreverent speeches and bade a fart for him'. For this abuse he was ordered 'to ask Mr. Wyldman forgivenness in church'. The victim was an otherwise unrecorded vicar or curate of Great Sampford with Hempstead.

A rare commotion shocked the pious and entertained the rest at Ugley in 1588. 'We present', the wardens stated, that 'Mr. John Bowlton our curate, hearing himself denounced excommunicate in the church, did disturb our vicar (George Darlow) in time of divine service, whereby he and our whole parishioners were driven to depart the church, leaving our service, and he termed our vicar "Foolish ass and dolt" for obeying the excommunication at the apparitor's hand.' The note, '*Quesitur viis et modis*' (to be sought by all ways and means) was the customary phrase indicating that citation could not be personally served on the offender; search in this case apparently failed to locate the insubordinate curate. Another preacher was humiliated in 1596, when Richard Bridge, a household servant of Layer Marney (probably of Peter Tuke of the Towers or Thomas Cammock[1]), 'during service lewdly, contemptuously and

[1] *E.L.: Disorder*, 186–7 (see also p. 135 below).

ungodly leaned against a pillar, facing the minister, staring, laughing and scoffing at him and his sermon'. At Bulphan on the last Sunday in Advent 1591 Henry Wakefeild 'openly rebuked the parson (?Edmund Williamson) for preaching false doctrine'.

A disturbance in Upminster church, but perhaps not during service, involved William Latham, lord of the manor of Gaines in that parish, who was a recusant.[1] Charged by the judge in 1574 that 'he did abuse Mr. Wassher his parson in church, reviling him', a witness named Frith averred his having heard the words spoken in the chancel in the presence of many. William Bawden of Upminster had informed against Latham, and at the next session he testified to the parties 'being at high words in the chancel and much angry talk', Latham saying to the parson, 'You are a knave'. Twenty-six years later he was in court again over a family pew dispute.

To hang horns over a doorway, as already explained, was to tell the goodman of the house that he had been cuckolded. More than one instance of such Elizabethan ribaldry was related in the previous volume.[2] When Richard Lamberd of Helions Bumpstead 'set up a horn in the chancel', did he do so to ridicule the minister? His act in any case required him to confess 'on Sunday next before the minister and six honest parishioners and promise that he will not do the like hereafter'.

Two presentments illustrate the antipathy of many lay persons to the use of the surplice, a dissenting opinion which was of course strongly held by some of the anti-vestments puritan clergy. In 1574 Nicholas Reynolds of Mucking 'mocked the minister for wearing the surplice'. The same view was expressed with caustic Essex humour by John Sharpe of Hatfield Peverel in 1586. He said, 'when he did see the minister wear the surplice, that the fool had gotten on his fool's coat, and did axe (ask) the minister if he would have it to keep him warm'. The buffoon did not respond to citation and was excommunicated.

Other personal insults took place in churchyards. Abusive epithets were thrown in 1584 against the minister of Layer-de-la-Haye, who was called 'an ungodly, unconciable wretch' (an otherwise unrecorded adjective); and in 1589 against Mr. Rosse, curate of Wakes Colne, who was called 'knave by Mr. Emerye, househould servant of Mr. Tiffin' (lord of the manor). 'Mr. Gordwin', minister of Lawford, was 'abused in words' by Robert Kettle of Lawford (1602). The wardens of South Benfleet, 'being credibly informed', presented Nicholas Elmes because 'he did very indiscreetly, uncharitably and unreverently contemn and abuse our vicar in the churchyard, with very opprobrious speeches and words of horrible oblique' (1596). What these words were is not vouchsafed, but the Great Chishall wardens had no compunction in reporting that William Prentice 'abused the minister in the churchyard by words, viz. he told him of his

[1] *E.L.: Disorder*, 188. [2] *Ibid.*, 69, 72, 108.

knavery and bade him kiss his arse', which direct hint Prentice denied having given. Purgation was apparently disallowed by the judge, who enjoined Prentice 'to kneel after the Gospel next sabbath and to confess' (1594). In 1600 Thomas Crowe of Broomfield 'misused Mr. (George) Parnell the vicar in the churchyard'. He had sold a cow at May Fair for Parnell, and told him 'he would see a cow in his belly before he would sell a cow for (unfinished)'. Penitential confession was enjoined.

While some of the clergy were slandered in consecrated places, several showed little restraint themselves. In 1574 Patrick Ferne, rector of Sandon, 'with others made great chiding and had many contentious words in service time'. He pleaded, however, that 'between service and sermon there was many outrageous words spoken against him, and he defended himself with words'. At the same session Edward Solme and John Tabor of Sandon and the parson 'were charged with a great brawling in service time'. Solme said, 'Service ended, and a little before the sermon, he answered one Tysdale who had said to them, "I defy thee, I defy thee, whoreson wretch"'; and Tabor admitted 'uttering angry speeches'. In each case the rector had to confess and pay 2s. to the poor. At the Assizes three years earlier he had been fined 3s. 4d. for quarrelling both in and out of church and 20d. for barratry.[1]

Thomas Turrel, curate of East Mersea, in 1582 not only omitted 'to say service at convenient times and did not walk the bounds of the parish' but also 'did order himself with hot speeches and unseemly words in the church, contrary to the Statute of Edward VI'.

An incident in 1591 presumably occurred in the church. Brian Atkinson, rector of Wivenhoe, 'being called by William Morley knave and rascal and hardly used by him and the churchwardens, and being provoked by their many abuses, did chide them and used hard words against them'. The judge ordered him to express his sorrow to Morley, which is not surprising, as the previous entry records the wardens having presented the rector both for suspected incontinence and for generally falling out with his flock.

A few of the more belligerent laymen did not stop at oral abuse of their ministers. The cloth did not protect them necessarily from physical assault. A Hempstead man with the unfortunate name of Thomas Savage in 1581 met the charge of his having 'laid violent hands on a minister' with the story that, 'passing by the churchyard, he did throw with a libbet at a walnut tree, and being reproved for his so doing by the vicar and the vicar offering to strike him he catched the cudgel out of the minister's hand and struck him within the churchyard'. The judge excommunicated Savage 'and decreed letters to be sent etc.', presumably forbidding entrance into

[1] *E.L.: Disorder*, 193.

his parish church. A libbet, meaning a stick to throw at something, was indeed *le mot juste*. On the other hand, when John Lawncellett of Danbury was accused in 1583 of 'beating the minister, abusing him with words and casting stones at him', he confessed and was released. We may perhaps assume, as the rector was Archdeacon Withers, that the victim was the curate. In 1588 John Bridge of North Shoebury 'did lay violent hands on Mr. (William) Hayward the minister'. A parishioner of St. Nicholas, Colchester, was presented in 1590, not only for playing bowls on Shrove Tuesday all the afternoon during service-time and refusing to come to be catechized, but also for 'striking and laying violent hands upon Mr. Ferrar, minister there', doubtless after being admonished. In the same year a man named Felton of St. Runwald, Colchester, was cited for 'striking of Mr. Cook minister and laying of violent hands upon him'. Not surprisingly, Joan Madyson of Buttsbury was excommunicated in 1597 for 'unreverently abusing our minister Mr. Simons by striking him on the head in such sort that she brake the same and made the blood run down'. Other charges lay against Edward Blackshawe of Helions Bumpstead for striking Mr. (John) Cowle, vicar there' (1581); William Sexton and his wife of Radwinter (1588) for 'striking William Pomfrett his minister', who must have been curate to William Harrison during one of his abscences, probably at Windsor, where he had become a canon of St. George's Chapel in 1586; (blank) Potter of Marks Tey for 'laying violent hands on Mr. Foster (an otherwise unrecorded) parson there and drawing blood of him' (1595); William Vernon junior, described as both of All Saints and St. Peter, Maldon, whom the wardens presented (1595) 'on a common fame and report that he jostled our minister Mr. Robert Palmer (vicar of the joint parishes) from the wall and bid him go his way if he were well, otherwise he would thrust him into the channel' (the kennel, or perhaps the estuary); and William Evans of Peldon for 'brawling and quarrelling with the minister on Easter Day in the church and churchyard; he did draw his dagger on the minister' (1597).

The clergy were not immune from being summoned to the courts for assaults alleged to have been committed by themselves. A number of them, as seen in the previous volume, were indicted at Quarter Sessions for physical attacks on parishioners or even for fighting among themselves. Three incidents occurred in 1584. Francis Warner, rector of West Mersea, 'struck our sexton in the church porch'. At the previous session Thomas Diglet, perhaps the sexton, had been presented for 'abusing the minister with strokes and beating him', so this may be a counter-charge. Henry Bell, clerk, of Great Horkesley, 'did fight and strike John Ball in the churchyard of Little Horkesley'. Humbly submitting that Ball was the first assailant and that he acted in his own defence, he was absolved. In the third case the verdict is not given: 'Mr. William Bambridge rector of

Tolleshunt Major and curate of Feering struck Mr. John Mullner of Thorrington, clerk'. (Bell and Mullner were evidently curates.) Thomas Howell, rector of Paglesham, was prosecuted in 1587 for 'brawling in the church of Burnham and for laying violent hands on Mr. (William) Chase, curate there'. The rector told the judge that he had already been suspended by the Court of High Commission; he was later deprived of his benefice. Edward Kynett, vicar of Ulting, was accused in 1597 of 'violently striking of William Barber's head with his dagger upon the sabbath day'. He pleaded self-defence and was enjoined to prove this on Barber's own oath.

The reader is probably wearied by the long chronicle of altercation, dissension and strife among laymen and of hostility to ministers, all in holy places: a chronicle to which the secular court records add even more riotous scenes. But he may have gained some satisfaction in being able to study an enlarged detail of a little-known portrait of Elizabethan society that has never been published before. A minor detail of the portrait, about to be described, depicts pew and bell-ringing disputes. Close to the main feature is the ugly delineation of indictment, slander and abuse of clerks in holy orders – to their faces but not apparently in church or churchyard, or behind their backs – which will be observed in the chapter on the Clergy.

Seating and Bell-ringing Disputes

Parochial custom and ancient usage governed the seating of the congregation. Both gave rise to controversy and occasionally to violence. 'Although the freehold of the body (i.e. the nave) of the church be in the incumbent,' Burn wrote,[1] 'and the seats therein be fixed to the freehold, yet because the church is dedicated to the service of God and is for the use of the inhabitants, the use of them is common to all the people that pay to the repair thereof. But the authority of appointing what persons shall sit in each seat is in the ordinary' (in our context, the two Archdeacons). He added, however, that by custom the allocation might be with the churchwardens. So much was clear, but after this relatively simple statement the erudite Burn had to spend five pages in trying to explain the law affecting private seats or pews, about which he was far from clear himself.

Prescription to the use of a certain seat could be claimed by the owner of a large house, provided that he could prove that his ancestors had 'time out of mind' repaired the seat. Such a pew 'belonged' not to the family but to the house.

From time to time the Essex courts gave orders to 'place the parishioners according to their calling', usually with no particulars, but in other cases

[1] Burn, *op. cit.*, i, 254.

lively doings are recorded. At Wakes Colne in 1594 a crisis had evidently arisen. 'There is great disorder', the entry runs, 'in the placing of the parishioners in their pews, the rich with the poor and not according to their calling.' The wardens were therefore instructed, with the minister's consent, to seat everyone 'according to their degree, ability and calling severally in their pews', and to notify the court of any recalcitrants. There had been trouble five years earlier, when 'Mr. Tiffin had set men a-work to pull down the stools being set up in the chancel by Mr. Munk and the rest of the parish'. Robert Monke was the rector, and William Tiffin, of the Middle Temple, was lord of the manor of Wakes Hall (his great-nephew, aged 16, wrote a Latin inscription on the mural tablet erected on his death in 1617, aged 85).[1]

At Coggeshall in 1598 'great disorder in the sitting' had broken out, according to Mr. Richard Constantine. On that occasion the judge 'decreed his commission to Mr. Newman (vicar), Richard Constantine, Nicholas Gray and six of the best of the headboroughs to place all the parishioners according to their discretion and place, account and reckoning'. Similar commissions with authority to act had been issued by the same archdeaconry court three years earlier to John Cole, the vicar, the wardens and fourteen parishioners of Helions Bumpstead and to Mr. Thomas Kyrby, the wardens and five other villagers of Henham 'to place according to wealth and ability'. But next year Giles Stubbing of Helions Bumpstead 'plucked up a seat in the church or removed the same', alleging that 'he paid as the actor for the narrowing or straitening of the foremost new stool in the body of the church, which was done by the award of Mr. Baker and Goodman Westleigh, high constables, and by the consent of the churchwardens'. He satisfied the court.

In 1577 the judge decided that the wardens of St. Peter, Maldon, with the consent of those of All Saints, 'should cause the parishioners to repair orderly to the parish church of All Saints on Sundays and holy days, and that the churchwardens of either parish (i.e. both parishes) should join together in all matters and causes whatever, and every parishioner to be placed according to his degree'. The parishes had in fact been united as far back as 1306! The reverse was the case with Great and Little Coggeshall, the latter having no church. In 1589 complaint was made against the Great Coggeshall wardens that 'they refuse to let the parishioners of Little Coggeshall have stools and seats for them in the church of Coggeshall'; to which the officers replied that 'there were sufficient stools assigned to the inhabitants of Little Coggeshall'. But the court insisted on seeing a certificate to that effect from the vicar and the wardens.

By far the fullest description of seating is found in North Benfleet parish register among the memoranda made between 1585 and 1595 by Thomas Meredith, the rector. 'At the time of the amending or new making of the

[1] *Ess. Rev.*, xxxix, 101–2; also *ibid.*, xxxv, 1–11, for later seat disputes.

stools or seats' in the time of his predecessor, William Savage (1572–82), the use of ten rows on one side and seven on the other was 'appointed'. Next to the chancel on the south, 'the upper stool or seat was made by the inhabitants for the use of couples to be married to sit in on the day of their marriage, and also for strangers of the better sort coming to the church'. The second was for 'the householders of Fanton Hall, Benfleet Hall, and Bonefields alias Bonviles'; the third and fourth for other farms; 'the three seats next adjoining for their servants'. Then, on the south side of the font under the belfry, the wives of several farmers sat in one row and maid-servants in the next two. On the north side of the nave, adjoining the minister's pew, sat his wife, next to 'the wives of the inhabitants of the said two halls', and those of other farmers in the second row. The third and fourth were for 'the men inhabitants' of two other farms and their men-servants; these farmers' wives sat on the north of the font, with maids in the two rows behind.[1] While it is interesting to note the custom about bridal pairs, which is not recorded elsewhere in Essex, the fairly general custom of segregating the sexes to opposite sides of the nave did not obtain in this church.

There were of course also individual trouble-makers. Affluent parishioners sat in front, and the exact siting was therefore a clear criterion of social position, which gave rise to many disputes among the status-conscious members of the congregation, some of which will be narrated.

In 1603, for example, at Horndon-on-the-Hill, a man who 'refused to take his place which was assigned to him by the vicar and churchwardens' asserted that 'he hath been heretofore placed in a seat wherein he sitteth', but the judge ordered that 'he sit in the seat appointed'; and a Mount Bures woman 'refused to sit in such convenient place or stool as by the consent of the chief of the parishioners is appointed'. In 1598, Margaret, wife of John Parke of Barking, was presented by the wardens 'for wilfully refusing to be placed in such a pew as was by us in our discretions thought meet for her, but will have a pew of her own choice'. She argued, 'For so much as her husband is charged towards her Majesty's service' (probably meaning the subsidy assessment) 'as greatly as others, she thinketh she ought to have as good a seat as they, for so her husband willed her to sit'. But she failed to convince the judge. Thomas Adams of Lambourne in 1595 would 'not be ordered by the churchwardens' and declared that 'he sitteth in the seat wherein his predecessors dwelling in the house where he dwelleth did usually sit'. He was again charged two years later with 'disorder and disobedience, by whose example others also begin to take stomach and to grow disobedient'. His own claim:

> Being appointed an inferior seat to that where he sat before, he hath of right (as he thinketh) continued his accustomed place in the foremost seat of the south side of the church; the causes (saith he) are these, viz. he is in all rates, taxes and im-

[1] *Ess. Rev.*, xlii, 63–4.

> positions equal with the best that sitteth in that seat; he is 32 years of age, of good fame, name and credit; and his predecessors in possession of the house and grounds which he holdeth, have for 60, 50 or 40 years last past continually for the most part sat in the same seat.

He produced as witnesses eight (named) parishioners, and two months later the archdeacon determined that he had established his claim.

A dispute in 1584 between Richard Gooday, gentleman, and his wife and Joseph Man and his wife about a pew in Braintree church came before Dr. Edward Stanhope, the diocesan chancellor, and Dr. Julius Caesar, who were appointed by the High Commissioners. They made their award, but details are not known.[1]

John Shipman, gentleman, and William Rooke, both of West Ham (in their wills they were both gentlemen), were involved in a feud that led to two presentments. In 1576, according to the wardens, Shipman 'will not keep his seat according to the orders of the parish'. His own version was that they 'removed him out of his pew, the which he hath held this twenty years, and troubled in the same pew by William Rooke, not being there placed by the churchwardens, also that Rooke threw his hat away which hung upon the pew door'. Next year Rooke was charged not only with throwing Shipman's hat and unseating him but also with 'molesting him whereby the whole parish was disquieted and the minister was compelled to stay his service through his rudeness, which he sundry times hath and doth use in service time'. Rooke, however, insisted that his ancestors had used the pew and that he 'chanced' to knock down Shipman's hat in entering his pew, which Mr. Shipman had 'wilfully and stubbornly entered, being not there placed by the churchwardens'. His statement was accepted and he was discharged.

Brother and sister were both accused by the same parish in 1588: Isabel Pragle, for 'not sitting in the pew where the churchwardens did place her and for intruding herself into another pew amongst the grave women'; and Richard Pragle, for 'using unreverent speeches to the churchwarden in time of divine service concerning the placing of Isabel his sister'. But as she 'hath not sitten in the same since she was forbidden', the case was dismissed. By his will, proved in 1617, in which he described himself as 'one of the ordinary yeomen of his Majesty's great chamber', he left 40s. to the vicar for preaching a sermon at his funeral.

A challenged seat in Debden church is mentioned incidentally in 1577 through the wardens having reported Mr. Edmund West for absence from service and communion. He explained that 'Cuttes keepeth him from his seat where his ancestors have accustomably used to sit, and therefore he desired that he might be permitted to go to Henham church'. The judge insisted on attendance by West and his wife at their parish church. He owned the manor of Mole Hall in Debden;[2] and Richard Cutte, by his will

[1] Morant, *History of Essex*, ii, 398n. [2] Morant, *History of Essex*, ii, 565.

dated 1592, refers to his lease of Debden Hall (from the owners of Audley End).

A long entry tells of a controversy at Hadstock in 1598. Dr. Thomas Puckering, the rector, came in person to protest that Thomas Christopher had disturbed his wife, 'a gentlewoman born of good friends and parentage'. Christopher had placed 'in disordered manner' the wife of one Jellybrond 'who hath offered maliciously divers injuries' to the rector 'upon a revengeful mind'. The judge ordered goodwife Jellybrond to her former seat, enjoined the man not to displace Mistress Puckering again, and directed that seating in the church be settled with the consent of the rector and of George Ferrand and John Butcher, 'two of the ancientest and chiefest of the parish'. John Jellibrond, as we have seen, had assaulted a boy in the same year.

'Broomfield: Why they do not appoint a seat for Mr. Bret according to his calling' is noted in 1603 'against the churchwardens', who duly attended the following session and were told to 'place Mr. Brett and his wife in the church according to their degree and calling'. When Mistress Woody took her seat in Great Holland church 'above' goodwife Keeble in the place where she used to sit, she punched the intruder with her elbow. Another altercation between rival seat-holders was reported at Great Bentley. John Mercaunt, according to the wardens, 'crowded' Edward Marvin out of his seat, 'and truly we think they were both in fault'; Mercaunt admitted 'shouldering Marvin from a seat of old belonging to his father's house', while Marvin declared that, 'sitting in his usual seat, Mercaunt did pull him by the shoulders, and he, willing (intending) to continue in his seat, did resist so far as he could'. Both these acts of petty jealousy occurred in 1596. Three South Benfleet men were prosecuted in 1580 for 'striving for their places in time of service'.

A well-known magnate was concerned in a more serious quarrel in 1600. William Latham, esquire, of Upminster, 'in the time of divine service did strive for a seat and the minister was disturbed there in that he unadvisedly used some speeches for the defence of his rights in the seats in the chapel there'. Latham personally appeared and admitted that this was true. The court 'adjudged him *maioris excommunicationis* according to the Canon'; ordered penance, 'On St. Thomas his day next he shall acknowledge his fault in unadvised rashness before the minister and churchwardens'; and directed him to appear again at the next court to certify performance of the order. Three other parishioners had also been cited. They admitted their guilt, 'saving that what they did unadvisedly was in defence of the right of their master, Mr. William Latham, and not of set purpose to disturb the minister', and they, too, were sentenced to the greater excommunication and the same penance. Latham's dispute is slightly puzzling. He had been presented to Quarter Sessions in 1586 as a recusant. To escape the £20 a month fines, perhaps he was one of the 'church papists' who attended service but not communion. As lord of the manor of Gaines in Upminster he may have felt the need to claim the manorial pew. As far back as 1574, as already related, he had been involved with the same rector, who held the benefice from 1562 to 1609.[1]

A Burnham woman in 1578 had refused 'to keep her seat according to the order appointed by Mr. Archdeacon'. Her husband pointed out that she 'was placed in a pew with two other women, whereof one hath a strong breath'! The judge accepted the plea. Another aspect was considered in 1600 when a man named Clerk of Old Meade in Henham, 'being of good reckoning and aged, thick of hearing, and so likewise his wife, being in one of the highest pews or seats whereby through distance of place he cannot well hear the sermon and service, desireth that he may be placed in some convenient place or pew near the pulpit or seat of the minister'. The sympathetic judge ordered a letter to be written to the wardens accordingly.

Physical destruction or removal was rarely reported. A parishioner of St. Leonard, Colchester, 'violently and without cause broke down the stool in the church'. In 1603, Robert Cammock, gentleman, of Layer Marney, 'pulled up certain stools in the church to the great offence of divers of the inhabitants who had interest in them and did usually sit in them'. Unfortunately it is not clear whether this apparently peremptory action was the aftermath of the violent incident of 1598, described in the previous volume, in which the wife of Peter Tuke of Layer Marney Tower and her servant assaulted Cammock's wife as she tried to enter the family pew, on to which Tuke's carpenter had affixed a lock.[2] No subsequent proceedings are recorded. The 'great complaint' about dilapidations at St. Botolph's church, Colchester, in 1584, also stated that 'certain stools are broken all a-pieces and thrown about'.

In 1597 the wardens presented 'Mr. Mulcaster, rector of Stanford Rivers, for pulling down the crease or knobs of a pew'. A pew 'crease' also figured in a complaint by the North Ockendon wardens two years later, on which the court took firm steps against Mr. Coyse, a parishioner, for 'setting up a pew to the annoyance of the church without the consent of the parish'. Mr. Repent Savage, as the Archdeacon's Official (he was also rector of Cranham), visited the church and inspected the 'noisome' pew: a proceeding never found otherwise in the Essex court books, though admittedly he only had to ride to the next parish. He then wrote to William Thwaites, notary public, who sometimes acted as the court registrar. Most unusually, too, a copy of the letter is entered in the act book:

> Mr. Thwaites, I pray you deliver the bearer hereof a copy of the act (i.e. minute) in Court done in the matter of presentment about Mr. Coise's pew. Upon the view of the pew I ordered that Mr. Coise or some for him should take off the uppermost pane or leaf of the said pew and cause the ledge (that being so taken off) to be set

[1] For seating disputes elsewhere, see C. Hill, *Economic Problems of the Church* (1956), 175–82.

[2] *E.L.: Disorder*, 186–7.

upon the pew again in decent and comely fashion manner. Insert this order in the act and deliver the same to this bearer in terms according to law. Thus wishing your good health, I rest yours,

REP: SAVAGE.

To my very good friend Mr. Thwaites at his house in Buttsbury these.

The 'act' accordingly recites that Mr. Savage, 'finding the pew to be noisome to many of the parishioners sitting near the same by reason of the height, did order the churchwardens to cut off the highest panel, pane or leaf, without spoil of the lower part of the pew, reserving the ledge or crease whole, and to set on the crease upon the pew again'. This course of action resulting from a relatively mild offence leaves no doubt that the seating arrangements in churches were regarded as an important element in ecclesiastical control.

While some were thus arguing about the seats in the church, others were misusing the bells in the tower. After the Reformation the Anglican Church forbade the 'superstitious' ringing of bells on holy-days or their eves, as abrogated by the Book of Common Prayer. But ancient customs were not always willingly given up, and among those that died slowly, despite the general prohibition, was the practice of bell-ringing on the eve of and on All Souls' (All Saints') Day (1 November).

At the visitation of the Archdeacon of Essex in 1563 a number of cases of unlawful ringing, mostly on that day, were disclosed. The sexton and another parishioner of Kelvedon (Hatch) 'rang a soul peal for Thomas Porter,' but were discharged on their promising not to do so again. The villagers of Willingale Doe 'rang the souls' peal on All Hallow day after service'. The wardens of Little Waltham, Broomfield, Widford, Stanford Rivers, Moreton, and Bobbingworth were also charged on account of 'ringing peals at Halloweentide or any other times unlawful'; while those of Stanford said that John Morris, constable, three men and a boy, all named, rang the bell. A Purleigh warden declared that four named men rang 'at Halloween Day'; those of Dengie named three men; and those of Woodham Mortimer 'cannot tell who did ring', whereon the judge ordered that Thomas White, the sexton, be cited to give their names. The visitation of the following year revealed two further cases: two Mountnessing men, for ringing on Allhalloween, and three Stanford Rivers men who 'rang for Glascocke as a soul peal' and were ordered to confess in church and give 6d. each to the poor. Yet again, in 1565, a Stanford parishioner, William Tinge (who had been suspected by the Ongar hundred jurors in 1562 of immorality[1]), was presented for 'ringing of soul peals' and had to pay 12d. to the poor. (A number of Stanford parishioners in later years were to appear as popish recusants.)

It is not surprising to find a reference to Lord Mordaunt, a well-known

[1] *E.L.: Disorder*, 197–8.

Catholic. In 1569, as seen elsewhere, he was against the removal of the rood in the church. The next entry reads, 'Mr. Whytney, Mr. Snowe and Mr. Walpole, servants to my Lord Mordaunt, the gardener and the brewer, rang on Allhallow night after evening, contrary etc., and fit ropes from their carts to ring'; but nothing further is recorded. A few soul-peal charges were heard many years later. In 1585, for example, three Ashdon men were accused of 'ringing in All Hallows night'.

The custom was not discarded at Henham, where ringing occurred in 1587. The defendant, William Glascock, alleged that 'he and others, being ready to ring a peal after evening prayer about Allhallowtide, Thomas Measaunte churchwarden there by force did take the bell out of his hands and striking him offered to trip up his heels, whereupon he leaving to ring was going out of the church and in the churchyard Measaunte said to him, "Sirrah boy, I will use you like a boy", whereunto he answered, "Boy, boy, on your face, for I am as good a man as you", and so he departed'. The case was dismissed.[1]

Bells had to be rung to give notice to the parishioners to assemble for the annual Rogationtide beating of the bounds. This was not carried out at Wormingford in 1590, so the wardens as well as the rector were summoned; the former said that 'the bells are in decay and not able to be rung', and they added that 'they wanteth a rope for the saint's bell.

Disorderly bellringing was presented in six parishes, all between 1596 and 1599. Whether some of the accused were over-enthusiastic ringers or high-spirited youths is not evident. Richard Baker of East Hanningfield (either a warden or a bell-ringer) 'suffered unruly persons to ring and jangle the bells out of due season'; and Thomas Robiont of Blackmore 'encouraged ringers to ring unlawfully' and had to give 6d. to the poor. John Humfrye, senior and junior, of Great Sampford, were charged with 'misusing themselves in a very bad manner in jangling on the sabbath day and for abusing the churchwardens when they were by him gently entreated to leave off', and the younger man also for 'swearing by God's blood that he would break the bells if he might not ring'. Joining with them in the jangling affair was the same William Turpin who had behaved irreverently during the sermon. None of them turned up in court. Search was ordered, with the result that the scribe noted at the next session, 'Turpin is gone for a soldier'.

Edward Pamflin and John Foxe of Widdington were reported because they 'rang in contempt of the minister and churchwardens admonishing them to forbear in respect of necessary business which was then to be determined of the parish in the church'. They were dismissed on their stating that 'they left off so soon as they were forbidden'. Robert Aylward

[1] Similar evidence comes from other counties, e.g. 'Among the mass of the people in Oxfordshire there was a widespread clinging to customs associated with the old religion. Ringing of bells on saints' eves and festival days was one of them.' (Brinkworth, *Oxfordshire Rec. Soc.*, xxiv, p. xxv, n.).

of Debden, presented for 'disordered ringing', was ordered 'hereafter to desist extraordinary ringing'. But a marginal note gives his contemptuous comment, 'I am bound by a better man than you to be at the court 40 miles off and I cannot appear. I will not appear and I will know it before a better man than you'. From this it would seem that he had been summoned to the court of the Bishop or the Commissary on a different charge. An identical presentment was put in against Richard Aylward, whose temperate answer was, 'The rest have rung two peals, one in the morning and the other in the evening upon the sabbath days; if that be contrary to the Injunctions I have offended'. He was warned not to offend again. Edward, John and Clement Aylward were likewise dealt with. Finally, the Pattiswick wardens were themselves summoned for 'not presenting such as did break the church door open and ringing unreasonably whereby the bells were broken'.

The festive Queen's Day, or Coronation Day, like fair-days, sometimes led to fights. A fracas in Stanway belfry on Coronation Day in 1588, one of extra jubilation over the Armada, resulted in William Cleere being presented. But, he claimed, William Newland 'did throw pieces (*sic*) at him and others there ringing, whereupon he and others came unto him and struggling with him, he did take Newman's arms and by force put him out of the church and there threw him down'. Ringing the bells on the Queen's Day was in fact compulsory and led to two other presentments. One came in 1590 from South Benfleet, where James Stephens had not contributed 12d. 'towards the ringers upon the Queen's Day'; and George Spenser, who had not given his 4d. towards their maintenance 'on the joyful day of her Majesty's reign', stated that he had been absolved before the Lord Chancellor, but was nevertheless ordered to pay the groat and an extra shilling to the poor for his negligence. The other, ten years later, was from Dengie, where William Wale, presumably one of the wardens, 'on the day of her Majesty's coronation tended altogether his wordly goods, neither sent his servant nor hired any to ring for her Majesty'.

4

Font to Grave

Baptism

It was the parents' obligation to have their infants baptized publicly on a Sunday or holy-day and the clergy's duty to admonish their flocks not to defer christenings longer than the first or second Sunday after birth, except for just cause. The font, and no other receptacle, should be used, and the child should be signed with the cross by the minister. A male infant should have two godfathers and one godmother, the numbers being reversed for a girl. The Church frowned severely upon christenings performed privately at home, and parents might resort to lay baptism only if the baby was in imminent danger of death.

The act books yield four reports of infants who had died unchristened. The parents were hardly to blame, in 1586, for 'keeping it 12 or 13 days and so died', for the father said that 'the minister, Mr. Seredge, was suspended'; this was true, William Seredge, the ultra-puritan rector of East Hanningfield, having been suspended by the bishop for not subscribing to the Articles and for refusing to sign with the cross at baptism. In 1584 Edmund Binder, the incumbent of Blackmore, was in grave trouble because 'two children died unchristened by his negligence, for that he would not christen them before Sunday following, and died in the meantime', as a result of which he, too, was suspended. Another of Seredge's parishioners was cited at the same session for 'having a child christened without the sign of the cross'. Seredge himself was first summoned for disobedience in 1591, and again in the following year, when his guarded reply was that 'he did not use the sign of the cross but doth not utterly refuse it, and for divers causes he doth omit the sign'. Thomas Lorkin, rector of Little Waltham, had also been suspended in 1584 for the same reason; but George Parnell, vicar of Broomfield, presented in the same year for a minor lapse, promised 'to use the cross orderly' in future and was discharged.

Three incumbents, none of whom is known to have been non-conforming in other ways, had to give their reasons for not using the font. The curious excuse of John Bound, rector of Great Horkesley, was: 'He left out the exhortations upon the words of the Gospel because it was 12 o'clock and they were ready to go to dinner, and he did christen it in a basin because he was a stranger, and the basin was tendered unto him;

otherwise he would have been contented to have christened in the font if water had been there.' He added that 'he had the consent of the minister there and did nothing in contempt of the (Book of) Common Prayer', so the judge told him to give 5s. to the poor. Bound had been reported by the wardens, 'being ourselves then absent', but it is not clear why he termed himself a stranger, as he had been instituted to Great Horkesley in December 1580 and the case came up in 1582, unless 'the minister' was a curate who functioned for a normally non-resident rector. If, as the wardens were accused two years later, 'This font would not hold water', it is hardly surprising that the rector accepted a more useful utensil! The curate of St. Botolph, Colchester, could not use the font for two christenings in 1583 because he was debarred from his church. The wardens had 'shut the church doors to Mr. Holland the minister and would not suffer him to baptize the children, whereby they were baptized in a basin'. The curate was also charged with baptizing them 'in the church porch, despite the churchwardens and in contempt of the Queen's Majesty's laws', and of course he explained why; they also presented him as a common swearer. In 1597 Robert Jenninges of West Ham was presented by the wardens: 'Our vicar did leave the use of the font and did christen in a basin in his own house a man child which by common fame was baseborn and brought from London'. He replied that, 'being himself sick and the child having lain twelve weeks unchristened, he did christen it in his house upon an extremity', on which he was discharged. The visitation articles of several dioceses demanded reports of any use of 'basins or other profane vessels.[1]

Edward Bullock of Great Tey had to answer the wardens' accusation in 1600 for 'having his child christened at home at his house by a strange minister, viz. Mr. Cooke minister of Langford'. The clergy list for this parish is deficient at this date, so it is not known whether Cooke held the benefice.

When Lawrence Lyde, vicar of Ardleigh, was complained of by a woman, 'because her child was baptized without any gossips' (godparents), he claimed, 'There were gossips', and was enjoined to prove it under the hands of six parishioners. Richard Millson of Dedham 'refused to have his child baptized', alleging, 'The vicar would not baptize it without the vow by God's fathers, to be made according to the Injunctions, were observed'. He was ordered to purge, defaulted, and so assigned penance.

In 1587 John Petchie and his wife of Fryerning were reported for 'keeping their child unchristened three weeks, and the wife brought her child to be baptized when she came to give thanksgiving' (i.e. to be churched) 'at the end of three weeks'. Said the father: 'Being disappointed of a godfather for his child, it was baptized by one godfather, the child then being in peril of death, and he did it not in contempt of the law', which was

[1] W. P. M. Kennedy, *Elizabethan Episcopal Administration* (1924), index, *s.v.* 'Baptism'.

accepted by the judge. Another father, John Warren of Great Chishall, replied in 1587: 'His child being born on Saturday was not baptized next sabbath day, although brought to church by sundry honest women, which was contrary to his liking and commandment, for that he was then provided of godfathers and godmother, but he said that, the next Sunday after, the child was baptized according to the laws.' 'Mr. (John) Horton, curate of Barking', was presented in 1579 for 'letting of children to christen and to be godfathers and godmothers, being not of sufficient age, contrary to the Queen's Injunctions'. The actual offence, however, may have been limited to a single occasion, as he was also charged with 'suffering Jane Upton daughter of Mr. Burres of Walthamstow to christen the said child', and she also had to answer for 'being godmother to a child and never received the Communion'. The Burres were Catholics. The court received a third presentment against Horton: 'He is a disquiet person amongst his neighbours and withholdeth certain church goods'; but nothing else seems to be known about him. Another curate, 'Mr. Wigfeild of Wix', was accused in 1585 of 'christening Andrew Debbenham's child, being an excommunicate person, a recusant of Much Oakley, not being born in his parish but in Much Oakley'. The father had opined that 'his child was christened before it was born'. In the previous year 'Anthony Barnishe gentleman would not suffer the curate of Fryerning to baptize his child, but sent for one Mr. (Samuel) Cottesford of Doddinghurst'.

The rectory of Springfield had been divided into two moieties from time immemorial and had two rectors. This anomaly gave rise to a case brought in 1580 against George Wood, rector of 'Springfield Ricardes', for refusing to christen two children. He defended himself by saying, 'The church hath two several cures and two several portions, and either parson is known to either parson, and there happened two children to come to be christened which were not in his cure or parish'. He was instructed 'to prove at the next session'. A concurrent charge was laid against John Beching, rector of 'Springfield Bossevile', with the same result, but Beching did not appear, was pronounced contumacious and excommunicated. Both rectors of what were generally known as Springfield Richards and Springfield Boswells occur in the clergy lists, and the latter name was recently commemorated in that of a new local road.

John Knight, rector of Goldhanger, was in court in 1589 because he baptized a child without any witnesses. Not unnaturally, the Fobbing wardens in 1576 presented 'Mr. Browne, rector of Fobbing, for maliciously saying that a child before he be baptized is not the child of God but the child of the Devil'. The solitary charge of 'not examining the godfathers and godmothers' refers to the two questions put to them about forsaking the Devil and all his works and about the Creed; it was made in 1567 against 'Mr. Johnson, the rector of Chignal Mary and James'.

Who would now censure the Elizabethans, forbidden to play so many of their time-honoured games, for indulging in a little irreligious fun? But idle gossip, it seems, reached the ears of the Ramsey wardens, who were constrained to intervene. The incident involved a woman (doubtless the cook, as her name is first) and three men, and although the court officers probably suppressed a chuckle it relieved the tedium of one session in 1590. 'They did christen a pig, being ready dressed to put on the spit, and called the pig's name Adam, as the crime (rumour) goeth'. Bucolic behaviour of this sort might be forgiven, but not that of Matthew Hailes of Burnham in 1587, who had 'caused his child to be brought to the church to be baptized, and would not let it be baptized unless he might have the word; the word being showed him, he went away in derision and would not suffer his child to be baptized'. The 'word' presumably refers to the baptismal service in the Prayer Book.

Occasionally the authority of the civil courts was sought, though ineffectively, in support of the Church on matters of baptismal doctrine. In 1581 the jurors of one hundred presented Thomas Redditch, vicar of Hutton, for not wearing the surplice or signing with the cross in baptism; eight years later Thomas Leggatt, gentleman, and Margaret Steven, widow, both of Hornchurch, were indicted for keeping an infant unbaptized for a year; and there are several similar cases, but of little interest.

In Tudor times christening was associated with various customs, some pagan or superstitious; unlike those connected with betrothal, however, the act books make no mention of such customs.

Catechism

Two centuries or more before Robert Raikes was actively promoting voluntary attendance at Sunday schools, all boys and girls had to go to church once or twice in every month to be taught the essentials of the Anglican faith. Little is known about this aspect of Elizabethan youth. The few illuminating entries are accordingly worth quoting, one of which is probably an echo of the minister's difficulty in keeping discipline: a task which must have been much harder when dealing with the juvenile mobs who turned up in the more populous parishes. Article 44 of the Queen's Injunctions (1559) ran: 'Every parson, vicar and curate shall upon every holy-day, and every second Sunday in the year, hear and instruct all the youth of the parish . . . in the Ten Commandments, the Articles of the Belief, and in the Lord's Prayer, and diligently examine them, and teach the Catechism set forth in the Book of Public Prayer.'

Delinquents, in roughly equal numbers, were ministers who were negligent in teaching or churchwardens who failed to send the boys and girls, and those who refused to attend for instruction or could not say their catechism. Many reports of slackness were received at the visitation of the Archdeacon of Essex in 1565. Thereafter a decrease is noticeable.

In 1572 the rector of Pitsea (Mark Sympson) rebutted such a charge: 'He have used diligently to teach the youth, and have been in the church at the time appointed, and none of the parish will come thither for that purpose, as appeared by certain of the parishioners affirming the same', on which he was discharged. When Roger Nowell, curate of Dengie, was accused in 1576 because 'the children be untaught the Catechism, for that he remaineth four miles from the church', the judge ordered that 'he shall remain near the church'. John White, vicar of Ramsey, confessed in 1584 that 'he hath not given warning to the parents to send the youth, and they that were sent he hath taught when he was at home and in health'. He was admonished to say divine services at 9–11 a.m. and 2–3 p.m. as well as to teach the Catechism. In the same year Mr. Golde, curate of St. Martin, Colchester, was commanded 'to take a catalogue of the names of the youth and to call them every Sunday and holy-day'; and a scathing presentment was put in from St. Nicholas, Colchester, to the effect that the youth 'will not come because of the simplicity of our minister; howbeit, they go to other places for instruction'.

Among youths who refused to come to be catechized were a few servants. One 'sat in his seat in church and would not come to be catechized'; and another claimed that he 'did not refuse, but was letted by his master's business'. Those who could not pass the oral test included a Great Bardfield boy who 'cannot say the Catechism' and a Lexden boy who 'cannot say it by heart'; both were 'to repair for instruction' to their respective rectors – John Jenner and Robert Searle. Only once do girls appear as failures: two of Colne Engaine who 'cannot say their Catechism' and, exceptionally, were ordered to undergo penance in church at morning prayer (1576).

John Peacocke of Abbess Roothing was charged that 'he in church disclaimed at the minister's catechizing, saying that he did nothing but prattle' (1589). When Thomas Foord of Lexden was prosecuted for 'not sending his children to be catechized' (1599), he said that 'he did not so dare, for fear that his children should be boxed about the ears, because Mr. Joyner (*sic*) the minister did so to the widow Warner's son, whom he boxed with five or six blows in the church, because he said that having received the Communion the others that had received the Communion were frow off from catechizing'. (Is 'frow' Essex dialect, not previously recorded, for 'frightened', or merely for 'throw' or 'through'? The writing is clear.) At the next session John Jenner the rector appeared and said that the father was very negligent in sending his children; he was directed to send his servants as well. During the vacancy following the death of the previous rector (Thomas Stanbanke) in 1566, the unnamed lessee of the rectory of High Laver was presented because 'the parson hath not put the parishioners in remembrance to learn the children'.

Betrothal

Every year the Church courts witnessed a procession of men and women who were involved in one or other of the many offences connected with marriage or failure to marry after betrothal. These 'matrimonial causes', as most of the laity's misdoings were called by the lawyers, show that some of the attendant customs and practices differed a good deal from those of the present age. Partly because of such customs, breach of promise suits were more successful. But, in courtship, love was by no means always the paramount factor. Hope of gaining land or goods was more influential with many men in their choice of a bride. This and other aspects are mirrored in some fascinating depositions. Unfortunately, no such details accompany the meagre evidence of sale of brides. Instances are not unknown even today, while Thomas Hardy gives a very late, though fictitious, example of the survival of the practice in Wessex until last century. We find in Essex a bizarre story of an Elizabethan monetary bargain to marry a widow about to give birth to another man's bastard twins, and to die in utterly miserable circumstances. Generally, however, when human passions rather than financial aims led to hasty betrothal or marriage, the court dealt with the affair as a sexual offence instead of a matrimonial cause, and such cases of bridal pregnancy were related in the first chapter. (See pp. 153–4 and plate no. 7.)

In Elizabethan times betrothal, or contract of matrimony, was a reciprocal promise to marry, of a firmly binding nature. The man was expected to say, 'I will take thee to my wife', the woman answering, 'I will take thee to my husband', 'I William take thee Mary to my assured wife and thereto I plight thee my faith and troth', or some similar phrase. Minors had to get the consent of their parents; those of age also were generally expected to do so, or any rate desired their 'goodwill' as well as that of close relations and friends. If the agreement was not taken before witnesses, the parties were liable to be excommunicated. In 1593 John Bossett of Dedham was cited for 'marrying Frances Butter without the consent of her friends'. The mutual giving of tokens was an ancillary custom, but not an essential or legal element in the contract.

Over one hundred disappointed parties are found to have sued for breach of contract, and some of the detailed statements portray couples being espoused. 'He should never forsake her and would buy her a petticoat'; 'He would be glad to have his mother's goodwill'; 'He would be as good as his word for the faithful promise he had made to her, and thereupon they plighted faith': such was the language at betrothal. But whatever may have been true of courtiers' seeking the hand of ladies, little enough romance attended the ordinary Englishman's wooing.

One unwilling woman deposed that the man 'was a suitor to her for marriage, and he gave her a silver whistle at Thaxted fair was a twelvemonth for a fairing, but not for any respect of marriage nor a token of any condition concerning marriage'. Silver whistles were very common articles of personal adornment. In several causes the women denied betrothal, one saying that 'she never made him any promise, but on her friends' goodwill'; all were declared free by the judge, who in each case forbade the man 'to meddle or have anything to do with her'. In another suit, brought by a man who alleged a contract 'and in token of the same she received divers tokens', the judge decided that 'there was no lawful matrimonial cause'.

The earliest depositions occur in a breach of marriage cause brought in 1561 by a man named Nevell against Margery Fyssher. John Edmunds of Woodham Ferrers, gentleman, aged 22, said that she, 'coming to Fresshe's house of Stow (Maries) parish, one Dandye and Margery sent for him and one John Parbye being then over a wharf (belonging) to the deponent; and Parbye coming to the house in the Lent, finding Margery Dandye Fresshe and his wife and one Thomas Camper in the hall, Dandye said that belike there is somewhat between Margery and the bachelor, and Margery being demanded said that she was willing to have him to her husband'. John Parbye of North Fambridge, aged 30 and above, and John Thrusshe of Stow Maries, aged 28, both confirmed the story. William Nevell the father deposed: 'About Shrovetide or the first week in clean Lent' (a term rarely used), 'Margery coming to his house, the parties plighted faith and troth and he gave his goodwill'. Robert Bankes of Woodham Ferrers, aged 35, stated that Nevell plighted faith and troth in his house on Thursday in the first week of clean Lent, and Alice his wife, aged 40, confirmed that they were 'sure together', and she 'gave her consent and was thereunto willing', presumably as another relation. Parbye's wharf was probably at the head of Stow Creek.[1]

Compulsory return of betrothal gifts in a case of alleged female fraud was decreed in 1564 against Joan Baker of Romford. She was prosecuted for 'contracting herself privily to get money of Geoffrey Wyllet of the same town, and in the pretence of marriage she used conference with him and others, only to have gain'. The items which she had to give back to him were 13s. in cash, a lockram kercher, a canvas apron, a pair of sheets, and two silver rings, and she was also ordered to certify when and where her (former) husband was buried. She insisted, however, that Wyllet had been 'asked' to one Jane Asshen, also of Romford, who was duly summoned and questioned whether she was lawfully contracted to Wyllet, 'Yea or no'. She said that he asked her if she would marry with him, and she said 'Yea', and thereon he gave her sixteen pieces of linen, viz. kerchers, rails, neckerchers, with a kirtle and a frock, and 4s. to buy a hat, and she also received a wedding ring with a purse worth 2s. 6d. Both Wyllet and Baker were enjoined to purge with three neighbours.

A presentment in 1565 is the only one brought against a cleric, and the

[1] Cf. *Trans. E.A.S.*, xxiv, 8.

result is unique in the Essex cases. The rector of Stock (Oliver Clayton) asked the banns of a couple, the man 'having made a pre-contract'. The judge then admonished both on learning that the woman 'would not have the other', for which she was ordered to pay the jilted bridegroom the sum of 2s. 6d. 'Contracted to a maid before being contracted to another' is typical of several ordinary breaches of contract.

Seven cases are found of previous contract with two, three, or even four of the opposite sex. One man, 'contracted to a wench or two, is now minded to marry' a third. A Greenstead-juxta-Colchester woman was accused of betrothing herself to two men named Wolvett 'at one time'. Thomas Kinge of East Ham, 'contracted to Mistress Pulliver's maid, Goodman Barrett's maid, and Onyon's daughter', stated that he had wedded one of them; 'to the others he had given money to be discharged of them' (1580). John Smith of St. Peter, Colchester, who was presented for being 'contracted to sundry women, viz. Alice Rosemary widow and three or four others', declared that 'she was first assured to him and then married another'. So the widow, also of Colchester, was cited, and both were to attend for examination. A month later she came, by then married to Henry Mayer of St. Nicholas' parish. There the case ended. When a South Weald maidservant who had 'made herself sure to three or four several men' produced John Fox of Braintree, stating that 'he had contracted marriage with her', the judge enjoined them 'to solemnize marriage before the face of the church before the Feast of St. Nicholas next'; and Anthony Barrett of Navestock and Fox were both presented for 'assuring' themselves to her, but no further action against the former is noted (1580).

Among the innumerable incontinence and bastardy prosecutions are several in which alleged contracts were mentioned. The earliest act book tells of a Brentwood couple presented for fornication in 1561. Questioned by the judge whether the woman 'ever had any tokens of him or no, she said she had a bowed (i.e. bent, see below) penny and a piece of gold'. He denied betrothal, but was given public penance in Brentwood market-place and in church. In 1565 John Samwell of Dunton, who had been unchaste with Edgata Thryeing, servant of Thomas Clemente, stated, 'He contracted marriage with her but does not wish to have it solemnized'. In directing them to marry as well as to perform penance, the judge also decreed that Clement should 'keep the woman until &c.' (i.e. the wedding), 'and for that the fact was done in his house, he (Clement) shall keep the woman upon her servant's wages, and after that she be brought abed they shall marry together', provisions not otherwise noticed.

A charge involving John Senior of West Ham and his 'wife' in 1584 reads: 'He was asked three times in the church to a maid called Joan Tyler and doth keep company with one Alice Hewes very suspiciously at unlawful hours and was taken by the constables and churchwardens with her in his own house and maketh no account of the maid which he was asked unto before, and it is thought that he was contracted to the maid.' The man, however, maintained that he was 'contracted to Joan Tyler and asked to her and would marry her if he could get the goodwill of her friends'. To support their denial of incontinence, John and Alice each had to find compurgators. Was this Alice Hewes the servant of the rector of Fryerning, suspected in 1565 of unchastity with him? (p. 219).

In a case from Great Oakley in 1584 the man declared, 'He was a suitor and in the way of marriage and contracted by Mr. (Thomas) Rochester (rector), and appointed the day of marriage and prepared the dinner, but Mr. Rochester would not solemnize the marriage because of the fame of suspicion of incontinency which was between them; whereupon they went out of the town and dwelt at Ramsey and lived together'. Presented in 1593 for not marrying a woman to whom he was contracted, another man replied, 'He mindeth to marry as soon as she is delivered of the child wherewith she is great by her former husband', and he was ordered to wed her before Christmas.

An unusually full series of depositions, taken in 1584 before William Farrand, doctor of laws and surrogate to the Archdeacon of Essex, bears ample testimony to the importance of Elizabethan betrothals. It tells of the tragic story of John Eaton, an old and apparently childless man, and Margaret Boulton, both of West Ham. They had made a formal contract as 'husband and wife', plighting each other's troth before witnesses, and had made all the preparations for the wedding; but on Whit Sunday, the day before the wedding was to take place, John died, apparently of a surfeit. Challenged by Margaret about rumours of his already being assured to two widows, as well as having made a deed of gift of all his property to a cousin, John flatly denied all, giving Margaret promises of a generous legacy. The cousin had evidently contested the betrothal, and the court found it necessary to examine no less than five witnesses, all of whom testified on Margaret's behalf.

The depositions and replies to the interrogatories, which were taken on four days in July and September, fill 17 pages. The statements are fairly similar and are not contradictory, so that only the first is given fairly fully, but minor differences of interest are quoted from the others. The case is narrated mainly in the deponents' own language. The 34 articles of the interrogatories, put after each had made his statement, are not recorded, and the replies are mainly of a negative nature, but all the deponents said that they did not know Richard Eaton (who was apparently John's cousin) and that Margaret had not paid their expenses to attend.

Robert Warde, husbandman, of West Ham, where he had dwelt about 21 years and previously at Blackwall in Middlesex, aged 40, deposed that he had known Margaret for about 20 years. 'One day a little after Easter last he, with Nicholas Boswell and a bailiff of Ware (Hertfordshire) whose name he knoweth not, was in her house about 10 or 11 a.m., all drinking with her and John. He heard Margaret and John confess that they had given their faith and troth and their hands and that they were as man and wife before God. It was commonly reported in Stratford Langthorne (in West Ham) that they would be married on Whitsun Monday. The dinner and all other preparations were made ready against the day, but John died on Whitsun Sunday at night 5 p.m. being 8 June 1584. Warde and his wife being at supper with John and Margaret, also one Roger Carter, in her house in Stratford on the Sunday before Whitsun, she said, "Goodman Eaton, I hear it reported in the town that you have made a deed of gift of all your lands and goods unto a kinsman of yours, and if you have done so I had as good keep me as I am as be married unto you". John answering did swear by his troth that he had not so done, and did take bread and did eat it, saying, "Whensoever I die, yea and if I die within an hour after, I do give you all my goods and £10 a year in land to you during your life after my decease, frank and free", John being then of very good and perfect mind and memory, neither sick nor yet molested in mind any way.' Answering the interrogatories, he admitted that he had heard that 'John was contracted to Adams' wife and widow Paine, but what gifts were given betwixt them he knoweth not, neither hath he heard any words of contract of marriage amongst them; John was drunk the night before he died: and he did vomit and scour after his homecoming from Margaret's house. John was apparelled in a jerkin, a pair of sheep's russet hose, and a black hat. The common report was that John died by reason of surfeiting, and whether he made any will he knoweth not.' Agnes, Warde's wife, who had dwelt at West Ham for about 23 years, and previously at Canborne in the Isle of Wight, said that John denied the deed of gift, 'and took a piece of bread and put it in salt and ate it', saying as before described, 'and thereupon gave Margaret his hand and kissed her upon the same'. Since then John had said before Nicholas Boswell and his wife that 'he had given her all his goods whensoever he should die'.

Roger Carter, minstrel, of West Ham, where he had dwelt about 28 years and previously at Queenhithe in London about three years and before that at Kirkaynton in Derbyshire, aged 43, also referred to John's having sworn 'by his troth and bread and salt'. In his replies he stated that he was 'a minstrel and licensed and getteth his living partly thereby'. Nicholas Boswell of West Ham, where he had lived about 14 years, before that at Stratford Bow about two years, Brentwood about 10 years, and Thames Street in London, aged 30, deposed that John said, 'Megg, thus it is, I bear you good will and I am an old man, and therefore I would not be mocked, and if it be so that you be as willing as I am I will make you my wife before we part'. She replied, 'Goodman Eaton, methinketh that you are somewhat hasty and therefore I would request a thing at your hand, which is this. I hear it reported that you are made sure to goodwife Addams and goodwife Paine, and that you should have one of them to your wife.' John then said, 'No, Megg, I am not sure to any, they do belie me that so report, for I mean to be three Sundays asked in the church, and if any can lay any claim to me then I will set thee at liberty'. After they had plighted their troth, Boswell requested John 'to give her an angel, he answering that he had not one about him but she shall have one soon'. Thomas Betson, carpenter, of Wanstead, where he had lived about two years, previously at Bulphan about eight years, Brentwood about 24 years, and Rotherham in Yorkshire, aged 71, said, 'About six weeks before Whitsuntide, he coming to her house, John secretly said to him that she should be his land's lord, for she is my lawful wife and I mean to marry her and I will that you shall pay her the rent. He (Betson) promised him a fat lamb to his marriage, and to take the best he had.'

John Hall, curate of West Ham, where he had lived for about three years, and earlier in London about 10 years, at 'Casseholter' (Carshalton?) in Surrey about six years, and 'Stopwalt' (Stopham?) near Chichester, aged 50 years, said that he had known Margaret about three years. 'About three weeks before Whitsuntide John came to him, being the minister of West Ham, and requested him to ask the banns of matrimony betwixt them openly in the church; and he and his wife being at supper with John at Margaret's house, John desired him to be in readiness against Whitsun Monday in the morning, would give him for his pains two Edward shillings besides ordinary duties to the church, and desired him and his wife to be at dinner with him. The Saturday before Whitsun Eve they prepared the wedding dinner, and in his conscience he believeth that if John had lived three days longer he had been married to Margaret.' William Mortimer, butcher, of Stratford Langthorne, where he had lived for about 30 years, aged 37, added that 'John and Margaret had bought meat of him for the dinner'; and Richard Staines, husbandman, of Stratford Langthorne, where he had lived for about six years, previously at Theydon Bois about 15 years and at Henham, aged 42, declared that 'John had bidden him to his wedding dinner and promised him a pair of gloves'.

Eaton apparently died before making the promised will, as none seems to be extant, and the result of the case is unfortunately not on record. It illustrates the mercenary aspect of marriage. The would-be bride, suspecting that the financial benefits of the match would be less than she had anticipated, demanded assurance on that account as well as denial of any existing pre-contract. She herself made no mention of love. But generally it was the man who weighed in the balance what he would acquire in land or livestock by way of dowry.

Another deposition, also taken in 1584, refers to the custom of giving a bent penny as a token of betrothal. Elizabeth Dixon of North Weald, where she had lived for about 27 years and before that at High Ongar, aged 60, being examined on the allegation on the part of Samuel Wright, said: 'Audrey Wodell about half a year last past came to her house about dinner time and requested her to go to Samuel and tell him that she must needs speak with him. Thereupon she told him her errand, who came to Audrey in the deponent's house. He asked her how she did, who answered that she did very well, she thanked God, and asking him if he would bestow a pot of beer of (i.e. on) her, "Yea, that I will", saith Samuel, and drew forth his purse and held his money upon the board, and amongst his money there was a bended penny, which Audrey did take up and said that she would have it. "No, that you may not", saith Samuel, "for it was sent from a brother of mine, and she that hath it shall have me too." Thereupon Audrey did receive it and did swear her troth and faith that she would have him and no other man, and gave him her hand upon the same, yea, if she would go a-begging with him she would not forsake him. There were present this deponent, William Dixon her husband, and no more.'

Among the various 'matrimonial causes', only two instances of banns of marriage being forbidden have been found. The first is related in the deposition of the girl's mother, Sabina Rame of Great Waltham, taken in 1577. This is what she said. 'By the space of a year and a half there hath been good will in the way of marriage between William Meade and her (daughter), of this deponent's sight and knowledge, and upon Sunday after Michaelmas Day was twelvemonth Meade in her house at Much Waltham, falling in talk with her, declared that he had obtained the good will of her daughter, and in talking of marriage requested her that she would grant her good will likewise to give her consent. She answered, "I perceive that you are both agreed", and seeing that it was their own match she was contented and prayed to God that they might do well. Thereupon Meade, taking Margaret by the hand, who then stood by, saying to her, "Margaret, now that I have your mother's good will also, I do here now take you to be my wife, and I do give you here my faith and troth"; and she, holding him still by the hand, answering, "And here I do likewise give you my faith and troth and do promise to be your wife". None being there present with them but this deponent, she thereupon requested them that they should go to her son-in-law Richard Drane and make him privy of it, that there might be a day appointed for the marriage; which thing they did; and afterwards they were accounted for lawful man and wife before God. And also the banns of matrimony was openly asked two several Sundays in Much Waltham church about Candlemas last, and the third Sunday they were forbidden by Nicholas Satch, who claimed marriage.' The extraordinary discovery of the long-lost Elizabethan parish register of Great Waltham, referred to later, enables us to follow the somewhat negative sequel. William did not wed his Margaret, nor is the marriage of either party to be found later in the register; but although Nicholas 'claimed marriage', meaning presumably that there was an earlier contract between him and Margaret, it was not consummated, and his marriage to Katherine Cripes is registered in 1585. It apparently proved childless, and he was buried in 1598. The other case concerned an Earls Colne woman, Katherine Wade, who in 1591 'forbade the banns of matrimony' with Clement Wiborow of White Colne, affirming that they were betrothed. The man admitted this, but 'sithence he was asked in church to Joan Smith of White Colne, notwithstanding he was sure before to Katherine Wade'. The judge inhibited him from marrying Joan.

After their banns had been published, several persons refused to marry the other party because they discovered a previous betrothal. A man, whose banns had been asked once, protested that he had not consented to their being read, and the judge accepted his statement. One couple was presented 'for publishing the banns a long time since, yet unmarried'. The Great Oakley presentment in 1599 reads, 'Enquire why the kinsman of Freburne questman, being solemnly asked in the church there to a singlewoman, should not proceed in the marriage, no banns forbidden'.

Not unnaturally there were also a few reports of men absconding after their banns had been proclaimed; to such entries a marginal note, '*Quesitur*' (he is to be sought), was made by the scribe, but no instance of successful search is recorded. First jilted, then frustrated through housing difficulties, Agnes Clarke was nevertheless summoned to account for a second delay. William Hix, she explained in 1577, 'was full asked to her in the church of Woodford, but, forgetting his promise made her before God, forsook her and married another, whereupon she hath contracted herself unto one William Turner, which mindeth to marry with her and she with him, but the cause of the stay of their marriage is for that she could not get a lease of her house at her landlord's hands, but they intend to marry before Michaelmas next'. The judge would allow no further postponement beyond Bartholomewtide (24 August). However, the same court seven years later did not insist on one man getting married, despite the banns. When examined, Nicholas Lynch of Theydon Garnon said that since the banns were read between him and Joan Robertes four years ago, 'he hath had no liking towards her and meaneth not to proceed'; and he asserted that 'he was never contracted to her and never received any token of her in the way of marriage'. The judge directed him on Sunday next to express his sorrow because 'he had abused the congregation in procuring the banns openly to be asked'.

The behaviour of her groom did not augur well for the wedding of Katharine Abbot of Romford in 1589. 'After they were made sure and betrothed together, and also being asked three times in church, he sold her goods and maketh a laughing stock of the matter, and braggeth that he will not marry her.' But the man, Robert Dewgard, also of Romford, declared that 'he did bear her good will in the way of marriage, and she likewise did bear the like'. They were enjoined to marry forthwith.

A reasonable excuse for postponing the wedding was advanced by William Colfild of Stanway in 1591, when the West Mersea wardens reported that 'he hath been contracted to Mary Straight ever since last Lent'. He admitted that their banns had been thrice asked, 'but she was in service with one Wilkinson her uncle and her covenant with him cometh (i.e. ends) not until Michaelmas next'; so they were given until the Feast of All Saints (1 November).

A Creeksea woman in 1598 apparently deceived her intended husband by managing to cover up certain physical defects. The wardens had presented William Walford of South Fambridge for not having wedded her, although some months had passed after the third reading of their banns. Failing to appear, he was declared contumacious and excommunicated, but later submitted himself. He then declared, doubtless to the surprise of the judge, 'I had purposed to have married her, but for secret causes and specially for that she is not sound in body nor hath any hair on her head, I will not proceed any further'. The judge 'considered the allegation' and apparently accepted this impediment to marriage.

A final illustration of betrothal proceedings, belonging to 1590, comes from the breach of promise suit brought by Joan Smithe against Nicholas Fulham. John Mond of Woodford, gentleman, where he had dwelt for about five years, before that at St. Giles-without-Cripplegate, London, about three years, and before that in the Queen's service about eight years, born in Cornwall, aged 42 or 43, deposed as follows: 'Coming to the house of John Lynnet at Woodford, with whom Joan dwelt as a servant, he found Nicholas, Joan, Thomas Skegges and his wife, and Edmund Saling and his wife, ready to sit down to dinner, and being desired sat down and dined with them, and after dinner they went into the orchard or garden', when Nicholas said that he and Joan were contracted to each other and were minded to marry at Michaelmas, 'for then his house came into his hands and possession, and for a further testimony they joined their right hands together. Nicholas asked Joan, "Joan, art thou contracted to take me to thy husband?", to which she answered, "Yea, I am content"; and then Nicholas said, "I do thank thee therefore, and I do here before these witnesses take thee Joan to be my wife"; and for a further assurance he drank in a cup of beer to Joan and she to him. Moreover, Nicholas did then and there confess that he had given her two pieces of silver (being shillings) in token thereof, and she did confess that she had given also certain tokens to him.' The deponent may be identical with John Mundes, a yeoman of Chigwell, whose will was proved in 1595. Thomas Skegge of Woodford, charcoal-burner (*carbonarius*), where he had dwelt for about 20 years, born at Stapleford Abbots, aged about 50, deposed in very similar terms, but in reply to questions said that 'he thinketh that Nicholas is married to another woman since the said contract, but to whom or where hence she came he knoweth not'.

From breach of marriage we pass to sinister 'sales' of brides and baleful bargains for marriage. In 1580 William Clark of West Ham was prosecuted for 'assuring himself to three sundry women, and one he sold away to another for 3s. or 40d., and now he has fled the country with Mary Atkins'. Eight years afterwards the West Ham wardens presented William Vaughan, because 'by common fame he bought one Katherine Popkyn, who is contracted to another man, and gave for her 5s.' While no specific contract was quoted, William Milles of Romford was brought to court in 1579 and indicted as 'a cozener of men's servants in promising them marriage'. Cozening, or defrauding, was a serious offence occasionally dealt with by the secular courts.[1]

These are mild incidents as compared with one, full details of which come from the deposition of a man who may be identical with the vendor of the small manor of Battesfords in Witham in 1633.[2] As a result, Quarter Sessions made a bastardy order. The extraordinary tale of the merciless treatment of a widow who died, leaving twin bastards, was related by William Freborne of Witham, when examined by John (Sterne), the Suffragan Bishop of Colchester (who was also vicar of Witham), in his capacity as a J.P. On 17 January 1600 Freborne confessed that, about six or seven weeks past, Thomas Saffold 'came for him from Maldon to Witham', with whom he went to Colchester to the sign of the 'Blue Pig', where he found one Agnes Burrow, a widow, who was pregnant, as she and others reported, by William Skarfe of Great Bentley, husbandman. 'Saffold was in hand with him (i.e. trying to persuade Freborne) to marry the widow', which he consented to do for £15, whereof he received £5 and took four bonds from Skarfe for the balance to be paid by instalments. Departing from Colchester the same day he was married, they went as far as the 'Crossy hand' (Cross-in-Hand inn at Marks Tey, shown on Ogilby's road-map, 1675) and thence the next day to Feering to the sign of the 'Chequer'. There he left her. She went to Edward Numan's house at Witham, where she lodged one night, and at the house of one Fowey four or five nights. 'Then being commanded by the overseers', Freborne 'carried her from Witham a mile beyond Colchester towards Wivenhoe, where he left her, hoping she would go to Bentley, where she dwelt; but the next day she returned to Colchester, where she got a passport from the Bailiffs for her passage to Witham, by virtue whereof she passed from Colchester to Lexden and so to Stanway, where she was lodged in the house of John Clear, the constable, upon Sunday towards night, where immediately she fell in travail and was delivered of child.' She sent for Freborne, who 'repaired to Stanway upon Tuesday morning, at which

[1] *E.L.: Disorder*, 97, etc. [2] Morant, *History of Essex*, ii, 110.

time he did earnestly entreat Clear to keep her in his house until she had recovered her strength, but Clear refusing, he caused her to be laid into a tumbrel and to be conveyed thence to Marks Tey, where she miserably died'.

Skarfe, now described as a yeoman, was arrested, and on 13 February he confessed to paternity and to the bargain with Freborne to marry her and to discharge the parish of 'all incumbrances touching her'. It was learned soon afterwards that Freborne had 'assigned the bonds to John Bynder for 5 marks, and 33s. 4d. more to be paid to him out of the £10, so £5 residue remaineth due'. Skarfe being 'bound to bring up the two children, she being dead, and Freborne is nowise to be charged with keeping them', the court ordered that they 'be kept at Skarfe's charges according to the bonds, 5 marks and 33s. 4d. shall be deducted out of the £10, and the residue being £5 shall be paid over by Skarfe to the overseers of the poor of Great Bentley, when due, to the use of the children, to be paid when they come to their full ages, with the profit that shall in the meantime grow by the said £5.' It is an unusually elaborate maintenance order. But why was Freborne apparently allowed to go scot free? Because he was a friend of the vicar? If not, it would seem, in the absence of other evidence, that the bogus marriage was a legal ceremony following banns or more likely by licence, so that the Church court could not prosecute him. Search in the early registers of the six Colchester parishes which are extant failed to produce Freborne's marriage entry.

In the same year a dowry was proffered but rejected, only the bare facts of which are vouchsafed in the archidiaconal records. Repudiating suspected misbehaviour with Ursula Lopar, Richard Dier of Margaretting disclosed that 'he never had any private company with her, but coming to goodman Ramme's house, with whom she dwelleth, as others did, Ramme did offer him that if he would marry her he would place them in a plot with six beasts'.

Marriage

Very faintly drawn scenes of bride-ales, of minstrels playing at a wedding in church, of morris dancers escorting a bridal couple will be observed in the chapter on Work and Play on sabbaths and holy-days in the next volume. That is all the court records portray of such merry-makings. The fifteenth-century 'Marriage Feast Room' close to Matching church is a solitary reminder of Elizabethan weddings. The cases now related concern breaches of the prescribed religious ceremony and sadder aspects of some marriages or of those that never took place, though there is the humorous, if impious, incident of ropes and nettles being carried before a bride.

Deviating from the rules for the marriage service, as laid down by the Book of Common Prayer, involved several clerics in the censure of the court, chiefly for celebrating weddings without a ring, to which some puritans objected; others were cited for marrying couples secretly. The charge against Ralph Bradley, curate of Berden, who 'omitted to use the ring' (1588), is matched by a number of similar examples. Ralph Barnes and Elizabeth his wife, 'suspected not to be lawfully married, wherefore the parishioners require to have a certificate of their marriage', led them both to court, where they confessed to having been married without the ring, on which the judge forbade them to consort together until they were properly wedded (1585). In 1588 'Mr. John Vicarie, vicar of Hatfield Peverel, stayed or stopped the marriage of one in the parish church when he was in the middle of the marriage'. His defence was that John Cracknell, a parishioner, 'refused to be married with a ring, also such duties as were due to him for his marriage, and did procure no other ring but a jet ring or horn ring for that purpose'. The vicar had demanded his 10s. fee. The case was not pursued. Two years later, Richard Cracknell of the same parish was presented for being married 'contrary to the Queen's Book with Joan Wilmot of the same without the ring'. Adjourned to the next session, Francis Fryer, vicar of Great Totham, who had performed the ceremony, stated, 'Having demanded a ring of Cracknell according to the Book, he had none, but did appeal to him; whereupon lest the marriage should not be finished for want of a ring, he proceeded without one'.

A wedding in 1602 was apparently ruined by the malice of a third party. William Gylchrist of West Ham 'upon Sunday 27 June last, when there was a marriage to be solemnized, he in derision of holy matrimony got a bough hanged with ropes' ends and beset with nettles and other weeds, and carried the same in the street and churchyard before the bride to the great offence of the congregation'. Sourness probably led Joan Swinyard of Bradfield in 1600 to 'mock John Copt and widow Hewett as they went to the church to be married'. But perhaps both incidents were typical of rustic fun evincing itself at weddings.

Other marriages were celebrated irregularly. It may be presumed that only a few of such cases reached the courts. An exceptional charge lay against John Asten, parish clerk of West Ham, in 1576, for 'assisting John Derington the minister, who unlawfully married himself'. He confessed that he 'ignorantly assisted as far forth as appertained to his office of clerkship and not otherwise, he thinking he might do so'. Next Sunday the clerk, who had no doubt witnessed other penances, had to acknowledge himself 'sorrowful and promise never to do the like hereafter'.

In 1584 William Tayler, vicar of Aveley, was rebuked because 'he married a couple and asked them twice in one day, and the next day asking them again married them without any licence'. Submitting himself, the vicar told this story about Richard Humber and Elizabeth Farrant, 'late of Bagshot (Surrey), widow'. The 'special cause that moved him to marry them so suddenly was that she, being servant in house with Mistress Barrett, who, hearing them asked, immediately after turned her out of doors, and the same Humber nor any other durst not keep her in their house for the displeasure of Mr. Barrett and Mrs. Barrett, and for the avoiding of further troubles that might happen in receiving of her, at the earnest petition of the same couple he asked and married them at a lawful hour, divers of the neighbours then present'. The Humbers confirmed his statement. All three were ordered penance by having to admit their fault before the Eucharist next Sunday. The Barretts were of course the owners of Belhus mansion, and perhaps Mistress Barrett, wife of Edward who was to die in the following year, had jumped to the conclusion that the maid was pregnant.

'Mr. Dow of Stratford in Suffolk', who was a puritan preacher and a prominent member of Dedham 'classis',[1] caused a flutter at Dedham in 1587 by marrying William Pulleyn and Barbara Waye, because she was 'voiced to be with child' and 'without licence or banns or penance done assigned by the authority of a competent judge'. William, Barbara, her father, and the Dedham wardens were all cited. The father said that his son-in-law came from 'Aldham in Suffolk beyond Hadleigh'. Barbara was 'searched by skilful women and not found to be so, and the banns were asked orderly'. So they all paid their fees and went home. 'For marrying one or two couples without banns thrice asking and without licence' brought Robert Marsh, vicar of Great Wenden, into trouble in 1597; and there are a few similar breaches of canon law governing marriage. An unclerical remark led 'Mr. Nowell, vicar of Pattiswick', to court in 1591. 'When Mr. Archdeacon's licence was delivered unto him to marry his daughter, being in his own handwriting', the charge recited, 'He said that he cared not a fart for this licence, or such like words'.

A small number of licences are recorded in the act books as having been issued by the two archdeacons acting as ordinaries exercising the right on behalf of the Bishop of London; for example, for the marriage of Edmund Goodale of Arkesden and Elizabeth Howland, the fees being paid (1597).

Production of licences was occasionally called for, if the legality of a wedding was in doubt. In 1578 Arthur Dent, curate of Danbury, would have been reproved by the Archdeacon for having married 'a couple about a month past, on a working day very disorderly, the woman being deaf and dumb', had he not asserted that he performed the ceremony, as he thought he might so do, by virtue of a licence issued by Dr. Bingham, the Bishop's Commissary; 'but he thinketh he hath done amiss, for which he is heartily sorry'. However, on exhibiting the document he secured his

[1] P. Collinson, *The Elizabethan Puritan Movement*, 223–7.

discharge. Eight years later, Hugh Inche, rector of Chipping Ongar, was censured because 'he married William Colford of Navestock and Ann Saling widow of Stanford Rivers in Stapleford Tawney church without the parson's consent, knowing that there was a controversy where she was dwelling'. He was able to answer, 'As concerning a pre-contract, about five weeks past he had married them in the church according to the Book of Common Prayer and with the ring, by virtue of a licence from my Lord of Canterbury, with the consent of the parson of Stapleford'. The couple had also been cited, and were excommunicated for non-appearance.

The court took a surprisingly lenient course in 1590 on learning that John Eborne, curate of West Ham, 'useth to take money for to marry folk that be dishonest and before they be lawfully asked'. He admitted that 'the party willingly for expedition offered him 4s. to marry him, also the party was of West Ham, but he knoweth not how long, but some alleged that he was not there above four days'. The curate had 'to restore the said 4s. into the poor men's box' and to acknowledge his guilt in time of service.

The romantic flavour of a runaway match in 1599 is sensed in the charge against Edward Gipps of Danbury 'for receiving a maid that one John Bitte stole away from Mistress Elmeare, and there she was found'. Bitte alleged that, 'being contracted to her, she came to him out of her mistress's ground, and he was married to her at St. Botolph-without-Aldgate, London'. The marriage certificate being produced, he was discharged.

Uniting two people in a private house was the charge laid against Bartholomew Glascoke, rector of Bobbingworth, in 1587. 'He married one Robert Masson, gentleman, and Margaret Borne, maiden, in Mr. Borne's house in Bobinger parish at Shrovetide last, or little before, without lawful licence.' The rector explained how, after the banns had been thrice asked, he performed the marriage 'upon necessity's sake', because she 'was sick and low before the solemnization, whereby she could not safely come abroad without great danger of her further sickness and recovery'. He affirmed that there were present 'divers of good credit and estimation' and that she 'is not yet very well recovered'. The judge warned him not to marry unlawfully in the future. A prosecution for incontinence against man named Collen in 1600 for 'begetting a harlot with child in Pattiswick' revealed that 'she was married in a chamber in the house of Guyver in Pattiswick or Stisted'.

Other secret or evening weddings were very occasionally discovered. In 1599 Thomas Castle, 'now or late curate of Great Sampford, solemnized a marriage between a couple unknown, without banns, clandestinely in the night time upon Coronation Day last, being procured thereto by Rooke Johnson with whom they did board'; and four years later George Barker and his wife of Feering were married at Little Braxted 'by candlelight by the minister, Mr. Farrer, by licence of the Ordinary', Farrer undertaking not to offend again. In 1566 a Purleigh couple were accused because 'they have contracted in a private place and have not solemnly celebrated marriage'. In 1600 Jane Chapman, a widow of Childerditch, had 'privately married John Chapman her late husband in a parlour in her own house by Mr. Arthur Grame their vicar'. She told the judge that three persons, whom she named, were present, but he sentenced her to 'major excommunicaton'. A little later, however, she submitted a humble petition for absolution, which was granted. The East Ham wardens presented two persons in 1599 because 'a common fame hath been raised by Katherine Gawen of East Ham widow that they were married under a bush'. The woman, when charged, said, 'Did my husband tell you that?'!

In 1580 Richard Bateman and his wife Joan of South Ockendon were reprimanded because they were wedded in West Thurrock church without banns being asked, 'which church is called a lawless church' (the parish lay in the jurisdiction of the Bishop's Commissary); the offence was aggravated by their pre-nuptial incontinence and by his having been previously contracted in marriage with Joan Ashley. The Batemans were commanded to confess their faults, holding the usual white wands. The church stood just behind the sea-wall, alone in the marsh and half a mile from the village street. Its registers before 1680 are lost.

The Church forbade the celebration of weddings during three seasons of the year. To aid their memory, a few ministers made a note of the prohibited periods in their registers. That of Cottenham in Cambridgeshire, beginning in 1575, preserves the lines of a clerical versifier:

> Advent marriage doth thee deny,
> But Hilary gives thee liberty.
> Septuagesima says thee nay,
> Eight days from Easter says you may.
> Rogation bids thee to contain,
> But Trinity sets thee free again.[1]

Expressed more accurately in prose, nuptials were debarred from Advent to the Octave of Epiphany, from Septuagesima to the Octave of Easter, and from Rogation Sunday (the 5th Sunday after Easter) to Trinity Sunday. Several ministers were censured for marrying parties during one or other of the close seasons. The cases yield nothing of special note, except that against 'Mr. Hilles, the Dutch preacher (at Colchester), for that he married three Dutchmen in the time prohibited without licence' in 1592, for which he was to be suspended. Attending two sessions later, he alleged that, 'by an edict or proclamation made in the time of King Edward last past, he and his countrymen were excused from the ordinary course of law and left unto their own orders and laws', which led to the lifting of his suspension. It will be appreciated that the Church's triple-period veto was highly inconvenient, if not a cause for anxiety, where the woman was already with child. But, as pointed out under Bridal Pregnancy,

[1] C. Cox, *Parish Registers*, 79.

little severity is apparent in the judges' dealing with cases of pre-marital intercourse between affianced couples.

More serious than marriage at prohibited times was marriage within prohibited degrees of relationship, though the section on Incest suggests that this sin was not regarded either by the clergy or the laity as so obnoxious as we should have expected to find. What offence had 'John Carrell, clerk, chaplain to Lady Grey of Pyrgo', committed in 1567? The bare note (in Latin) reads, 'In a matrimonial cause promoted by Joan Mell'.

Five instances of excommunicated persons being married have been found. A domestic servant of Lord Wentworth of Little Horkesley had married a smith who 'keepeth his shop of smith' on Mile End Green near Colchester. The wench had had a bastard child and was an excommunicate at the time of her marriage (1589). The scribe noted, 'Enquire who married them and where?' In the same year John Jollye and his wife of Earls Colne 'did enterprize to solemnize matrimony together, being excommunicated by Mr. Adams, vicar of the same'; in the other cases ministers were guilty: Nicholas Daye, vicar of Cressing, 'for marrying widow Catche and her now husband Beckwith', both excommunicate, and 'he is gone' (1590); and George Rogers (curate), of Rayleigh, for marrying an excommunicated woman of Laindon (1600).

Churching of Women

The Prayer Book rubric before the office for the purification, or churching, of women reads, 'The woman, at the usual time after her delivery, shall come into the church decently apparelled, and must offer accustomed offerings; and if there be a communion, it is convenient that she receive holy communion'. Refusing to go to be churched was not a common offence. Routine cases call for no comment, but the court books disclose several instances of strange behaviour.

Jane, wife of John Minors of Barking, who had kept her child unbaptized for a whole month in 1597, claimed, 'It was foul weather, I dwell three miles from the church'. In a further charge the wardens expressed their concern at some length:

> She very unwomanly came to be churched at the end of the month, together with her child to be baptized, and feasted at a tavern four or five hours in the forenoon; and in the afternoon came to the church rather to be seen than upon any devotion as it seemed, for whilst the minister was burying a corpse she went out of the church unchurched unto the tavern again. And when she was spoken to by the clerk to return to church again and to give God thanks after her delivery, she answered, 'It was a ceremony'. The which abuses, seeing they are so public and notorious and the example unpunished, may prove dangerous. We pray that you would enjoin that her satisfaction may be also public to the content of many of good worth.

On her denial the judge deputed 'Mr. (Richard) Wignall (vicar of Barking) and others to hear and determine' the matter and to certify the court. This was done, and the woman was discharged.

In 1589 an Inworth wife had said, with cynical simile, 'A woman going to give God thanks orderly according to the Book of Common Prayer with her neighbours about her was like unto a sow with pigs following of her or like to a bitch that went to salt'. In court she offered the further opinion that the laws 'were neither good nor godly nor ever ought to be obeyed'. The registrar added this unusual note: 'When she appeared, nothing could be found against her but the book turned over, and so for 8d. she was discharged.' Perhaps nobody came to substantiate her imaginative, if irreverent, remarks.

Once, in 1586, the court accused a husband, Edmund Fanninge of Hatfield Peverel, of being 'a hindrance to his wife in giving thanks'. Ordered to purge himself of the offence, he defaulted; his wife also failed to certify her having been churched. Joan Thrussell of Danbury, also presented in 1586 for not giving thanks after her delivery, made the curious reply that 'by reason of her being a green woman (p. 284) she did frequent Terling church' (about seven miles away). Danbury church was the scene of an incident, which we might have related under Church Disturbances. In 1578 Katherine, wife of Stephen Whithed, 'came to church on Sunday to give thanks for her child-bearing at the sermon time, and whilst Dr. (George) Withers was at the sermon she with a loud voice demanded of Dr. Withers, "If he were ready to do his duty she was ready to do hers", whereby she troubled him in his sermon and caused the people to make a laughter; and the same Stephen for his part with obstinate words maintained his wife in her lewd (i.e. rude) fact'. Her sentence: 'To confess that she is most heartily sorry in using such unseemly speeches and abusing the worshipful Dr. Withers, promising amendment' – 'worshipful', because he was Archdeacon of Colchester as well as rector of Danbury, which lay in the other archdeaconry.

Not coming to be churched 'decently apparelled' or accompanied by other women resulted in several prosecutions. A South Benfleet wife 'came very undecently, without kerchief, midwife or wives, and placed herself in her own stool, not in the seat appointed, by the which she showed herself desirous in coming so like a light woman, so that she returned not churched'. Her defence was that she acted 'according to the book which she best liked, and said that in places from whence she came the use in such neither did and was at any time otherwise'. Another wife 'went to church to give thanks disorderly in her petticoat with one only woman meeting her by the way and sat in her usual pew far from the minister and not in the right seat, and her husband maintaining her therein'. More briefly in other entries, 'She came to be churched undecently and unwomanly without any woman with her', or 'She went with her husband alone and no women'. Coming 'with a kerchief over her head' was not deemed decent; and in another case the accused explained that she wore a 'kerchief not for any superstition but for warmth'. There was an ancient custom at Dunton, according to which the woman gave a white cambric handkerchief to the minister as an offering at her churching.[1]

Occasionally the minister committed the offence of churching at home instead of in church. For doing so in 1571 Richard Glover, curate of St. Botolph, Colchester, had to give 2s. to Robert Bird, 'the collector of the Hospital of Colchester'. On the other hand, William Frith of Upminster complained that William Washer, the rector, refused to come to his house when his wife was too ill to give thanks in church, and he urgently petitioned the judge in his private chambers, who instructed Mr. Lambert, vicar of Hornchurch, 'to go quickly to Frith's house'. Clerical offenders also included (Edward) Boardman, who would 'not church child-wives' (i.e. lately delivered) by the prescribed form, and Philip White, rector of Fobbing, who 'refused to purify Nicholas Marten's wife when she came to be churched'.

Throughout the centuries the pangs of childbirth have often forced the unmarried mother to name the father: some depositions of midwives in bastardy cases may be related in the next volume. A different sort of unguarded but sympathetic cry led the wife of a man called Gilbert of Inworth in 1589 to be charged; she said 'at a woman's labour that the laws were neither good or godly not to be obeyed'.

Living Apart

It was regarded as a sin for married couples not to cohabit. 'Living asunder' was allowed by the Church only if the aggrieved spouse had sufficient grounds to obtain a decree of judicial separation. The extent to which the archidiaconal courts awarded such decrees will be seen in the following section. The act books also tell the story of wife-beatings, broken marriages, self-exile and separations without either party having recourse to divorce. Some entries are in vivid terms; others are terse, the sober language screening domestic quarrels. The majority concern married couples 'living apart (contrary to the laws of the land)', or 'living asunder'; or the husband 'leaveth his wife and liveth most wickedly'. In most cases the court ordered them 'to cohabit together again' or 'to be reconciled to each other', sometimes adding optimistically, 'treating one another affectionately'. Simple refusal to live together was a relatively rare charge, of which about 30 cases have been noted. Often the accused spouse produced a counter-accusation against the other.

A presentment in 1574 for 'turning away his wife, saying that she is not his wife', brought the alleged justification, 'He turned her away, for that

[1] Morant, *History of Essex*, i, 219.

she would not be ruled'. Exceptionally, in 1587, Anthony Gaskin of Little Bromley was given a choice: 'To use his wife lovingly and like an honest man, and her children, or else to pay 2s. weekly so long as he shall keep from her company.' On the other hand, in 1589 Edward Bennitt of Mistley (perhaps a weaver of that name whose will was proved in 1610) asserted that 'he was willing to cohabit with his wife, but she will not cohabit with him', and in 1583 Thomas Finch of Great Burstead explained that 'the fault is not with him, but she hath gone from him, and he is content to live with her, but knoweth not where she is'. When John Bell and his wife Joan of Fobbing were 'detected for living asunder this year and this half' in 1588, she appeared, declaring that 'he did use her hardly with unreasonable stripes, but now they are both willing to cohabit together as Christians'; so the judge demanded a certificate to that effect.

Within reason every husband had the right to chastise his wife if he disapproved of her behaviour: if she was a scold and her neighbours disapproved, there was always the ducking-stool to cool her tongue. There was rarely divorce for cruelty. But some wives left home after they had suffered too much injury or dreaded assault. Mary, wife of Thomas Bellsted of Boreham, alleging that she was in fear of her life, was told to attend and explain (1577). William Staine of High Ongar was presented for 'misusing his wife with stripes contrary to all order and reason' (1587); and John and Joan Bull of Fobbing, who had 'lived asunder for two years, and the cause was that he did use her hardly with unreasonable stripes', were however 'willing to cohabit again' (1588).

Among the few cases in which both parties were prosecuted is that against Humphrey and Joan Bailey of Leigh in 1590 for 'living slanderously asunder'. Joan declared that they had not been lawfully married, and that 'by deceit he compelled her thereto, and now will not suffer her in his sight and beateth her, so that she is not able to abide him for fear of her life'. She further alleged: 'He hath heretofore when they lived together brought home certain goods that she supposed he had stolen and would have compelled her to keep them close (i.e. secretly), or other vile things, which she denied to do, and therefore was glad to depart from him.' The woman was discharged, while her husband was excommunicated.

But it was not always the male partner who was the tyrant. Edward Rawlins and Cecily his wife of Rayleigh 'live asunder in several (i.e. separate) parishes' (1597). But, the wardens added, 'The greatest fault is in Edward, for his wife is willing to dwell with him, if he would suffer her'. Edward thought otherwise: 'He discontinueth from her for fear she would poison him.' Despite the risk of consuming her culinary concoctions, he was ordered to go back to her. A Little Ilford man, too, living apart from his wife, averred that 'he standeth in fear of his life for her' (1597).

Occasionally the husband's excuse was his wife's alleged adultery: 'She being with child which he saith is none of his'; or, more pointedly, 'She was brought abed of two children within seven weeks after she was married, he saying that they be none of his', which led to her being excommunicated; or the woman was charged with 'living from her husband to the offence and grief of her neighbours, and she is also a harbourer of two lewd daughters'.

Objection being made against William Markes of East Doniland for 'living asunder from his wife', he declared in 1589 that she was 'a woman many times besides herself and will not be ruled, that he hath procured her to come to him, and after the same in her madness hath departed from him without cause'.

For reasons unstated, Henry Reade *alias* Davye and his wife Margaret were cited in 1562, when he 'affirmed that forasmuch as he hath married his wife he will never forsake her, but do with his body what they will'; and another husband assured the court that he would gladly keep his wife, 'but she wanting government doth absent herself'.

When John and Cecily Browne of Rayleigh were summoned in 1575 for living apart, the man said that 'he hath refrained from her company for the space of half a year, for that he thinketh she doth not love him'; but the wife argued that 'he doth refuse her without cause'; the judge ordered him to receive and treat her with marital affection. In the same year Thomas Lovekin of Mundon 'obstinately refuseth his wife without lawful impediment'. Yet, later in the year, he sought to divorce her for adultery. These two cases seem to be the only evidence of wives complaining about loss of conjugal intercourse. William Wheeler of South Weald explained in 1597 that 'his wife used such company that he liked not of, and he often warned her to forbear and she would not'; but he was told to cohabit with her. Another wife complained that her husband 'without any just cause did put her away from him'.

Two husbands abiding in parishes which rarely figure in the act books were able to explain their not living with their wives. John Cotton of Langley was 'living scandalously from his wife' in 1587; but, he said, she had gone to live with Thomas Bennett, her father, at Windsor. The Cottons were a family of some substance in the area. Is he identical with John Cotton of Great Chesterford, esquire, who made his will four years later, leaving an annuity of £25 to his wife Judith, subject to another annuity of £7 payable to their son John?[1] In 1591 Stephen Newton of West Bergholt stated that he had been 'household servant to Mr. Wallgrave Abell of Bergholt' for the past four years, and his wife was 'a very outrageous and unreasonably contentious woman, very unquiet, and such as with whom he cannot rest in peace; and notwithstanding he doth provide for her, allowing her for her maintenance £6 yearly or a house and ground to that value, whereof she made choice'. The judge, satisfied with the truth of his statement, discharged him.

[1] E.R.O., D/ACW 1/55.

Charge, answer and decision in a case against John Gyon the elder of Coggeshall in 1588 read: 'He doth not divorce his wife'; 'She will not live with him, but dwells in Waldingfield'; and 'To ask the aid of the judge of that place to call his wife and to charge her to repair to his company'; and the registrar noted, 'She cannot, for fear of her health'. Waldingfield lies only a few miles over the Suffolk border; but when the Wix wardens reported Henry Bolton, cooper, for living apart from his wife for one and three-quarter years at Spalding in Lincolnshire, the court apparently felt that it would not be worth the trouble to prosecute him.

A woman described as servant to Mr. Braunshe of Theydon Garnon, who 'liveth not in order with her husband', replied in 1579 that he was 'living and servant with the Right Honourable the Earl of Worcester in Wales, and for want of a house she came to London to her friends, but she mindeth to cohabit with him as shortly as she can'. Two West Hanningfield women were jointly prosecuted in 1569 for 'living from their husbands, being serving men, and they are suspected of a common crime'. Both wives alleged that 'their husbands do live with their masters and do sometimes repair to their companies'; and they produced a letter from Eustace Clovell, esquire, the active justice of the peace of Clovile Hall in that parish. They were accordingly discharged, and the wardens instead were cited to explain their presentment.

Strangely enough, only one case of a deserting husband is recorded. A woman, charged in 1594 with living apart and not receiving communion, said that 'her husband went away from her two years at Whitsuntide last and she cannot learn sithence where he is'.

A singular response was made in 1595 by Ellis Wright of Fobbing, whose wife 'keepeth' (liveth) at Havering: 'By reason of the young years of his wife he hath placed her with a friend till his (*sic*) state and ability be better'; they were directed to cohabit. Could this refer to a child-marriage, of which there is no other evidence in the act books? In contrast, Alice Rede of Ulting, who had separated from her husband ten or eleven years ago, claimed in 1579, 'It is not in her default and she is a very old woman', and she was dismissed.

Divorce

A surprising result of examination of the archdeacons' court books is the significant number of 'divorce' cases, all of which will be recounted. The Church recognized two kinds of divorce – *a vinculo matrimonii* (from the marriage bond) and *a mensa et thoro* (from board and bed, or cohabitation). The former could be sought on grounds of consanguinity or affinity within the prohibited degrees of marriage, because the union was void *ab initio*; it could also be claimed for permanent impotence. Divorce *a mensa et thoro*, or judicial separation, in which the marriage was not dissolved, was by far the more frequent kind and could be sued in consequence of adultery or extreme cruelty; in such cases the wife was entitled to alimony. In both categories the Church forbade intercourse with a third person after divorce by either party, and they were obliged to give an undertaking to that effect. Any subsequent marriage after judicial separation would be declared void.

Three divorce petitions were received in 1563–4. Henry Mynkes was sued by his wife Katherine on her plea that she was 'in danger of her life and cannot live with him as an honest woman ought to do'. She was granted separation, and he was ordered to return the goods which she had brought to him at their marriage. A somewhat imperfect entry records the suit of Mr. (blank) Harrys for 'separation *a vinculo matrimonii*' (a technically incorrect phrase, and implying only normal separation). The court ordered him to pay 8s. to his wife 'for the expense of herself and children' until the case had been settled. Harrys had defaulted in purgation and so was ordered penance. The judge decreed that she and her children 'shall be placed at Cokars within two days', apparently to be 'boarded' there, and he was enjoined 'never to come in the company oj the said Fenner's wife', with whom he had committed adultery. The previous entry relates to a charge against Thomas Hamond of Woodham Walter for suspected incontinence with 'Mistress Harrys', but no proceedings are given. In neither case are the parties' abodes stated, and it may be that they relate to the influential Harrys family of Maldon. 'Cokars' may have been the home of Edward Coker, one of the two Maldon borough bailiffs in 1558.[1] Another ambiguously phrased case refers to Thomas Twide (or Twyede) and Buntynge's wife of Buttsbury, having been charged with suspicion of incontinence; the husband appeared and declared that they 'bore good love one to another; about seven years ago she went away from Bowentynge's by the space of six days, and at that time Bowentynge got her again by a divorce as she saith at London, and by that divorce they have continued both married'.

The earliest divorce entry, in 1561, somewhat obscurely records the judge's decree by which the husband had to pay an unstated sum, presumably as alimony, and the wife had to deliver his goods which he seemed to have left in his house. In the same year there is found one of those rare but bare references to a physical or sexual defect. 'Because of her impediment, viz. that he and she shall not be in house together in that he and she can not have copulation as man and wife, wherefor she frankly of good will desired to be divorced in the court, on which the judge pronounced a sentence of divorce *a thoro et mensa*'. The husband's name was Richard Gollinge, but no abode is given and he did not leave a will. In a second case of abnormality Richard Nycolas of Purleigh was cited in 1566 for absenting himself from his wife. He asserted that she was 'not a woman

[1] *Ess. Rev.*, xxiii, 63.

lawful for a man's use'. The court ordered that she be searched by women, who adjudged her 'not to be a woman', i.e. probably male. He then sought divorce, 'freely offering £8 (a year?) for her help (*ad eam auxiliacionem*), and bound himself to pay this sum'. The judge's response is not given. Is it conceivable, though improbable in the first of these two cases, that the court was dealing with women in a trans-sexual condition, centuries before society definitely accepted the existence of sex changes? The Purleigh spouse may possibly have been a pseudo-hermaphrodite. Although descriptions of hermaphroditism and other kinds of sexual deficiencies and inadequacies are fairly common in medieval medical literature, original English references are virtually unknown. The alternative interpretation is of course some form of vaginal malformation including its diminutiveness or absence.[1]

The most illuminating case came from Danbury and was heard by Archdeacon Cole personally at his visitation court at Romford in 1566. Both husband and wife, of the name of Alborowghe, had been cited because of their quarrelsome life. The man's version was that she did not wish to come to his bed, and 'threw water over his head'. Hers ran, 'Her husband hath oftentimes been abroad a nights and days, spending away his thrift, and when he cometh home he abuseth her and beateth her'. She then declared that on the very day (of the session) he had said that 'if she would tell anything against him to the judge he would keep her with stealth, and whereas he hath given her meat and drink he will give her water and bread'; and on oath she added that 'he had put a knife to her throat and a halter about her neck'. On her petition and fearing for her life, and because 'he saith that if it (were not for) the Queen's laws he would do otherwise with her', the Archdeacon granted her a divorce *a thoro et mensa*, in full court published the sentence, and asked 'Mr. Emerye of the same (parish) to take the goods, the one half to her, until they do better agree'.

Although no suit for divorce because of the husband's impotence is specifically noted, it may have been the intention in 1585, when Robert Smythe of Kelvedon had to answer the 'objection that he hath been married to Alice his wife for twelve years, and during that space he hath not had carnal use of her body, neither hath he done the duty of the man to the woman'. This he admitted, 'because he hath defect in his body and is not able to perform that duty of carnal copulation by reason that it is not with him as it is with other men, by reason of his defect'. The judge directed him to attend again at the next session, but the case then vanishes without further record. The eminent French surgeon, Guy de Chauliac, has an extraordinary passage in his *Chirurgia magna* (1363) about examination of alleged impotence (for legal purposes), in which he recommended

[1] I have to thank Mr. E. Freeman, Sub-Librarian, The Wellcome Institute of the History of Medicine, and Dr. J. Randell, for advice on this paragraph.

the surgeon to engage the services of 'a damsel that is wont to such things', basing his diagnosis on her report of what happened in bed.[1]

In 1585 John Jerningham appeared in an important case which also included a charge of bigamy, and a curate of East Ham and two other parties were also involved. The proceedings began with Thomas Rogers of Theydon Garnon being accused that 'indirectly for a sum of money he was bound to consent to a divorce between himself and his wife'. He 'showed a copy of the sentence of divorce before Dr. Hunt and Dr. Cesar for the exempt (jurisdiction) of St. Katherine (London) for adultery committed between her and John Jerningham esquire'. There followed the case against John Gerningham (*sic*) and Julian Rogers *alias* Fouler of Hornchurch, 'she being Rogers' wife of Theydon Bois'. Learning, however, that the cause was pending before Lord Hunsdon, one of the Queen's councillors, the judge dismissed both parties. Edward Hopkin of Hornchurch was also in trouble for 'lodging them together in his house, knowing that they were not man and wife'; and, more seriously, John Peyton, curate of East Ham, for solemnizing their marriage in East Ham church 'contrary to law and at an undue time and at the time when Jerningham had another wife living and Julian another husband as sithence it hath been known', for which the curate was suspended. The cause cannot be followed in the Privy Council minutes as the volume for 1583–6 is lost; but in the previous volume John Jerningham, esquire, 'one of her Majesty's servants', figures several times during 1581–2 as a debtor who had complained against Edmund Bedingfield of Huntingfield in Suffolk for detaining money due to him.

Of the remaining divorce cases, the act books give only brief factual statements. John Wademan, described as a servant with Mr. Wieat of Theydon Garnon (the visitation book of 1565 gives Francis, whose will was proved in 1568), was cited in 1566 because he was 'divorced from his wife by Mr. Huicke, doctor of laws, Chancellor of the Bishop of London, as he says and appears in the detection (presentment) of the churchwardens'. Under 1569 is a note, 'To make a testimonial under seal of the divorce between Henry Asser and Elizabeth Pynkman *alias* Asser, for he and she hath paid and the judge contented'. At a session two years later, in a suit 'Michell *versus* Michell *alias* Tolie', no parish or other details being given, 'sentence of divorce etc. was read as appears in the act on the file (*philium*)'. When Richard Salye of Langham brought a cause for divorce against Margaret his wife, described as of Layer Breton, in 1570, she did not appear; after five later sessions to which she was summoned she remained excommunicated – but apparently not divorced. In 1575 Thomas Lovekin sued Agnes Lovekin, *alias* Tistone, who was prosecuted in a cause of divorce *propter adulterium*, but the wife failed to attend to hear the sentence. Again, as in an earlier case, the decree was read in the

[1] Translation edited by Mrs. Margaret Ogden (*Early English Text Soc.*, no. 265, 1971).

presence of the Official and four witnesses who were apparently court officers. Richard Haliwell of Great Totham, accused of 'living disorderly from his wife' (1589), was ordered to cohabit and dwell with her; but in this and the next instance the judge added, 'or else to show cause why he should not do so or to sue her in a cause of divorce'. John Curtice 'of South Fambridge or Shopland', another deserter, asserted that she was 'a woman of evil life and conversation (conduct) and hath had a child by another man since he married with her, since which time he hath not kept company with her' (1592); again the decree ran, 'Seeing that he hath taken her to be his wife, he shall continue with her or else divorce her by order of law'. In 1599 Grysel Cowper of West Ham was cited, with the note, 'She is divorced, but lately hath a child'.

A suit which resulted from a husband's incest with his niece is related under that subject, and divorce is referred to in other contexts under Bridal Pregnancy and Bigamy.

No clear conclusions can be drawn from the Essex evidence, despite the relatively good material on an aspect of Elizabethan life for which so little is otherwise known; and the subject still awaits study of Church court archives elsewhere. But, although divorce *a vinculo matrimonii* is used in two of the cases which we have quoted, there seems little doubt that all the decrees were for judicial separation only, and none for full divorce in the modern sense.

Bigamy

Whereas bastardy could be punished by Quarter Sessions as well as the Archdeacons' courts, the spiritual sin of bigamy first became a civil crime a year after Elizabeth's death, under the Act of 1 James I, c.11.

As would be expected, the majority of the prosecutions lay against men. The earliest could be either bigamy or incest: John Tomson of Barking, presented at the visitation for having 'married two sisters' (1561); but the apparitor certified that 'he can find none such of the name'. Several were cited on the ground that their lawful wives were suspected to be alive; one was ordered to purge himself by the testimony of as many as eight neighbours; another, by seven. A Barking couple were both accused because 'they would marry together', although he was rumoured to have a wife living (1579). He claimed, however, that she had died about two years ago, and the judge accepted his statement. A third Barking man had a wife still living in Suffolk, a fact of which the churchwardens had 'great proof' (1591). He had been presented at the Bishop's visitation, they added, 'but nothing done'. Two men confessed their sins; one was also a brawler and swearer, while the other pleaded having committed bigamy when in 'extreme sickness and not of perfect wit'. John Courtman of Tollesbury, not satisfied with having two 'wives' alive at Wells in Somerset and 'upon the bank in Southwark', had 'wooed two widows, the one in Tollesbury, the other in Goldhanger'; but the judge's ruling is not given. Wedding widows could be profitable, as the woman was entitled to her dowry of one-third of her husband's possessions.

In 1592 the court considered a triple charge against Jasper Dormer, described as a gentleman of Stanford-le-Hope, for absence from church, marrying his wife in Stanford church 'in her mask', and 'for having two wives alive at once, and not divorced'. At first contumacious in failing to attend, he later admitted having married 'about sixteen years agone' Margaret Battell at Eastwood, with whom he continued about eleven years, and 'about a year ago he was married in Rushmere church near Ipswich to Agnes Ive, with whom he continueth, and both are yet living'. His sentence: To stand in Romford market on Wednesday in a white sheet, with a writing on his head about his guilt, and to bring a certificate of his penance from the bailiff at the next court.'

'Believed lost at sea', the perennial dilemma of so many sailors' wives, brought William Anderson and Joan his wife of Maldon to court in 1590 on the charge that she 'hath another husband living'. Explaining that she had married Anderson eleven years ago, because her former husband, George Carpenter, 'went beyond the seas about sixteen years since and she had letters about eleven years since that he was deceased', she 'now understandeth that her former husband is alive'. The judge admonished the Andersons 'not to cohabit together between this and the next court', and Anderson was warned 'to propound in form of law against the said Joan and to see further process'; but the matter was apparently not determined by the court.

A case brought in 1588 disclosed that both parties of a broken marriage had become bigamists. Rowland Tempest of Great Wakering had 'married a woman whose husband is alive'. The circumstances, according to Tempest, were that he had 'married with Amy the wife of Nicholas Osborne, who more than a year gone went from his wife and married with one Prudence Thorocke yet living; and he and Amy thinking Osborne to be dead as the common report went and as his nearest friends had reported'. Osborne being alive, the judge had no alternative but to direct Tempest 'to absent himself from the company of the said Amy'; who herself was separately charged as Rowland's 'pretended wife'.

When Ralph Hall of Great Chesterford was charged in 1580 because 'he being married to one Agnes Bygrave is now married to one Agnes Fysher, Agnes still living', he alleged that 'about nine years past' he was married to the latter at Great Chesterford, 'from whom for her adulterous living with one John Chapman and others he was lawfully divorced by Mr. Becon, Chancellor of Norwich, as showed to the judge under the seal of the Chancellor'. The prosecution of Henry Reade *alias* Davye of Wethersfield (a well-known local family) and Margaret, 'his pretended wife', in

1562 may perhaps imply bigamy, though not so termed. He swore that his wife was 'imbecile' and unable to come without peril of her life; but the judge insisted on their joint attendance at the next session.

Of the twenty-two charges found, only three lay solely against women. In 1577 'Margery Dunston *alias* Myller *alias* Blakeley' (of Wennington?) was presented because 'she married one Thomas Blakeley about two years past and it is not certainly known whether Dunston her first husband be dead, who parted from her company about twelve years sithence'. She contended that 'there hath been diligent enquiry for Dunston but she is certainly persuaded that he is dead'. The charge not being proved, the court decided that Myller 'cohabit with her until it be otherwise found that Dunston still lives'.

Allegations of bigamy against two ministers will be mentioned under the Clergy. Perhaps as a result of objections to the marriage banns, steps were taken in 1578 by the court to prevent a couple from committing bigamy. John Loggen of Barking 'hath proceeded to the banns of matrimony and intendeth to marry with one Mary Hewett, his first wife called Jane being yet living'. 'But', replied Loggen, 'she is gone from him and married to another man now dwelling in Kent, wherefore he thinketh that he might marry again.' The judge thought otherwise and 'inhibited him from marrying again during the lifetime of his lawful wife, except he may be lawfully divorced'. (This is not the same case as that of Barking, 1579.)

No case of trigamy came before the archdeacons, but a solitary reference to 'John Courtnaye, for having three wives', without further record, occurs in the Quarter Sessions rolls in 1583.

Such was the incidence of bigamy in two-thirds of a large county in so far as it was discovered in a century long before innumerable forms, telephones and income taxes gave the criminal little opportunity of escape: provided that the Elizabethan absconder went afar and steered clear of the vagrancy and settlement laws, he had a good chance of never being found out.

Burial

The Courts Christian were concerned with burial for two entirely different reasons – mundane and spiritual. By custom, interment inside the church or chancel was allowed where the deceased person belonged to a leading family. Burn's cautious phrase was a 'person of extraordinary merit, of which merit the incumbent was the most proper judge'.[1] A few such people figure posthumously in the act books because a relation had failed to pay the fee for breaking the floor or had not covered up the grave-hole. By ancient prescription, the privilege of burial inside the building had become attached to many manors and substantial houses.

[1] Burn, *op. cit.*, i, 186.

William Robert of Hawkwell 'buried his wife in Dengie church and will not pay the duties therefor neither yet cause the grave to be pavemented again' (1574). Christopher Mercer, vicar of Little Wakering, was presented by the wardens of Canewdon for 'not paving of the chancel where his wife was buried' (1587). John Cockley of Great Chishall was in default for 3s. 4d. for the burial of his child in the church, but paid up in court (1598).

People of substance formed a very small minority of defendants in the archidiaconal courts, but similar default brought a number to answer. Mistress Priscilla Rushe of Woodham Walter, because 'her husband's grave lieth uncovered in the chancel', was ordered to 'repair before St. John's Day' (1575); Christopher Blake of Great Baddow had not 'paved' a grave in the church (1590); Mr. David Hamner of Little Warley had failed to make his wife's grave in the chancel (1593); Thomas Prince rector of Great Chesterford had not 'paved' his wife's grave in the chancel (1595).

John Knight, rector of Goldhanger, was presented by the wardens because 'there wanteth two graves to be covered in the chancel, and our parson should repair the same' (1591). Another case (1590) confirms local historians' assumption that Manningtree chapel had no graveyard, as it was only a chapel-of-ease to Mistley. The 'old' wardens of Manningtree were not overlooked by their successors because of 'three graves in the church of Mistley uncovered with brick or pavement by reason the churchwardens of last year received money for them and have not covered them, neither allowed the money to cover them'. One confessed having received 5s. from executors. Six years earlier, Robert Glascock of Manningtree 'did bury his wife in the church and did not cover her grave and hath not paid the noble' (6s. 8d.). Again, it is Mistley church that is referred to, and this is further confirmed by his will (proved 1596), in which he termed himself a gentleman, and desired to be buried 'in the parish church of Mistley near Frances my first wife'.

In 1586 William Laytham of Cranham (he owned the small manor of Berdens) had 'refused to pay for the burying of two of his children in the church and breaking of the ground'. He stated that 'he refused to pay it to Mr. Widgarten for that he is not a friend but offered it to his fellows', and he was instructed to pay 'according to the ancient custom', which was of course a general one. Joan Cowle of Hempstead, widow, was charged in 1599 not only with 'digging up the church for her husband's burial' without the wardens' consent, but also for not paying. Next month Mr. John Westlye appeared and paid 16d., apparently as an act of charity (the Westleys owned one of the Hempstead manors). In 1578 John Cliff, executor of Edmund Tyrrell's widow, had to answer because 'the place in the church of Rawreth where Mr. Tyrrell was buried lieth unseemly uncovered'. But 'Mr. Brasier rector of Ingatestone attended the Court and undertook to repair before Michaelmas'. Cliff is known to have been one of Sir William Petre's executors. Tyrell was an overseer of Petre's will[1] and was lord of the manor of Beches in Rawreth; he had died in 1576, and was buried in the south aisle. In 1580 Richard Eve 'of Chignal Mary and James', executor of John Eve of Bedells Hall (in Chignal St. James), was reprimanded because 'there is not a stone laid upon his grave'. He said that John, while he lived, was himself executor of Thomas Eve, late vicar of Little Leighs, and that Thomas was buried in the chancel, 'which grave is yet uncovered'; he was ordered to cover it before Easter.

Despite the subject of death, there is much colourful detail in Elizabethan wills about 'sepulture', including burial of affluent testators in church or chancel; this will be related in the next volume. The great majority of people were of course not buried in coffins but were laid in a grave, the corpse being wrapped only in a woollen 'shroud'.

The spiritual aspect of burial is reflected in consequence of various usages differing from those set out in the Prayer Book, either in the absence of a proper service or in the unlawful burial of excommunicated persons. A strange indictment brought Thomas Tirrell, curate of East Mersea, to the court in 1581. 'He is unquiet among his neighbours, also he refuseth to bury the dead, accounting them his neighbours as dead, and therefore saying, "Let the dead bury the dead".' In 1584 John Knighte of Fryerning 'brought one of Mr. Butler's men, being dead, and for that the minister of the town, who had no authority to bury the said corpse (for that he dwelt not in the parish); Knighte buried it without any minister being present, contrary to law, as it is commonly reported'. He denied the charge, 'saying that he was one of them that brought the corpse to the church, and he requested Mr. Clercke to bury the corpse, and he refused to do it; and upon his refusal the corpse was buried by others, and not by him, but by whom he knoweth not'. The result was that he had to purge with three neighbours, John Clarke was curate of Fryerning,[2] and the deceased servant's master was presumably John Butler, J.P., of Thoby Priory in the adjacent parish of Mountnessing.

Under 1587 four presentments for unlawful burial by laymen are found. The first came from Bradfield and lay against Bartholomew Jennynges, a yeoman there, for burying of two soldiers found dead in his field or marsh by the high constables, without Christian burial or a note of their names in the register book, because 'there was no convenient churchyard near at hand, and that they did savour (i.e. smell), did bury them for pity's sake in the field'. At the next session Robert Wharton, also of Bradfield, who was accused of 'burying a soldier in a ditch in the fields', was admonished and dismissed. The others came from Colchester. Richard Langley of Trinity parish 'did bury in church without the form of burial in the Book of Common Prayer; the minister, Mr. Gold, was absent' (Robert Good,

[1] Emmison, *Tudor Secretary*, 290. [2] Dr. Anglin's thesis, 349.

rector). The latter, however, said that 'he was at home, but was not desired to come, and that Thomas Langley was the father of the child'. Marmaduke Young of St. Botolph 'buried the dead without prayers'; and Henry Vincent of St. Giles 'did bury John Pye without prayers, Mr. Cocke their minister being absent'. Next year the wardens of SS. Peter and Runwald, Colchester, were cited to explain why 'there hath been no divine service these two years, neither is there no minister at this present, and there was a child died with cold, not be gotten to be buried by any minister'. (The benefice of St. Runwald was so small that the advowson had lapsed to the Bishop in 1544; St. Peter's church, on the other hand, was reckoned as the chief church in the town, but presentation had also lapsed temporarily to the Bishop, who collated Thomas Taverner in 1589.) Also in 1588 the Dedham wardens reported William Elmes 'for burying the dead', adding, 'One Mother Gyrton of the parish, being dead, he (Elmes) being sexton did make a grave for her, and there she was laid in by them who brought her to the church, without the service of burial. William Butter, a layman of the same town, did put in the earth and filled up the grave, and said he would answer for that his so doing. Elmes said he durst not do it, by reason that he was in trouble for the like before.'

In 1589 two Romford defendants, Thomas Charvile and John Bennet, referred to the family which lived at the manor house of Stewards in Romford and to the troublesome puritan schoolmaster. 'At the request of Mistress Quarles they did bury a maidservant of Mr. Quarles without any ceremony and not according to the communion (*sic*) book.' Charvile asserted that 'he being one that did help to make the grave, Mistress Quarles did command him to throw earth upon her; and he demanded who should bury her; Mr. Leche standing by answered, "All we here present", who then threw the earth on her and covered her'. The maid's dame was the wife of James Quarles, Surveyor General of the Victualling of the Navy, who died in 1599. Three years after this incident, Mistress Quarles was to give birth to Francis, the future pious poet and author of *Divine Emblems* (1635). The active party was John Leche, the master of Romford charity school, a frequent defendant in the court.

In 1593 'Mr. Bainbrigg, minister of Norton Mandeville' (Thomas Bainbrick, holder of the curacy), was in mild disgrace, but explained that 'he did not go to the grave according to the Book of Common Prayer by reason of a great wind, and not being well he durst not go into the danger of taking cold in the air, but he saith that he read the whole service'. He was enjoined on the next Sunday to acknowledge that 'he had omitted his duty in not burying the dead corpse of one Father Cooke'. Two years later the court learned that 'Mr. Shawe, rector of Chingford, hath not served the cure about three Sundays since Christtide, and parishioners die and some are fain to stay still unburied till a minister be gotten'.

Notice of death had to be given to the minister. Failure to do so led to presentments in 1572 against John Woodward of Woodham Ferrers, who, 'when his wife lay in passage and so departed this world, gave no knowledge to the minister to come to her and counsel her in the time of her sickness'. His defence, which was accepted, was that 'his wife died so sudden of the squinzy that he could not make the parson privy' (squinzy, or quinsy, was suppurative tonsillitis). Against normal customs one churchwarden anticipated the dealing with mortal remains in 1589: John Miller of Great Horkesley 'did intermeddle to serve the carcase of a dead body of one (blank) an old woman before any other came unto her, to the great offence of the whole parish'.

A macabre incident interrupted a funeral at Wrabness in 1598. The wardens brought Thomas Bett, a parishioner, before the court because 'he did go into the grave made for the body of Edward Godfrie and did there arrest the body with very unseemly, unrelevant and intemperate speech, whereby our minister would not bury him or read the burial service for him'. Bett was ordered to produce four compurgators. The rector was also presented for 'denying' the burial. According to ancient folklore, the burying of a debtor might be held up by 'arrest'; but there was no legal foundation for such action. It is possible that the case arose from a late survival of the superstitition, but more likely the accused was giving vent to his dislike of Bett for the last time: in churlish contrast to Hamlet's sorrow at Yorick's graveside.

It was the churchwardens' duty to see that a bier was always available, and in 1597 those of Witham, which 'wanteth a hearse', were told to provide one.

By Canon 67 (1603), 'when any is passing out of life, a bell shall be tolled, and the minister shall not then slack to do his last duty. And after the party's death (if it so fall out), there shall be rung no more but one short peal, and one other before the burial and one other after the burial'.[1] Of the three references to knells, two originated in 1603, a few months before the Canons were issued. The first, 'not paying the clerk's wages for the knell and ringing at the funerals of his wife and daughter', resulted in an injunction to pay the fee; the second was brought against John Todde, vicar of Great Bentley, 'because he would not let the bell be tolled or knell rung when the corpse of Humphrey Searles' wife was brought to be buried'. In 1599 Robert Hanger of Walthamstow, 'indebted to the parish for ringing of a knell at the death of his son, 16d., obstinately refuseth to pay, contrary to order and custom'.

Tolling the passing-bell was for some unexplained reason disregarded by John Coker, sexton of Goldhanger, in 1591. 'Requested to ring the bell for John Birtche when he lay upon his deathbed, he did refuse'. This he denied and was assigned to purge with three parishioners. No certificate

[1] Burn, *op. cit.*, i, 96.

of his purgation was received at the next two sessions, but at the third he was up again, for 'disturbing Roger Cowper, one of the churchwardens, and offering to strike him and miscalled him otherwise' (perhaps for reporting him the first time); he was then suspended from ingress to the church. The court, however, received a counter-accusation by Coker that he had been slandered by Cowper, who had to answer no less than seven additional charges for defamation, as already related.

Two prosecutions for illegal ringing are found in 1585, one from each archdeaconry. Thomas Robient of Blackmore, cited for 'encouraging of ringers to ring unlawfully', answered that 'the next day of the solemnization he caused some of his neighbours to ring one peal, which he thought he might do', a plea which was accepted but he had to confess in church and pay 6d. to the poor. Guners Grevers of Great Bardfield 'called us the churchwardens knaves and fools in the church for forbidding him to ring more than one peal after Mr. Sergeant Benlowes' burial'. He was suspended from ingress to the church and commanded 'to ask the churchwardens openly for their forgivenness'. His tart retort: 'I had rather see the churchwardens' hearts out', on which penance was prescribed, but he contemptuously answered, 'I will not do it'. The fine tomb and house (Place House) of William Bendlowes, serjeant-at-law, may still be seen at Bardfield.

A peculiar entry was made in 1597. 'We present Richard Swetman of Ingatestone,' the wardens stated, 'as author of disorder in that when one was drunk he caused the bell to be tolled.' To this he replied, 'There was a friend of his which had an impostume broken on him the night before and he found him without breath, and then he caused him to be tolled for'. (An impostume is a purulent swelling or abscess.) If he believed the man to be dying, his plea was justified, but the judge ordered penance.

Swetman may not have been a humorist, but death and burial customs produced some buffoonery at other funerals. Practical jokers or the like had to appear on four occasions. John Copland of Coggeshall 'caused the bell to be tolled as though he were at the point of death, yet being in health' (1586). Admitting the trick, he was instructed to acknowledge his guilt before the minister and the wardens. Two other townsmen had also been cited: Ralph Reve, who said he was 'the messenger to go to the clerk to cause the bell to be tolled', and Robert Pickett the church clerk. William Francis of Wivenhoe 'caused his boy to ring the bell as if he had been dead but denieth that he was either then drunk or at any other time' (1592). Enjoined to find as many as six compurgators, he failed to produce them. Doubtless when he obeyed the order to confess 'in face of the church' the congregation relished the change from the many penances. A prank at East Tilbury in 1600 led the warden, 'upon the report of the sexton', to present four men and women for 'carrying William Goodin upon the old hearse in the churchyard', and a fifth for 'aiding in ringing the bells'.

The doggerel made up by John Sherwood of Dedham (or was he reciting an unrecorded version of a popular rhyme?) doubtless failed to amuse the judge who had unsuccessfully tried to secure his attendance, because the registrar noted, 'He is in the Queen's works at Harwich'. This must refer to the strengthening of the fortifications against the threatened invasion by the Armada: the case came up in January 1588. At any rate, he was charged with 'burying of the dead, being a layman', and the words he used were:

Three blind mice, a hog and a dog,
A pig in a pocket,
The miller and his man,
For a diddle diddle,
Go knave go,
One knave bury another.

In earlier days, on the death of a parishioner, it was customary in some places for executors to give the minister the best, or second best, beast or article of clothing. In theory this was a recompense for tithes that he had omitted to pay during his lifetime. Whereas the lord of a manor claimed by right the best beast as a heriot, the giving of a mortuary depended entirely on the custom of each parish. Where it prevailed, a mortuary was held to be a debt for which the minister could sue in the secular courts. But by the Act of 21 Henry VIII, c.6 (1529), its value was fixed as money payment: 10s. if the deceased's movable goods were worth £40 or more, graduated to nothing if worth less than £6 13s. 4d. Lists of mortuary payments are written in a few Essex parish registers, and by old-established custom of the Sokens parishes the 'best upper garment' was still being given as late as 1707 at Kirby-le-Soken.[1]

Apart from the charge of extortionately taking 10s. which Thomas Austen, vicar of Aveley, had to answer in 1598 both in the archdeacon's court and at Quarter Sessions,[2] the act books give only a solitary case, under 1589. Robert Edmunds, rector of East Mersea, was accused because 'without authority and warrant he retained in his possession a gown of Nicholas Adye, late of East Mersea, deceased'. The rector alleged that, 'by an ancient custom used in the parish of East Mersea and also of West Mersea, viz. that everyone dying there, not having dwelling in the same parish by the space of a year and a day, there is due to the parson his best garment'; and Adye 'had not dwelt there by the space of a year before his death'. The judge awarded the gown to the rector. While awaiting trial, he had been directed by the court to leave it with widow Cowdge, 'the hostess of the White Hart at Colchester'. So the custom was upheld.

[1] Emmison (ed.), *Catalogue of Essex Parish Records* (1966), 142.
[2] *E.L.: Disorder*, 90–1.

5

The Church Settlement and the Visitations of the Archdeaconry of Essex, 1561–65

A reasonably good picture of the effect of the Religious Settlement of 1559, though virtually confined to about one-third of Essex, is afforded by the records of one archdeaconry for 1561–65; but there is none showing the immediate reactions of the clergy and laity to the Settlement as laid down in the Act of Uniformity and the Royal Injunctions of 1559.

Three act books have been preserved for the Archdeaconry of Essex for September 1561 to April 1562 and for August 1563 to April 1565, also one for the Bishop's Commissary in Essex and Herts. (with cases from about twenty Essex parishes) for July 1561 to July 1562. The four books give the proceedings taken at the visitations, chiefly as a result of the parochial presentments, as well as the minutes of the normal inter-visitation sessions. A different form of record (and the only one of its type for our period) is contained in a thin register into which were fair-copied the returns from the parishes within the jurisdiction of the Archdeacon of Essex, received at his autumn visitation in 1565; but the act book recording action taken on these reports is not extant.[1] Preserved also are three 'visitation books' for the Archdeaconry of Colchester, 1586–88 and 1597–1603, but they contain only the names of the clergy and churchwardens.[2]

All five volumes have a fair amount of detail showing the various defects in carrying out the regulations of 1559 on the part of the churchwardens and the laity – chiefly alterations in the church fabric, furniture and vestments to conform with the prescribed order of worship, parishioners' non-attendance, and clerical non-residence and plurality. A more general picture of dilapidated churches and chancels from 1566 onwards is afforded in the chapter on the Buildings. The interesting question arises, How effective were the visitations? Although much credit is undoubtedly due to the sustained efforts of the archdeacons' courts, it is very difficult to generalize, and the answer may fairly be left to the reader's judgement.

Visitation records for archdeaconries elsewhere in the country yield very similar evidence. Nor do those for the following century differ greatly

[1] There are also Colchester archdeaconry visitation records for 1540–45 in the E.R.O., but many of the entries are illegible. Extracts were printed in W. H. Hale, *A Series of Precedents and Proceedings in Criminal Cases, 1475–1640*. For a more accessible summary, also Essex details of the royal visitation of 1547, see J. E. Oxley, *The Reformation in Essex*, 145–52.

[2] See *Ess. Rev.*, xxxii, 132–37.

in the overall picture they present: the lack of care of churches, chancels, churchyard walls, and church furnishings, non-residence of the incumbent, and so forth, are all commonplace items. The post-1603 detailed visitation books for the rural deanery of Colchester, 1633, the Archdeaconry of Colchester, 1683, and the Archdeaconry of Essex, 1683–86, which are the only other pre-1700 Essex returns that have been preserved, are printed in full.[1]

No printed or manuscript visitation articles (i.e. questionnaires) for the Essex archdeaconries are known to the writer, but those for the Archdeconries of Colchester, 1633, and Middlesex, 1582, were published.[2]

The Catholic Church structure which Mary had taken such pains to restore was mainly levelled to the ground in 1559 by the Acts of Supremacy and Uniformity. Elizabeth secured from Parliament the renowned Settlement – the *Via Media* between the drastic reforms under Edward and the equally stern measures under Mary. Thenceforward the worship and doctrine of the Anglican Church were to be based on Edward VI's Second Prayer Book, as slightly revised by a committee of divines presided over by Sir Thomas Smith (the future builder of Hill Hall, Theydon Mount), and in turn restored in 1559. A uniform service thus became compulsory: a double obligation – on the clergy, to adhere strictly to the ritual laid down in the Prayer Book; on the laity, to attend Morning and Evening Prayer and to receive the Lord's Supper. But some details of worship, as will be seen, were not rigidly established until well after the issue of the Injunctions.

After the violent and rapid swings of the politico-religious pendulum, the great mass of the ordinary people welcomed the compromise and conformed. There remained on the one hand those who adhered to the Old Faith, and on the other those who deplored nearly all ritual. There was a fourth category, sometimes overlooked by historians: the ungodly, who were indifferent to the Church Settlement and figure so frequently in the archidiaconal archives. The clergy, to some extent, also fell into the same four groups. The vast majority took the oath and observed the prescribed services. A small number of devout Catholic priests resigned their benefices soon after the Settlement that left them no alternative, so they virtually pass out of the story. The Puritan clergy, difficult to define precisely in any Elizabethan decade, appear one after another as offenders against the regulations. Ironically, they attended the courts in company with their clerical opposites – gamesters, drunkards, brawlers, lechers – most of whom were presented by their own churchwardens.

'The Prayer Book', in the words of the most detailed book on ritual, 'conceives of each service in the liturgy as the work of the whole body of

[1] *Trans. E.A.S.*, xi (1633); xxiii (1683); xix–xxiii (1683–86). For a detailed note and bibliography of visitations, see D. M. Owen, *The Records of the Established Church in England* (1970), 30–35.

[2] Copies of both are in the E.R.O.

the faithful; medieval churches with their screens separating clergy and laity, and the laity from the altar, tended to make the faithful largely onlookers and the liturgy the peculiar and exclusive work of the clergy. It was clearly impossible to pull down the churches and build others more suitable, and the authorities instead took the course of re-arranging our churches for the congregational liturgical worship of the Prayer Book.'[1]

Edmund Grindal, the first Elizabethan Bishop of London, exhorted the clergy and churchwardens in his diocese (including of course Essex) to demolish the stone high altars and to provide a communion table in its place: an iconoclastic disaster which deprived England of so much good work. Under the Injunctions roods and rood-lofts had to be taken down. Any shrines and images, mural paintings or other pictures that had survived the Edwardian destruction were now to be removed as idolatrous; but the stained glass was accorded some respite.

The vicar of Radwinter faithfully chronicled the stipulated changes in a concise passage, with a valuable reference to stained-glass:

> Bells and times of morning and evening prayer remain as in times past, saving that all images, shrines, tabernacles, rood-lofts and monuments of idolatry are removed, taken down and defaced; only the stories in glass windows excepted, which, for want of sufficient store of new stuff, and by reason of extreme charge that should grow by the alteration of the same into white panes throughout the realm, are not altogether abolished in most places at once, but by little and little suffered to decay, that white glass may be provided and set up in their rooms. Finally, whereas there was wont to be a great partition between the choir and the body of the church, now it is either very small or none at all, and to say the truth altogether needless, sith the minister saith his service commonly in the body of the church, with his face towards the people, in a little tabernacle of wainscot provided for the purpose.[2]

An illustration of his last point is seen in the court order, made in the same year as Harrison's second edition of the *Description* (1587), for Great Chesterford church in his own deanery: 'To make a pew for the minister in the body of the church to read divine service.' It is to the credit of the Elizabethan clergy and wardens that the stained glass was not smashed in many churches. Iconoclasm had gone far enough, some thought, whether tolerant or just practical-minded; but much of what was then left was swept away by the Cromwellian wave. Fortunately, a few white-washed mural paintings have now been recovered and restored, as at Great Canfield, Little Easton, Fairstead and Little Baddow; and we still have the renowned work at Copford church.

Dealing first with the records for 1561–62, this is what they tell of ritual disobedience. The churchwardens of Hatfield Broadoak still retained 'Latin books of superstition'; John Norryes of Shellow (Bowells), accused

[1] G. W. O. Addleshaw and F. Etchells, *The Architectural Setting of Anglican Worship* (1948); see also H. Gee, *The Elizabethan Prayer Book and Ornaments* (1902). Cf. a series of Lincolnshire returns made in 1566, of church furniture destroyed (E. Peacock, *English Church Furniture*, 1866).

[2] Harrison, *op. cit.*, 35–36.

of having in his hands 'certain books of supersition' belonging to the parish, refuted the charge, and the rector was instructed 'to deface all such books as shall be found'; but John Cree, warden of Leaden Roothing, was able to assure the court that 'the church books be defaced and sold to one Cavell of High Easter, a grocer', whose mundane use for the parchment leaves is obvious. The Stebbing wardens, presented because they had 'sold of the church goods to the value of 20 marks', replied that they had sold 'a cross of silver and a chalice to the value of £6, which is and must be bestowed in the mending of their steeple and church', and they were absolved. Henry Whyte of Little Henny owned land called Cross Croft which had been 'given for certain lights to be burned in the church'. But 'he hath condescended and agreed that he will continually (for that he doth acknowledge it to be a due) pay it yearly for ever to the churchwardens during his life'; in other words, the money rentcharge imposed on the land by the legacy for the lights would be paid into the church funds. These five extracts are from the Commissary's book. In the other book for the same period we find that Edward Nallinghurst of Great Baddow had 'a book of papistry' and Robert Harris of Black Chapel (in Great Waltham) also kept 'divers papistical books', which he was ordered on the following Sunday in the chapel to deface in the people's presence. The only mention of stained glass occurs incidentally. John Rayllde of Buttsbury, informed against by Walter Dawtrye for drunkenness, declared that Rayllde 'said once to the parishioners, when they would have defaced the images in the glass windows, that it was no harm'. Jervice Hylton, rector of Cranham, denying his parishioners' presentment, was enjoined by the judge 'on Sunday to say before them that he did not say *De Profundis*' and to give 4d. to the poor men's box.

Breaches of the Settlement regulations recorded in the act book for 1563–65, apart from the common offences already mentioned, are very few. The court was mainly concerned with altars, communion tables and books, and for these we draw on the act book for 1566 as well as that for 1563–65. The Injunctions of 1559 had decreed that 'the holy table be decently made and set in the place where the altar stood, and so to stand, saving when the Sacrament is to be distributed; at which time the same shall be so placed within the chancel as whereby the minister may be more conveniently heard'. Many stone altars had accordingly been removed. The Settlement, in this as in other ways, attempted a compromise. (As late as 1572 'Chignal SS. Mary and James' had 'no communion table, but a plank lying upon two trestles, undecent'.) Two Kelvedon (Hatch) men were presented 'for that they take on them to remove the table to the place where the altar stood', and a little later the table had still not been set up properly. The farmer (lessee) of Canewdon was charged because 'the place where the altar stands is not paved'; the wardens of St. Lawrence, because the same place had not been 'whitened, nor the steps going to the same paved'; and those of Dunton for 'the hole still at the high altar.' The rector of Rochford was presented because 'vestigia in the chancel' were not removed, which must refer to some remaining traces of images or other 'superstitious' ornaments; and Robert Ynglande of Grays Thurrock had to exhibit his account of the 'church ornaments sold by him for money', the court ordering him to state the name of the purchaser of the 'copes and holywater stock' (stoop). The Cranham wardens 'lack a communion table', for which they were ordered to give 20s. to the poor, a pretty heavy fine, and to do penance in a white sheet. Those of Stapleford Abbots had failed to provide a table of the Commandments and a 'calendar' (of the Church festivals). Dunton and Rettendon lacked a 'decent pulpit'; and both parishes as well as East Hanningfield had no table cloth; Purleigh and Buttsbury had no table of Commandments.

Thomas Bayarde of Mucking and Christopher Eaton of East Tilbury appeared as defendants in a cause of defamation promoted in 1563 by Henry Hoye of Mucking. Eaton had said: 'Hoye did make a shrine of the copper cross and did worship it as a god. These words were spoken in Horndon (on-the-Hill) market'. He added: 'The order of punishment that Mr. Cole (the Archdeacon) did assign Hoye, viz. to stand in a white sheet, he would see it done or else bring Mr. Cole before them that should cause him to be as good as his word.' Bayarde declared: 'Hoye had a velvet cope in his custody and no account of it, and Hoye and Richard Fawcknar had the goods of the church and would not make no accounts of it, also that one Hawle and Hoye did sell away the chalice in hugger mugger.' First recorded in the *Oxford Dictionary* forty years earlier and meaning 'clandestinely', the actual spelling 'howggar mowggar' suggests that Essex folk pronounced it in a way not paralleled elsewhere. No further process in this cause is found. A solitary presentment in 1564 resulted in the South Weald wardens being ordered 'forthwith to cause the superstititious images to be defaced'.

Disobedience in buying books and the like (see p. 260) was presented by Steeple, Magdalen Laver and St. Lawrence, for the Homilies; 'The two tomes of the Homilies, a Bible of the largest volume, and the Paraphrases of Erasmus' were not provided at Ashingdon and had to be bought by the wardens under threat of excommunication; Hockley lacked a similar bible; West Ham and Greenstead had no Paraphrases; North Weald, Blackmore and South Fambridge, a copy of the Articles (of Religion); Fryerning, the Injunctions; and St. Peter, Maldon, 'a register book' (the first book duly starts in 1566). Re-inforcement of these provisions was ordered somewhat later by the next Bishop of London: 'In 1577 and in 1586, Aylmer searched the parishes for old service-books, for vestments and monuments of superstition, asking for a list of the names of those who had such in their possession.'[1] The Injunctions made no mention of the Royal

[1] W. P. M. Kennedy, *Elizabethan Episcopal Administration* (1924), lxv.

Arms, which had been set up in many churches over the rood screen near the end of Henry VIII's reign by the more ardent reforming parishes. After Elizabeth's accession they were usually set up in place of the rood.[1] The interesting presentments for unlawful bell-ringing at Halloweentide have been narrated at the end of the chapter on Religious Offences.

We may now examine the register into which were copied the parochial returns made at the visitation of the Archdeacon of Essex in 1565. But why, except for chancels, does the visitation book omit details of defective church fabrics? The slightly incomplete returns for 139 of the 145 parishes in the seven deaneries disclosed thirty-two chancels in some degree out of repair. (This figure excludes presentments of chancels which still needed white-liming and paving after the removal of the altars.) The majority merely stated that the chancel was 'out of reparations' or 'in decay', or it needed tiling or glazing, without further details; but 'shortly it shall be done' is added for South Ockendon. Wickford reported that 'the chancel windows this winter fell in decay and so are, but this summer are promised to be amended'; and at Lambourne 'one great glass window is decayed', referring perhaps to the east window. The roof or tiling of several other chancels was definitely in need of attention. At Woodham Ferrers 'the birds come in and they make a foul church'; at East Ham 'the fowls come in and bewray the communion table with their dung'; and at North Weald 'the chancel is dry hanged with tile whereby it snoweth in some time'. More serious was the condition of the chancels at Ramsden Bellhouse ('in great ruin and decay'), at Chingford ('the arches of the chancel wall are in decay and so fallen down'), and at Steeple ('fallen down').

In three instances the lay rector was named. At Dagenham 'the high chancel is not repaired as yet, Justice Browne (Sir Anthony Browne) to be at the charges thereof'; 'Richard Bowland should do (it)' at Margaretting; and the chancel of East Tilbury was 'in great decay whereby the church is much annoyed, the Queen's Majesty being patron'.

While so many churches were deteriorating through neglect, enforced inconoclasm and other destruction had been taking toll inside the buildings as a result of the Royal Injunctions.

Delays in removing the rood loft were referred to in several parishes. 'Certain boards over the rood loft remain unpulled down' (Bulphan); 'One part remaineth as yet undefaced' (West Horndon); 'The rood loft is pulled down one part of it, and the rest is left for fear of the church falling' (West Horndon); 'The holes of the rood loft where the posts were in be not stopped up as yet' (Loughton). At Vange, 'The quire is unpaved and the place where the altar stood not whited, but is as it was when the altar was plucked down, and it is all unglazed'. 'The place' (or 'the

[1] See the article on 'The Custom of setting up Royal Arms in Churches '(*Trans. E.A.S.*, vi, 22–27).

chancel') 'where the altar stood is not paved nor the wall whitened', or a similar phrase, occurs twelve times. Only at West Horndon church, 'Some part of the altars be taken away and defaced but some part there are yet remaining'. A unique entry is made under St. Peter, Maldon: 'There is an altar standing still in the spittle, to the offence of the people, the bearer thereof is one Edward Harvey of Langford.' (The slight remains of the leper hospital still stand.)

'The imagery in the glass windows are not all defaced' was the position in Stanford Rivers; and 'There is a beam whereon was wont to stand a light before an image called Our Lady, which Mr. Tyrrell will not suffer to be pulled down' at Little Warley; these are solitary items. Perhaps John Tyrrell, the Catholic lord of the manor, still hoped that the religious tide would turn once again and he would then be able to replace the light.

The renowned Saxon church of Greenstead-by-Ongar was the only one the wardens of which confessed to having no communion cup (its present cup is dated 1739). The communion tables were not in order at Little Thurrock ('not lawful'), or Childerditch and Stapleford Tawney ('not decent'), while those in four churches lacked covers; and unsatisfactory reports about the pulpits came from Loughton, Stanford Rivers and Ashingdon ('insufficient' or 'not decent').

A 'bible of the largest size' had not been acquired by the wardens of three parishes; a psalter or a service book in another three parishes; and the *Paraphrases of Erasmus*, or the *Book of Homilies*, or both, were still lacking in eleven parishes. Chingford wardens admitted, 'The Latin books remain in the vestry undefaced'; Great Waltham reported that they had 'sold one chalice to maintain their church withal'; and Runwell stated, 'All the church goods are heretofore sold saving since the visitation last we translated our chalice into a communion cup', as explained in the section on Church Plate.

Disobedience regarding vestments was reported only from South Ockendon, where 'there be certain vestments and other church goods used in the time of popery undefaced'. Great Baddow had 'sold unto Mr. Latham of Sandon certain copes and vestments', of which no details are given. For a third parish, however, what is probably the last list of pre-Reformation Essex church vestments is recorded: 'South Weald. There were sold by the bishop's warrant one cope of white damask, two vestments of blue velvet, one old cope of blue damask, one vestment and a cope of bridges (Bruges) satin, two old tunicles of Turkey silk, two old vestments of fustian, and one altar cloth of imagery work', which were sold to four named men. (A tunical was worn by a sub-deacon over the alb at the Eucharist.) The inventory of all the church goods (including plate) of South Weald, 1552, had listed nineteen vestments, of which 'the cope of white damask and the vestment of the same', together with 'the cloth to the communion table', were the only items of this kind authorized by the commissioners to remain in use; the rest, as elsewhere, were to be appropriated.[1] It looks as though the articles in the 1565 list, most of which are identifiable with items in that of 1552, were surreptitiously withheld at the time. In 1580 Thomas Hobson of Prittlewell and Henry Tyler of Southchurch were accused of 'detaining certain copes and vestments, when they were dwellers in Sutton, and never made any account of them to the parishioners, neither have delivered the same'. Hobson appeared and admitted that he had 'his part of a cope and a vestment about the value of 5s. for his part, which were defaced about twenty years past'. This sum he was instructed to pay to the church-wardens. Eight years later William Felde of West Mersea was presented for having 'a cope which he keepeth of a superstitious mind'. Thus some of the last known vestiges of Romish practices were suppressed. Doubtless a few remained, secretly preserved by faithful Catholics.

The walls or fences of twenty-five churchyards were related to be 'in decay' (Stapleford Abbots 'in great decay'), in need of repair, or lacking in part. At Little Warley, the liability for maintenance was for 'the east part, which the farmer (lessee) of Childerditch Hall has always made'; at Hockley, 'the vicarage must fence the churchyard from the mansion house to the stile that goeth down to the parsonage'; part of the Shenfield church-yard fence was the parson's responsibility; and at Greenstead-by-Ongar, 'Mr. Wood should make the fence of the churchyard, about a rood thereof'. At West Tilbury, 'the churchyard walls are broken down and are (i.e. ought) to be repaired by the parson and the parish'. The South Ockendon return stated that 'the churchyard house is burned, so that the fence of the churchyard there is open'. A churchyard gate was unrepaired or lacking in two parishes.

Fourteen parsonages (i.e. rectories) and vicarages were in need of attention. At Ramsden Bellhouse, 'the mansion (i.e. dwelling) house is in great ruin and decay'; the North Shoebury 'vicarage house is in decay and needeth both timber work and groundselling'; and the Bradwell-juxta-Mare 'parsonage is out of reparations in tiling, daubing and timber work'. In addition, five parishes referred to the barn, stable, or 'houses' (outhouses) being out of repair or fallen down; at Cranham, for instance, 'the barn was burned and is not yet builded, contrary to the Injunctions'.

Of the 139 parishes which sent in their 'bills' in 1565, 36 specifically stated that their minister was non-resident – a disgraceful state of affairs, though a few lived in their other benefice. Nine of the 36 had failed to distribute the prescribed one-fortieth part of the income of the benefice to the poor, and two had not 'kept hospitality'; one resident was also in default for his 40th. The vicar of Hockley (Rowland Noble), who 'dwelleth at Kirby Kendal' (Westmorland), had been absent ever since the Queen's accession, 'saving once', and was to be cited; George Colborne, parson of

[1] *Trans. E.A.S.*, n.s., ii, 181–83.

Little Warley for five years; and the parson of Shenfield for 1¼ years, 'neither do they know where he is' (William Newhouse was deprived in 1567). The parishioners of Stapleford Abbots declared, 'They know not whether their minister be licensed to serve or not, or whether he be learned', which suggests that although the residence of the rector (John Bennet, 1560–72) was in his other and neighbouring parish of Epping, he never or rarely appeared at Stapleford Abbots. The rector of Great Warley (John Sherebourne) was not only absent but 'left his benefice unto rude and unlearned persons from Michaelmas last unto Our Lady Day last'. Two parishes were apparently almost bereft: Havering stated, 'They have a reader whose name is John Brockas, and no minister'; and Mundon, where the vicar (probably Henry Williams) was non-resident, 'We have no curate, but a sufficient reader'. The parson of Wickford had three benefices, 'one in Runwell, another in London'; but the parish exonerated him from non-residence because 'Mr. Wright' (the rector) 'and Mr. Bryce' between them had delivered the 'four quarter sermons'. Henry Wright, in fact, even preached elsewhere, as Downham parish stated that, of their four sermons, two had been given by 'Mr. Ankle' and one each by Wright and Brice, possibly because Segare Nicholson, the rector, was on his death-bed (his successor was instituted in September 1565). On the vexed matter of pluralism, nine incumbents each possessed two livings, but two of these were stated to be resident in the parish which made the return. It is possible that a few others were non-resident, or seldom resident, because of the number of parishes which returned a lack of the minimum of four quarterly sermons. Eight parishes had had none and four only one; five had two sermons, and one parish, Stapleford Tawney, had three, 'the one by Mr. Douglas the other two by Mr. Mullins' (John Hanson was rector).

The campaign against the clergy who had not delivered their quarterly sermons is seen to have begun in June 1564: at least twenty-four incumbents were presented before the end of 1566, together with the farmers of the rectories of seven further parishes. The same two act books for 1563–66 name sixteen non-resident ministers, four of whom were pluralists, including the rector of Dengie (Edward Morecroft), who was in Italy, and a fifth, the rector of Woodham Walter (William Dawes), who held three benefices; in addition there were six other pluralists, the rector of Runwell (Thomas Forster?) holding also the benefices of Wickford and St. Stephen, London. (A few pluralists were prosecuted in later years, for example, John Becham, rector of Springfield Boswell, in 1576: 'He is not resident upon his benefice, not letteth it to a sufficient curate.')

'The youth hath not been instructed in the catechism as they ought to be' was reported by eleven parishes: in four of them it was the parson's or the curate's fault. South Ockendon admitted, 'The parish is somewhat slack in sending their youth to be instructed by the curate on the holy days and Sundays', and at Stanford Rivers 'there are no children brought in as yet to the minister'. The Bowers Gifford officers were prepared to share the blame with the curate, 'who hath taught the youth and instructed them in the catechism on divers Sundays and holy days, but not so often as the Injunctions doth will him to do, neither hath the parish resorted to the curate so oft as the Injunctions commanded'. At Stapleford Abbots the youth were not taught the Commandments, and at Buttsbury 'the parson hath not examined the parents neither the godfather nor godmother of their belief in the time of baptism nor when they should receive, neither hath instructed the youth in the catechism'. South Benfleet thought poorly of their vicar, who was 'not meet to instruct the children'.

Three schoolteachers of a sort are mentioned. At Ramsden Bellhouse, 'one Mr. Spacie sometime their curate teacheth children their absye (i.e. ABC), whether he be licensed or no they know not'; and at West Tilbury 'John Goose teacheth certain of the youth of the parish the absy and to read, unlicensed'. Horndon-on-the-Hill presented that 'a Thomas Mericke doth keep a school without licence of any Ordinary', i.e. bishop or archdeacon.

'The declaration touching the principal Articles of Religion' had not been read in five parishes; of these, Bowers Gifford not only referred to the Articles but also to the Queen's Injunctions, which had not been read every quarter.

So far we have seen what defects the Visitation of 1565 disclosed mainly through the neglect of the clergy, churchwardens and lay rectors. Coming to the laity, the largest number of absentees from service (11) was at High Ongar. Four are named in each of three other parishes, but the remaining places reporting non-attendance mention fewer or only single absentees: a total of only 31, apart from South Weald, which parish 'is so great that they (i.e. the wardens) know them not by name, but they know none to be obstinately absent'; it certainly was a large one and included the market-town of Brentwood. A Chigwell man was presented for carting 'a load of stuff on Sunday being Christmas Even' as well as being away from church on two other Sundays. This, however, is far from being a complete picture for the archdeaconry. Although a few persons had merely missed one Sunday, some parishes evidently saw fit to present only the worst offenders or those who had been 'slack'. At North Benfleet a man and his wife were accused of not receiving communion for two years and for absence from service on twenty Sundays in the past year; Shenfield mentioned three who either 'kept ill rule in service time' or 'danceth the morris in service time'; and East Hanningfield, which named only one person for four Sundays, added, 'The churchwardens have not levied the sum of 12d. for every one absenting himself from the church'.

The returns make it clear that a much larger number had failed to receive communion. In those parishes for which figures are given, the defaulters total 96, of whom a few had communicated only once in two years. Cranham stated, 'None of the parish have received three times in the year, but at Easter they have received all'; North Weald, 'All the parishioners have not received this late year three times'; South Weald, 'A great number whose names we know not have not received thrice in the year'. Among other places, 'Many have not received three times for default of a minister' at Great Warley, 'divers' at Bradwell-juxta-Mare and Shelley, and 'divers' of the youth both men and women not three times' at Wennington, a somewhat exaggerated phrase for a parish with a very small population. The seven absentees at South Shoebury included 'the parson's wife', and 'my Lord Morley's man' and 'Mr. Silyard's man' at West Hanningfield. A Ramsden Bellhouse man's offence was due to another having 'requested of the curate not to minister the communion to him until he had talked with the justice to know whether he might have law of him or not'; and 'Mr. Woodd (of Broomfield) being troubled in the law hath absented himself two Sundays'. Three non-communicants were specially named as 'an evil liver', 'an unquiet woman', or 'a troublesome woman'. One parson received a woman 'who was out of charity with her neighbours'; such persons being forbidden by the Church to have the sacrament, instances of which we have already noted.

Beating the bounds at West Tilbury led to the parish reporting, 'John Goose' (the unlicensed teacher referred to above) 'hath spoken certain words against the going about in the Rogation Week to see the limits of the parish, saying, "Is there an idol here to be worshipped that you have a drinking here to the offence of the hearers?"' According to the Injunctions, which forbade 'feastings, handbells and lights' during perambulation as savouring of 'superstitious' practices, the charge should have been laid against the parish, not against Goose.

The parish officers were in no way concerned with probate of wills, which was always rigorously controlled by the Church courts. But their returns revealed several cases of non-payment of legacies to the poor. Details will be given in the next volume, which will deal with Wills and the Poor generally.

Turning to moral offences, the eleven bastardy cases included one about parents who subsequently married and one runaway father. Walthamstow stated that a man had committed bigamy, a child having been born ten days afterwards. Four pregnant wenches were mentioned, two being maidservants who had left their masters. Harbouring pregnant girls is referred to five times; at Cranham 'the parson keepeth a suspect woman in his house'; and a Romford wife 'played the harlot and is driven out of the town'. Very few other sexual offences were reported: four cases of suspected incontinence, two of suspected adultery, and at Stanford-le-Hope 'they think it not convenient' for two unmarried persons to 'dwell together'. On the other hand, seven married couples who 'lived apart' were named; of these, a woman 'brought a testimonial of her honesty', and a man who 'doth not use his wife according as he ought to do, neither keepeth her company', perhaps had a sexually unsatisfied spouse who complained about her marital rights.

The visitation returns produced four drunkards. They included, in the words of the wardens of Chignal 'Mary and James', their 'parson, a drunkard and a haunter of alehouses and not meet to serve any cure' (William Johnson). Stanford Rivers was pestered by two 'scolds' (one of each sex); Chipping Ongar by two 'brawlers and scolders' (man and wife); and at Ashingdon a man and his wife were 'breakers of Christian love and charity between their neighbours'. Slanderers were reported from two parishes. Prittlewell's return concentrated solely on John Vincent, a butcher, who not only 'did misuse the vicar and did opprobriously miscall him', but was also 'an ungodly man and hath tempted divers women to lewdness; furthermore, he did not receive (communion) this twelve months'.

It is with the removal of rood-lofts (and even roods) that later books reveal more evidence of wilful procrastination; removal of the screen was optional. For some years after the 1565 Visitation reports about rood-lofts continued to be made, such as 'The rood loft not clean defaced' (Bobbingworth, 1570) and 'Not pulling down the residue of the rood loft' (Widford, 1569). The most outstanding case concerned that at West Horndon, which had been presented in 1565. Home of Lord Mordaunt, a staunch Catholic, no action had been taken to comply with the instructions. 'The rood not pulled down' (1569): a glaring instance of disobedience. From Ingrave, too, whence one of the wardens appeared (also 1569), the Archdeacon demanded to know 'why the rood loft is not clean plucked down'. He was informed that 'he (the warden) told my Lord Mordaunt thereof, and he said that Mr. Official should send some to pull it down. In 1572 the West Horndon wardens were again charged because 'some part of the rood loft standeth'. At the next session they declared that 'they had taken it down accordingly', and were dismissed. In the same year the loft remained at Upminster. 'The rood is still standing' was the indictment against the South Benfleet wardens in 1574, and this and rood beam at Rayleigh were to be removed forthwith. The final presentment is recorded in 1581, when 'the bottom of the rood loft' had to be dealt with in that tiny Catholic stronghold, Little Sampford. Preserved clandestinely by the wardens, the rood-loft in North Weald church is the sole complete survival in Essex.[1]

Among the very few post-1565 presentments for infringements of the Settlement is a composite one against John Exceter and William Fuller,

[1] *R.C.H.M.*, *Essex*, ii, 198 (confirmed by general index).

wardens of Shenfield in 1568, because 'the churchyard lieth open that a child was pulled out of the ground, the altar-stone standeth in the chapel, and they lack a cover for the communion cup and a book of homily of the first tome'. Exceter was also charged with carting on Sunday, for which he had to give 3s. 4d. to the parish poor, but was later released from payment.

Apart from the very few remaining pre-Reformation examples of imagery reported at the visitation of 1565, popish idolatry is not referred to later, except incidentally in 1583, when both the wardens and the rector of Fyfield were cited, and the successive entries are among the more informative found. Against the wardens: 'Their church windows is so painted that the minister cannot see to say service in the afternoon, it is so dark; their Ten Commandments are hanged up so high that they cannot read them; also the youth of the parish doth take up the stools where the parishioners should sit, and they lack room.' Against the rector: 'The pews in the chancel is pulled down and the roof of the chancel lacketh reparations; also there standeth a ladder in the middle of the chancel where the communion table should stand.' Was this consequently the time when the stained glass, which had survived the Reformation, was replaced by ordinary glass?

6

The Clergy

Liturgical and Ritual Offences

The Act of Uniformity (1559), with the prescribed order for Divine Service in the Book of Common Prayer, and the Royal Injunctions (1559), followed by Archbishop Parker's first visitation (1559) and the two Archdeacons' first visitations, had set the ecclesiastical stage in Essex, much as elsewhere, for the trial of dissident members of the clergy. Wilful nonconformity and disobedience or slackness on the part of layman have already been related in the chapter on Religious Offences, together with minor transgressions by clerics and laymen in the sections on Baptism, Marriage and Burial. We shall now try to describe briefly the various aspects of clerical nonconformity in the period after the visitation of 1565.[1]

Church historians have concentrated chiefly on the reactions of the clergy to the Settlement and on the puritan and other 'godly' ministers, as seen in the central and diocesan records.[2] Some use has recently been made of archidiaconal archives in relation to the clergy, but research has been negligible in so far as the conduct of the laity was concerned: hence our attempt in other chapters to cultivate this little-worked soil. The potential yield having regard to the rich Essex ground was obviously high: only the reader can judge the quality of the crop we have tried to produce. But he will now receive a poorer harvest from the clerical 'glebe', because we have scarcely tilled the broad acres of doctrine, liturgy and ritual, partly because they are somewhat peripheral to the general theme of Elizabethan life.

The main reason, however, is that much of the ground has been thoroughly worked over by Dr. Anglin in his thesis, 'The Court of the Archdeacon of Essex, 1571–1609':[3] He is at present extending the scope by a more comprehensive study on the administration of the Essex spiritual courts and the clergy, which will also include the material for the Archdeaconry of Colchester and much complementary evidence from the records of the episcopal Consistory Court and the secular courts. Some of

[1] I am grateful to Mrs. D. M. Owen for her helpful comments on this section.

[2] In particular, *The State of the Church . . . in the Diocese of Lincoln*, ed. C. W. Foster (*Lincoln Rec. Soc.*, xxiii, 1926).

[3] J. P. Anglin, 'The Court of the Archdeacon of Essex, 1571–1609: An Institutional and Social Study' (Univ. of California, 1965); copy in the E.R.O.

the Essex archidiaconal archives have also been used in a broader context by Dr. Collinson in his invaluable work on the Puritans.[1] Earlier writers on the Essex clergy, while not having the Essex archidiaconal material at their disposal, made available a great quantity of original records, some of which have never been reprinted elsewhere.[2] A fairly recent and exhaustive study for Leicestershire, on somewhat parallel lines to Dr. Anglin's research and drawn chiefly from the Lincoln episcopal visitation and court books and the Leicester archidiaconal court books, provides comparable evidence.[3] Other books cover a much wider field, and there is a good deal of specialist literature on the Elizabethan clergy and non-conformists.[4] These, then, are the justification for our very inadequate treatment of the strictly religious offences of the 'godly' ministers in marked contrast to the wordly sins of other clerics, related later in this chapter.

All the clergy, churchwardens and sidesmen were under an obligation to attend the spring visitations and the autumn synods. The Essex act books periodically give lists of the clerics and parish officers who had failed to answer the summons. The clergy were also frequently convened by the archdeacons for other sessions, 'where they were subjected to special examinations or given additional duties or assignments to perform'.[5] Among these the matter of preaching was prominent. 'In spite of the early anxiety of the Crown and the ecclesiastic hierarchy as to the dangers of too much preaching, the demands of the puritans for a preaching ministry were gradually met by the Church through a systematic and controlled programme which attempted to provide conformable preachers in as many parishes as possible.'[6] This sustained campaign was largely effected by requiring the clergy to obtain licences to preach, which were withheld from many ministers who were unable to provide evidence of adequate academic education and training. Some details will be given shortly.

[1] P. Collinson, *The Elizabethan Puritan Movement* (1967). See also his 'The Puritan Classical Movement under Elizabeth I' (Ph.D. thesis, London, 1957), and 'The Godly: Aspects of Popular Protestantism in Elizabethan England' (one of the papers presented at the Past and Present Conference on Popular Religion, 1966), copies of both of which he gave to the E.R.O. library. The latest work is L. J. Trinderud, *Elizabethan Puritanism* (New York, Oxford U.P., 1971).

[2] The foundation work, often quoted in our present and previous volumes, is T. W. Davids, *Annals of Evangelical Nonconformity in Essex* (1863); also chapters 2 and 3 of H. Smith, *Ecclesiastical History of Essex* (1933), who corrected and added some material omitted by Davids. A brief general account of the Essex clergy in our period is in *V.C.H., Essex*, ii, 34–45.

[3] C. D. Chalmers, 'Puritanism in Leicestershire, 1558–1633' (M.A. thesis, Leeds, 1962), a copy of which was lent to me through the good offices of Mr. G. A. Chinnery, Archivist, Leicester Museum.

[4] Among others, Christopher Hill, *Society and Puritanism in Pre-Revolutionary England* (1964); P. McGrath, *Papists and Puritans under Elizabeth I* (1967); R. A. Marchant, *Puritans and the Church Courts in the Diocese of York* (1960); R. B. Manning, *Religion and Society in Elizabethan Sussex* (1969); R. C. Richardson, *Puritanism in North-West England: A Regional Study of the Diocese of Chester*.

[5] Dr. Anglin's, thesis, 199. [6] *Ibid.*, 209.

Dr. Anglin has produced statistics for the Archdeaconry of Essex which prove that the efforts of the Church in this direction gradually led to an improvement:[1]

Parishes with qualified preachers

1583	1586	1589	1592	1598
43 p.c.	43 p.c.	50 p.c.	57 p.c.	72 p.c.[2]

It was a duty imposed on all unlicensed holders of benefices to procure at least one sermon each month, and licensed preachers were encouraged to provide sermons in the neighbouring parishes which were bereft of them. (This provision was independent of the obligation on all the clergy to deliver or procure quarterly sermons against the papal authority.) The visitation book of 1565 and the act books generally name scores of parishes which were without sermons. The courts occasionally gave limited leave to parishioners thus deprived of religious edification to attend churches where sermons were delivered, but they kept a careful watch for any 'conventicles' where preaching did not take place in church. In some towns and parishes with a strong puritan laity, 'lecturers' were appointed to give them extra spiritual teaching; for example, George Gifford at Maldon, Edmund Chapman at Dedham, Richard Rogers at Wethersfield, Tristram Blaby at Stanford-le-Hope, and a succession of them at Colchester. Their unorthodox activities led to various disputes with beneficed clerics and anti-protestant laymen.[3]

Medieval Essex was noted for its radicalism. This nurtured religious dissent, and the county became one of the chief centres of puritanism. While this is well known from the State Papers and other sources, Dr. Anglin is the first to exploit the court books of one Essex archdeaconry, and he has given in his chapter on Clerical Nonconformity a mass of new and detailed evidence of various infractions by individual ministers. Many of their names are familiar from those of the twenty-seven puritan ministers who signed an earnest appeal in 1584 to the Privy Council for protection from further persecution of some of themselves and other Essex ministers by Archbishop Whitgift. (It was not an isolated act; similar petitions were submitted from ministers in Norfolk, Lincolnshire and Oxfordshire.) Shortly afterwards, seven members of the Council, referring to 'the lamentable estate' of the Church in Essex and the number of

[1] Dr. Anglin's, thesis, 211.

[2] Cf. figures for 1576 in three archdeaconries in Lincoln diocese (Foster, *op. cit.*, p. xix):

	Lincoln and Stow		*Leicester*	
	Latin	Sacred learning	Latin	Sacred learning
Sufficient or moderate	154	195	13	12
Insufficient or ignorant	135	113	91	93

For Devon and Cornwall, 1561, see A. L. Rowse, *Tudor Cornwall* (1941), 324.

[3] *Elizabethan Life: Disorder*; Index *s.v.* 'lecturers'; cf. Rowse, *op. cit.*, 334.

'zealous and learned preachers suspended' in Essex, drew the attention of the Archbishop and Aylmer, Bishop of London, to the 'notoriously unfit' ministers, who were not censured. Petitions to the Council or to Lord Rich were sent by large numbers of the chief laymen of several Essex hundreds.

The puritan clerics' damning account,[1] to which we shall refer more than once, is headed, 'A survey of sixteen hundreds in the County of Essex, containing benefices 335; wherein there are of ignorant and unpreaching ministers 173, of such as have two benefices a-piece 61, of non-residents that are single beneficed 10, preachers of scandalous life 12 – summa totalis 225'. (Davids unwittingly failed to print also the names of the twelve 'preachers of scandalous life'.) The hundreds of Becontree, Harlow and Witham are missing – a total of 34 parishes. It is followed by a much fuller description, including notes of suspension by the Bishop, of the 38 'sufficient, painful and careful preachers and ministers in Essex, who have been sundry times molested and vexed, partly for refusing the late urged subscription, and partly for not wearing the surplice and omitting the cross in baptism and the like'. ('Subscription' refers to the twenty-four articles of examination drawn up by the Archbishop.) Some of their names will be found in this and other chapters of the present book.

Clerical violation indeed centred mainly around the surplice, the sign of the cross, and the ring in marriage. Thomas Knevett, rector of Mile End, Colchester, for example, confessed to all in 1587. The sections on Baptism and Marriage name a number of offending puritan ministers. The 'vestiarian controversy' and the other ritual and anti-ceremonial factors in their dissent are matters of general knowledge, and the Essex records merely add precise particulars.[2] In place of such superfluous trappings, the puritan ministers concentrated on biblical study, preaching, prayer, and other holy 'exercises'. Arising from such principles came the Classis Movement of the 1580s, and it is fortunate that the proceedings of one such quasi-presbyterian group – the Dedham Classis which drew its members from the Essex-Suffolk borders – have been preserved and published.[3] The leading member of the Dedham Classis was probably Dr. Edmund Chapman, the church lecturer, with Richard Parker, vicar of Dedham, acting as secretary. The Church authorities were confronted with other 'classes' at Braintree and elsewhere, but that of Dedham was the most influential.[4] There was some participation by substantial and reliable laymen, and the Dedham ordinances provided for quarterly visitations by

[1] Davids, *op. cit.*, 88–104; also 77–8, 81–3, for several petitions to the Council. These surveys were published in *The Seconde Parte of a Register* (ed. A. Peel, 1915); those for Lincolnshire and Buckinghamshire are summarised in C. W. Foster, *op. cit.*, xxxiii–xxxvi.

[2] For the dispute in 1564 involving John Nowell, Dean of Bocking, see Davids, *op. cit.*, 64.

[3] R. G. Usher, *The Presbyterian Movement in the Reign of Queen Elizabeth as Illustrated by the Minute Book of the Dedham Classis, 1582–1589* (1905). For the Classis Movement in Leicestershire, see Mr. Chalmers' thesis.

[4] Collinson, *op. cit.*, esp. 222–39.

the ministers and these 'ancients', accompanied by the constables, of suspected houses in the poorer parts of the town.[1] Powerful members of the Braintree conference were Richard Rogers, curate and preacher of Wethersfield, and Lawrence Newman, vicar of Coggeshall. A revealing diary, kept by Rogers, has been printed.[2]

In his account of the puritan clergy within the Essex archdeaconry, Dr. Anglin attempts to divide them, according to the available evidence, into two groups: those directly involved in the Classis Movement, and those who were not so associated but whose liturgical practices warrant their being regarded as puritans.[3] For the nonconforming clergy in the Archdeaconry of Colchester (as well as that of Essex), the reader may turn to the account of the 'painful and careful preachers' already mentioned; and it must be emphasized that this contains a great deal of detail to which Anglin's material is of course complementary. Their intransigence towards the established Church gave rise to much trouble, which appears to magnify their numbers; but they were essentially a relatively small minority. Anglin shows that, despite the demise of the classis system in 1592, puritanism among the clergy remained unabated at the end of his period in 1609, and he concludes that the Church courts in Essex failed to achieve their conformity. The remarkable fact is that, although some of the beneficed clergy were suspended and a number of curates were readily silenced on the judges' own authority, few incumbents were actually deprived, and some of these not until the next reign. In the Archdeaconry of Essex the deprivations were limited to William Asheton, rector of Wennington (1581), John Hopkins, vicar of Nazeing (1589), Anthony Tirrell, rector of Dengie (1606), William Buckley, rector of Little Leighs (1609), and William Negus, rector of Leigh (1609). A distinguished Tudor historian expresses a somewhat different view: 'The Vestiarian Controversy ended in victory for the official Church and the bishops, and conformity seemed established. The battle was entirely over externals, but it had an ominous side. On the one hand the Puritans, defeated in the Church, attempted to gain their ends in Parliament. On the other, the bishops' disciplinary action concentrated the attack on them. . . . By the early 1590s the bishops had won: the classis was virtually dead, the clergy nearly all conforming.'[4] We therefore await with interest the result of Dr. Anglin's study of the Colchester archdeaconry act books.

Despite the archdeacons' courts being so much concerned with uncompromising ministers, the numerous prosecutions for refusal on conscientious grounds yield few matters of lively interest, unlike entries bearing on other offences. They are nearly all bare, prosaic statements.

[1] Collinson, *op. cit.*, esp. 354.
[2] M. M. Knappen (ed.), *Two Elizabethan Puritan Diaries* (1933).
[3] Dr. Anglin's thesis, especially appendix iv, 432–57.
[4] G. R. Elton, *The Tudor Constitution: Documents and Commentary* (1960), 433, 436.

Sometimes the registrar did not bother to note all the counts; for instance, that against the unnamed rector of West Horndon in 1566, for 'not having sermons, contrary to the Queen's Injunctions, and for many other causes as appear in the wardens' detection'; referring to William Harwood, who had been instituted in 1542 and was to hold his benefice for almost fifty years. The twin subjects of liturgy and ritual lack depositions of the kind found, for instance, in suits for defamation, breach of promise of marriage, or tithes. In other words, the transgressions of the clergy under the Act of Uniformity and the associated orders contribute little vivid detail to our study of Elizabethan life. Such cases as break through the brief factual items relate mostly to stubborn puritan ministers; but negligent clerics also appear. The more informative prosecutions will now be related.

In 1564 'the rector of Stock' (Oliver Clayton) was accused because 'he turneth his face at the Communion as he did at mass time, and he affirmeth that he hereafter will stand in no such sort'; on which he was ordered to confess in church and to give 12d. to the poor. On Christmas Day 1581 'Simpson curate of Clavering', who was apparently Thomas Simpson, the vicar, was in no peaceful mood. 'Without a surplice he did minister the Communion to sundry communicants which did stand and sit and were gloved, and (when) the churchwardens offered him the surplice he refused and did throw away the same. Ten years later, the wife of Richard Parker, the puritan vicar of Dedham, had evidently abetted him in pretending that his surplice had been burnt – by accident; being cited, he promised that if that was not so he would produce it to the wardens – and it was duly delivered up by her! A curious presentment in 1566 discloses that the vicar of South Benfleet (John Garratt) was in trouble 'because he doth not observe the Injunctions and will not minister with a surplice, and came to the house of Henry Wood with his bow and arrows to seek him'.

The same remarks about formal language apply to the relatively few indictments which reached Quarter Sessions – mostly for not wearing the surplice. In 1577, for reasons which are not clear, John Lodge, rector of Quendon, was charged with 'wholly refusing to say divine service'. Near the end of our period, in 1602, Geoffrey Josselyn, vicar of Good Easter, was before the County Bench on two counts: for saying service and administering communion without the surplice, and for 'laying hand and unreverently expelling John Hardy out of the church at the time of celebrating the communion'. In neither instance is the verdict noted. It was at the Epiphany Quarter Sessions, 1586, that what appears to be the grand jury's presentment deals solely with three ritual offences. William Lewyse, clerk, of Steeple, and Robert Edmondes, clerk, of Mayland had both refused to wear the surplice, the latter 'saying rather than he will wear it he will lose his living, and doth also refuse to church women'. Lewis was the rector, but it is not known whether Edmondes was the vicar or a curate. The remaining item concerns a Chelmsford shoemaker named Glascocke who, on Shrove Tuesday, contemptuously rent certain leaves out of the prayer book relating to public baptism belonging to one Collen in his presence and that of others. Being questioned about the reason, Collen declared, 'Because it is naught; there is in it named the water of Jordan for the washing away of our mystical sins; if that water washeth away sins, then Christ died for us in vain'. Such sayings savoured of sedition.

An unusual charge was laid in the archdeacon's court, 1579, against Matthew Skirton of St. Giles, Colchester, that 'by fraud and colourable means he took out of the church of St. Leonard, Colchester, without the consent of the churchwardens, borrowing the church keys of Mr. (Thomas) Upcher parson, he went into the church and took out the font cover from off the font and carried it away'. He was ordered to return it to the font – a fifteenth-century example.

In some of the smaller parishes the wardens were probably unaware of the exact official ritual under the Settlement, and their ignorance encouraged more than one minister to follow his own tenets. In an exceptional case, which reached the Assizes in 1583, an indictment recited that Stephen Beamand, rector of Easthorpe, had neither worn the surplice nor used the Prayer Book, but 'had seditiously celebrated there other services', and in so doing had been aided by Thomas Pudney, husbandman, and Richard Cranefeld, ploughwright, the churchwardens. Such a minor and probably passive infringement of the ecclesiastical laws by these humble rural wardens was only 'seditious' in the narrowest sense, and was accordingly omitted from the account in the chapter on Sedition in the previous volume. In fact, some of the more serious charges of liturgical offences committed by clergy and laity have already been printed in that context: oral remarks, whether deliberate or careless, which expressed dissatisfaction with the Settlement brought many defendants before Quarter Sessions or the Assizes for sedition; a few having been passed from the spiritual to the secular courts.

The rather repetitive kind of presentments for breaches of the Prayer Book orders that occupied the ecclesiastical judges' time thus have their counterparts in similar charges that reached the temporal justices, especially on the obsessional views over the surplice. As already explained, it is hoped that Dr. Anglin's careful analysis of the offences which were tried in either or both of such courts with overlapping jurisdiction will appear in due course.[1] But only a few of the delinquencies showed much in the way of departure from the several norms.

One refreshing change from the commonplace reports is seen in that against Thomas Elmot, or Elinot, of Great Holland in 1572. 'He taught them that, after evening prayer it is lawful to go to cart on Sunday, that

[1] Dr. Anglin's thesis, chapter 3, 'Allied Jurisdictions'.

the holy days appointed he wished to be taken away, for they were idolatrous and superstitious, and that upon All Saints' Day after morning prayer it was lawful to go to work.' Clearly, such opinions could not be tolerated by the archdeacon's court, and he was ordered to find nine compurgators (almost a record number) 'of honest neighbours of the parish', a phrase which suggests that he was a layman, not the curate. But it is equally clear that he was in no conciliatory mood, for the next entry records his having accused in turn two villagers as 'common talkers in church in service time' and one of them for disturbing the minister in church.

Another series of charges against the clergy arose from failure to hold services on Sundays, holy-days, or on Wednesdays or Fridays. At least twenty cases are found in the act books, but further research would be needed to decide how many lay against puritan clergy and how many against indolent ministers, especially where the evidence is as contradictory as that in the various accusations, about to be related, which Godfrey Burgin, rector of Little Wenden had to answer. Edward Bynder, the licentious curate of Blackmore, in 1589, admitted that, because 'there was speech that there should be an attachment for him (i.e. arrest), he durst not come into the church', and he was suspended; the reasons for which are given elsewhere. The charge against Henry Sledd, vicar of Eastwood, was that he 'doth not keep his church on the Lord's Day, so that we have had no divine service on divers Sundays, whereby the inhabitants are fain to repair to other churches, to the great offence of the congregation'.

Exceptional circumstances obtained at Chadwell. On 17 November 1579 'the parishioners gathered together to hear service, for it was the day of the beginning of the Queen's Majesty's reign, upon which day there should have been service said according to order described by a special book for that day set out, but no service by the negligence of the parson being absent'. Francis White, the rector, explained that he 'was at London upon the urgent and necessary affairs of his mistress, Mrs. Cooke of Giddy Hall, but notwithstanding he appointed Mr. Nellson, curate of Little Thurrock, to say service, who disappointed him of service, but he missed not service of any contempt'. His mild sentence was to confess his negligence next Sunday and to hand over 12d. to the poor. The lady in question was Anne, widow of Sir Anthony Cooke of Gidea Hall in Romford and mother of the distinguished wives of William Cecil, Lord Burleigh, and of Sir Nicholas Bacon, Lord Keeper.

While criticism may well be justified on account of the energy devoted by the courts and some of the clergy to the vestiarian and other ritual controversies, the reverse undoubtedly applies to the efforts of the Anglican Church to supply the parishes with qualified preachers. It is not generally appreciated that relatively few congregations in Elizabeth's early years had proper sermons, partly because a licence was required to preach. We have quoted Dr. Anglin's figures of licensed preachers from 1583 onwards, revealing a gradual improvement in the Archdeaconry of Essex. The act books of the other archdeaconry yield evidence of the disciplinary measures taken to enforce the need for adequate training of the less educated clerics. It is outside our scope to evaluate or even to summarize it. There are in fact some hundreds of entries showing the court's insistence on the production of licences to preach, and the registrar took the trouble to note the dates of licences thus exhibited as well as the name of the ordinary who had granted them. Almost as many entries name those who were reported (and sometimes suspended) for unlicensed preaching. The same Colchester act books for the last two decades contain long annual lists of the preachers and of the non-preachers who were 'tied to the exercises', i.e. the courses of theological study supervised by those academically qualified: their parishes are usually, but not always, given. The impetus probably came from the issue of the Canons of 1571, which provided for a review of preaching licences.

A few examples must suffice. 'Mr. (Richard)[1] Forthe parson of Great Holland doth not preach nor hath not of a great time, and the curate now lately come called Mr. Drinkworth doth expound without licence, on the accusation of the wardens' (1603); and 'Mr. (John) Manninge minister (curate) of Hadleigh, presented for that he refuseth to show the churchwardens any licence for his preaching' (1602). From a group of parishes to the east of Colchester came three charges (all in 1589) involving an excommunicated curate: against (Richard) Harrison, rector of Beaumont (who had been deprived in 1586 but was two years later restored to his benefice), for 'placing Mr. Waine his curate, being an excommunicated person, he knowing thereof', his answer being that 'Waine one day preached he knowing not that he was excommunicated'; against the wardens of Thorrington, for 'suffering Mr. Wayne to say service being excommunicated'; and against 'Mr. Richard Waine, late curate of Weeley and now of Thorrington, suspended at the Visitation for not exhibiting his theological exercises and stands excommunicated *duplicater* for not appearing to reply to the articles of contempt'. Even in their own parishioners' eyes, some ministers were found wanting; witness the scathing presentment by the Ramsey wardens in 1584: 'John White, our vicar, is not able to deliver any doctrine but by bare reading of the letter, neither do we know that he is diligent and useth conference with preachers to grow to ability'.

It was incumbent, in fact, on the wardens to report, or they were reported themselves for, any irregularity in this respect. Those of St.

[1] The writer has often supplied in parentheses (from Newcourt and supplements in *Trans. E.A.S.*, vi, vii) christian names and 'rector', etc., but some 'ministers' have not been identified as beneficed clergy or curates.

Lawrence had 'suffered Mr. (Thomas) Heape to preach, being unlicensed', their defence being that they did so 'before the licence came from my Lord's Grace of Canterbury, not knowing that it was contrary to law' (1588); those of Inworth 'suffered Mr. Tunsted (curate?) to say service and preach, he being suspended by my Lord of London' (1589); one of West Tilbury 'suffered ministers to say service not authorized', who pleaded that 'he was ignorant and cannot read', and was enjoined first to ask the preacher to show his licence (1597). In another instance, Henry Weler and another warden of Great Burstead were presented because 'they do refuse to hear one Mr. (William) Simons, which is appointed reader in the absence of Mr. (William) Pease (vicar), for not hearing divine service from him' (1600); readers could be appointed under the Canons of 1571.

The act books clearly testify to the courts' determination to instil a deeper knowledge of the Scriptures in the minds of the non-graduate clergy; this applied to beneficed ministers as well as curates who lacked a preaching licence. They were obliged, after studying a given passage, to produce in court their written 'exercise'. This is exemplified by two notes in 1585 that 'Richard Disborough, curate of Fingringhoe, exhibited his exercise upon the Epistle of St. Paul', and 'Jeffery Banbrick of Mount Bures, curate, hath showed his exercise on the 6th chapter of the 1st. Epistle of Timothy, and he hath the next chapter to certify before 8 April'. In 1591 John Newton, curate of Black Notley, was enjoined 'to certify on the exercise on the 1st. chapter of the Epistle of Paul to Timothy', and his having done so is duly recorded. Far more numerous are the entries of suspension of ministers who had failed to show their written exercises, especially in 1588. Two extracts will serve to illustrate: 'Mr. John Lucas, rector of Salcott Virley (now Virley), for not exhibiting his theological exercises' (1588); 'Mr. Roger Goodwin, curate of Layer-de-le-Haye, stands suspended for not certifying upon his theological exercises' (1592).

The term 'exercises' was, however, used in a wider context and referred to the groups of neighbouring ministers who met for the purpose of religious discussion. These provided a favourable atmosphere for the growth of puritan and presbyterian principles; they also engendered comment on the abuses in the Anglican Church. Some regulation became necessary, and in 1576 Archbishop Grindal, on his election, issued orders accordingly. The Queen had already signified her express disapproval of these 'prophesyings' or 'conferences', alternative names for such assemblies. The first edition of Harrison's work, which appeared in the following year, includes a passage that, unlike his usual forceful style, is patently cautious. Referring to their being started 'for the examination or trial of the diligence of the clergy in their study of holy scriptures', he continues: 'Howbeit such is the thirsty desire of the people in these days to hear the word of God, that they also have as it were with zealous violence intruded themselves. . . . The laity never speak of course, except some vain and busy head will now and then intrude themselves with offence, but are only hearers; and as it is used in some places weekly, in other once in fourteen days, in divers monthly and elsewhere twice a year, so is it a notable spur unto all the ministers thereby to apply their books' (then concluding with characteristic invective), 'which otherwise (as in times past) would give themselves to hawking, hunting, tables, cards, dice, tippling at the alehouse, shooting of matches and other such like vanities.' But in his second edition (1587) he added a paragraph, attributing to Satan the rise of adversaries who had 'procured the suppression of these conferences'.[1]

In the interval between Harrison's editions, Grindal strenuously opposed Elizabeth's strong dislike of the assemblies, but this had the result of his being placed under sentence of suspension himself. His successor, Whitgift, a man of rigid orthodoxy, at once issued articles in 1583 aimed against nonconforming ministers. They are referred to, two years later: 'Mr. Cottingham, curate of Dovercourt, exhibited letters testimonial of his diligence in the exercise of divine service, according to the form prescribed last by my Lord's Grace of Canterbury.'

The moderating effect of the Settlement in Elizabeth's early years had been largely nullified in the 1580s by the stern action taken against the Catholics and the Puritans. On the nonconforming clergy and laity in Essex, the reader can do no better than consult Dr. Collinson's intensive study, which is particularly valuable for its discussion of the exercises and conferences.[2]

What is one to make of the multiple charges against Godfrey Burgoyne (or Burgin), rector of Little Wenden, in 1585? 'An insufficient minister; could not administer the communion aright; leaveth out part of the Lord's Prayer; an alehouse-haunter; a blasphemer of the name of God; keepeth company with suspected persons; keepeth company with papists.' A sweeping denunciation, made by John Feltwell. But, according to a petition from many inhabitants of Great Wenden which they were to submit to the Privy Council six years later, Feltwell was 'a very troublesome and contentious person who prosecuteth divers frivolous suits against them to their great charge and vexation', and this view was confirmed by local justices.[3] In face of the counter-charge, Feltwell's evidence may have been false and malicious. At the next session, however, the Little Wenden wardens presented 'Mr. Godfrey Burgin for that we had no service the last Sunday, being 3rd October, being a communion by his appointment

[1] Harrison, *op. cit.*, 25–26.

[2] Collinson, *The Elizabethan Puritan Movement;* for some further details about the clergy in the Colchester archdeaconry, see *Ess. Rev.*, xxxii, 132–37 (chiefly 1580s). A good account of the conferences or 'prophesyings' in Leicestershire is given by Mr. Chalmers (see p. 191, n. 3), 62–70.

[3] *E.L.: Disorder*, 57.

provided, which by reason of his absence was undone'. To this the rector alleged that, 'coming from the Quarter Sessions upon the Friday he fell sick and tarried at Mr. Long's at Dunmow until the Sunday and could not travel by reason of his sickness'; from which charge he was dismissed. But on the same day further offences were related. He had been absent from his church on three Sundays or holy-days and did not say service on Wednesdays or Fridays; he very seldom administered communion, and when he did so it was not according to the Prayer Book because he administered the bread without the wine or used certain prayers between the delivery of the bread and that of the wine; he had not read the Queen's Injunctions, nor gone the perambulations, nor kept his register book of christenings, weddings and burials; and he was a contentious person and frequented alehouses. So, after all, the wardens confirmed what Feltwell had confronted Burgin with. But this was the rector's reply: his absence was due to his being engaged in litigation through 'one Feltwell who molested him; on St. Andrew's Day he left a sufficient man, one Mr. Wilkinson, to preach, and one Mr. Clarke vicar of Great Wenden did serve the cure that day; he hath oftentimes on Wednesday and Fridays repaired to the parish church to say service and there hath been no person to hear service; he hath twice or thrice at least administered the communion; he read the Injunctions twice since he was parson of Little Wenden; he hath walked the perambulation; he hath frequented the alehouses or inn only for his victuals and dressing of meat and drink and not otherwise; there wanteth a book of register but since there was one he doth his duty; he confesseth that upon St. Stephen's Day he did first deliver the bread and between the delivery of the bread and wine he used the Lord's Prayer and other prayers by oversight and forgetfulness, and that he left out the gospel and epistle upon 18th July'. Apparently therefore he gave a straightforward and honest admission where he was at fault; at any rate, the judge dismissed him on these counts also. But, two years afterwards, the wardens reported him again because they had had 'no service on seven (named) holy-days and Sundays and neither any service on the weekdays since St. Luke's Day'. Despite his alleged alehouse-haunting and general slackness, he is not mentioned in the puritan ministers' petition of 1584, possibly because his offences came to light just after its being compiled. He died in his rectory in 1598.

'Divers' offences were alleged against several other ministers. In 1567 'Mr. Johnson, rector of Chignal Mary and James', who had been instituted in 1555, was again in trouble for 'not saying service on Friday and Wednesday; not examining the godfathers and godmothers; not examining the brides; going in the perambulation with a surplice; the parsonage and chancel are in decay; and for divers other causes'. The court decided that his case must be referred to the bishop within the next twenty days. In 1580 William Drywood, rector of Downham, had to answer because 'the chancel wanteth shingling, tiling and glazing, and divers other things presented'. These were amplified at the next session: 'He hath procured not above six sermons these two years and a half in his parish church; he denied to receive (communion) four sundry women which should have given thanks for their child-bearing, who came to the church to that intent; he putteth his hogs, horses, kine and sheep into the churchyard, whereby it lieth very undecent and the graves rooted up; he doth use to rail and mis-term his parishioners, saying that they were like hogs and dogs.' To this the rector stated that he had 'procured his sermons as he believeth, saving one absence'; the rest he denied. The puritan ministers' report stigmatizes him as a gamester.

Another cleric in trouble on various counts was Philip Gilgatt,[1] vicar of Boxted. In 1590 the wardens' report ran: 'He hath procured Mr. Farrer, parson of Langham' (Thomas Farrer was a staunch puritan), 'to preach three times within this fortnight, contrary to Her Majesty's commandment and my Lord Bishop of Canterbury and my Lord Bishop of London, without licence or authority; also he hath baptized Agnes Northen without the sign of the cross or wearing the surplice, and saith that he will not make the sign of the cross for none of us all.' His disarming answer reads: 'Mr. Farrer hath preached there sundry times, being parson of the next parish and a licensed preacher of a long time; and he baptized the said Agnes Northen without the surplice for that she was brought to be baptized in the end of the service, the surplice not being tendered or laid forth before he began service, and he laid his hand upon the face of the child and used the words of baptism as appeareth by a presentment subscribed unto by Bradlie and another, churchwardens.' At the same session he was presented because 'he hath been a brawler and a slanderer where he can find no cause; he standeth outlawed; and he hath a shed in decay belonging to his parsonage'. To this Gilgatt said: 'As for the last part, the presentment is true; as for the rest, he is only complained and presented by William Bradlie as a private man without subscribing his name unto the detection, being his extreme enemy; and Bradlie and the other churchwarden and sidemen in their bill exhibited the same day have not presented him for any such matter; and he desireth to be discharged and law and justice done.' The brief result was merely an order to wear the surplice and to repair the shed. The appendix to the general petition of 1584 includes his name among the 'unpreaching ministers'.

An outstanding case of intransigence on the part of a curate is found in 1601. William Farrington, curate of Stanford Rivers, was questioned 'whether he had read divine service since that it came to his knowledge that he was suspended'. His reply was that 'judicially then and there he

[1] Newcourt, *op. cit.*, ii, 80, and the puritans' report of 1584 both give 'Silgate', but Gillgate (Gylgate) is found in three wills (*Trans. E.A.S.*, vi, 140; *Brit. Rec. Soc. Publns.*, 78, p. 173).

did acknowledge that after he had seen the letters denunciatory of the said suspension and had a copy of the same at the hands of Mr. (John) Nobbes, parson of Stondon, he did read divine service publicly in the parish church of Stanford Rivers, and he would read divine service still notwithstanding the said suspension, for he was commanded so to do by his master Mr. (Richard) Mulcaster, parson of the said parish, who promised to bear him out and save him harmless'. On this the judge ordered him to appear at the next session to see further process, but nothing more is recorded. The series of charges brought against him by the Chipping Ongar wardens two years previously will be quoted shortly.

There is the even more extraordinary case of William Seredge, the puritan rector of East Hanningfield, who withstood the prosecutions of the archdeacon's court for various ritual misdoings for eight years between 1584 and 1592, as well as indictment at the Assizes for refusing to make the sign of the cross in baptism. For non-appearance at the spiritual court, he was temporarily suspended and was also excommunicated for his contumacy, but finally submitted and was absolved, only to be excommunicated and absolved again, and later coming under the same interdict a third time. Dr. Anglin traces the long series of presentments in detail, with the various technicalities involved.

His thesis offers several reasons for the puritans' victory in the main. Among them was the ineffectiveness of the courts, which had no power to deprive, this being the prerogative of the bishop. Episcopal action was spasmodic, sometimes lenient; Edmund Grindal, Bishop of London (1558–70), was sympathetic, whereas John Aylmer (1577–94) was antagonistic. But the bishops in general were influenced partly by the lack of support from Parliament, which included among its members powerful puritan leaders. In the early part of our period, Thomas Cole, Archdeacon of Essex, 'was himself a flagrant nonconformist'.[1] Even George Withers, Archdeacon of Colchester, demonstrated his leanings by writing in 1583 to Lord Burleigh concerning his bishop's stern attitude. At county level, Robert Lord Rich was probably supreme, and as patron of many of the benefices to which he had appointed puritan-minded clerics he was able to moderate much of the prosecution of his more obstinate nominees. At parochial level, many of the churchwardens turned a blind eye to their ministers' ritual irregularities, were slow in presenting them, or were themselves reported for allowing sermons to be given by unlicensed preachers.

It is difficult, in the face of a certain amount of conflicting evidence, to estimate the degree of exaggeration by the clerical signatories of 1584 about their alleged persecution. Dr. Anglin, writing only of the Archdeaconry of Essex, is inclined to think that the puritan ministers were only moderately harassed. But it is abundantly evident that, over the whole county, they were

[1] Collinson, *op. cit.*, 68.

given ample opportunity to conform, even if only partially. Admonition, rather than disciplinary punishment, was generally tried, sometimes over long periods still further extended by their initial or even repeated default in answering citations and by the slow court procedure. The very few deprivations were the desert of the ultra-refractory objectors.

The vestiarian controversy and other ritual bigotry seem trifling stuff by current standards of judgement. One of the fairest modern versions runs: 'Although the Puritans' position was legally of course untenable, their earnestness, their high morality, and the undoubted power of their preaching evoked sympathy which the vehemence of their views might otherwise alienate from their cause.'[1]

In the next section the views of the devout as well as the dissolute laity about their lecherous, quarrelsome or drunken pastors will be quoted. They are all on record because of the clerics being presented or themselves or the wardens charging the parishioners with defamation. The voice of the puritan ministers' flocks unfortunately is rarely heard except indirectly and weakly, when they were augmented by followers from neighbouring parishes who were presented for absence from their own churches. Perhaps the most significant expression came from the little port of Leigh on the Thames estuary. William Negus had recently been instituted (1585) to the benefice on the presentation of Lord Rich, but was soon suspended by Bishop Aylmer for refusing to wear the surplice. On learning this, twenty-eight of his principal parishioners sent him a petition: 'We do entreat you,' they wrote, 'as you render our souls, and as you regard this account that you must render unto God for them, not to forsake us.' The surplice may have been a 'rag of Rome' to the zealous ministers, but the men of Leigh showed religious commonsense in seeking to retain their leader. Negus in response exhibited practical judgement by conforming, temporarily at any rate, though he eventually proved obstinate and was deprived in 1609, as already mentioned. In contrast, three of William Shepherd's flock at Heydon (now in Cambridgeshire) in 1580 betrayed their devout rector when he inadvertently drew an analogy between Jesus and Jesuits, forgetting the latter's sinister meaning.[2]

Infringements of the Church's tenets by laymen have already been considered, mainly under Religious Offences, especially for non-attendance at service and communion, with brief accounts of conventicles and recusancy; a few who refused to kneel or bow appear incidentally among those who disturbed services; and a few more in the chapter on Font to Grave, which also mentions some clerical transgressions.

[1] *V.C.H. Essex*, ii, 37, in the article on 'Ecclesiastical History of Essex', by the Rev. J. C. Cox and J. Horace Round: it is too gentle to have emanated from Dr. Round's pen! (Mrs. Owen adds, 'Or from Dr. Cox's!').
[2] *E.L.: Disorder*, 48–49.

Falling somewhere between doctrinal and moral offences was simony – the unlawful buying or selling of ecclesiastical preferments or emoluments. Only two charges have been found. In 1561 the vicar of Hawkwell (William Marshall, who died three years later) was accused, but no details are vouchsafed. Under 1600 the act book records the showing in court of the Bishop's mandate for the induction of Richard Buckenham, S.T.B., to the rectory of Great Bromley, vacant by the death of Peter Wentworth, the patronage having lapsed for this turn to the Queen because of 'the irregularity of simony' (*pravitatem simonie*). Again nothing further can be gathered. Wentworth had been a pluralist, having also held the rectory of Abberton but had resigned the benefice nine years earlier.

Abuse and Defamation

Our chronicle of Church Disturbances revealed widespread anti-clericalism, expecially by way of abusive language in church or churchyard. Even more foul or slanderous epithets were cast at some of the clergy in unconsecrated ground and were set down in wardens' presentments against the offending parishioners. We now relate the more serious sayings about the ministers' morals. Such statements are found either in charges against these slanderers or gossipers or in defamation suits brought by the victims. It is abundantly clear from internal evidence and from the strictures in the general report of 1584 about the 'unpreaching ministers' that a small minority of the clergy failed conspicuously in their calling. Occasionally, however, the abuse is seen to have arisen not through their overt delinquencies nor local tittle-tattle but because of their having reproved erring parishioners. What follows is therefore a medley of truth and lies, on which the reader may give his own verdict, having knowledge or hindsight of earlier or later incidents in which ministers were involved.

Much dissension at Barking involved the vicar, Richard Tyrwhytt, in bringing a suit for defamation in December 1563 against Robert Rychmonde, William Bexwell, Mr. Wyle, Anne Foster, Nicholas Pratt, George Male, Robert Stokdale, John Walker, and Rychmonde's maidservant. On appearing, he declared that they had 'put in certain articles against him, the one for incontinency with Robert Rychmonde's wife and the other for a common sower of discord'. All nine parishioners also attended and their version was that 'the vicar would have had to do with her'. To that, Tyrwhytt explained how both Rychmonde and his wife had defamed him by saying that the accusers 'should say that Mr. Vicar came out of Foster's house with his hosen down and his gown about him'. The court excommunicated Mistress Rychmonde and directed the others to answer further regarding the charge against them. Nine months later the vicar himself was excommunicated 'for contempt of court viz. in railing on

Mistress Rychmonde and in calling Bexwell knave'; but he came, submitted himself to correction, begged absolution from the sentence, and was granted it. Immediately afterwards the judge excommunicated the woman again, this time also 'for contempt of court viz. in pulling the vicar by the beard in full court', and she was also told to give 12d. to the poor. The court, however, was far from satisfied with the slander affair, and in February 1565 both parties were summoned again to receive penance decrees on account of their earlier contempt. The woman first sought and obtained release from excommunication. She was then assigned 'upon Sunday to acknowledge her fault in the church that she hath abused the court to make contentions in the open court to the grief of the parishioners'. Tyrwhytt got a similar sentence, plus a fine of 3s. 4d. for the poor. Exactly a year afterwards 'Tirwitt' was excommunicated a second time, for absenting himself both from the archdeacon's 'synod', or visitation, and from 'the reading and last convocation' (*lectura et convocacione ultima*), but the registrar noted that he was present at the synod, 'as he said'. Tyrwhytt had apparently succeeded John Gregyll as vicar in 1560, when the latter was imprisoned for a short time as a suspected papist.[1] On his death in 1584, Tyrwhytt was described as sub-dean of the Queen's Chapel.[2]

In 1571 Richard Reynolds, parson of Lambourne, was called 'a very knave and a very villain'; four years later Richard Ryder of Fyfield declared that 'he did see Mr. (Edward) Bordman (rector of Fyfield) and Mr. Huttoffe's wife down together under the hedge': a charge which was discounted because the judge ordered Ryder to ask both parties' forgiveness on the next Sunday; he had, however, been in court the previous year for alleged drunkenness. In 1577 'opprobrious words' were spoken against the rector of Wrabness (Thomas Sayer), in his case anticipating graver crimes to be related in due course. Angry rather than slanderous words were given by an aggrieved parishioner who in 1576 'misused Mr. Vicar of Kelvedon' (Thomas Simpson). Nicholas Francis's contention was that, 'upon occasion of certain talk which the vicar had spoken to a widow to whom he was a suitor by reason whereof the match was brake off, being offended with the vicar, she did upon a Sunday morning before service reprove him with sharp words'. Despite this plea, Francis had the further mortification of undergoing the usual penance at morning prayer. In the same year Gabriel Hone of Danbury, often a church absentee, 'railed on the minister and the sidemen, calling them protestants pratlingstants'; he was probably the curate, as it was unlikely that such pointed remarks would have been levelled against the rector, Dr. George Withers, who was also Archdeacon of Colchester. Hone claimed, however, that 'he was absent one day, and he reported to the minister that they were not protestants but pratlingstants that do use to tell lies', and had to purge. Having

[1] *V.C.H. Essex*, v. 225. [2] *Trans. E.A.S.*, vi, 134.

failed to produce not only compurgators but also a certificate of performance of penance, he was excommunicated.

In 1579 three clerics were slandered, each by one of his parishioners: the minister of Great Stambridge, a 'saucy jack'; the minister of Stifford, a 'knave'; and Mr. (Edward) Card, vicar of Bradfield, 'by Cock's (colloquial for God's) soul, an arrant knave thus to bring us to the spiritual (court) to spend our money': one of the many attacks on official fees.

Gilbert Spede of West Bergholt was an unusual character. In 1581 he not only 'thou'd' the minister (probably Richard Kyrbye, the rector) to his face but 'also burdened (charged) him that he should (i.e. did) say that the Book of Common Prayer was not to be read, which the minister doth account to be slander to him'. ('Thou' used familiarly by an inferior was insulting.) Spede was further accused of possessing 'an unlawful book of soothsaying, palmistry and such like, etc.' Less coarse in speech than rustics, as would be expected from such a man, he asserted that he had merely told the minister that 'for his good will he would be glad and rejoice, but for his ill will, a fly for him'; and he denied commenting on the Prayer Book.

In 1584 as many as nine ministers received rude language. Five men and women spoke 'slanderous and reproachful words' about Ralph Kinge, rector of Little Bromley; Francis Cheveleighe of West Hanningfield called 'his minister knave'; a Great Chesterford woman addressed 'Mr. Hawton our minister' (not the vicar) 'knave and lying knave and other opprobrious words to his discredit'; Richard Wells of Great Tey, presented for not receiving communion for a year, declared that the vicar (John Hall) was 'an evil person, a naughty pack that keepeth and houstereth naughty persons in his house' (he resigned shortly afterwards); ending with a wide sweep, 'and the parish is a naughty parish'. Counter accusations were shouted in Blackmore, John Fuller being charged with 'calling the minister whoremaster knave', his defence being that 'Mr. (Edward) Binder openly abused him in church'; but when Thomas Prince, vicar of Great Chesterford, had been 'evil spoken of', the wardens tactfully added, 'whether he hath deserved it or no we know not'; both will appear again on more definite evidence.

Although the vicar of Great Sampford-with-Hempstead was one of the 'unpreaching' parsons, the Church could not tolerate a layman, William Lagden of Hempstead, 'openly to report that those who received Communion with Mr. (John) Luddington were rotten members and rotten sheep'. A man named Belvis of Goldhanger 'very contemptuously' said to his unnamed curate, 'You should be a minister, you are a minisher', unconsciously echoing a comment made twenty years earlier by Becon, the protestant writer, about a greater man, 'He is not Episcopus, not a Minister, but a Minisher'.[1] The exact meaning of 'minisher' in this

[1] Thomas Becon, *Works* (1564), preface (quoted in the *O.E.D.*).

context is not clear, but may be 'one who belittles'. Mr. (Henry) Robinson, rector of Fairstead, had the misfortune in 1585 of being called 'a farting priest' by Thomas Scott, who himself had been adjudged an adulterer four years earlier, when he was assigned public penance.

'Mr. (Thomas) Rochester, parson of Great Oakley', was accused on separate occasions in 1584 by two of his flock. Thomas Maydston 'used contemptuous speeches' against him; but all he admitted was 'some falling out between them'. The other, Thomas Mellys, said that he 'was a common barrator and so he would prove him'; and he was sued by Rochester for 'asserting that he was a lewd person as any this hundred miles, and if he himself were a whore Mr. Rochester would ride forty miles to do him a good turn, and in particular Mr. Dr. Joanes, Mr. Thorne, Mr. Dickens, and others'. Two of these are clearly recognizable as clerical neighbours – Richard Jones, S.T.B., rector of Manningtree, and William Thorne, vicar of Great Bentley. Three years later it was the turn of John Rochester, curate of Great Oakley (perhaps Thomas's son), who alleged that, 'By the procurement of Thomas Mellis and others, he remains in durance in the Castle (Gaol) of Colchester, whereby divine service was not said the same day'. Whether John Rochester, gentleman, who was patron of the benefice, was identical with the defendant is not certain.[1]

At a session in Walden church in 1585 the Official himself (Dr. William Bingham) charged Lancelot Ellis, vicar of Wimbish, because 'he publicly in court said to Mr. John Knight, curate of Great Sampford, "You are a sauce box", against the form of the statute'. A few weeks afterwards, when Knight was termed 'late curate', he was presented for 'not subscribing to the Articles' and arguing about transubstantiation. Ellis, who had succeeded Parson Harrison in this benefice four years earlier, was himself slandered later on. A somewhat different form of abuse led Thomas Pratt of Hornchurch to be cited in 1585: 'He used unseemly speeches against a preacher, viz. that he misliked the sermon of Mr. Diccons, a good preacher, saying that they liked nothing in his sermon but a vice or such like.' Simon Cook, rector of Great Birch, who was to be in prison three years later, made out in 1585 that he was the victim of a malicious slander. Accused of 'adultery or fornication with the wife of one Brocke, attorney of Easthorpe', an adjacent parish, he firmly disavowed the charge, adding that 'his (i.e. Brocke's) wife being a notorious harlot, for her own defence or shadowing (i.e. concealment) of her lewdness, gave out such speeches most falsely and most slanderously, but of late being thereof examined before two justices of peace and two ministers hath confessed that therein she had slandered him to cover her shame'. He was thereon discharged. Cooke had been instituted in that year.

A woman of St. Leonard, Colchester, 'in the open street uttered many slanderous speeches against our minister, Mr. (Thomas) Lowe' (rector); a

[1] R. Newcourt, *Repertorium* (1710), ii, 97.

8, 9
ELIZABETHAN CHURCH FURNISHINGS

The Elizabethan period was a barren one for the building of new churches (in Essex, only Woodham Walter) and the provision of new furnishings, except for plate. The illustrations above show two of the very few examples in Essex churches. Two communion cups were shown in the *Elizabethan Life: Disorder*.

8 Pulpit at Chipping Ongar, showing the panels carved with jewel ornament and arabesques, late sixteenth century (p. 242).

9 Poor's box at Dovercourt, dated 1589 (p. 264).

10–12

THREE PAPERS FOUND IN THE COURT BOOKS

10 (top)
Certificate by Henry Cor(n)e-beck, clerk, 1596, of the receiving of the Lord's Supper by Bartholomew Brock, gentleman, 'with the greater part of the parishioners of St. Trinity' (Colchester); on the Sunday before Michaelmas his wife received it at home because of her sickness.

11 (left)
Original presentment by the churchwardens for carting on St. Bartholomew's Day; for absence from Communion for five years; for absence from Divine Service; and for sending to fetch corn and absence from Morning and Evening Prayer.

12 (right)
Another presentment of two women (one whose husband is at sea, the other being single) for lodging a stranger from London in their houses – a 'crime (i.e. rumour) . . . which is very evil thought on'.

Weeley man called 'Mr. Wayne (apparently the curate) his minister, knave'; a Messing man, admonished for being away from church, 'railed on Mr. (John) Harris the minister, calling him damned idle dog and he had as lief hear a dog bawl as to hear a minister to say service'; and a Little Thurrock man 'abused the minister in words'. These four defamers were all cited in 1587.

Next year James Thomlinson of Trinity parish in Colchester was in court. He had 'misused Mr. Robert Goode (the rector), calling him drunkard, saying that he was like unto one drunken Cocke, the butcher, who is known to be a notable drunkard, and that Mr. Goode did inform the matters unto this court as he did promote matters by way of information unto the Chequer (Court of Exchequer) to the benefit of this court; also his wife said in the street that Goode was a whoremaster and had a whore at Harwich and bade him give her a gown as he had done before'. Goode was one of the 'unpreaching' ministers, 'also sometime a mender of saddles and panels', another word for saddles.[1] Another of his parishioners, Anthony Aleswaye, was accused of 'calling Mr. Goode, Pope', and was excommunicated for non-appearance. A woman, herself presented as a common scold, called Stephen Roberts, curate of Salcott, 'knave, three times'; he, too, was another 'unpreaching' minister and 'an alehouse haunter'.[2] Also in 1588 (William) Pynder, rector of Stock, had the epithet 'a vile priest' bestowed on him by Nicholas Bush's wife, and William Sexton of Radwinter 'misused Mr. Pomfret clerk, his minister', presumably in Harrison's absence.

Year after year Essex clerics encountered much the same treatment. In 1590 the wardens charged Jeremy Burton of Elmstead for 'railing openly in the street against our minister (Reginald Metcalfe, vicar), calling him quarreller and suchlike words when he was admonished to keep his church, for that he is often absent, and for keeping ill rule in his house as playing at cards or tables on the sabbath days; also he never cometh to church on any holydays'. This shows Metcalfe in a favourable light. (Five years later, when he was indicted for stealing cheeses, the bishop appealed to the county justices on his behalf, asserting that there was a conspiracy against him.)[3] Burton failed to appear and was excommunicated; ironically, he then attended church, and being excommunicate was commanded by the vicar to leave, in accordance with the law. In the same year three members of the Pewterer family, husband, wife and son, of Langham, 'railed on Mr. (Thomas) Farrer our minister, slandering him without cause divers times' (he was a puritan in trouble for not wearing the surplice[4]); an East Donyland excommunicated woman slandered 'Mr. (Brian) Atkinson minister (rector) of Wivenhoe, a preacher, saying that he was a whoremasterly knave', and also termed 'Mr. (William) Kyrbye her minister (rector of East Donyland) a perjured knave'.

[1] Davids, *op. cit.*, 98. [2] *Ibid.*, 97. [3] *E.L.: Disorder*, 294. [4] Davids, *op. cit.*, 110.

An East Mersea woman declared of 'Mr. (Robert) Edmonds her minister', that 'he could say well in the pulpit, but when he was out of it he was the very Devil'; Richard Fuller of Langford 'abused the minister, viz. Mr. Graysborowe, with unreverent speeches and unseemly behaviour': clearly a case of coarse slander, as Fuller was presented on five further charges; John Harr of Tollesbury 'reported of Mr. (Bartholomew) Moodye (rector) that the scurvy priest had abused him' (all 1591). A Witham man named Spradborowe exclaimed to Samuel Wither, vicar of Cressing, 'Thou knave, scoundrel and shitten fellow' (1592).

The vicar of Great Tey was an object of one virago's vulgar spleen, which we learn from the report in 1591 against Elizabeth Hindes a parishioner, describing her as 'a common scold and sower of discord among neighbours, and especially between Lionel Foster minister there and his parishioners, and of these vices and offences she is commonly suspected and defamed in the parish'. Foster had succeeded John Hall, the 'naughty pack'. In a separate charge on the same day, she was presented as 'a common abuser and railer, calling Mr. Foster a minister of the Devil, a bloodsucker, brawler, liar, knave, etc.; and of late she went into the houses one after another of Mr. Chishall, William Welles, William Forde, John Lea, Thomas Phipes, Henry Barick, widow Summerson, and into the smith's forge and the tailor's shop and divers other places, and there reported and defamed Mr. Foster to be a notable liar and a lying vicar; and saith that her husband commanded her so to do. She likewise in the churchyard very unchristianly railed against Mr. Foster with most filthy speeches, calling him bloodsucker, knave and arrant knave and spitted at him, and banned and cursed like a mad woman.' Three years earlier, Foster had been reported for incontinence with Braberton's wife, but it looks as though the vicar of a parish plagued with such a peripatetic slanderess as Elizabeth Hindes should be given the benefit of the doubt.

Of the next character, Zachary Some of Sandon, the Quarter Sessions records disclose that he belonged to a family of inveterate poachers, and Zachary himself was to be imprisoned in 1595 for attacking John Pascall's warrener at Danbury.[1] Three years before this conviction he had been arraigned in the spiritual court for 'uncharitably abusing the minister of Sandon, calling him prattling fool for preaching against drunkenness; saying moreover that he could, if he had authority, within a fortnight space, make as good a sermon as he'. On the same day, he and a West Hanningfield man had to answer for 'unreverently behaving themselves in church on a Saturday night by throwing of pessocks (i.e. hassocks) at the sexton's head, and thereby brake his head'; and Zachary also for harbouring a pregnant unmarried parishioner, who, he said, had gone away to Stock and he was not aware of her condition.

The wardens of Stondon (Massey) had no doubts about the effrontery

[1] *E.L.: Disorder*, 245.

of Edmund Lincolne, who in 1596 'most irreverently in terms misused our minister as if he had been the most vile and bad fellow in the country, and that in his own house'. In the same year, by a coincidence, (blank) Lincolne of Elmdon, many miles away in the other archdeaconry, 'being an excommunicate and being warned to depart would not go out presently but said he would stay awhile, and his wife being called to depart she used these words that Mr. (Thomas) Clowghe (vicar) was an old dolt, old fool, drunkard, and this was in the church. Further she said that Mr. Brownrigg, preaching at Elmdon, said thus, viz. Like vicar, like preacher'. The report of 1584 had certainly put him down as 'no preacher'.[1]

Five embarrassing cases came before the Colchester archdeaconry judge in 1597–98. A Bradfield woman, according to the wardens, 'openly reported that Mr. (John) Richardes our minister did knock at her chamber window in the night time, with other foul and slanderous speeches, which she can declare upon her examination by you better than we can by our writing'. Nevertheless she was assigned to confess her defamation in church. A Peldon wife admitted the charge of 'not receiving the Communion and for abusing the minister, calling him thief and wretch'; but she added, mysteriously, 'He came more like a thief than an honest man, because he did break up her house door in the night time when she was in bed for certain books (*sic*) who scolded in the church'. The accused was Dorcas, wife of the John Lawrence, who had 'charmed a thorn out of a maid's leg' (p. 79). The judge commanded her to ask Mr. Ashpole forgiveness and to receive before the next court. (The clergy list for Peldon is defective.) A second minister of East Mersea, this time Mr. Garye, was slandered by villagers. One named Goodwyn 'reviled the minister or curate, calling him drunkard and whoremaster and other reproachful speeches'; the other, John Owting, declared that 'he was a drunkard, kept a whore in his house, and had lain with his maid and gotten her with child before, he was a cup companion, a breakhedge, a dicer, and played all his money and laid his dagger to pawn, which he saith he will prove'. A less scurrilous but more meaningful remark brought Gabriel Sadler of Walden to the court: 'He did use these words of contempt to Mr. Lancelot Ellis, vicar of Wimbish, that he did no good neither was there any goodness in him, and that vicarages and parsonages were for poor men's livings better than for him', a statement which he denied having made.

'Mr. (William) Pasfeild our minister' (vicar) of Tolleshunt D'Arcy was subjected to 'railing and reviling speeches' by a housewife (1598); and Henry Rayner of Terling, who was accused of 'abusing Mr. Minister and giving him the lie' (1599), retorted that he was 'urged by Mr. (James) Robinson giving him the lie first', on which the judge assigned him to reconcile himself to the other party.

Robert Ayleward of Debden showed an imaginative mind in expressing

[1] Davids, *op. cit.*, 90.

his opinion of the rector in 1599. The wardens' report was, 'He used contemptuous and unchristian words against Mr. (Richard) Hodshon his minister, viz. that he wished that the church door keys were molten hot in Mr. Hodshon's belly, and being reproved for the same answered again and said that he wished that they were in his own belly if he did not think as he spake, or words to the like effect'. Briefly, in 1602, we learn that an Aveley wife railed against the vicar; that Thomas Weekes, a cooper of Horndon-on-the-Hill, 'very unreverently abused Mr. (Robert) Willmott, our vicar, at the Lion'; and that village gossip accounted 'Mr. (Thomas) Newman, (vicar) of Canewdon, a beggary (*sic*) priest'. The adjective implies 'contemptible': in 1596 John Gore, a layman of Holy Trinity, Colchester, was presented for 'his slovenly beggarliness', which was not an offence under the Church's canons, so he was discharged.

There is remarkably little evidence of efforts by the clergy towards the reconciliation of estranged couples. One rector who made such an attempt in 1602 received abuse, when a Springfield man was presented because he and his wife 'would not be persuaded to live otherwise, after they knew that it was very offensive in the parish, but gave very bad speeches when they were admonished to lead a better life, and especially to Mr. (William) Danyell our minister'. Eight years after being reviled as 'a farting priest', Robinson fared even worse from a woman named Drane of Fairstead. Prosecuted because 'she did make her husband a cuckold the first night she was married and was dancing with a young man all night, and then Mr. Robinson, parson of the same parish, rebuked her for so doing, she answered and said unto him "Hold your peace, for you were the first!"' Calumny or truth, but damaging in either case, the wardens again did not spare the rector's discomfort.

Among the various age-old problems of justice which the archidiaconal courts tried to solve was that of maidservants charging their clerical masters with attempts on their virtue. One master, perhaps two, at any rate decided to take the initiative and sue for defamation, but the court books give only the wenches' stories of their being assaulted while busy in domestic tasks. 'The answer of Bridget Pakeman' in 1570 ran:

> She dwelt some time at Wrabness, first with one Godfrey and after with Mr. (Thomas) Sayer, parson there, three quarters of a year, during the which time Sayer would have ravished her, first flattering her and embracing her when she was turning a flooring of malt and promised her if his wife died of child he would marry her and attempted to handle her shamefully, taking up her clothes. Another time on the kell (kiln) as she was heaving of malt, at which time using her as before she fell out with him and was going away from him but he coming after her stayed her. And another time about Midsummer she having gathered a bundle of rushes and gathering up the old rushes to have strowed the hall, Sayer came to her, his hose being down, and did shamefully use her, at which time she was forced to take him by the members to save herself, wherewith Sayer gave her a blow on the ear and therewithal departed. Howbeit she denieth that he had his pleasure of her at the time.

Another example of malicious slander? The maid's 'answer' seems to imply that she was the defendant, but the court book has entries 'against Sayer' as well as for 'Sayer versus Pakeman', while the obscure language apparently indicates that the churchwardens had presented their rector. The case dragged on from session to session after the judge had accepted 'answers on oath as in a certain paper schedule' given in by Sayer and 'decided to deliberate'. The servant girl, perhaps scared out of her wits, absconded and 'stood excommunicate', and Robert Heyward, one of the Wrabness wardens, was also given the same sentence, presumably for not attending to substantiate the original presentment. The entries finally peter out, so that the rector may have considered his reputation had been cleared. The Pakemans were a well-established Wrabness yeoman family. Fourteen years later, Sayer was accused (though acquitted) of rape.[1] Six years after that, he was incarcerated: 'The cure is not served by reason of the imprisonment of Mr. Sayer, rector', reported the wardens; whereupon the judge decreed that 'the fruits and tithes of the church be sequestrated for sustaining a curate'.

The other suit was brought before the Essex archdeacon's court in 1578 by James Ballard, clerk (who was rector of Leyton), against Margaret Griffin for defamation. (Leyton was not in the archdeaconry, but her abode, not given, must have been.) Her statement was that 'upon a Sunday morning about a month past, she being in his chamber a-spitting a piece of meat for him, and thus being about her business, he having his hose untrussed suddenly pulled her unto him and took her between his legs, and would have had to do with her but by force she got from him'. The judge ordered the parties to attend the next session, but then there is silence.

A second scandalous report about the vicar of Great Sampford as well as his spouse led to Anne Scot's citation in 1584. 'She openly said that Mr. Luddington's wife was with child at the time of marriage, for she fell down in the church, and God knoweth what became of the child, and that Mr. Luddington was shut up close in a chamber with one Lettice Horne whilst she the said Anne went about other business by the space of two or three hours.' In milder language, the wife of Mr. Drywood (rector of Downham) was 'an unquiet woman' (1577). These presentments introduce the controversial matter of clerical marriage. Elizabeth's well-known antipathy was expressed by the extraordinary provisions in her Injunctions of 1559. 'Whereas there hath grown offence and some slander to the Church by lack of discreet and sober behaviour in many ministers, both in choosing of their wives and indiscreet living with them', it was ordered that in future no priest or deacon be married before the intended bride had been examined by the bishop and two justices of the peace of her

[1] *E.L.: Disorder*, 197.

neighbourhood and 'allowed' by them and also produced evidence of the goodwill of two kinsfolk or her master or mistress: the last in itself a token of ministers' low social status at the period. Irrespective of their royal mistress's opinion on priests' unions, their parishioners occasionally voiced strong views about the morals of clerical marriage and clerical wives: views that were doubtless shared by other members of the laity. No light is thrown on the dubious question of actual inquisition by J.P.s or even less likely by the bishop.

A subtle form of slander is gathered from depositions taken in 1569 from two Upminster parishioners. Stephen Barnard, labourer, who said he had dwelt there 'half of his age of 40 years' and was formerly of Brentwood, alleged that Margery Whyte last June 'came to his house after they had been at sheep-shear, and being offended because she was not bid to one Coles to sheep-shear as she was wont, said of Mistress Wassher, "Humphrey, Mr. Latham's man, cannot so soon lay his hand on Mistress Wassher's head, but straight way she will fall down backwards", whereby he judgeth that by reason of those evil words her good name must needs be worsened'. Adria Turre, who had lived there for 24 years, formerly at Hornchurch, aged 60 or more, deposed that 'about St. Peter's tide last', Margery had spoken identical words. 'Indeed I did say those words of her', the defendant exclaimed in court, 'and I will never deny them'. The victim was clearly the wife of William Washer, rector of Upminster; William Latham was the chief landowner in the parish.

Defamatory words spoken in 1600 against the recently deceased Nevendon rector's widow were set out in the deposition of Nicholas Burre, 'poulter' (poulterer), of East Horndon, aged 58, who had dwelt there for twenty years and before that at Shellow Bowells. 'On a Tuesday in the afternoon in July last,' he declared, 'coming into the yard of John Hampder at the sign of the Crown in Billericay, where his horse stood, and having made his market and put his wares in his basket, there were in the yard Elizabeth Wilkinson and Jeremy Wittham, both of Nevendon, chiding together. Wittham said to Elizabeth, "Thou art an arrant whore and I will prove thee an arrant whore", William Lone and one Mr. Richman being also witnesses. Wittham did maliciously slander her in uttering such speeches as he believeth, and she was then the wife of Mr. William Wilkinson, parson of Nevendon.'

Occasionally the clergy – or their wives – were slandered generally. Seven charges of this sort are found. The first arose merely out of drunken chatter. John Lone of Rayleigh was 'a slanderer of the ministers, calling them prattling knaves, a swearer, sower of discord and a disquiet person' (1579); he pleaded that he was 'sometimes overcome with drink'. Robert Long of Salcott 'said that ministers' wives were whores and their children bastards' (1571). For this he was given public penance, 'to stand two

Saturdays following with a paper upon his head in Colchester market and there openly acknowledge his fault and the like in the parish church of Salcott the two next Sundays'. The other slanders, with the same double theme but spoken more than a generation after priests were allowed to marry, perhaps reveal that some of the Anglican as well as Catholic laity still preferred celibate clergy. John Mous of Little Stambridge was accused of 'using bad speeches towards the minister and for reporting in the presence of many persons of good credit that all priests' wives are whores and their children bastards, and that is no fame to abuse their bodies for that they are whores' (1592); also of not living with his own wife. John Wakelin and John Wakelin, both of Hempstead, 'said that ministers ought not to marry and their children are bastards' (1596). Benedict, wife of George Mayers of Bradfield, expressed a similar belief, fortifying it, as she imagined (though a historical untruth), with 'They did not marry before this Queen's reign' (1599); she denied the charge and had to purge with three neighbours. The final instances are of a different character. Elizabeth, wife of John Heckford of Elmstead, was presented (1591) 'for a slander against her honest neighbours and in such railing manner against those that profess the Word of God, saying, "A shame, take all professors, for they are all dissemblers and liars'". So, on denying these words, she had to find four of her worthy friends to purge her remarks. In contrast to the expressed desire of some puritans who went to other churches solely to hear sermons was the opinion of Thomas Halles of Hempstead, who said (1598) that 'men are the worse for hearing of sermons', which, on his admission, earned him penance before the wardens and two parishioners.

The Elizabethan clergy thus received from the laity an abundant offering of slander and hostility, but it is perhaps surprising to find that sharp clerical tongues brought so few of them to court for the same offence. In 1561 an East Tilbury man sued Christopher Eaton, the vicar, for 'defaming him by saying he would make him a red coat', but Eaton asserted that he merely said that 'he would serve a red coat on him, meaning a citation'; this possibly suggests that apparitors wore distinctive garb. Brian Atkinson, rector of Wivenhoe, who had been accused by the wardens in 1590 for incontinence, was shortly afterwards presented for 'falling out with divers of his neighbours, as with William Morley and others'. He said in his defence, 'Being called by Morley knave and rascal and hardly used by him and the churchwardens, and being provoked by their many abuses, he did chide them and used hard words against them'; the judge sentenced him to express his sorrow. Henry Ellis, minister (evidently curate) of Tollesbury, in 1599 denied having slandered a parishioner, 'saving that he did tell Courtman the presenter in church that he lied and that he was once in Campion's house and played at the tables there'; whereon Ellis had to produce eight compurgators – an equal number of clergy and laymen. He prayed the court's absolution, but the judge, because of his scolding words 'in giving the lie in the church', suspended him from ingress in accordance with the statute. The scribe noted in the margin, 'Mr. Ellys said that he had injustice done to him in divers respects'. At the next session Ellis appeared again, alleging that 'this presentment is only done by goodman Courtman, who is a notable enemy and is excommunicated lawfully, and so hath stood for two months, and also that he (Ellis) is a minister and thereupon without any witnesses he may not be detected (i.e. ought not to be presented) or called to law'. But the purgation decree was reaffirmed.

Moral Offences

In introducing the long series of charges against the Essex clergy for immorality and kindred vices, two points must be emphasized. Almost as many clerics were cited, not as a result of such failings but because they refused, through the dictates of conscience, to observe the rules laid down under the Elizabethan Settlement and subsequent orders. Only one, Richard Parker, the puritan vicar of Dedham, appears in each group – for suppressing his surplice but not his sexuality. Between these two categories of course lay the great majority of the clergy, who committed no fleshly sins, wholly conformed in liturgical practices, and therefore seldom appeared before the archdeacons' tribunals. The number of morally corrupt clerks in holy orders must also be set against that for all the parishes in the two archdeaconries for the whole period – a number which included more short-term curates than beneficed clergy – and the total probably exceeded two thousand, even allowing for the many poorer benefices being vacant for some years.[1]

While the low educational and social standards of the clergy at the beginning of our period and the later general improvement are well known,[2] the ethical qualities of the Essex clerics apparently showed no such rise; indeed, if judged solely by the number of cases – an unreliable criterion in itself – they tended to decline. In this our findings differ somewhat from those of several other writers, including Dr. Anglin, whose research covered only one Essex archdeaconry. In other words, the gradual replacement of those craftsmen and tradesmen[3] who entered the Church in the early years by men of superior academic and economic status was seemingly not accompanied by a reduction in the transgressions attributed to them. The pathetically poor qualities of many of the clergy in 1560 were

[1] There were well over one thousand incumbents and curates in the Archdeaconry of Essex alone (Dr. Anglin's thesis, 204–6).

[2] See esp. C. W. Foster, *op. cit.*, xviii–xxi, for Lincs., quoted *supra*, p. 192, n. 2; and F. W. Brooks, 'The Social Position of the Parson in the 16th Century' (*Journal of Brit. Archl. Ass.*, 3rd ser., x, 1945–47); Christopher Hill, *Economic Problems of the Church* (1956), 218. [3] Davids, *op. cit.*, 88–105, names several of such origin.

acknowledged by Archbishop Parker when writing to Grindal, Bishop of London: 'Occasioned by the great want of ministers, we and you both, for tolerable supply thereof, have heretofore admitted into the ministry sundry artificers and others, not trained and brought up in learning, and, as it happened in a multitude some that were of base occupations.' Harrison, seventeen years later, bewailed the poverty of many of the clergy and referred to 'our threadbare gowns'.[1] Even in the decade after Elizabeth's death the benefice of Broomfield was worth only £35 a year; and an Essex curate was receiving only £5 6s. 8d. and his diet.[2]

The weight of incrimination or suspicion laid on the Essex clergy for sexual offences cannot, however, be dismissed as insignificant on any count. Even allowing for some of it being grounded on mere gossip, over twenty clerics were brought before the courts on definite charges. These included three for bastardy, including an apparent case of pre-nuptial intercourse with a widow, one for adultery as well as perjury and bribery, one for being taken *flagrante delicto*, three for attempted seduction, one for suspected lewdness with two wenches of whom one was only ten years old, four for liaisons with their maidservants, one for a reputed brothel, two for attempted rape, and two for bigamy.

'Too many ignorant men of doubtful morals: the Elizabethan clergy were a mixed lot' is the pithy comment of a leading Tudor historian, who also writes: 'The defeat of the papacy, the victory of an anti-clerical laity, reduced the clergy in circumstances without, however, removing all the scorn and distrust which the old clerical pretensions had produced.'[3] Some of the clergy therefore earned little respect, which accounted for the even more numerous reports of their receiving oral censure or abuse from extrovert parishioners. A few of these, as we have seen, were adjudged false and led to the victimized clerics in turn bringing defamation suits. We now narrate the more objective charges, including drunkenness and the other non-sexual offences. A large number of the clergy were indicted at Quarter Sessions and Assizes for various crimes and offences;[4] if their names do not occur also in the archidiaconal archives, they are not referred to in the present volume.

Much of the time of the Elizabethan clergy was spent on their glebe and gardens. Their wives, like Parson Harrison's, were busy with household tasks, brewing, and the countless needs of families which were largely self-supporting from their own resources. In these ways many clerical families lived much like their parishioners, with whom they were in more intimate daily association than those of recent generations. The details of their misdeeds, the suspicions their behaviour aroused, and the coarse abuse they received, all serve to complement what we have already learned

[1] Harrison, *op. cit.*, 38.
[2] H. Smith, *Eccl. Hist. of Essex*, 273; A. T. Hart, *The Curate's Lot* (1970), 55.
[3] G. R. Elton, *England Under the Tudors* (1955), 421. [4] *E.L.: Disorder.*

about the lives of the Essex laity. Again, it is a one-sided account of human failings, but it helps us to penetrate deeper into the minds of some of the clergy and their parishioners.

Charges against the clergy for sexual immorality were somewhat fewer than those which the laity had to answer for defaming them for such acts, but relative numbers are immaterial, as some cases could be assigned to either category. Their flocks were unlikely to overlook clerical sins, whereas most of the illicit liaisons of the parishioners, despite the astonishing number that came before the courts, probably escaped presentment.

The three earliest cases are from the only Elizabethan court book of the Essex Commissary. The devout must have been shocked and the irreligious stimulated in the Easters. Edmund Styleman, vicar of High Easter, was presented for fornication with Elizabeth Lyvinge (1561). Under purgation he brought Lawrence Clayton, rector of Aythorpe Roothing, William Whyte (rector) of Sheering, Roger Clayton (rector) of White Roothing, Ralph Watson, curate of Great Easton, and four named laymen whose abode is not given, one of whom may have been the 'Mr. John Aylett' charged next year with bastardy. But none appeared at the next session and all were pronounced contumacious. The judge, referring to the grave peril of perjury, charged Styleman on oath and admitted him to self-purgation (a privilege rarely granted), after which he was restored to his former good reputation. Having already reached his three score years, he was to live another five years; High Easter had had him as vicar for exactly half a century, so he must have been born before 1500! Thomas Browne, vicar of Good Easter, was in deep disgrace (1562). In court he confessed that 'he had made a contract with Alice Kelly widow and hath already asked the banns between them three several times, and further saith that he hath gotten her with child.' Submitting himself to correction, the punishment ordered was that 'upon Sunday next he shall in his parish church read the whole homily of adultery and there declare to his parishioners his offence, desiring them to pray for him'. He was further enjoined to marry her on the Sunday after Trinity Sunday, and the case was then dismissed. Browne had been instituted in 1560 and resigned in 1565.

A pregnant woman accused the vicar of Braintree (1562). 'Katherine Baker hath lived incontinently and is with child by Sir Robert Basseloe.' Appearing in court, she submitted that he was the father of her child and 'none other but him'. Although clerical marriages had been reluctantly allowed three years earlier, was there possibly some question of her being unrecognized as the wife of the vicar, who himself had been instituted under Mary? The judge ordered her to attend again at the next session to hear his sentence of penance. (The 'Sir' is of course the medieval courtesy title for a non-graduate cleric, rarely used as late as this.) Basselow was deprived of his benefice three months later.[1]

There was rumoured unchastity between John Sadler, rector of Dunton, and his servant Ellen Hylton (1562), which both denied. The rector was assigned to purge by four clerics and four laymen; the maid, by four women. Robert Brown, rector of Fobbing, whose name is otherwise unknown, was suspected with John Perrye's wife (1563). Having declared his innocence, he had to purge himself by producing three clerical and three lay supporters at the next synod. Alice Hewes, servant of Lewis Maddock, rector of Fryerning, was likewise suspected (1565). She claimed that she was his blood-relation (*consanguinea*) and that she lived with Hewes Meredythe; she was discharged. In a charge against the unnamed rector of Hadleigh for incontinence (1565), no details are given, but must refer to Robert Rowland.

An extraordinary story was told by the rector of Creeksea in 1565. Eligeus Nollard had alleged that 'the vicar of Mayland and Okeley (*sic*) was taken on a-bed with a wench in goodman Stammar's house' A grave statement that would normally, as here, have led to the accuser's deposition being taken. In this case Nollard's testimony was certainly questioned, but his answers have no direct bearing on the charge. Flemish priest – tailor – priest again: such was the sketch he drew of his life. Aged 44, he affirmed as follows. 'He was brought up from his youth to 13 years in no school, but in Ypres in the school whereof was Mr. Francis and there learned grammar and accidence, and was of the age of 11 years at his coming and there continued two or three years. At the 13th year, anno 1535, he was admitted into the White Friars of Arras and there continued till the age of 23 years, at which time he was made deacon at Ypres under the Suffragan of Tyrwyn (Tournai) and subdeacon also in the church called St. James. He was made priest in the Bishop's chapel of Arras by the Suffragan, and after that continued to the White Friars again, but how long he cannot tell. At Ypres he forsook his friar's coat and so went to France and begged from town to town, after which time he never went to any school but continued a beggar in France three months. He hath said mass. Afterwards he went to Brabant, and at Calais he learned to be a tailor, and so learned the science whose name was Joyse the tailor at Markes in the market place. He came over at the loss of Calais into England and there served in the ministry.' There are several puzzling features. The case was heard at a session held at Maldon on 3 March 1565, when 'Mr. Loye rector of Creeksea' was presented for 'serving two cures and leaveth Creeksea unserved', but the institution of Nollard as rector is given as June 1564, 'on the death of the last rector'.[2] And while Mayland is close to Creeksea, why 'Okeley' (Great and Little Oakley are many miles away)? Robert Edin had been instituted vicar of Mayland in 1562, but the length

[1] Newcourt, *op. cit.*, ii, 89. [2] *Ibid.*, ii, 201, 412.

of his cure is not known. Was Nollard's accusation made the excuse for trying to find out whether he still had Romish leanings?[1]

In another abnormal charge (1566), 'Mr. Herne', vicar of Aveley (Robert Heron), was accused of having committed bawdery (*fovet lenocinium*) with his maidservant; his wife was suspected of incontinence; and his mother was pregnant in his house. Denying a rumour of incontinence, Thomas Chambers, rector of Langford, was directed to produce seven neighbouring priests at the next court (1569). In this exceptional case, however, he 'instantly' submitted a petition from himself and 'the other minister friends' and secured his dismissal. John Mader, rector of Tolleshunt Major, was presented (1579) upon a fame of 'living incontinently with one Priscilla King *alias* Harris and another wench about ten years of age'. John Mather, instituted in 1572, immediately resigned his benefice.

Among the ministers named in the censorious report compiled in 1584, immoral behaviour of four incumbents was mentioned: 'Mr. (Nicholas) Walles, parson of Pentlow, now in trouble for incontinency'; 'Mr. Halls (Edward Hall or Hales), vicar of Witham, incontinent'; 'Mr. Warrener (Francis Warner, vicar) of West Mersea, an adulterer'; and 'Mr. (John) White, vicar of Ramsey, presented for his scandalous life upon certain articles directed from the Queen's Majesty's Council, and also indicted for a common barrator'.[2] None, however, seems to have been cited before the Archdeacon of Colchester's court, except White. The charge laid against him, also in 1584, ran: 'He hath a very low voice; he is a troublesome man among his neighbours and disquieteth them by law unjustly and giveth them evil example some ways by his conversation of life; he is of a scandalous life.' Included in this indictment was that regarding his inability 'to deliver any doctrine but by bare reading of the letter', already noticed; on that, 'letters testimonial of the Bishop of London to preach, dated the previous year, were submitted, and he was discharged'.

Edward Binder, the 'whoremaster knave' of Blackmore, was presented (1586) because 'he pays honest women to commit adultery with him'; also more specifically for adultery with Ellen Rame. He was unsuccessful in declaring his innocence, and both parties were obliged to perform public penance. He was subsequently suspended. When Thomas Prince, vicar of Great Chesterford, was accused of fornication (1586), his denial was accompanied by the allegation that the bastard's mother had falsely laid paternity on him. The court enjoined his purgation, which had to be supported by four ministers and two parishioners, but he failed to produce them, the reasons for which will become apparent later. He was excommunicated and penance in his own church was decreed: 'He shall stand in the chancel door from the first lesson of morning prayer until all the service be said and a sermon preached, his face turned to the people

[1] See *Essex Recusant*, v (1963), 39–40. [2] Davids, *op. cit.*, 89, 94, 97, 98.

and a white rod in his hand, and then shall kneel down and ask God and the congregation forgiveness and promise hereafter never to give occasion of offence.' It is to be noted that this humiliating confession was to take place while another minister officiated in his place. The puritans' account described him as 'a man of very evil report'.[1]

Excommunicated for not answering his citation (1587), Henry Palmer, rector of Widford, had been presented for suspected sin with Alice, wife of William Dale, but attended next month and was absolved from the interdict. He admitted that he kept her company, for which he expressed his grief, and was discharged on being warned not to consort with her. The report had described him as 'heretofore a serving man or a soldier, a gamester, and pot companion', who had been 'called to the spiritual court for the same'.[2] Thomas 'Sare' (Sayer), the profligate rector of Wrabness, had to answer yet another citation, this time based on 'a common fame of incontinence with Mercy Ladbrooke', who had told two persons that he had committed fornication with her (1587). James Thwaites appeared as his special proxy and claimed that the presentment was insufficient in law, on which the rector was absolved and the case dismissed. The old lecher died in his rectory in 1608 after holding the benefice for forty-three years.

The court had been notified (1588) that 'Mr. (John) Harris, vicar of Messing, hath attempted to dishonest goodwife Pemerton of Messing and to have lain with her, that Mr. Ferris (*sic*) telling her that she was an idle wife she said she would keep her house better were it not for him, and that if she were called in question she would say more'. Ironically, a male parishioner had called him 'damned idle dog' in the previous year. Next year Harris was prosecuted for 'abusing his wife and pinching her (when) with child'. Drink and sex were the failings of William Kyrby, rector of East Donyland (1588), 'accused by Maydstone's wife to be a common alehouse haunter and a frequenter of a harlot's house, viz. Pitcher's wife there, who is suspected to be a light woman and a harlot'. The Pitchers were to be cited for the next session. About the same time, Cook, his neighbour at Great Birch and just as dissolute, called him 'fool and ass'. Accused of incontinence with Fish's wife (1588), Richard Wayne, curate of Weeley, failed to answer his citation and was excommunicated, but was later admonished that 'hereafter he doth not keep company with Fish's wife but only in public places as the church or the market', so that he must have submitted to the court.

The predicament of Richard Parker, the youthful vicar of Dedham, a prominent member of the Dedham 'classis' and an earnest puritan, was exceptional. The story of his downfall has been told by Dr. Collinson and is based on the archidiaconal records and on those of two other Church courts not used in the present book. 'Since the early months of 1588, he had been in trouble. First there were reports of an immoral association

[1] Davids, *op. cit.*, 90. [2] *Ibid.*, 99.

with the miller's wife of the next village, Stratford St. Mary (Suffolk), and these were examined by the bishop's commissary. Although Parker cleared himself of this charge with the help of a deathbed confession made by the miller's wife, a year later the whole town suspected an attempt on the chastity of two married women of Dedham: the wife of Robert Thorne, a sidesman, and the wife of one John Martin, a poor man who rented a shop and the rooms above it in part of Parker's bachelor vicarage. For his misbehaviour with Mrs. Thorne and certain "filthy speeches" overheard by a maid, Parker had been presented to the archdeacon and enjoined penance. Questioned by the more substantial townsmen about his dealings with Mrs. Martin, he admitted that he had "asked her the question, but, quoth he, I protest before God that I never did the deed with her". This was at midsummer 1589, the very time of the last recorded conference (of the classis). In November, Martin brought proceedings, and by the end of the year the vicar "with weeping eyes" was begging one of the churchwardens to "stand his friend and consider his estate, being a young man, and that his credit once taken away, he was utterly undone". The case was heard in the consistory court in May and July 1590, and by October Parker had resigned the living. Twelve years later he became vicar of Ketringham in Norfolk.'[1]

The prosecution of John Goldringe, rector of Langdon Hills (1589), for adultery and involving also perjury and bribery, reveals some remarkable features that will be recounted under Purgation.

Mr. (Francis) Sea, vicar of Ulting, was accused (1589) of 'retaining in his house one Green's wife of Colchester and thereby they live slanderously together'. The vicar brought her to court, and the judge ordered her to show the will of (blank) Green, late of Colchester, deceased, presumably as proof that she was a widow. Margaret Green, also presented, said that she was 'with Mr. Sea upon necessity, otherwise through her husband's fault she was like to starve'.

Charged on suspicion of adultery with Avice Page (1591), Thomas Howell, rector of Paglesham, maintained his innocence and was directed to produce six clerics to swear with him in purgation, of whom four were to be beneficed clergy in the deanery of Rochford. Brian Atkinson, rector of Wivenhoe, designated a 'whoremasterly knave' by an excommunicated woman (1590), was suspected of immorality with a Brightlingsea wife, and was also presented by the wardens as a man 'of evil and scandalous behaviour, to the offence of the parishioners and elsewhere, as we hear' (1591). Repudiating the charges, he had to secure the testimony of five clerics within the deaneries of Tendring, Colchester and Lexden. He was further accused of falling out with 'divers of his neighbours'. Whether the vicar of Ulting's trouble had merely arisen from his being a bachelor or

[1] Collinson, *op. cit.*, 438–49, quoting also from documents in the Greater London Record Office and the Guildhall Library.

widower with a housekeeper living in or not, the clergy were always liable to be called to account for such a woman; and this could have been the case when a plea of not guilty was put forward by William Winkfield, curate of Wix, presented for suspicious misbehaviour with his domestic servant (1592).

Although the rector was apparently not cited, Elizabeth, wife of Thomas Elliott of Farnham, was reported (1594) for 'living a long time with one Mr. (Leonard) Some, parson of Sheering, and hath been admonished by the parishioners and hath promised not to come to each other's company any more, yet have met together sithence very suspiciously'. Search for her was evidently unsuccessful. She seems to have been the wife of a yeoman of Hasely Farm in Farnham, whose will was proved in 1597. Prince, vicar of Great Chesterford, again presented by the wardens, was the subject of further suspicion (1594), 'upon a fame for begetting Joan Grigges of Ickleton (Cambridgeshire) with child, which we believe not to be true, because she challenged one Coote of Ickleton and said she would lay the child at his master's gate'. But a marginal note adds, 'Robert Coote is now at Chelmsford, late of Ickleton, who begot Joan Grigges' child'. Robert Hewetson, rector of Pitsea, was rumoured to be living dissolutely with Ellen Tate his maid (1596), but he secured absolution and his reputation was restored. James Wallinger, curate of Langdon Hills, however, was apparently guilty (1599) on 'a common fame among honest and credible persons' that he 'liveth incontinently with Susan Hales, single woman, of Grays Thurrock, and (as it is reported) he was taken in bed with her in his own house between 10 and 12 in the night by the conspiracy (i.e. joint effort) of others'. At the same time, as will be seen shortly, the wardens also put in a damning description of the misuse of his tongue.

A shocking story about Stephen Roberts, curate of Salcott, who, as also will appear later, had been described as a knave and alehouse haunter in the 1580s, was revealed in the deposition of Elizabeth Bird of his parish (1596), preserved in the Quarter Sessions records. A warrant had been issued, for the arrest of herself and one Perce because of their 'disordered lives', at the instigation of her husband. The curate counselled her to go away for a time, 'for if you do not', he said with a sinister hint, 'you will go to the gaol or else be whipped'. She went to Tollesbury and was followed by Roberts, offering to 'make her a testimonial'. Enticing her away, he read it in a wood, where he attempted to rape her. He had been trying to seduce her for two or three years, but she would not consent. A little afterwards, 'knowing that all the people where she kept were abroad at harvest, he came over the pales, and would have used her as she was wont, but she would not suffer him but made it known to the neighbours'. Another Salcott man gave further adverse evidence. Roberts had been bound by his own recognizance a fortnight earlier to appear, but defaulted. Yet, three days after the woman's statement, he had entered into another bond on behalf of Peter Roberts, a tailor of his parish (his brother?), to ensure Peter's taking service with a master; again he defaulted. Two weeks later and a week before the Michaelmas Sessions, he was indicted in general terms as a common barrator and disturber of the peace. At the next sessions his name was included in the composite writ for the arrest of numerous persons, but no more is learned about him.

When (William) Buck, vicar of Rainham, was presented (1599) by the wardens of Hornchurch on 'the common fame that he and the wife of goodman Harte of North End do live incontinently together', the court commanded that they must in future 'normally never resort to each other'.

The disgraceful fall of William Bangor, curate of Stanford Rivers, is of special interest, because his case was heard by both the spiritual and the secular courts. Accused (1599) of immorality, he declared his innocence. Details of the unusual proceedings that followed are also given under Purgation. His reputation was thus restored – in theory. But there was a little bastard and some question of his being the father. Who would maintain it? That was for Quarter Sessions to decide. At the Midsummer Sessions Bangor, so the record runs, 'affirmed in court that no witness had been hitherto examined for his part, therefore the court requests Sir Henry Graye, Sir Robert Wrothe, Mr. Doctor Dove (Thomas Dove, vicar of Walden), Mr. Smythe and Mr. Turner, or any three of them, to examine the matter of bastardy for a child begotten on Dorothy Barrett, and to certify their proceedings at the next Sessions, the Bench then to make a definite order therein, and meanwhile the reputed father and the mother to pay 6d. weekly each until the next Sessions'. The curate found Richard Luter, gentleman, of Kelvedon, who was lord of the manor of Myles, to stand bail for his next appearance, the recognizance being taken before Grey. The justices were duly informed of the result through a letter from Grey, Wrothe and William Smith as follows:

> They have examined Bangor and his witnesses, but could not find any matter that should tend to his purgation or clearing from the said charge, or that the woman was familiar with any other person than Bangor, and they thought it superfluous to examine any witnesses that should accuse him, the same being already procured. They caused Bangor and the woman to be face to face, who after great persuasions used by us for her to say no otherwise than the truth with great commination of punishment of God if she should wrongfully accuse him, she most confidently affirmed upon her salvation that Bangor was the father of her child and no other. But concerning a stock of money which Bangor alleged she had, with which she should bear the charge of keeping the child, they cannot understand that she has any stock or any goods or lands to maintain herself but by her labour, and if any charge should be laid upon her it would quickly revert to the parish. Therefore they desire some further order for the relief of the parish, which is greatly surcharged with poor people.

The order is not on record. The only other facts known about Bangor are that he had been licensed to teach grammar in the previous March[1] and

[1] Dr. Anglin's thesis, 342.

13 A LONG-LOST ELIZABETHAN REGISTER

'Lost' as far back as 1703, this register of Great Waltham was offered for sale by an unknown person in 1961 and acquired for public custody by the Friends of Historic Essex (p. 263). The last entry shows the union of two substantial families in the parish.

114

14, 15 PENANCE AND PURGATION

14 (upper)
Hugh Johnson of Wanstead, wearing a (white) sheet and holding a white wand, has to 'confess his fault in receiving a harlot into his house and suffering her to go away unpunished'. Grave sexual offences resulted in more humiliating forms of public penance (pp. 281–91).

15 (lower)
Suspected of incontinence with William Cordall, Joan Bowier of West Ham denies the charge and is assigned to purge herself with five neighbours (*sexta manu* denotes six oaths, including her own) (p. 292).

held the curacy at Stanford Rivers from April of that year until April 1600. What became of him cannot be ascertained.

'To lead an Elizabethan curate astray and then denounce him to the ecclesiastical authorities became in some parishes a recognized sport among the more undesirable elements of his congregation.'[1] The author of this passage does not give his source. It is a moot question whether Essex rustics, despite their propensity for coarse humour, had actually victimized any of the five accused curates in this way; but a vicar seems to have been duped by his drinking companions, as will be seen shortly.

Two charges of clerical bigamy are found. Religious life at Hadstock must have been at a low ebb early in 1589. 'Mr. Brame, curate of Hadstock', was cited because 'he hath two wives living, whereof one at Canterbury, and for that his letters of orders (ordination) are suspected to be forged, and he useth to play at cards Sundays, holydays and workdays'; to which is added, 'He is doubted to be minister'. At the same session he was also charged for 'not catechising and he hath not catechised this three-quarters of the year not passing once or twice'. Many villagers were summoned on the same day for church absence, including several ale-house-haunters, and three others also incriminated Brame (?Braine) by declaring that he had said, 'They ought not to present any man without warning, by the common articles'. In 1593 the wardens of East Horndon presented as a fact, not fame, but failed to prove, that Robert Hunter, the rector, 'had two wives alive'. Appearing, he explained that, 'in the time of Queen Mary's reign, before he was made minister, he was married to one Margaret Wattes, that she died as he hath heard about twelve years agone, and that within three or four years after her departure from him he was married to Elizabeth Turner of South Weald in the parish church there, with whom he lived 28 years. He married her (while) Margaret Wattes was then living, for that he saith Margaret was then the lawful married wife of Richard Mingsden of Maidstone in the county of Kent.' He was also detected that 'he giveth ill example of life by unquiet living, beating and chaining of his wife to a post, and is a slanderer of his neighbours'. The registrar noted, 'To bring the Lord Bishop Grindal's order for the allowance of his second marriage'.

It is clear that some of the clergy were much given to excessive drinking, gaming, swearing, and quarrelling. Abundant evidence of this, from indictments at Quarter Sessions, was related in the previous volume.[2] For drunkenness or alehouse-haunting, eighteen came before the Church courts. The report of 1584[3] accused nineteen ministers of habitual inebriety or frequenting alehouses, a few being 'notorious'; they include

[1] A. T. Hart, *The Curate's Lot*, 62. [2] *E.L.: Disorder*, see index of subjects.
[3] Davids, *op. cit.*, 77–78, 88–105.

six or seven whose cases occur also in the act books. The majority of those in the Church records held benefices; the remainder were curates, who could ill afford the habit. Some have already been noticed for indulging in illicit philandering as well as intemperate quaffing.

A strong plea for a more sympathetic view of the stipendiary curates, however, has been made by a recent writer. 'Deprived of their provision of books and the opportunities for study,' he writes, 'with few home comforts and no wife, they almost inevitably gravitated to the village alehouse during their brief leisure hours, where, after a hard day's work in the fields or about their pastoral duties, they could unashamedly mix with men of their own class, enjoy its warmth and good fellowship, and drown their sorrows in a friendly atmosphere.'[1]

The verdicts and sentences are not always given, but in the earliest case the punishment was humiliating. In 1564 Mr. (William) Lynch, rector of Beauchamp Roothing, presented 'for being a drunkard', was reprimanded by the judge because 'he hath not walked so wisely as he should have done', and was ordered not only 'to forbear coming to the alehouse and to give 20s. to the poor' but also to confess his fault 'on Friday next in the market of Chelmsford with a white sheet and a white rod'; also, 'for missing four sermons', he had to find a further 26s. 8d. for the poor: two very heavy fines. When Christopher Dryver of Stock was charged with not receiving communion in 1566, he declared that 'he and his wife were not in peace because the rector of Stock is a drunken man': a reference to Oliver Clayton, who had been instituted only a few months earlier. Mr. (Edward) Bordman, rector of Fyfield, was reported in 1574 as 'given to drunkenness' as well as to neglect of his duties. Two years later, when censured for administering the communion although excommunicate, he was enjoined to purge with six neighbours after denying that he was 'a common drunkard and a disquieter of his neighbours'. The same two charges were laid in the following month against Mr. (Ralph) Whitlin, rector of Corringham, whose compurgators were to be three clerics and three laymen.

There seems little doubt that Richard Atkins, curate of Romford chapel (a chapel-of-ease to Hornchurch), was too fond of the alepots. Having been cited in 1585 for being 'two times drunk in this month', managing to produce 'five honest men of the parish of Hornchurch' to testify for him, and securing his dismissal, he was up again next year on a fresh charge – 'so drunk that he could neither examine the youth in the catechism nor say evening prayer but would have said one lesson twice'. This time he failed to attend, was pronounced contumacious, and was excommunicated. An even more striking entry in 1587 about the bigamist curate of Hadstock reads that he 'is given to drunkenness, and he was so this court day and divers other times'. In 1576 Richard Spenser, curate of Greenstead-juxta-Colchester, was summoned for drunkenness, did not attend, was

[1] Hart, *op. cit.*, 35.

excommunicated, submitted, and was ordered penance. The sentence ran, 'To stand up before the preacher at the end of sermon in St. James's church (Colchester) and openly confess his faults, and shall write without the book such places against drunkenness as Mr. Challener the preacher shall instruct him, desiring the people there present to pray to God for his amendment'.

There was a minor wave of reports of clerical drunkenness in 1588. Mr. (William) Owin, rector of Fryerning, was 'an alehouse haunter'; Thomas Mynckes said that 'Mr. Roberts, late curate of Salcott, was a tosspot, alehouse haunter and table player'; and Thomas Stempe, curate of Burnham, who was presented for 'frequenting the alehouse and had no service on a Sunday in the afternoon', was found guilty and subjected to penance. Of this trio, the second went farther downhill as a would-be rapist in 1596.

In the following year, George Rowland, a Great Braxted parishioner, proclaimed Mr. Fountain the curate as being 'a scandalous minister and a drunkard, by reason whereof his conscience cannot permit him to receive Holy Communion at his hands in this good time of Easter; he was drunk in Osmund's house'. Further counts against him alleged (1) that 'he is in the alehouse at inconvenient times and will be overtaken with drink and useth hard speeches of his neighbours'; (2) that 'he did not catechize the youth of the parish, and the parishioners are unwilling to come to church because of his ungodly life'; and (3) that he 'did cast a figure, and he is continually absent from church' (cast a nativity, or tell a fortune).

Why Simon Cooke, rector of Great Birch, was incarcerated in Colchester town prison in 1588 is not clear. The indictment in the Church court ran, 'Not having that regard to his calling and function as he ought to have hath heretofore, he kept company in alehouses with some whose conversation (behaviour) was not answerable unto his calling, whereof some of them as he thinketh have been given to drunkenness, albeit as he saith never drunk in his company; and by reason thereof he was laid in prison by the bailiffs of Colchester'. The scribe added, 'The judge by reason of his imprisonment as for other causes etc. gave Cooke a salutary warning'. But that was not all, because it was also alleged that 'he was taken in bed with a woman in Suffolk', a charge which he denied. At the next session he produced 'Mr. Bartholomew Moodye, William Banbrick, Robert Holmes, William Robinson, clerks'. His compurgators were the vicars of Tollesbury and Tolleshunt Major and the rector of St. James, Colchester, but the last has not been identified. The judge decreed that he had been canonically purged and that testimonial letters to that effect be issued.

In 1590 Edward Goodwin, curate of Thorrington, was presented by the wardens of Wivenhoe for 'being so drunken at our town that he was not able to stand, nor go, nor yet rightly to speak', a convincing phrase. But James Whelehowse, vicar of Little Baddow, submitted in 1597 a disarming defence: 'Being in company with divers of his friends, they violently urged him to drink more than was fit', which secured his release. A series of complaints was preferred against one curate, who not surprisingly had a somewhat peripatetic career. In 1598 the Woodham Ferrers wardens stated, 'Mr. James Boxar, our hired minister, is a haunter of taverns, alehouses and other suspected places and much given to be drunken, to the grief and offence of the whole congregation'. Next year, 'now of Hadleigh', the Danbury wardens enlarged on the theme: 'He was so drunken that he either let the book fall into the grave or threw it in'; and, on another occasion, he boasted of his drunkenness and said that he was 'fitter to be a drunken companion than a minister'. In 1600, Mr. (Christopher) Mercer, vicar of Little Wakering, was cited as 'a common drunkard, giving very ill example of life' ; and again in the following year on an even graver charge, 'Being excommunicated, he did administer the Communion at Easter last and was drunken before he went to bed'.

The Essex puritan ministers' survey of 1584 indicted fourteen clerical gamesters, of whom five were among those also noted for alehouse-haunting. The archdeacons' books record seven, of whom two occur in the same report. John Layland, rector of Thundersley, 'playeth at cards and dice all the week long' (1563). (John) Brown, rector of (East) Horndon, 'enticeth men's servants to play for a shoulder of mutton' (1564), confessed, and was punished: 'To stand in the mid pace of the church with his surplice and a white rod in his hand, confessing that he hath done evil in alluring the youth to play at tables, and to give 20d. to the poor.' Mr. (Thomas) Martyndall, rector of South Shoebury, was 'a dicer and carder whereby he lost this Christmas £3' (1565). An unnamed curate of Grays Thurrock 'plays at painted cards' (1566); he was enjoined 'to desire the parishioners to pray for him'. George Elmer, curate of Canewdon, was 'a haunter of alehouses, a drinker, and a player at cards and tables' (1586). Dr. (Robert) Salisbury, rector of Great Holland, had to answer for being 'a gamester and a player at tables and at alehouse', as well for not catechizing and reading the homilies (1585). Stephen Roberts, the dissolute curate of Salcott, was reported for 'playing at tables all the day' with one of the sidesmen (1587); two parishioners, presented for the same offence, protested that they had done so on his solicitation.

Among the clergy given to swearing or brawling, or both, four were accused in the report of 1584, of whom the notorious Levit, rector of Leaden Roothing, was also incriminated for gaming, hunting and fighting.[1] He was beyond reform, and died in 1591 before his indictment for counterfeiting a coin reached the Assizes.[2] James Wallinger, the lecherous curate of Langdon Hills, according to the wardens in 1599, was reported at the same time 'to be a common swearer and a blasphemer of the name of God and a man whose tongue is full of ribaldry and filthy speeches, to the great discomfort of his coat and calling and to the evil

[1] Davids, *op. cit.*, 92. [2] *E.L.: Disorder*, 82.

ensample of others; item, a common brawler and a debate maker, and a sower of sedition between neighbour and neighbour'. He was suspended.

Akin to brawlers were barrators, who were disturbers of the peace and quarrellers. In 1598 two vicars were charged as common barrators and as such laid themselves open to indictment before the secular court. Mr. Christopher Goffe of Great Waltham was 'indicted at the Assizes as the report goeth', which he denied; but the Assize file is missing. The other was Thomas Austen of Aveley, who 'standeth indicted for a common barrator at the last Quarter Sessions' and was now charged afresh in the spiritual court for not saying prayer or service on Wednesdays and Fridays. He had in fact come before the justices of the peace for levying an exorbitant mortuary fee on a parishioner.[1] Disharmony prevailed at South Hanningfield rectory in 1592. John Pokins and his wife were both presented for 'very often brawling and scolding together and have not lived quietly as man and wife ought to do'. The rector attended and declared that 'his wife was a very disquiet woman and hath been void of her perfect senses'. Perhaps the most quarrelsome of all was William Pinder, another rector of Stock. In 1587 his parishioners even petitioned the High Commissioners to settle their differences and to order him to answer for the controversies he had created in the parish.[2]

A multiple accusation was tendered in 1599 by the Chipping Ongar wardens:

> We certify how one William Farrington, clerk, of Chipping Ongar, as he saith, liveth idly in our town without serving any cure, contrary to the Articles and laws ecclesiastical.
> Item, we present him for not receiving the Sacrament in our church for three quarters of this year, of purpose going out of the town every Communion to avoid it.
> Item, we present him to be a malicious, contentious and uncharitable person and a railer of our minister and of most of the inhabitants that profess religion, calling them all heretics, hypocrites, such as he hath ever in every place detested, clowns, etc.
> Item, we present him for his often absence from prayers on the sabbath days in contempt of our minister and for his usual departure out of the church at such time as he cometh, before the people be dismissed, contrary to the Articles.

Later in the year he was detected for teaching school in the adjacent parish of Fyfield, being unlicensed. Next year he was licensed as a curate by the Chancellor of the diocese, but having no degree was obliged to take exercises. Two years later, then curate of Stanford Rivers, he was suspended for taking services after having been inhibited at the recent archdiaconal visitation.

The four series of wills of the Essex Church courts[3] for the Elizabethan

[1] *E.L.: Disorder*, 90. [2] *Ibid.*, 69–70, 144.
[3] Those of the archdeaconries of Essex, Colchester, and Middlesex (Essex & Herts. jurisdiction), and of the Commissary Court of London (Essex & Herts. jurisdiction), deposited in the E.R.O. (Emmison (ed.), *Index to Wills at Chelmsford, 1400–1619*, Brit. Rec. Soc., vol. 78, 1958).

period include 79 wills of Essex clergymen, but none relate to any of the men referred to in this chapter. The dissolute rector of Wrabness, Thomas Sayer, made his will five years after the end of our period and finished it (1608), 'thus beseeching the Almighty Lord to give me a portion of his everlasting kingdom'. The wills proved in the Prerogative Court of Canterbury yield 21 Essex clerics' testaments,[1] only one of which concerns us in this book: Peter Wentworth, rector of Great Bromley, who will appear in our last chapter on Contempt. Clerical wills were mostly proved in the Consistory Court.[2]

[1] Photostats of all Elizabethan Essex wills in the P.C.C. (now in the Public Record Office, about 1,000) were recently purchased by the Friends of Historic Essex and will be deposited in the E.R.O. when the present writer has finished using them.
[2] These wills are deposited in the Greater London Record Office.

7

The Parish Officers

While the clergy looked after the spiritual needs of the laity, the churches and church affairs in general were in the hands of the wardens and their assistants – the synodsmen, sidesmen, or questmen. The duties of the churchwardens were manifold and heavy, as are apparent from the countless presentments for disrepair of the fabric or neglect to provide proper furnishings and articles used in worship.[1] There was therefore sporadic reluctance in accepting the office, despite its being an honourable one. An added reason, unconnected with the care of the buildings or services, caused many to seek exemption, and this will be referred to shortly.

The vast majority of parishes elected two wardens annually. Barking had four, one for each of the Town, Ilford, Chadwell and Ripple wards. Chelmsford, by ancient custom, appointed three, the third serving for Moulsham. Only a few other large parishes had separate churchwardens or chapelwardens for independent townships, such as Romford in the parish of Hornchurch. The wardens were normally chosen by the joint consent of the minister and the parishioners.

In some places, as with the constable and other manorial officers, the duty was known in advance because of a regular rota of farms and other large holdings, the occupiers of which served in turn. There was no property qualification, but, unlike the offices of constable and surveyor of highways which were usually regarded as humble, that of churchwarden was rarely given to a poor parishioner.

Excuses offered to the court for not taking office provide sidelights and some may be compared with similar answers for absence from church. A 'servant to Mistress Bradbury and much absent, thereby not fit for office' (Littlebury, 1588), worked for a family with much property in the Littlebury area. James Watts, 'servant to Mr. Harvye of Cressing Temple and daily attending upon his business, so he cannot attend the office' (Tollesbury, 1594), refers to Francis Harvey, an active J.P., and may imply that Watts was his clerk. John Bacon, 'household servant with Sir Thomas Lucas' (Greenstead-juxta-Colchester, 1598), was evidently employed at St. John's Abbey, Colchester, which was Lucas's house. Richard Keeler stated that he was 'farmer to Mr. Bankes, lord of (the manor of) Manningtree, and much employed in his business, so as he cannot intend

[1] Their duties are set out more fully in the Canons of 1571.

(*sic*) to the office of churchwarden; also he lately came to the town and is not fully acquainted; and also an innkeeper' (Manningtree, 1597); one or other of the alternatives he put forward led the judge to order the election of a substitute. 'Cannot attend to the office' was the excuse given by George Howes of Mile End, Colchester (1593), who had been excommunicated for not appearing at the recent Visitation and explained that he was 'the attendant and retained servant of Lord Darcy' (of St. Osyth's Priory). A carpenter, 'much from home' was exonerated, the judge deciding that, 'in case two of the parishioners came not to be churchwardens', he would nominate two himself (Layer Marney, 1590). A similar plea, 'much from his parish so as he cannot attend to the office', was also submitted by William Sdvanne (*sic*) of Wrabness, 'seafaringman', who gratuitously advanced the names of two men 'continually at home' (1599); and in the same year a Greenstead (by Colchester) man stated that he was 'a bachelor and a servant to his mother and by no means fit to the office', when the court ordered 'another honest neighbour being a married man to be called in his place'.

Holding another parochial or manorial appointment or having served as warden for two years or longer was a more justifiable objection. John Howland of Wicken Bonhunt complained in 1586 that 'he was constable of the parish and so hath been for five or six years, since which time about Hallowmas last he was chosen by Mr. Swinho parson there churchwarden there, and that if he were not constable he would be willing to be churchwarden, for he saith he cannot serve two places at a time'. He named six 'honest men fit for that office and without any office in the parish', and desired to be discharged. The same request was made in 1600 by John Cookes of St. Martin, Colchester, who 'hath borne churchwarden more than a year and of late he is chosen constable by the Bailiffs of Colchester', and he alleged that 'Goodman Jackson is a sufficient man and not in any office except an overseer of the poor'; Jackson was to be cited. 'There is no reason why he should use both offices' was similarly put forward by an Elmdon constable in 1594; and George Sache, elected a warden of Great Tey in 1588, expressed the view that 'he is a collector for the poor there and also a trained man, whereby he cannot intrude to the office of churchwarden'.

Nicholas Clerke, who had been chosen for Great Totham in 1590 but had failed to attend five consecutive sessions and was declared contumacious, was discharged because 'it appeared to the judge that he is an attorney'. The statement of a Coggeshall warden named Clerk in 1596, is also of interest. 'He is now of the 24 of Coggeshall but lately dismissed by the company, and that always the churchwardens have been time out of memory of man of the 24': an early mention of the body which governed the parish in much the same way as the well-known 'Company of the Four and Twenty', or select vestry, of Braintree.

Old age was advanced on three occasions: by Mr. Thomas Spackman of Chigwell, 'above 70 years old, weak in body, and not able to execute the office' (1592); by William Welles of Greenstead (by Colchester), aged 74 and 'unable to serve' (1597), whereat the judge ordered another to be found; and by William Moore of Pattiswick, also 74 and 'continually troubled with the colic and besides sickly and not able to travel', with the same result, on which 'Mr. Nowell' (an otherwise unknown incumbent) and the wardens were instructed to elect a substitute. In 1588 the court decided that 'two parishioners of White Colne be cited to function by reason the old churchwardens were so simple (i.e. either humble or half-witted) and poor men'; and in 1597 a Langenhoe man alleged inability to serve because of his poverty. So did a Lexden warden, 'a poor and labouring man', who sought exemption in 1591 because he had already acted, 'a year, happen two years past'. If somewhat vague about his term, he had no doubts about a substitute, for 'there are divers sufficient men in the Queen's book' (the subsidy lists), who in his opinion were 'meet to serve, which have no office neither served sithence he was churchwarden, as Mr. Stowers', five named villagers, 'and others, yet out of course he was of late chosen again' ('course' probably refers to the rota). The judge ordered that the second man among those suggested should enter into office; and similarly the minister and parishioners of Tolleshunt Knights in 1589 were told to choose another in place of one who had acted for two years. Only one other warden, William Hall of All Saints, Colchester, seems to have excused himself because of length of office; he declared in 1598 that 'he served six or seven years together about five years past and Andrew Clover is willing to be churchwarden in his place'.

The annual Easter meeting of another Colchester parish was evidently not clear about whom they had appointed. Nicholas Bennold, 'elected as is pretended' (so he alleged in 1590), declared, 'The sabbath day by a common vestry there was chosen Robert Smith gentleman and one Monson and not him, but only he was warned yesterday about 1 or 2 of the clock to be here' (in court to take the oath). He was ordered to prove his statement.

A few parishioners decided firmly to object to their having to serve. John Trussell of Purleigh 'will not be churchwarden' and was excommunicated (1566), and Thomas Geffery of Wickford 'obstinately refuseth to be churchwarden, notwithstanding he was chosen by the consent of the parson and parishioners' (1575). Very determined was Edward Riche of Langford, presented (1599) for 'drinking himself drunk to the end it might be a reasonable excuse for him not to be churchwarden (1599).' His allegation runs, 'He is lame and cannot come or travail about the office and offers to give 13s. 4d. to the poor to be discharged'. Instead, he had to purge with five credible men.

On taking office, willingly or unwillingly, the churchwardens, with the sidesmen, had a duty very different from looking after the church: that of presenting every kind of ecclesiastical offence, committed or even suspected to have been committed, by any parishioner, including the minister. How numerous and heterogeneous were the offences under the court's jurisdiction we have already seen. But many wardens failed in this inquisitorial responsibility. Ordinary human psychology lay behind much of this. Why should they, before being stripped of their brief authority, alienate the goodwill of their friends or earn the hostility of their neighbours? The point needs no stressing, but this facet of Elizabethan life, utterly incongruous with modern concepts about moral or other informers, has often been overlooked by social historians. A few entries taken at random will explain why so many wardens were themselves censured by the courts for not acting in this way; suppressing reports of parishioners' immorality has already been exemplified. 'He threatened the wardens because they did present him for working and for absence from church on Sunday'; 'They did not present one Joan Sturgin who dwelleth in a little house in the churchyard for quarrelling and fighting there' (All Saints, Colchester, 1590); 'Bob Avis, for carrying away his maid, the same being under their noses and knowing thereof': doubtless she was pregnant (Markshall, 1595); 'For not presenting divers things corrigible as those who did camp (i.e. played football) there upon Sunday 3 May last' (Feering, 1601). Even more naturally, a few wardens abused the privilege of office in keeping silence about their own transgressions. In 1596, for example, Roger Banckes of Great Wenden was cited 'for suspicion of incontinency with Margaret his maidservant, yet never presented, he being a churchwarden' (his 'partner' was likewise summoned, but discharged). But most wardens, as their oath obliged them, duly submitted their reports about misdoings, for which many were rewarded, as related under Defamation, with slanderous or abusive language; or even told, in another context, when the judge ordered an offender to apologise, 'I would rather see the churchwardens' hearts out'.

Equally numerous were those who were guilty generally in not bringing their quarterly presentments, 'detections', or 'bills'. In 1587 the Colchester archdeaconry registrar compiled a list of the wardens who had not brought in their bills at the previous Christmas. Four years later, he wrote, 'Memorandum to send out excommunications against all churchwardens which have not given in their quarter bills'.

William Seredge, vicar of East Hanningfield, was himself presented in 1587 (as so often for other offences) for not giving warning to the wardens 'to look to their duty in service time, for such as are absent'; he forgot, he said, but would be more diligent.

John Wenden, one of the Wakes Colne wardens, reported his fellow, who 'would not present' church absentees in 1587, 'and would not see them, but winked at it'. The wardens of Mistley-cum-Manningtree defaulted in 1600, for 'in their quarter bills they have not presented anything at Michaelmas or Christmas, and yet the church windows want glazing, the leads decayed, service book wanting, and a chest with locks and keys according to the canons for the new register book'. But in 1576 William Savering of Stock had gone too far in the opposite direction. 'He made a bill of presentment last year against their parson Oliver Clayton and presented it to my Lord Rich, which he ought not to do, being one of the churchwardens.' Robert, 2nd Lord Rich, was a leading Essex puritan; Clayton, unlike his successor, was never in trouble with the Church authorities. A townsman of St. Nicholas, Colchester, was charged in 1593 with 'bewraying' (fouling) his fellow warden's presentment: a pity that the reason for his ire is not vouchsafed.

It was no easy matter for the wardens of some of the populous parishes to estimate the quantity of bread and more especially wine, which it was their duty to provide. In a few rare instances, perhaps as a safeguard, clerics entered the names of the communicants in their register. The earliest Romford register has eleven pages of lists for the last two decades of the century, but those for other parishes are mostly confined to the following century. The prevalent politico-religious attitudes of Elizabeth's time might well have dictated the desirability of compiling annual parochial lists of communicants and of those confirmed or in need of confirmation: an extra clause in the Act of Uniformity making such lists obligatory and Elizabethan England would have become the demographer's Utopia.

In 1584 'Mr. Genor' (John Jener, rector) of Great Bardfield, as well as the wardens, were directed to explain why 'certain of the communicants wanted wine upon Sunday after St. Andrew's Day'; their answer was, 'By reason that a greater number did communicate than they looked for, as that divers could not have wine, because there was but one pint provided by them'. The Church could not tolerate such inexcusable deprivation of its members' rights, and the judge decided, 'Some Sunday before the next court, they shall read a homily or else preach a sermon concerning the reverent and orderly receiving of the sacrament, and Mr. Genor and the churchwardens shall openly confess their faults'. Under 1599 the act book has a note, 'Cite the churchwardens and minister of Terling for that through their default in not providing wine there departed divers or many to the number of thirty without the Communion'. Faced with the same predicament, the officers of another parish solved the problem in a most reprehensible manner. In 1600 the Great Tey wardens 'mingled beer with wine for want of wine for the Communion'. While admitting their inadequate provision 'by reason of the great number of communicants coming without expectation', they claimed that the mixing was done without their consent by the sexton, who was cited for the next session, and in the meantime they had to perform penance.

On several other occasions wardens were reprimanded for failing to provide bread or wine; or both, as at West Bergholt in 1590. Those of Hatfield Peverel in 1584 confessed that the minister had given them warning, but each 'trusted to his fellow churchwarden to provide'. And in 1579 John Paterson, one of the Boreham wardens, explained, 'On the first Sunday in November the communicants after service ended being ready to receive, they were rejected for want of bread and wine; he affirmed openly that he would not out (*sic*) no money for it and would not prepare any, for that he could not tell how to come by his money again'. Both were punished by public penance in their own churches. Similarly in 1596 those of Elmstead 'refused to provide bread and wine'; this they denied and were commanded to produce five men to testify with them. Five years afterwards William Riche, 'late churchwarden of Elmstead, upon Christmas tarried at home, and a Communion being appointed, did not bring the wine and bread, whereby the Communion was disappointed, and likewise the Sunday after Easter'. One would have imagined that the sacramental elements were placed overnight in the church chest. Even so, this man, perhaps a late sleeper, would have held up communion as the three keys were by law kept in the custody of the minister and the two wardens. Another defendant was Thomas Minkes, warden of Salcott, who in 1593 'carried away the wine from the minister which was left at the Communion'.

To complete the account, we must refer here to four cases bordering on profanity in connexion with the Lord's Supper. While not entirely anticipating Marie Antoinette's own ingenuous solution, John Atkynson, rector of Nevendon, was even more reprehensible and was duly prosecuted in 1567 for 'ministering with loafbread and cakes, to the disturbance and unquietness of the parishioners'. He was judicially sentenced 'to stand in the pulpit after the reading of the Gospel and confess his fault'.

If the crowd of communicants at Great Tey received the Blood of Christ in the form of wine mixed with beer, those who received at Springfield in 1564 drunk an unholy potion. A worse charge was laid against 'Mr. (George) Cokerell, rector of Springfield, and (blank) Harrys, clerk'. Harrys was accused 'for that he administered the Communion in beer'. Both were sentenced to public penance on the following Sunday with the usual white rod and white sheet. Cokerell held the moiety of the rectory known as Springfield Richards. Another charge was that of desecration of the Body of Christ. In 1595 Joan Wheeler of Dengie 'brawled in the church on Whitsun day before the Communion and did not eat the bread of the Communion but put it in her pocket at Easter last was twelvemonth'; Edmund her husband attended and denied the indictment. What is one to make of the obscure presentment by the Hawkwell wardens in 1565 of an unnamed curate for 'no worse faults than to minister with ale'? 'Minister' normally means to administer communion. In this context it might possibly imply alehouse-haunting with his friends, and if so it is another example of sardonic Essex humour. No more can be gathered from the court book.

It was inevitable that some wardens failed or even refused to render their accounts at the synods. Nearly twenty pairs of delinquents have been noted; all had to rectify the matter. Doubtless, a few had lost the scraps of paper on which they had jotted down their disbursements; others found money sums a headache, could not balance their accounts, or would not produce the cash balance. William Stammers of Prittlewell in 1600 withheld the accounts from the new warden 'by reason of sums of money which he hath laid out for the parish' (1600). The East Horndon wardens explained that 'the parishioners will not come to reckon with them' (1590), which did not surprise the judge as the population was very small, and they were allowed to submit their unaudited accounts directly to him. John Tiball of Ramsden Bellhouse would not receive the accounts of Nicholas Tabor and (blank) Fuller, late wardens, because he 'was not chosen by their parson'.

Other wardens defaulted in their obligations with regard to the ordinary necessities. At Hadleigh, for instance, 'There wanteth a bier to carry dead bodies to the church'. In 1578 the court had evidently some reason for suspecting that the vestments at Dengie were inadequate and demanded their production by the wardens and the curate: 'They brought in their surplice, which surplice is torn and very undecent and uncomely; whereon the judge, for that they neglected their oaths, ordered them to confess their fault and prepare a new surplice of holland cloth of 5s. the ell containing eight ells, before the Feast of All Souls'; at the next session, however, they were directed to provide a new surplice containing six ells at 2s. 8d. the ell. A few failed 'to deliver the church goods' to their successors. But by far their commonest neglect was 'for the reparations' of the church, an offence which ranged from 'grave decay' or 'in ruins' to lack of minor repairs.

An original and very censorious letter about two Creeksea churchwardens (one, a former sidesman) was pinned into an act book at 1572. It is addressed to 'Mr. Rust, Official to the Right Worshipful Dr. Walker, Archdeacon of Essex' (William Rust was also vicar of Felsted and headmaster of the school), 'Dengy' is written in a different hand at the top, but must refer to the deanery of that name, as Arthur Harrys lived at Creeksea Hall and the wardens' names are also those of Creeksea families. The right-hand side was slightly defective when it was printed by Archdeacon Hale over a century ago (the original is lost):

> Salutem in domino. This is for to let your Worship understand that Jasper Anderkyn who was churchwarden hath done nothing of that which he was appointed by your Worship at Midsummer to do. For the churchyard lieth to commons and all other things in the church is undone. But that Mr. Harrys did buy the bible, we should have had nothing done. A man so negligent in his office I never knew none, being so much c . . . as he hath been. I pray you deal with him so that may be a

precedent for them that shall have the office; for they will but jest at it and say it is but a money matter. Therefore let them pay well for the penalty which you set on their heads. The cause why I do write thus unto your Worship is that you be not abused in your office by their much intreating for themselves, for Jasper Anderkyn stands excommunicated. And here is one William Panton who was one of the sworn men and how is chosen to be the churchwarden, and he hath also negligently forgotten his oath, for whereas he should have looked for the coming of others, he himself was absent the . . . of June, the 6 day of July and the 13 day of July and the 20 day of July, and going out of the church at mid service, idle well a-proved. And 25 day of July which was St. James day and the 27 day of July and many other times that I have not well noted, because it belonged to the churchwarden and the sworn men. And thus much I have given your Worship to understand that you may the better examine them when the parties come before your Worship. I pray you, learn Panton the way to the church, for he is a young man and sharply rebuke him and he will be a precedent for others.

By me John Mather.[1]

We must certainly not, however, give the impression that Elizabethan churchwardens were generally neglectful in their duties. So far from that, the archdeacons' courts had to reprimand only a small proportion of backsliders. Against them must be set the total number of office holders during the period. The two archdeaconries contain 247 parishes of the 416 parishes in the county. In the long years of Elizabeth's reign, allowing for gaps on the two series of court books, well over 15,000 Essex churchwardens were appointed. Their office was no sinecure, and we owe many of them a debt of gratitude for discharging the unpaid task of looking after the fabric and furnishings of their churches, despite the many reports about dilapidations. They were guardians of parochial dignity, responsible to the Anglican Church for providing some of the essentials of corporate worship.[2] But most of the colourful ritual had gone with the Reformation. In the Colchester archdeaconry court book under 1543 we read of one of the Coggeshall wardens' assistants. They presented 'Thomas Paykoke that he hath broken an ancient and laudable custom of the parish in making torches that hath been used time out of mind of man'. The man who had refused to serve as 'one of the torchwardens' in being elected was probably owner of the early sixteenth-century house, later the 'Fleece' inn and still surviving. It lies on the west side of John Paycocke's richly-ornamented house, which had been built by an earlier Thomas, the clothier merchant, about 1500,[3] and now belongs to the National Trust.

The annual autumn synod had to be attended by the minister, churchwardens and sidesmen of each parish, the last assisting the wardens in making their presentments. 'Sidesman' is not a corruption of synodsman, as so often stated, and 'sideman' is the earlier form, first found in Foxe's *Book of Martyrs* (1570). Alternative titles were *testes synodales*, questmen (i.e. enquiry men), or sworn men. Not much is known about their activities

[1] Hale, *Precedents,* 155.
[2] For a few other entries in the act books, 1570–1640, see *Ess. Rev.*, li, 145–50, 200–04.
[3] Cf. article on 'Paycocke's House' (*Trans. E.A.S.*, 311–21).

in Elizabethan times, but various references in other chapters illustrate their work. The number was not fixed by law, but like churchwardens two seems to have been usual, though depending actually on the ancient custom of each parish.

Various excuses, as with some wardens, were offered when elected questmen had been cited for not fulfilling their office: John Sherman of Thorrington, because 'he is in the service of Mr. Knightlye and thereby cannot attend to the office of a questman' (1588); Esias Knight of Tollesbury, 'a seafaring man and much from home, a poor man and sickly, and not able to serve' (1589); and Henry Cleveland of St. James, Colchester, 'collector for the poor and a trained man and a sworn man for the council of the town, whereby he cannot intend (*sic*) upon that office but desireth to be dismissed' (1589). In the same year William Sander, elected as *testis synodalis* by the Coggeshall wardens, declared that 'he was not of Great Coggeshall but of the hamlet of Little Coggeshall or St. Nicholas' parish in Little Coggeshall, being of the peculiar jurisdiction of Canterbury and therefore not tied to be a questman or subject to the jurisdiction of this court'. Richard Bennett, 'chosen by the vestry of the parish of West Ham to be a sideman' in 1584, refused to act, 'but the churchwardens request to have him according to order'. There was evidently disharmony in the parish, as the wardens themselves were presented next year because 'they will not conclude (i.e. settle business) with the sworn men, according to their oaths'. It was reported from Tendring in 1582 that Thomas Hills, a questman, had been 'absent divers times from the church'; and from Henham in 1594 that John Perrye, a questman, had been 'very negligent in coming to church', and he was ordered 'to join with his fellow questman to make a bill'.

That minor but traditionally self-important functionary, the parish or church clerk, had a variety of duties which might include writing the church accounts, the draft parish register and the vestry minutes as well as assisting in the services by leading the singing and so on. His office was in the hands of the parson, or if non-resident in that of the curate. It was a freehold, held for life. The only qualifications required were that he was a man of 'honest conversation' and could read and write. By fairly general custom he received alms which every parishioner was expected to give, in bread, eggs, or otherwise in kind or in money, at Easter, Christmas or each quarter. In course of time the voluntary alms became 'wages', and about twenty persons are recorded for refusing to pay such wages. In 1598 two men of Barking 'wilfully denieth the payment of the usual clerk's wages to Father God our town clerk' and were ordered to pay: a puzzling name but twice clearly written, probably for the surname Good or Gould. 'Not paying the clerk's wages for the knell' at a funeral occurs once: but tolling the passing bell was usually the sexton's duty.

Apart from such references, parish clerks rarely claimed the attention of the courts. Only on two occasions, both in 1580, do the records reveal an inability, for which they were not unnaturally presented: the clerks of Bradwell-juxta-Mare and Woodham Mortimer were both reported because they 'cannot read'. But a Romford parish clerk was in trouble for teaching without licence. The act books are singularly bereft of colourful incidents about these dignitaries, whose office was lowly but steeped in parochial custom.[1]

Looking after the interior of the church and its contents, bell-ringing and grave-digging were the chief tasks of the sexton, who is an occasional figure in the records. Appointed by the minister, he received 'wages' in kind or money in much the same way as the clerk. A few were unlucky in not receiving payment from one or two parishioners, such as the man who 'refused to pay the sexton's wages, very often demanded, and will not pay but bids the churchwarden do what he can, for he will not pay, which wages is but 4d.' The presentment by the Beaumont wardens in 1598 of 'Scattle the sexton, for intruding himself to read evening prayer, Mr. Gabriel Elkin, minister, present and thereto appointed' is unique; Elkin was the curate. One sexton took upon himself to make a grave and bury a woman without the burial service; another refused to toll the passing bell. In 1584 the wardens of St. Botolph, Colchester, reported that 'Thomas Ward our sexton is a railer, a blasphemer, a swearer and a slanderer, and suspected of drunkenness'. While Petruchio, who was to tame the shrew, 'threw the sops all in the sexton's face', we are vouchsafed no details of the alleged assault by one parson on the sexton. Robert Smythe, sexton of Coggeshall, with William Harr a fuller and others, was cited, also in 1584, to attend as witness against a woman who had broken into the church with a pole at twilight in order to release a boy accidentally shut inside. Little more can be gathered about these useful but humble officers.

[1] For details, see W. E. Tate, *The Parish Chest* (3rd. edn., 1960), and the Taunton act book, 1623–24 (*Som. Rec. Soc.*, xlii, 19–21).

8
The Buildings

Churches and Chancels

The archdeacons' records add immeasurably to our knowledge of the people of Elizabethan Essex, especially the ordinary folk and the clergy. Unfortunately the same cannot be said about the fabric of the churches, though there is more about the bells and plate.

The Essex court books, like those of every other area, abound with presentments of churches in need of repair, but they are mostly brief and uninformative. Of the hundreds of entries, the great majority deal with fairly minor defects, and it is very doubtful whether these have any interest either for the architectural or for the parish historian. The story of 'ruinous' Essex churches begins as far back as the record of the personal visitation of the Dean of St. Paul's to the Chapter's own churches in 1297![1]

Churchwardens' accounts of all periods chronicle the continual need for trifling repairs and are usually more specific about their nature than the court books. Wardens' records for the Elizabethan period are extant for eight Essex parishes; nearly all of these are on deposit in the Essex Record Office, and some have been published, in full or by way of extracts.[2]

Nearly all our old churches were built, enlarged or rebuilt in the medieval period, giving England its treasured heritage. Those Elizabethan squires and affluent parishioners who were inclined to good works directed their activities rather to charitable foundations, some of which involved immense sums. Many less substantial people, too, gave in their lifetimes or left in their wills sums of money for similar social objects.[3] Donations or bequests for the fabrics or furnishings of churches were less frequently made. In the next volume, which will incorporate a mass of material on social life drawn largely from wills, about two hundred legacies to Essex churches, chiefly for repairs, will be referred to or quoted. Other testators, however, were more disposed to make bequests for sermons, and much more so to leave money for the relief of the parochial poor. A novel post-

[1] *V.C.H., Essex*, ii, 12–15.

[2] Emmison (ed.), *Catalogue of Essex Parish Records* (E.R.O., revd. 1966), has details of those that have been printed. For two recent short illustrated descriptions of selected churches, see A. C. Edwards, *Essex Churches* (E.R.O., revd. 1966), who kindly read through this section, and K. D. Box, *Twenty-Four Essex Churches* (1970).

[3] The most comprehensive account of the changed attitude is that of Professor W. K. Jordan, *Philanthropy in Rural England, 1480–1660* (1961).

Dissolution feature is the provision by substantial testators for handsome, if ostentatious, monuments commemorating themselves or their families.

The building of new churches in Elizabethan England was a rare event. In Essex, Woodham Walter is the sole example; this mellow red-brick building was consecrated by the archdeacon of Essex in 1564. The period was remarkably barren in providing new furnishings, as fonts and pews. The big exception of course is communion plate; but why, for an age in which supreme importance was attached to the sermon, and especially in puritan Essex, have we virtually no surviving Elizabethan pulpits except that at Chipping Ongar? (See plate 8.)

In the following pages we shall refer only to churches reported to be in 'great decay', 'likely to fall down', or 'in ruin': such a selection of course depends wholly on the arbitrary language of churchwardens or ministers. It is, however, improbable that wardens exaggerated structural defects, for the removal of which they were responsible. It represents only a very small fraction of the items in which the usual terms were merely 'in decay' or 'out of reparations'. It also excludes several hundred entries about broken windows or 'in need of glazing', which are of no significance. Our drastic selection about seriously dilapidated churches will be found to relate to about twenty-four parishes. About half this number concern chancels. Where the description of such churches in the *Inventories* of the Royal Commission on Historical Monuments[1] bears, or seems to bear, on the information in the court books, a relevant extract is given. The reader is reminded that the court books cover only two-thirds of the Essex parishes – those in the archdeaconries of Essex (south and central Essex) and Colchester (north-west and north-east, but not north, Essex): the omitted parishes are referred to in the Introduction and indicated on the map as well as being distinguished in the Index of Places.

Although it is a well-accepted fact that many churches were in a structurally bad state at the beginning of the reign, most of the reports or charges fall within the last fifteen years. In each section all the badly decayed fabrics are noticed more or less in order of date, followed by the few other cases of interest. The court usually instructed the wardens to effect the necessary repairs within a few months and to certify their having done so. As lay rectors and 'farmers' (lessees) of the rectorial tithes, who were liable for maintenance of the chancels, are not generally well documented, entries which name them will be given.

'Gingmountney' (Mountnessing) reported, 'The church is ruined, viz. the steeple' (1566); the act book records, 'To repair before Midsummer'. In the same year Loughton steeple was so 'ruinous' that the bells could not be rung. (Steeple means the tower, with the spire, if any.) 'Asheldham

[1] Essex is covered in four volumes (1916–23), cited as *R.C.H.M., Essex*; some corrections are being made in *V.C.H., Essex*, iv onwards. A useful early account is G. Buckler, *Twenty-Two of the Churches of Essex* (1856). For tombs, see F. Chancellor, *The Ancient Sepulchral Monuments of Essex* (1890).

steeple lieth half unshingled' (1576), and again, 'The steeple is in great decay' (1578). The entry accusing the Woodford wardens of neglect has a note, 'The church is like to fall down' (1579). St. Martin's church at Colchester was in similar or worse condition: 'Our church will all things belonging are very unrepaired and ready to fall down' (1587). The efforts of later wardens evidently failed to restore it, and another charge was made, to which the answer was, 'Our church is greatly in decay and we are not able to make it' (1591). That it 'probably fell down in the seventeenth century' was the opinion of the Commission's inspectors.[1]

Four centuries before their church was to be totally destroyed by fire (1971), the Alresford wardens also pleaded poverty: 'The steeple is ruinous and our church not so well tiled as it ought to be, but our parish is very poor and we cannot invoke them to make a rate for the reparation' (1587). A few weeks afterwards the court learned that Lawford church was 'greatly decayed and the steeple is fallen down'. Somewhat later the wardens presented three rate defaulters, including Samuel Sparhawke, 'for not paying his rate to the building of the steeple', whose blunt reply was, 'Before the steeple fell down, the ground which he hath was in the possession of one Elmes, and he hath not lied to the same charge' (1603). The tower 'was extensively altered early in the sixteenth century'.[2]

Elmstead tower was in a similar state: 'The steeple is decayed and the bells may not be rung' (1582); 'the steeple is ruinous and in decay and ready to fall down' (1589); 'the church is in decay and the steeple is down to the ground; Mr. Pyrton is the farmer' (lessee) (1593); and still later: 'the church and the chancel are in great ruin and one or two bells are broken' (1603). 'The tower was probably never completed' is the comment in the *Inventory*.[3]

The Ramsey wardens were accused of 'not repairing the bell tower (*turris campanalis*)' (1588). Belfries were a continual source of trouble. In some churches they were not strong enough to sustain the ringing of the heaviest bells. It is noticeable, however, that none of the larger timbered belltowers, for which Essex is justly renowned, was reported for structural weakness during our period. Thomas Colfield, one of the Stanway wardens, was in disgrace 'because he would not do his office, but did suffer the top of the steeple to be in decay and some of the bells ready to fall down, which be in great ruin, contrary to some of the parish's mind' (1591).

When the Little Oakley wardens presented, 'Our church and church steeple are in decay, being part fallen down', one warden, John Browne, pleaded that he was 'a poor man and not able to make a rate without the consent and privity of Mr. Mannock, farmer of Oakley Hall, and John Herd, John Sallowes and Abraham Condell, who are the best of the parish' (1593). The *Inventory* dates the tower as *circa* 1490–1500, adding that it was

[1] *R.C.H.M., Essex*, iii, 37. [2] *Ibid.*, iii, 151–2. [3] *Ibid.*, iii, 94.

partly rebuilt in modern times.[1] Of East Mersea church there is a brief note of its being 'in great ruin in many parts' (1596). A more informative report was put in by the Aveley wardens: 'Our church and steeple are in great decay, especially in a party gutter between the north aisle and the chancel and the frame where the bells are hung' (1598). The wardens of Great Braxted were censured for 'not presenting that the church was in ruin and that it rained in' (1602); and those of Mile End, Colchester, because 'their church is in ruin' (1603).

Long-term inactivity in attending to essential maintenance is well illustrated by what happened at Widdington. In 1594 the church was 'in decay', and five years afterwards the ex-wardens were reprimanded for 'leaving the church in ruin when they went out of office'. A century later, at the visitation held in 1686, it was reported that 'the tower of the steeple is cracked'. Yet another ninety years and matters had apparently gone from bad to worse, for the parish register, under 15 May 1771, gives the entry: 'The whole steeple, from top to bottom, with ten feet in breadth of both sides of the body of the church fell down.'[2]

Although this brief account is restricted to fabrics in a bad state of repair, mention may also be made of the presentment in 1566 of 'Mr. Eaton (the lay), rector of Broomfield, because the chapel is not repaired', as the present north chapel is modern.

The wardens' ancient responsibility for the fabric was concisely expressed in the Canons of 1571: 'The churchwardens shall see that the churches be diligently and well repaired with lead, tile, lime and glass, that neither the minister nor the people, either in the holy ministry and worshipping of God or in celebrating the heavenly mysteries or in receiving and hearing the Communion, be troubled with tempestous weather'. The effect of some Elizabethan tempests may be of interest to meteorologists. The summer of 1588 had been marked by a succession of storms of almost unprecedented violence which wrecked many of the ships in the Armada. But the first six extracts which follow refer to a later storm which can be exactly dated. The accounts of Sir John Petre of Thorndon Hall near Brentwood have two entries that mention damage to the half-constructed 'two new great stables and saddle-house which were blown down with the great wind upon Twelfth Even, 1589' (i.e. 5 January 1590).[3]

Little Baddow. The church in decay by reason of the last wind (January 1590).
Fobbing. The church and parsonage want repair (after the) last winds (1590).
Horndon (-on-the-Hill?) The belfry wanteth repair by reason of the last great wind; they craveth a time (1590).
St. Lawrence. The church wanteth reparations and tiling the chancel, by reason of the great wind (1590).
Wivenhoe. The chancel in the lead is in decay by reason of the last great wind, in such sort that the benefice is not able in very short time to repair the same (1590).

[1] *R.C.H.M.*, *Essex*, iii, 172. [2] *Trans. E.A.S.*, xix, 22.
[3] Mr. A. C. Edwards kindly drew my attention to these entries (E.R.O., D/DP A21).

Mistley. There is a glass window that is broken by the great tempest of wind, but it shall be amended with speed (1590).
Earls Colne. Their church was reved (damaged) by the last wind (1594). (One of the wardens certified three weeks later that the church was repaired; there had been a severe gale on 27 May.)
Woodham Mortimer. Some few tiles were blown off from the church the last great wind, as yet unrepaired; we humbly crave a day to be assigned to us with favour (1600).
Little Ilford. Part of the church is uncovered by the tempest of wind (1600).

The same and other storms doubtless resulted in the next group of entries. Wormingford church was 'in decay and doth rain in in many places' (1589); at Wivenhoe, 'it raineth in' (1590), and 'it doth rain in some places in our church, and our forebell in our steeple is broken' (1591); at Great Chesterford, 'it raineth in an aisle in the chapel, which is broken very much and rotten with rain' (1599); at Strethall, 'it raineth into the chancel' (1599); Mr. (John) Beryman, rector of Rochford, presented the wardens because 'it raineth in over the minister's head in the church where he readeth divine service' (1602).

The urgent need for other roof repairs was often reported. In a few instances details are given. Richard Langlye of Holy Trinity, Colchester, was accused by the wardens of 'taking away lead off the church without the licence and leave of any of the parish' (1588). At the same session an Alresford warden was summoned for disrepairs, but quickly arranged that another parishioner, Thomas Hewes, was cited as the culprit: 'The cause is that he detaineth 137 cast of plain tile and 50 gutter tile, which John Paine while he was churchwarden there laid in the church porch, touching the reparations of the church, and yet Hewes presented Paine in not paying.' 'Robert Wroth, esquire, of Chigwell' was presented because 'the church wanteth tiling and paving and the walls cracked, and are to be repaired by him, farmer of the parsonage' (1590). Sir Robert Wroth was lord of the manors of Chigwell, Luxborough in that parish, and Loughton. But why he should be responsible for the church ('church' is repeated in clear writing) is puzzling, unless one assumes that the scribe twice wrote 'church' in error for chancel. It is well known that the lessee of Chigwell rectory, the penitentiary of St. Paul's, was bound to repair the chancel and the parsonage; by the terms of his lease he also had 'to find the lessor, if he was disposed to preach here, lodging, maintenance and horsemeat for himself and two servants for four days and four nights every year'.[1] Wroth, at any rate, ignored the summons to attend. The wardens of Earls Colne were told to act because 'a shot of lead off the vestry and off the church was stolen or taken away, and it raineth in to the ruin and destruction of the church and the vestry' (1596).

Many an Essex church spire at one time or another was in need of being re-shingled (shingles are wooden tiles). For example, at Pontisbright (now called Chapel), 'the steeple wanteth shingling' (1586); and at White

[1] Newcourt, *op. cit.*, ii, 141; *V.C.H.*, *Essex*, iv, 25, 30–32.

Notley, 'the steeple wanteth shingling, and there is a little hole so broad as their hats that they will repair as soon as they can' (1597).

Of church and chancel windows, smashed by the elements or by mischievous boys (four were named as having broken the church and chancel windows of Rayleigh in 1580), a few of the many entries will illustrate this ever-recurring need. At Little Warley, 'the chancel windows are broken, viz. half a dozen quarrels' (small panes, usually diamond-shaped), 'whereby owlets cometh in and thereby with dung bewrayed' (1571); at Tolleshunt Knights, 'the pigeons come in at the broken windows' (1583); at St. Botolph's, Colchester, 'the glass windows of church and chancel are so broken that the church is more like a dovehouse than a place of prayer, for which cause both the preachers and others have made great complaint' (1584). Later, and all in 1600, the wardens were ordered 'to repair the windows of the chancel which are moored up' (Dedham); 'the church wanteth some pargeting and whiting, and the chancel wanteth some pargeting, glazing and whiting' (Little Bromley); 'the chancel wanteth tiling, glazing, pargeting and whiting (Wix); 'the church wanteth whiting, pavementing and other ruins' (Great Oakley).

Actual destruction is registered on two occasions. Seven parishioners of Fryerning were directed 'to certify that they have builded a new church porch when they pulled down the old' (1589). Their allegation was that 'the porch was pulled down with the consent of the whole parish'; but the judge commanded them 'to build up another good and sufficient porch in the same place before Midsummer Day'. Presumably this was done, and it is to be regretted that this rare example of an Elizabethan porch has not survived. Peter Pond, warden of Fryerning, had been charged that 'he with others, sold away the church porch'. This he admitted, but added that it was not much used and was only a little porch, and that 'it was sold by Edward Hilles who appointed and named the price, and Robert Clercke and Roger Brett the other churchwarden, and he (Pond) gave not his consent'. A note states that it had been bought by Thomas Richardson. When James Atwod of East Tilbury was accused of 'carrying away the chapel of Little Thurrock' (1577), 'he denieth, but confesseth that there was such a chapel in the churchyard twenty years past, and then it was pulled down by the Queen's surveyors'. Is this an otherwise unrecorded chapel?[1] Here may also be noticed the indictment of Thomas Till of Coggeshall 'for carrying away a great hewn stone from the porch of the church and applying it to his own use' (1599), which led to a court order to restore it.

John Pake, lessee of the lay rectory of Broomfield, in 1586 disputed liability for repairing the 'decayed stools' in the chancel, averring that he was bound only to repair the parsonage and that the stools in the chancel should be repaired by the vicar: a claim which was allowed. Provision of a

[1] Not in the lists of Essex (medieval) chapels (*Trans. E.A.S.*, xvi, xx).

pew for the family of the rector of Wicken Bonhunt in 1583 caused quite a fuss. First the wardens were presented because the church 'lacketh a pulpit and a convenient place to say the service, the chancel is in ruin, and the parson's wife lacketh a place to sit in for her children'. At the next session they were commanded 'to pull down the stairs near the rood loft and to assist Mr. Swinho in making a seat for his wife at the lower part of the stairs'. Then, next month, the judge deputed Edmund Sherbroke, rector of Hadstock, and Thomas Dove, vicar of Walden, 'to view the parish church and to appoint a place to build pews for Mistress Swynho and Mr. Swynho's children'.

As explained later, the whole parish was responsible for the repair or rebuilding of the seats, and any major restoration involved a special rate. In 1592 Thomas Auncell senior of Kelvedon was prosecuted for 'refusing to sit in the place appointed by the churchwardens, likewise for not paying of his rate'. Two parishioners of St. Nicholas, Colchester, in 1570 were each reported because 'he payeth not for his stall', but it is not clear whether they were private family pews. These are the only references to payment. Personal liability, however, is definitely mentioned in 1587, when Eugene Gatton of Mucking, gentleman (a member of an old-established family there), had not 'repaired the place or aisle where he sitteth in the church'; also in 1596, when the Rettendon wardens' declaration, 'There is a pew made by Matthew Evered and it did breed contention', elicited the answer, 'He did repair a seat which did and doth belong to the house he dwells in'.

Wardens' responsibilities extended to keeping their church interiors 'clean and holy, that they be not loathsome to any, either by dust, sand, or any filthiness' – words taken from the Canons of 1571. That this precept was often disregarded is reflected, for example, in reports that Lawford church was 'not orderly but filthy, and the churchyard also' (1584) and Great Tey church was 'not cleanly kept' (1592).

By a local usage, the wardens of Messing were apparently not liable for one item of 'furnishing' of their church. In 1599 they presented Mr. Cockett, the farmer of the rectory, for 'not finding good and sufficient pesbolt for strawing of the church this winter time, according to usual custom as we have had it always heretofore from the farmer of the same parsonage'. He appeared and denied the custom and was directed to attend again to see further process, there is no later entry. Of peasebolt, Tusser wrote in his *Husbandrie* (1573):

> With strawisp and pease-bolt,
> With ferne and the brake,
> For sparing of fewel,
> Some brewe and some do bake.

A similar custom seems to have obtained at Great Chesterford, the wardens of which complained against the farmer of the rectory in 1587. 'Whereas', they presented, 'we have had straw for the church, now we cannot have it from the parsonage as we had; the parsonage is in the Lord Thomas Howard's hands.' The Howards, of course, owned Audley End and its vast estate including most of Great Chesterford and were patrons of the living.

While the maintenance of the nave, aisles, tower and porch was the responsibility of the parishioners through the churchwardens, that of the chancel lay with the rector, or, in the case of vicarages, with the lay rector, who was usually also the patron, or his 'farmer' (lessee). According to one writer, 'as early as 1559, a fifth part of clerical income was ordered by the royal visitors to be spent on decayed chancels',[1] but none of the numerous bishops' articles of enquiry specifically refers to this, and the Essex archives also make no mention.

The visitation by the Archdeacon of Essex in 1565 revealed many dilapidated chancels (but as already stated no churches). The only pre-1565 entries in the act books show how Thomas Davyes, an otherwise unrecorded rector of Ashdon, was ordered to repair the chancel and the parsonage house (1562); and the wardens of Steeple stated, 'My Lord Ryche is patron of the benefice, where the chancel is clean down' (1564), but no order was issued to so important a magnate. It was in fact a joint benefice, comprising Steeple church with the chapel of Stansgate; and the pre-Dissolution patrons, the priors of Bicknacre and Stansgate, presented *alternis vicibus*. Did Rich manage to delay matters till 1567, when rector Hugh Joanes was deprived and his successor was presented by Sir Humphrey Mildmay? The church was pulled down, and a new one, incorporating much of the former church, was built on a fresh site in 1882.[2]

Six chancels were reported in brief terms between 1566 and 1572: Richard Palmer, farmer of the rectory, because 'the chancel lacks repair' (Stanford-le-Hope); 'The windows in the chancel in decay and the timber work, through default of Mr. (Edmund) Wythipole, the patron' (Walthamstow); Robert Eaton, rector, because the chancel was in decay, and he promised to repair (Springfield); Mr. Sorrell, owing to the ruinous chancel (Great Waltham), who replied, 'The college of Oxford ought to do it' (Sir Thomas Pope, the founder of Trinity College, Oxford, to which he had recently given the rectorial tithes);[3] 'The chancel ought to be mended by Robert Wright and Thomas Manle as feoffees of the Free School of Brentwood' (Dagenham). The sixth case relates to a church which vanished three centuries ago. The rector of Little Wenden was presented because the chancel 'lacketh tiling and glazing', but 'William Helder, the farmer, undertook to remedy the defects' (1570). One later reference to the doomed church is found. Robert Colman of Little Wenden, prosecuted for not paying towards the church repairs, said that he had only three acres of

[1] W. P. M. Kennedy, *Elizabethan Episcopal Administration* (1924), lxxviii.
[2] *R.C.H.M.*, *Essex*, iv, 151. [3] Newcourt, *op. cit.*, ii, 631–2.

land and had paid 2s., so he was discharged. After the Restoration the combined income of the parishes of Great and Little Wenden was scarcely adequate to maintain even a single minister; Little Wenden church was very low and ruinous; Great Wenden vicarage and Little Wenden rectory were both almost uninhabitable, the former being in the worse state; and the churches were less than half a mile apart. The inhabitants of both parishes, with the consent of the patrons, therefore petitioned the bishop to unite them. In 1662 he decreed that the benefices should be joined under the name of Wendens Ambo, that Little Wenden church and Great Wenden vicarage be pulled down, and that the materials be applied to repairing Little Wenden parsonage.[1]

Vincent Harris of Maldon had allowed 'the chancel of Mundon and the chapel annexed to the same' to fall into 'great decay' (1572). (In his will, proved in 1574, he bemoaned the heavy costs of his lawsuits 'in defence of the title' of the lease of the manor of Mundon Hall with the rectory and tithes devised to him by his father, William.) Some years later the wardens reported: 'The glass windows of the chancel are out of reparations and are to be repaired by Mr. Harris our parson (i.e. lay rector), also the palments (pavements) of the chancel are broken up' (1598). Apparently little action, if any, was taken, as 'Mr. Thomas Harris of Mundon was presented for the chancel and chapel thereunto annexed, for that by no means they can be repaired or amended but be very noisome to the whole parish' (1602). The chancel was rebuilt early in the eighteenth century, but the whole church is now (1972) in a similar condition to that of the chancel exactly four centuries ago.

When notified that 'he, being farmer there, ought to repair the chancel', John Browne, gentleman, of Kelvedon disclaimed liability (1573), asserting that he was 'only by virtue of his lease bound to repair the buildings that are upon the site of the manor and not otherwise, and that the Bishop ought to repair the same as his predecessors have hitherto done, as he is informed'. Christopher Hanworth, farmer of the rectory of Creeksea, was presented because 'the chancel and the chapel is in great decay, which chapel was built by old Mr. Harris, and Mr. Hanworth receiveth the tithes to the use of Mr. Osborne of the Exchequer' (1575). A marginal note, 'To speak with Mr. Osborne', is interesting as indicating that the archdeacon was prepared to deal informally with substantial impropriators or lessees. Three years earlier, when the unnamed rector had been cited because of the state of the chancel, the judge had ordered him 'to give out of his benefice yearly 33s. 4d. until it be repaired'. But, two years after Mr. Hanworth was alleged to be liable, the rector of Creeksea was presented for the decayed chancel. He admitted that it had 'fallen down', and was ordered to repair it before Pentecost. At the same time 'the church wanteth reparations' and the wardens were given a

[1] Newcourt, *op. cit.*, ii, 649; Morant, *History of Essex*, ii, 593.

similar instruction. In 1580 the rector was cited again, 'for the chancel is falling down and the mansion house (i.e. the rectory) is ruinous'; which shows that 'falling down' and 'fallen down' are after all relative terms not to be construed too literally. Another lay rector, 'Mr. (Richard) Francke, All Saints, Maldon, suffereth the chancel to run greatly in decay' (1585). When the court learned (1579) that Chadwell chancel 'lacketh shingling', it was alleged: 'it cannot be repaired this winter time for that the shingles cannot be now laid, and it hath not been long unrepaired', which was accepted.

William Egelffelde, farmer of the rectory of East Tilbury, was reported as 'the chancel is greatly unrepaired and the lead carried away, whereby it lieth uncovered' (1574). His reply was that he and Edward Camber 'have a lease from Mr. John Hatton of Gravesend of all the tithes, and Mr. Hatton hath covenanted to discharge them from repairs'. The judge ordered repairs to be carried out by 'them' (presumably the lessees), despite the covenant; but nothing was done, and the wardens then tried to put the onus on Camber as sub-lessee (1577), by which time the chancel had become 'very ruinous'. He in turn refused, named Egelffelde as co-lessee, and stated that widow Clarcke of Gravesend 'had the lead'.

There seems to have been a determined effort in 1574–75 to tackle the problem of decayed chancels in the Essex archdeaconry. No less than ten other clerical or lay rectors were cited.

Ramsden Bellhouse. The farmer (unnamed): not repairing the windows.
Norton Mandeville. William Pawne, gentleman, of High Ongar: wanteth reparations, which should be repaired by him, often presented.
Lambourne. The rector: ready to fall down.
Maldon, All Saints. Mr. Franke of Hatfield: in great decay in glass paning and in leaden gutters.
Rainham. Katherine Frith widow: doth want repair.
Springfield. Robert Eaton (rector of a moiety): promiseth to repair.
Fyfield. Edward Bordman, rector: in great decay, not pavemented.
Hockley. Mr. Edmund Tyrrell, farmer of the rectory: lacketh white lime and shingling, often presented.
North Shoebury. Rector or farmer: in great decay.
Walthamstow. Edward Dawson, farmer: in great ruin. Dawson, one of the farmers, appeared and alleged that the chancel lacketh a little reparation, but it shall be amended forthwith.

In 1580 two of the biggest Essex landowners come into the picture as lay rectors. As for Mountnessing chancel, both 'Mr. Brasier and Lady Petre' were charged with not repairing it (1580): linking vicar Anthony Brasier with dowager Lady Petre, widow of the former Principal Secretary, of Ingatestone Hall, who had presented Brasier, was perhaps a matter of leniency to her. At any rate, both failed to attend and were pronounced contumacious, with penalty reserved. After entries at the two following sessions, in which only Lady Petre's name is given, the case does not appear any more. It was also the vicar, Robert Dixon of Little Leighs, who was cited in the first place (1580). 'I take', said Dixon in appropriately obsequious terms, 'that the Honourable Lord Rich should repair the chancel, but requireth a sufficient day'. The judge, equally hesitant, enjoined the unfortunate vicar 'to prove' liability. But five years later the same vicar had to appear again, when he pleaded extreme sickness (*valde indebitate ac canceratum*), whereat the court, 'on account of his poverty', so the entry runs, 'assigned him to bestow the fifth part of the value of his benefice upon the reparations of the chancel' and to carry them out by All Saints' Day.

There is a brief reference to Wicken Bonhunt chancel being 'in ruin' (1583). 'As for our chancel', declared the wardens of St. Martin, Colchester (1583), 'our parson hath carried away our glass twelve months ago, and we cannot get it again, nor our chancel repaired neither'. When John White, vicar of Ramsey, was cited in 1584 for negligence, he replied that 'the chancel is so broken that the east wind coming in from the sea doth so drown his voice that he cannot be heard'. In 1585 two chancels in the other archdeaconry are mentioned. That of South Benfleet 'wanteth reparations'. The lay rector having been named, there appeared Humphrey Drywood, who stated that 'Dr. Goodman is the rector and lives in the city of London, so that he cannot readily come to this session', but he was assigned to repair. As the patrons were the Dean and Chapter of Westminster Abbey, Goodman must have been the lessee. The other case refers to the now famous Saxon church of Greenstead-juxta-Ongar with its timber-walled nave, but then unrecognized as probably the oldest wooden church in Europe. The presentment, however, relates to the condition of the chancel, which in 1585 was described as 'wanting reparations in glass, door and floor', causing 'John Levett (lay) rector of Greenstead, or farmer' to be cited, who said that he was 'but a deputy to Mr. Philip Morrice, the farmer, and the same Mr. Morrice affirmeth', so Levett was discharged. The *Inventory* states that the chancel had been rebuilt early in the sixteenth century.[1]

The church of White Colne formerly belonged to Colne Priory, which had never ordained a vicarage but served the parish by a monk. At the Dissolution it became a donative or perpetual curacy in the gift of the Earls of Oxford of Hedingham Castle. 'William Adams vicar' (incorrectly so termed) was presented on account of the chancel being 'in ruins, and the vicar ought to repair it' (1584). He admitted decay, but said, 'My Lord of Oxford should repair'. Five years later 'Mr. William Barnard, farmer of the rectory', was summoned. Instead there appeared 'John Churche, gentleman, who affirmeth that his father, being curate for many years of the parish church, did during his time repair the chancel when it was in decay'. At the next session 'Mr. Adams curate' attended and was ordered to repair. William Adams' name is given in the very imperfect clergy list, but Churche's name is new.[2]

[1] *R.C.H.M., Essex*, ii, 112. [2] Newcourt, *op. cit.*, ii, 186.

Two cases, both of which occurred in 1588, show that the maintenance of some chancels was shared between occupiers. Kelvedon chancel being in decay, William Pratt of Bradwell was held liable because he had '40 acres of arable land in his occupying belonging to the parsonage and all the tithe corn on the same ground', and he was ordered 'proportionately to repair'; and William Appleford had to repair an unspecified part of Witham chancel in respect of his 'holding 30 acres tithe free belonging to Kelvedon Hall'. A presentment in the following year, 'Our chancel is in decay and Mr. Lounlye, rector of Great Tey, should repair it' (1589), refers to the lay rector and patron, whose name is also recorded as James Lomelinus.[1]

A parson of South Ockendon inherited a structural responsibility, of which he was immediately made aware. 'George Drywood rector: the chancel lieth unpaved and the windows unglazed, very ruinous, and one of the parsonage barns is fallen down, and a bridge over the parsonage moat is in great decay' (1590). His rejoinder was that 'he hath been there but a small time and hath not received any benefit as yet'; he had in fact only just come to the parish.

Springfield rectory was exceptional in being divided into two 'portions', or moieties. 'Mr. (William) Daniel rector' (of Springfield Richards) was called to account for 'his part of the chancel wanting some shingles, which were pulled off by the boys' (1595). The second moiety, Springfield Boswells, apparently had to maintain the other part: a fact that is learned from the citation of 'Mr. William Tailer, rector of Springfield', because 'the north part of the chancel is out of repair' (1600). He stated that he had been 'convented before Mr. Whittell, Commissary to the Lord Bishop of London, for the same'. There was also another defect: 'Part of the pavement in the north side of the chancel is unpaved in the place where Mr. William Mildemaye was buried, by the negligence of Mr. Mildemaye's widow, wife of the said Mr. William Taylor, as we can learn.'

As already mentioned, Pontisbright was a chapel-of-ease to Great Tey, and complaint was made against 'Robert Durden, farmer of the rectory of Great Tey', both chancels being 'in great ruin' (1602); he admitted liability. The warden of the tiny parish of 'Salcot Virley', now called Virley, was himself charged for failing to present 'the ruin of the chancel' (1602). He produced his 'bill' (return), and was discharged; presumably the clerical rector was then cited, but there is no record of this.

Lawford chancel was 'in ruin', and 'Mr. Hawys the rector' (William Hawes) had to deal with it (1603). Fortunately, the fine fourteenth-century chancel remains intact. On its north wall is carved an extraordinarily interesting babery – a 'chain' of figures, mostly male, each balancing the next above. Two are managing to play a musical instrument: one stands precariously on another's head; the other is held aloft by his leg! A present-

[1] Newcourt, *op. cit.*, ii, 573.

ment was brought against 'the rector impropriators or farmers of the rectory of Holy Trinity, Colchester', because the chancel was out of repair (1603). James Thomlinson, lay rector or lessee, attended and alleged that 'he hath not any money in his hands and that tithes will not be due till Lady Day'. An early entry stating that 'George Swayne is bound in 100 marks for repairing Rayleigh church and payment of all dues to the church' (1561) probably indicates that he gave an indemnity or bond on taking a lease of the rectorial tithes.

Reciprocal rights and liabilities were the subject of two cases that arose near the end of the century. 'The chapel in the north side of our church belongeth unto Horndon Place, which is now in the tenure and lease of John Tolekearne, farmer of Horndon Place'; so the wardens of Horndon-on-the-Hill declared (1597), adding, 'which chapel is and hath been ruinous both in the lead and glazing'. It would seem therefore that the fifteenth-century north chapel had been built by an early owner of Horndon Place, which was a small manor associated with, and evidently carved out of, the manor of Ardern Hall, at which the Queen had probably been entertained in 1588 when she visited her troops at Tilbury.

The present Blackmore church and chancel are structurally part of the nave of the former Priory, dissolved in 1525, which originally extended further to the east. Some depositions by four old parishioners taken in a suit brought in 1583 by Thomas Smith, lord of the manor, in the archdeacon's court, supply a few fresh details to the known dispute that arose from his attempt to appropriate the chancel. William Wayte, labourer (aged 80), where he had dwelt for about 60 years, formerly of Great Bardfield, said: 'He did perfectly know the religious house called Blackmore Priory, which before the dissolution was adjoining to Blackmore church, which Priory was pulled down in the time of this deponent's remembrance whilst he was a dweller there, about 40 years past. Sir Brian Tuke, who purchased the same house of the late king Henry VIII, did pull it down, and by the persuasions of the parishioners for the enlarging of their church and by his sufferance the same part of the church which was used for a chancel was counted parcel of the same religious house and left standing for the causes aforesaid. Afterwards Sir Brian sold all the same monastery with the demesnes unto one Mr. Smith, father of Mr. Thomas Smith, now lord of the same Priory, about 30 years past, and during his lifetime the parishioners had the use of the same part of the chancel by the sufferance of the same Mr. Smith. And likewise Mr. Smith, party hereto, suffered them to have it, until about two or three years past they did claim the same to be parcel of the parish church and no part of the Priory, whereupon Mr. Smith enclosed the same up and holdeth it in his own possession.' He added, 'Part of the posts of the pulling down is yet standing, but always the parishioners have had the use of the same part of the chancel so enclosed by Mr. Smith'. Thomas Samon, husbandman (about

60), where he had dwelt from birth, likewise declared that he 'doth perfectly know that that part of the chancel which is now enclosed by Mr. Smith was parcel of the same Priory and left standing but stood open, but enclosed from Blackmore church until about 30 years part'. John Symond, husbandman (about 80), where he had lived for about 75 years, formerly at Brentwood, said that 'Mr. Smith by reason of controversy between him and parishioners did shut up the chancel'; and Geoffrey Wyat, husbandman (about 60), where he had dwelt since birth, said the same.

In 1599 Robert Mordaunt of Hempstead, the first lay patron and rector of Great Sampford with its annexed chapelry of Hempstead, evidently made abnormal claims to the 'chapel'. According to 'goodman Lagden, the churchwarden, Edward Flexman hath set a lock upon the chancel door (so) that nobody can come into the chancel, whereas the minister and the parishioners heretobefore time out of mind of man hath come unto the chancel by the same door; and this is by the means of Mr. Robert Mordaunt; also Mr. Mordaunt hath by policy (cunning) gotten away the vestry door key of Hempstead church from the churchwardens and hath locked it up'. At the next session Flexman acknowledged the truth of Lagden's statement and was dismissed.

The ceaseless struggle to maintain these ancient buildings, judging by the number of entries, was as prominent in the courts at the end of the period as at the beginning. As Dr. Anglin has pointed out, 'Progress was slow, and considerable periods existed between the original presentment of the dilapidation and the certificate of its repair. Difficulty was especially encountered in securing repairs for edifices in some of the parishes leased to farmers and in those which were impropriate. The Crown and the Dean and Chapter of St. Paul's were especially slow among the impropriators. Eleven presentments for the need of repairs were made against the Crown's farmer alone for the rectory of East Tilbury between 1574 and 1600.'[1]

To end, we quote one of the very few presentments which mention structural work: strictly, it falls under Churchyards, but logically belongs here. The wardens of Wix complained about Daniel Spencer, a carpenter of their parish: 'The churchyard is annoyed with timber through his default in not building the roof of the church according to covenants, having received most part of his money' (1596). But the carpenter was not to be intimidated: 'The timber lieth there and not set up by reason he cannot get his money due for the setting up of the same, and the churchwardens should pay him.' So the judge ordered their citation, and the outcome was an instruction 'to finish the building up of the frame and to certify'. The *Inventory* states that 'the foundations of the north aisle were reported to have been uncovered in recent years'.[2] Is it possible that the

[1] Dr. Anglin's thesis, 219–20. [2] *R.C.H.M., Essex*, iii, 234.

date of the removal of this aisle coincided with that of the rebuilding of the nave roof?

This miscellany of extracts about Elizabethan Essex churches and chancels has added, as we anticipated, relatively little to what can be deduced from careful study of the actual fabrics. The Church hierarchy was chiefly interested not in restoring ancient churches but in maintaining the services and ensuring the attendances to the full in accordance with the Act of Uniformity. As long as wardens and rectors kept the walls, roofs and windows of their churches and chancels reasonably sound against the elements and the interiors whitewashed and free from all Romish paintings and furnishings, all was in order: to have allowed any images or pictures to remain after the general devastation was a form of ritual disorder, as already related under the Church Settlement.

In the section on Rates, other churches are named, and it may be that the levying of a rate for repairing church or tower, in contrast to rates for bells, furniture and other church requirements, is a criterion of serious defects; but there are too many entries to quote. The rate for the 'decayed steeple' of Saffron Walden church, for instance, seems to fall into this category (1585).

Plate

Fairly typical of the whole country is the chronicle for Essex of the almost wholesale loss of medieval church plate at the dissolution of the religious houses, guilds and chantries under Henry VIII and Edward VI;[1] purchase of new plate under Mary; and sale, exchange or adaptation or acquisition of communion cups in Elizabeth's early years. The county is fortunate, however, in having its own story available in a detailed and well-illustrated survey made shortly before and after the First World War.[2] Some of the interesting treasures, including examples of Elizabethan cups and patens, are now periodically displayed and have been seen in exhibitions, for example, at the Shire Hall and Prittlewell Priory Museum.

Edward VI's commissioners performed their task with extreme thoroughness. Whether, by Elizabeth's time, any pre-Reformation or Marian Essex plate had escaped their notice and was being used, secretly or in the more remote parishes, is largely hypothetical; at any rate, none had survived to this century except for two medieval patens. On the other hand, the published catalogue of fifty years ago revealed that no less than 123 early Elizabethan cups (72 with covers) were still preserved, many

[1] The Essex inventories at the Public Record Office have all been printed in full (*Trans. E.A.S.*, O.S., iv, v; N.S., i–iii).

[2] *The Church Plate of Essex*, ed. W. J. Pressey (1926); also gives transcripts of the inventories of plate of the monasteries, guilds and chantries, and abbreviated notes from the inventories (chalices and patens only) of 1552 (appendices A–C). See also his shorter account in *Ess. Rev.*, xxx, 95–105.

of which are of beautiful design and fine craftsmanship. The widespread change, apparently sponsored by Archbishop Parker, which led to the substitution of the 'fair and comely cup' for the 'massing chalice', was effected mainly in 1561–64.[1] Virtually all the early Elizabethan plate was bought (or exchanged), but two cups, at Earls Colne and Great Wigborough, appear to have been re-fashioned, perhaps at Colchester, from vessels previously in use.[2]

The act books of the 1560s and the visitation book of the Archdeacon of Essex of 1565 have furnished some information about the obligation placed on the parishes; but those of the Archdeaconry of Colchester are extant only from 1569 (apart from 1540–45). Very few of the entries appear in the printed account, so every reference is now given.

Before doing so, the churchwardens' accounts for two parishes may serve to illustrate the change-over. At Great Dunmow in 1558, they sold two chalices weighing 23¼ oz. for £6 15s. 5d., the entry for which is followed by 'Paid for the communion cup weighing 17 oz. lacking 12d. in weight after 6s. 7d. the oz., £6 7s.'[3] Next year the 'chief inhabitants' agreed that the wardens should sell crosses and the like, weighing a total of 110 oz. worth 5s. 4d. the oz., i.e. £29 6s. 8d., 'to pay debts that were owing to divers of the parish and for the reparations of the church'. Then, in 1560, the accounts record the receipt from 'Mr. Muschamp goldsmith at the sign of the Ring with the Ruby in Lombard Street for a gilt chalice with a paten gilt weighing 23¼ oz. at 5s. 4d. the oz., £6 4s.' and 'Paid to him for a cup of gilt weighing 19¾ oz. at 6s. 8d. the oz., £6 11s. 7d.' It is this cup that was listed in the parish inventory of 1580. A few months later, the vessel narrowly escaped being stolen, when the church was burgled, and the thieves 'attempted to have broken into the vestry but they prevailed not to have had the communion cup, Thanks be to God'.[4]

The earliest mention of plate in the act books occurs in 1561, when the wardens of Stebbing were presented because they had 'sold of the church goods to the value of 20 marks'. They admitted having disposed of 'a cross of silver and a chalice to the value of £6 which is and must be bestowed in the mending of their steeple (i.e. tower) and church'.

From 1563 onwards a good deal of light is thrown on the purchase of communion cups. Where these survive the fact is noted. Among the defects found out at the Archdeacon's visitation in the autumn of 1563, East Tilbury and Horndon-on-the-Hill each lacked a communion cup, and the wardens were commanded to provide one before All Saints' Day.

The visitations of 1564–65 were presided over personally by the archdeacon, who covered his area between April 1564 and March 1565. The wardens of Hornchurch, Romford and Havering (the two latter being chapels-of-ease to Hornchurch) were all ordered 'to prepare a communion

[1] Many of these cups and patens are also illustrated in *R.C.H.M., Essex.*
[2] *Ibid.*, page v. [3] E.R.O., D/P 5/2/1. [4] D/P 94/5/2.

cup of the same weight that the chalice is before Whit Sunday on pain of excommunication and to present in their next detections'. Those of Greenstead-by-Ongar had to provide a cup 'before the Sunday after Michaelmas' under a similar penalty, while Steeple and St. Lawrence wardens were 'to prepare a communion cup by fourteen days after this day', and 'for their not having of the cup they shall give to the poor 6d. apiece' (Steeple) and '3s. 4d.' (St. Lawrence). The orders for Little Warley, Pitsea and East Horndon were identical with that for Hornchurch; and Grays Thurrock had 'to turn the chalice into a communion cup'. South Ockendon, Stow Maries and Ingatestone lacked cups, and were presumably given the same directions. The wardens of Fryerning declared: 'Sir William Petre will help them to have it changed that was their chalice by Midlent Sunday, and Thomas Spryengfyeld hath taken upon him to do it'. (Unfortunately, the detailed account-books of Sir William Petre of Ingatestone Hall cease in 1562.) In the case of Buttsbury, an entry of 1564 states that 'Roger Bexwell will consent to the sale of their chalice and Rumbold Taverner will be contented to have the chalice sold and to give 12d. to the poor'.

Church Plate in Essex records that seven of these parishes still possessed the cups. viz. Buttsbury, Hornchurch and Romford (all dated 1563), Horndon-on-the-Hill (1567), Little Warley and East Horndon (1564), and Pitsea (1568).

The special visitation register of 1565, as mentioned, has the solitary confession by the Greenstead wardens about their having no cup. The autumn visitation of 1566 disclosed that Woodham Walter 'lacked a communion cup', which was to be acquired before Christmas. That of the following year found Leyton, North Fambridge and 'Theydon' without covers to their cups, and the Woodford wardens stated that they had 'no communion cup of silver'. Also in 1567 William Bates of Purleigh was presented for 'detaining the chalice', and the wardens of Ingrave and Widford still lacked a cup in 1569, which they were ordered to get. By this time it may be assumed that the church plate in the archdeaconry of Essex had been completely regularized, as no further presentments of the kind are seen.

Later references to church plate in this and the other archdeaconry deal with different aspects. In 1576 South Benfleet received a legacy of £6 13s. 4d. (10 marks) from John Letton, a parishioner who described himself in his will as a yeoman. An executor handed over this substantial sum, when the judge ordered that 'they shall have a bible of the largest volume, a communion cup, and all other their necessary books, and to repair the churchyard'.[1] Archbishop Grindal had very recently issued his articles of enquiry with the aim of ensuring that every church had such a bible ('Cranmer's Bible'), together with the *Paraphrases of Erasmus*, the *Homilies*, and a

[1] For the entry in the court book (with photograph), see *Ess. Rev.*, xxx, 103–4.

'decent cup and cover of silver'. This timely bequest enabled the wardens to fulfil their requirements, also to put into proper order their churchyard which, as earlier entries show, had for a long time been in a neglected state. Thus South Benfleet acquired its typically Elizabethan cup, dated the same year, which is still preserved.

We have a possible record of one pre-Elizabethan cup, if 'chalice' is so interpreted. Thomas Hatchman of Boreham, one of the late wardens, was prosecuted in 1576 because 'he withholdeth a chalice and 4s. 5d. of the church goods from the churchwardens'. He contended that 'he keepeth the same for that there is money owing him by the parish' and was ordered to surrender them. In the same year Richard Minors went so far as to 'have laid to gage' (i.e. pawn) the Woodford cup 'for 30s. that is owing to him'.

A somewhat similar defence was submitted by Thomas Westbrook in 1585, when the warden of 'Great Sutton' was presented because the parishioners lacked a silver communion cup. As far back as 1569 the same man had promised 'to prepare a cup of his own cost if he may have it in his own custody'. This the court allowed, 'until such time' as the parishioners had paid for it. Next year, however, he was reported as 'in default'. By 1580 the position was no better. In 1585 the then warden accused him of having 'carried it away, as he saith, for debts owing to him, but he knoweth not of any'. Shortly afterwards Westbrook admitted having the cup, but asserted that the parish owed him 36s. 6d., apparently for part of the purchase money. They still 'wanted' a cup in 1597. The matter seems to have dragged on until 1613, when the rector stated that an earlier warden had kept a cup in his hands, but the parish had had the use of it for fifteen years. This had evidently been acquired in 1601, the date of the existing cup.

There was trouble, too, at Coggeshall. In 1579 Bernard Bisley and John Sander, the former churchwardens, 'did detain the communion cup, whereby divers and sundry communicants have been put by for lack of the communion cup'. Bisley was ordered to deliver it up before the next Sunday and to pay 2s. 6d. for the use of the poor. In 1598 the wardens of All Saints, Maldon, told the court that Thomas Webb, 'late churchwarden, is gone out of the parish and carried away the communion cup and cloth'. The order reads, 'Because they have not used that direct means which the law requireth to recover the same, the churchwardens shall call a vestry and shall make a rate and provide a cup and cloth'.

Wendens Ambo still possesses a cup dated 1589 and a cover dated 1568. Where a cover is of a different date, it is usually later. Here the reason is apparent from the rather full entries in the act books under 1588. Little Wenden lacking a cup, the wardens certified shortly afterwards that they had provided 'a comely communion cup', but several months later six parishioners were presented for refusing to contribute sums of 2s. 8d. or less towards its purchase. At the first of these sessions George Day of Great Wenden and John Felsted of Little Wenden had testified that 'there was delivered 10s. or more to Father Bankes of Great Wenden about 24 years past towards the buying of a communion cup for Great Wenden and Little Wenden by the parishioners of Great and Little Wenden, but to whom it was delivered he remembereth not. Mr. Bankes remembered no such money delivered neither did he receive the same.' Apparently the cover did not need to be replaced, only the cup.

When the late officers of Great Holland were cited in 1597, they alleged that 'the communion cup was lost or stolen away through the default of Robert Peachye now churchwarden'. The usual order was made. A century later, the act book for 1683 stated that the parish then possessed 'a chalice and cover of silver with 1571 on the top of the cover', so it was evidently recovered. Thefts of the beautiful cups of Wickham St. Paul's and Margaret Roothing, both dated 1562 and both recovered, are described in the previous volume, where they are illustrated.[1]

The printed description of the Essex church plate has an appendix of extracts relating to plate in early printed wills. The penultimate entry belongs to the beginning of our period. John Bourcher's will was proved about April 1559, but he made it a month before Mary's death. The testator bequeathed money to buy 'a chalice, with a paten of silver'.[2] His bequest marks the virtual end of the long era of legacies for ritualistic purposes. Thirty years afterwards, when William Sorrell of Great *alias* Old Saling, yeoman, made his will, he forgave all the debts due to him from the parishioners, including that 'in recompense of the communion cup'.[3] Its date is 1573; perhaps he had paid the bill when a churchwarden.

Because of the keen interest aroused by a sale of plate that took place in 1971, a postscript will briefly mention the circumstances. Apparently made in 1507, an inventory of the Saffron Walden almshouses in 1524 included 'a mazer with silver and gilt'. This is the vessel from which Pepys drank when he visited the town in 1660: 'They brought me a draft of their drink in a brown bowl, tipt with silver, which I drank off, and at the bottom was a picture of the Virgin with Child in her arms, done in silver.' Owing to its exceptional value, the account of Essex church plate records the mazer in some detail, concluding, 'The authorities have in recent years wisely withdrawn the bowl from use, and it is now kept at one of the banks in the town'; until shortly before, it had been used by the governors at their annual election and on some other occasions, 'the custom being that each person drinking out of it gave a shilling to the town crier who handed it round'.[4] Three years after the book was published, the almshouses trustees sold it for £2,900. At the recent auction it fetched £22,000; the new owner ntends to retain it in England.

[1] *E.L.: Disorder*, 278 and plate 24. [2] *Church Plate of Essex*, 318.
[3] Noticed during preparatory work for next volume.
[4] *Ch. Pl.*, 264; see also *Ess. Rev.*, xxvi, 98.

Books, Registers and Chests

By Article 6 of the Injunctions of 1559 partly reiterating those of 1547, every minister was responsible for providing at the parish charges 'one book of the whole Bible of the largest volume in English', also the *Paraphrases of Erasmus upon the Gospels* in English (1523), 'and the same set up in some convenient place within the church where the parishioners may well commodiously resort and read the same, out of the time of common service'. The bible was Cranmer's (or the 'Great Bible'), and his *Homilies* (1547) were also provided. In 1563 the *Second Book of Homilies* was first issued by Convocation, and in the same year it was decreed that a translation of Foxe's *Book of Martyrs* (1563) be purchased by the wardens of every parish. To these were also added Bishop Jewel's *Apology* (1562) and the *Defence of the Apology* (1570) for the English Church. The Canons of 1571 refer to the provision of 'the Holy Bible in the largest volume (if it may conveniently be), such as were lately imprinted at London', that is, the 'Bishop's Bible', revised under Parker's auspices and published in 1568; this only partially supplanted the earliest versions.

Many entries in the court books reveal how some parishes lacked one or other of these books. An adulterous Brentwood man, in addition to undergoing penance, volunteered to give a copy of Foxe to South Weald church or Brentwood chapel – thirty-seven years after young William Hunter's martyrdom at Brentwood in 1555. Had an earlier copy been stolen by a devout Catholic? Three earlier orders imposed on lechers provided their parishes with the *Book of Martyrs*: see under Penance. In Chelmsford cathedral library, however, another treasure is still in good condition: Erasmus' *Paraphrases*, probably the only copy in the diocese that has survived in parochial custody.[1]

The archdeacons' act books tell a good deal about the keeping of parish registers. Whatever may be said about neglect in later centuries, the Elizabethan Church authorities exercised strict control over registration and custody, and they deserve a tribute for administrative efficiency.

The tenth clause of the Injunctions of 1559 enforced the keeping of registers of baptisms, marriages and burials, which had been initiated by Thomas Cromwell in 1538. It also directed that the churchwardens should provide a coffer, or chest, with three locks and keys in which the register would to be kept, the minister to have one of the keys and the wardens the others. Each Sunday the entries for the previous week were to be written by the minister in the wardens' presence.

The court archives before 1576 have no reference to registers except

[1] This and other early books, including William Lyndwood's *Provinciale* (*c.* 1505), Erasmus' *New Testament Annotations* (1535) and Luther's *In Genesin* (1552), are in the same library. I wish to thank Mr. E. O. Reed, J.P., F.L.A., Borough Librarian and Honorary Cathedral Librarian, who arranged for their being exhibited in 1969, for generous facilities.

that the wardens of St. Peter, Maldon, were presented at the visitation of 1566 because 'they do not keep a register book'. (The register entries date from ten years earlier, in the form of the usual transcript made in 1598.) Whether the visitation articles included enquiry about registers is not definitely known, but the act book for 1576 includes three lists of registers produced by the wardens at the visitation of the archdeacon of Essex. They relate to the parishes in Dengie and Rochford hundreds and Ongar deanery. The books for about half the number of parishes were 'sufficient'; the rest, 'insufficient', so new registers were to be ordered. The Rochford parish entry reads: 'The book exhibited by Thomas Write and John Eve churchwardens, sufficiently kept, but they are appointed to buy a new book well bound in sorrel in 4 quires of paper, new written out before the Feast of Easter'. Burnham, in Dengie hundred, still possesses its paper register from 1559, being the transcript made in accordance with the judge's order of 1576.

The wardens of the tiny parish of Markshall were accused in 1579 of lacking the *Paraphrases* and a register book, and their church was out of repair: the church was demolished in 1933. Its register begins in 1582, but in the form of a transcript made in 1738, the original long since lost.

Enquiries were made in the archdeaconry of Colchester in 1583, as a result of which the wardens of four parishes (three in Colchester) were ordered: 'to prepare a new book for christenings and burials' (St. Giles); 'to prepare a register book with quires of paper covered with leather' (St. Nicholas); 'to buy a new register book with clasps' (St. James); and 'to provide a register book of six quires of paper, well bound and covered, before Easter, and to write this book according to the order' (Great Bromley). 'Mr. (Robert) Dixon, vicar of Little Leighs, to show his register book to the judge to peruse in what order he hath kept the same', noted in 1590, further illustrates strict supervision. None of these original paper registers has survived.

There is a little evidence of mutilation or detention. John Knight, rector of Goldhanger, was accused by the wardens in 1591 because 'he had the register book at his house and rent out of the same one leaf and writ another in the same place thereof, but whether it be agreeing to the leaf that he rent out we know not'. More curious are some entries about the register of St. Peter, Colchester, in 1596. The John Smith who had a strong urge to contract himself in marriage to 'sundry women' was incriminated at the same session: 'He did cut out leaves out of the register book there.' This is followed by a charge against John Smith of St. Nicholas, *janitor* (doorkeeper, or possibly school usher): 'He carried the said register to the said John Smith of St. Peter's to cut out the same leaves.' The latter was to be questioned, but after his non-appearance at the next two sessions the record is silent. In 1591 the wardens of Mile End, Colchester, admitted, 'The minister called there several sabbath days to have it but could not have it'. *Per contra*, John Pilborowe, gentleman, of Hatfield Peverel, was presented in 1585 for 'keeping and withdrawing the register book from us the churchwardens'; and both he and Mr. John St. John, the 'old churchwardens', by the then wardens in 1589 because 'they cannot get the register book out of their hands'.

A constitution issued by Convocation for the province of Canterbury in 1597 and shortly afterwards approved by the Queen directed the more careful keeping of parish registers. Parchment registers were to be purchased, and the earlier ones on paper were to be copied into the new parchment registers from the beginning (1538), 'but especially since the first year of her Majesty's reign' (1558), which explains why so many of the extant registers start in the latter year. The permanent loss for biographical and genealogical research may be attributed either to the laziness of ministers or to the parsimony of wardens of the more populous parishes where a fee was paid for transcription.

Both injunctions were rigorously enforced (except of course the option to copy only from 1558) in both archdeaconries. Only two parishes, Stow Maries in 1598 and Chadwell in 1600, were indicted for not having procured a parchment book: both registers have been preserved, and the entries start in these years, the paper books having apparently been destroyed even at that time. Indeed, most of the original paper registers were probably thrown away. Later ravages of damp and rodents and the long succession of incumbents, curates and churchwardens, to whom the fragile or crumpled leaves must have looked like rubbish, have taken their heavy toll. Despite all this, there have been preserved in Essex paper originals for sixteen parishes, though only seven date from 1538;[1] none of these parishes corresponds with any mentioned in this chapter.

Wardens had to produce their new registers at the visitation and to show that the pre-1598 entries had been copied, the transcript being 'signed in the prescribed form'. The act books record the parishes which had thus exhibited their books. Mr. Greene, rector of Markshall, stated that 'it is not yet finished'; the judge ordered him to show the book at the next session: with its small population, John Greene could have had only a few leaves to copy. Mr. (William) Harris, the vicar of Messing, cited because the wardens 'hath required the register book of the minister and hath not delivered it to them', complained that 'he is not paid for the writing', but was instructed to exhibit it.

The wardens of Little Wenden stated in 1599 that the register had been stolen, and they were ordered to provide a new book. Starting at 1602, it was continued as the register for Great and Little Wenden (Wendens Ambo) from 1662, when the parishes were united.

[1] Emmison (ed.), *Catalogue of Essex Parish Records* (E.R.O., revd. edn., 1966), 5. This book gives the earliest dates of the surviving registers of all parishes. For a few additional details about the register entries in the act books, see *Trans E.A.S.*, xix, 10–13.

An interesting record of 1598 shows how much the new parchment books cost. The deputy registrar for the Colchester Archdeaconry brought to the court a supply in five different sizes, which were sold as follows: books containing 100 leaves 12s. 6d., 80 leaves 10s., 60 leaves 7s. 6d., 50 leaves 6s. 3d., and 40 leaves 5s. The largest volumes went to Manningtree and Dedham; Witham had one with 80 leaves, Kelvedon one with 60, and so forth.

A remarkable discovery was made in 1961. The present writer, while County Archivist, learned through a book-dealer that the parish register of Great Waltham for 1560–1701 was available for 'sale' by its private 'owner', whose name was never disclosed. Negotiations with his agent enabled the Friends of Historic Essex to acquire it for a relatively small sum, after which the society added it to the other registers of Great Waltham which had been deposited in the Essex Record Office about twenty years earlier. The register for 1703–82 has a contemporary note at the beginning that the older volume was 'lost' when the new one was started in 1703! That it should turn up, and in very good condition, after more than two and a half centuries, is almost incredible (plate 13). Its disappearance was perhaps connected with the extraordinary prosecution of John Oswald, the vicar, in Doctors' Commons in 1698 by Sir Hugh Everard of Langleys for alleged immorality, drunkenness and neglect of duty including errors in his register, for which he was found guilty owing to prejudiced proceedings. No less than twenty neighbouring incumbents later testified as to his good character; and Oswald was obliged to print a full account of his case, explaining how it arose out of a dispute with Sir Hugh about tithes.[1]

After 1597 annual copies of registers were sent to the bishop. Well known, such 'bishop's transcripts', as they are called, are of the utmost historical and genealogical value, but Essex, so rich in nearly all other classes of archives, is virtually bereft of early transcripts. There is only one echo. In 1604 Mr. (Robert) Searle, rector of Lexden, was presented by the wardens because he 'kept the register (so) that we cannot have it to send the transcript into my Lord Bishop of London's Office as we should do'; order was given accordingly to the rector.

A very small number of clerics listed in their registers the names of their communicants – or absentees[2] – but no separate book has survived. That such were kept in a few parishes is learned from the charge in 1591 against John Shoncke and John Nevell, chapelwardens of Havering, that 'the communion book of the chapel' (the mother church was Hornchurch) 'is rent and torn'; so they were told to provide a new one.

[1] *Some Memorandums of Matters of Fact* . . . (2nd edn., 1709), a very rare pamphlet, a copy of which is in the E.R.O. library.

[2] *Catal. of E.P.R.*, index, s.v. 'communion', 'communicants'.

The history of the Essex church chests – the medieval chests for keeping the precious vestments and missals, the register chests, the 'poor men's boxes' (plate 9), and the strong coffers for holding deeds and evidences–has been told in a well-illustrated work.[1] The book gives some extracts from the act books and wardens' accounts.

Neglect led to a few orders for providing a register chest with locks at Terling (1599), Eastwood (1602) and South Ockendon (1602), also at the last 'a box for alms'. The chest at Layer-de-la-Haye in 1587 had only one lock, the key being kept by the sexton, so the wardens had to provide accordingly; nevertheless the register was subsequently lost.

A singular story about the Canewdon chest is preserved under 1601 in reference to that licentious vicar, Thomas Newman. The wardens reported: 'He was consenting and privy to the picking the lock of our parish chest wherein we keep our evidence and writings, out of which chest there was certain evidences taken away at the same time that the lock was picked which concern the lands belonging to the poor; and one Robert Parker now deceased, a smith, did confess before my Lord Riche that Mr. Newman and one Mr. Kinge did cause him to do the same. Further we say our same vicar is very slack and negligent in going perambulation for these two years past.'

We are proud to have the famous thirteenth-century church chest at Newport, with its elaborate carving and painted lid. For two or more centuries parish registers and account-books, and later the massive bundles of poor law settlement papers, were stored in these large wooden (often iron-bound) chests, but the iron boxes which parishes had to provide for their registers in 1813 led to many ancient chests being discarded.

Bells

A very comprehensive account of the Essex church bells, their inscriptions and their founders, published over sixty years ago, amplified a series of earlier articles that dealt mainly with inscriptions and was limited to the Archdeaconry of Colchester.[2] The Elizabethan archidiaconal archives reveal several hitherto unknown items of interest, but they disclose less about bells than plate. As with communion cups, the entries chiefly concern acquisition or detention, but there is a little more information in the presentments for unpaid rates. Unlike cups, however, 'new' Elizabethan bells can rarely be identified with any of the surviving ancient bells. As far as is known, none of the early Essex churchwardens' account-books refers to new bells being made, though there are many items, as elsewhere, of minor expenses for new ropes and the like.

[1] H. W. Lewer and J. C. Wall, *The Church Chests of Essex* (1913).

[2] C. Deedes and H. B. Walters, *The Church Bells of Essex* (1909); *Ess. Rev.*, i–vii (1891–97). The Essex parish church inventories (Edward VI) at the Public Record Office list many bells; these are printed in full (*Trans. E.A.S.*, O.S., iv, v; N.S., i–iii).

In 1579 two West Tilbury parishioners, Robert Jackson and a widow, 'refused to pay money that they were assessed for the making of the bell'. The sum of 18d. was due from the former, who 'very unreverently used himself, saying that the judge did him wrong', on which the court suspended him from ingress to the church; but the irate Jackson had the last say, 'affirming that it was but 18d. matter'. In 1587 two Great Wenden parishioners declined to contribute 'to the casting of the bell', one for 18d., the other for 8d. Two years earlier a brief note in 1585 shows that the Tollesbury wardens were ordered 'to cast the bells before Michaelmas'. John Lyne of Tolleshunt Knights refused to pay 16d. 'towards the casting of a bell' in 1588. A rate for 'providing a bell' for the parish church of Mile End near Colchester in 1589 led the wardens to cite Leonard Parishe of Colchester to pay 5s. in respect of his 50 acres of land at 1d. an acre and four other men'. Next year Thomas Stonard of Kelvedon refused to pay his rate of 3s. 4d. 'towards the shotting of a bell'; William Laston, another parishioner, assessed at 8d., also demurred, alleging that 'the bell was broken by extraordinary ringing and jingling and not by ringing in orderly ringing according to law'; and Thomas Wilson (8d.) and Edward Bawby (6d.) were likewise cited. In 1591 the East Donyland wardens presented 'Mr. Wiseman of Great Wigborough because he was rated at 16d. towards the shotting of the bell and will not pay it'; and a similar charge was made against Erasmus Golding for 16d. and John Harvey for 6s. 8d., both of East Donyland. (Mr. D. Hughes, director of the Whitechapel Bell Foundry (founded in 1570), kindly explained that shotting a clapper means that the stem of the clapper is cut into two pieces and rewelded to alter its length or to repair a fracture.) At opposite corners of Essex in 1598 five Barking townsmen refused to pay the rate for repairing the church and 'new casting of a bell broken wilfully', and John Osboston *alias* Osborne of Manningtree and Mr. Francis Thumblethorpe of Mistley would not give 6s. and 2s. 6d. respectively 'towards the new casting of the great bell' of the former church. Nicholas Faunte of North Ockendon in 1602 failed to pay his 13s. 8d. rate for the casting of a bell. Except for the earliest case, no subsequent proceedings are found and it may be assumed that the defaulters paid up.

Another presentment serves as a link between bell-rates and bell-ringing (mostly unlawful), some incidents of which have already been related: in 1590 George Spensar of South Benfleet was charged because he had not contributed 'towards the maintenance of the ringers on the joyful day of her Majesty, being rated at 4d.'. He was ordered to pay the 4d., plus 12d. to the poor 'for his negligence'. Perhaps he was not so loyal as the others or perhaps he disapproved of the 'Queen's Day' because the celebrations often led to disorder.

A few parishes were reported to have bells that were broken or 'in decay', including those at Wormingford (1590), two at Marks Tey which the wardens were 'to cause to be made new again' (1598); and 'the great bell is ruinated and broken' at Great Chesterford (1598). Other bells were mentioned in the section on churches out of repair.

The most informative case concerns the re-casting of a Great Stambridge bell by John Dier. In 1584 John Langer and Robert Mountaine were presented because 'when they were churchwardens they did put forth one bell as it is thought to the value of £10, which bell they have not as yet'. Their reply was that it 'was cracked, whereupon they put it out to mending and is now in mending with John Dier of Much Baddow a bell-founder, and they have offered to bring it home so that the parishioners will hear the chimes'. The court ordered that 'they shall hang up the bell again at the equal charges of the whole parishioners'. Great Stambridge's oldest existing bell is dated 1783. Dier made many bells in the last quarter of the century: eleven each in Essex and Herts., ten in Beds., two in Hunts., and one each in Cambs., Bucks. and Suffolk.[1] The historian of Hitchin states that 'the Dyer family were bell-founders in Hitchin throughout the 15th, 16th and 17th centuries';[2] John may possibly have lived for a short time at Great Baddow: three of his undated Essex bells include one at Little Baddow. A few weeks later (1584) occurs an entry which may also relate to a bell made or re-cast by Dier. A Stock man was prosecuted for refusing to pay a rate for repairing the church and 'changing of a bell'. The oldest bell is inscribed 'John Diar and Robert Wickes made this bell 1577'.

The story of an angry Cambridge bellfounder who reclaimed his unpaid 'great bell' for Little Bardfield is traced in a series of entries beginning in 1595, when Alexander Harrington, late warden, was charged with 'selling away or taking away the great bell and not presenting the same'. He answered that 'he did take the bell down and laid it to give to a bell-founder a week before Easter last, and this he did for money that the parish did owe to him'. Despite the court injunction to restore the bell, the wardens stated two years later that 'there is but two bells and one bell is carried away'. Excommunicated for contumacy, Harrington at last put in another appearance in 1598, when his defence ran:

> There is due to him as churchwarden £6 for the charges of the reparations of the steeple, the bell and other charges of the church, which was paid by Mr. Smith of the mill, four parishioners refusing to pay the rate. Further, there is due to the bellfounder, Mr. Nicholson of Cambridge, towards the shotting and the metal of the bell by the parish £5, and Mr. Nicholson with his consent and delivery did send a cart and certain men to take down the bell which with his consent he did carry away, and Nicholson hath in his custody the said bell for the said money.

Harrington and four parishioners who had refused to pay the rate were instructed to attend the next session, when he was ordered once more 'to bring the great bell and to hang the same up in the steeple again'. The defaulters complained that the rate was not lawful, but 'they will pay if

[1] Deedes and Walters, *op. cit.*, 83. [2] R. L. Hine, *History of Hitchin* (1927), i, 98n.

Harrington re-hang the bell'. As no later proceedings are found it must be assumed that the precept was carried out.

John Grove of Blackmore was presented in 1575 because he had agreed with the High Ongar wardens that 'his cart went to fetch home the bell', but had not done so. There was a dispute in 1584 about a bell belonging to Little Bromley church sold 'to one Paye for about the sum of £12', for which John Elye of Weeley, late warden of Little Bromley, was summoned to account. Two years later the South Ockendon wardens admitted that 'there was lately a bell sold, being broken, by the whole consent of the parishioners'. In 1569 four men of St. James, Colchester, were presented for 'delivering a great bell, but the money not accounted for'. Alleged misappropriation led to a charge in 1603 against Hugh Lobell of Holy Trinity parish in Colchester: 'He hath a bell belonging to the churchwardens which he applieth to his private use as for a clock'; to which he said, 'Gatelye late churchwarden did offer and leave it with him to sell'; but the judge commanded him to 're-deliver the bell' to the new wardens. Among various defects at Dunton church, notified in 1596, 'the belfry lacks a bell'; and there was no bell at Salcott in 1602.

A second reference to a clock may be noted. In 1601 William Thresher of Aveley was called to account 'for that in his time of being churchwarden the clock of the church was carried to London, pretended to be mended and so set up as beforetime, but what is become of it we cannot tell'; he was discharged on declaring that that it had been restored to the church.

Churchyards

The churchyard, as well as the church, was the freehold possession of the parson, who could sue anyone committing trespass. It had to be 'decently enclosed', especially to prevent incursions of livestock. The maintenance of the wall or fence was generally the liability of the parishioners, less often that of the incumbent; always under the supervision of the churchwardens. Who was actually responsible depended on the ancient custom of each parish. Those who owned houses adjoining the churchyard usually had to maintain their part of the enclosure. Otherwise the remainder, if any, of the fence had to be repaired according to a recognized apportionment, which in some parishes lay with certain farms and houses and was sometimes recorded in a detailed list.[1] For example, the first entry in the 'declaration' written in North Benfleet parish register runs, 'Fenton Hall' (Fanton was a Domesday manor): 'from the great elm on the east to the churchyard gate at the south-east corner, 3 rods 10 feet; and on the south 6 rods 2 feet'.[2]

[1] The rector of Netteswell wrote such a detailed record about 1580 in his register (*Catalogue of Essex Parish Records*, 163).

[2] *Ess. Rev.*, xlii, 64.

Richard Underwood of Kelvedon was instructed by the court in 1595 'to exhibit the roll whereby all the parish is set their parts to repair the churchyard fence'; and in 1587 the pale of Great Braxted was 'in decay, and by reason that our book is lost we know not who should make the defaults'. Harrison's churchyard at Radwinter in 1586 'wanteth new fencing', and Edward Momford, churchwarden, was ordered to repair it.

Several villages whose officers were cited for unrepaired fences at first pleaded ignorance, but after being pressed by the judge came back with a clearer answer. Robert Heard at Stifford, having in 1597 pulled down a tenement abutting on the churchyard, 'whereby it lieth open', was enjoined to fill the gap. So also in 1589 was 'one Thompson, who dwelleth with Lord Morley without (i.e. outside) the jurisdiction (of the court) and standeth excommunicate, and did take away a house from off a piece of ground which did fence the churchyard of Tolleshunt Bushes' (Tolleshunt Knights). Two years earlier it had been 'in decay, and the manor of Barn Hall' (owned by Lord Morley) 'and those that farm the farm' were given as the responsible parties, John Derington being named as the lessee. In 1597 Thomas Blatch of Great Waltham was summoned for 'suffering a fence to lie open to the churchyard, which by covenant he hath made with the parish for to make, and withheld the yearly rent of 4d. for his eavesdropping, otherwise called a wall, abutting upon the churchyard, for the spell of seven years'. The 2s. 4d. due he was ordered to settle. The court heard of another agreement at Stapleford Abbots when Mr. Raynold was reported in 1598 for not 'fencing of one part of the churchyard, which he hath done four and twenty years'.

A crafty attempt to escape liability at Fobbing led to Geoffrey Stent having to answer for 'coming upon the churchyard to make his fence and for turning the beard of the hedge from the churchyard as though the parish should make it, when it was wont to be made by the landholder and to be turned the other way'. In this rare sense 'beard' is defined as 'the bushes which are stuck into the bank of a new-made hedge, to protect the fresh-planted thorns';[1] and the side of the quicksets on which the dead bushes were stuck would indicate the ownership of the hedge. In 1570 Mr. Thomas Clough of Elmdon (the vicar), presented by the wardens for not repairing part of the fence, refuted liability, which he claimed was that of the parishioners in general.

Depositions are recorded in 1600 in the case of Henry Bright, churchwarden of Bulphan, against Anthony Ramsey of the same. Phineas Wicks of Bulphan, husbandman, where he had dwelt for 24 years, born at Great Burstead, aged about 53, stated: 'About 22 years ago he, dwelling with Mr. (William) Lowen, the parson, came into the churchyard, and there was Goodman Peppercorne, who then was farmer and dwelt in the farm-

[1] Halliwell, *Dictionary of Archaic Words*; cf. F. W. Austen, *Rectors of Two Essex Parishes* (1943), 58, referring to Stock.

house of John Hurte called Slowe house, making the fence at the west end of the belfry, and thinketh that the fence ought to be made by John Hurt or his farmer and that no part is made at the common charge of the parishioners, also that Ramsey hath held Slowehouse and about 30 acres of ground for 6 years'. Thomas Drywood of North Ockendon gentleman, where he had lived for 6 years, before that at Danbury 5 years, and before that at Bulphan 10 years, born at Dunton, aged about 50, also deposed: 'About 24 years ago, he then dwelling in Bulphan Hall, being amongst others called upon by the churchwardens to repair the churchyard fence as they ought severally to do, did view every man's part, and it was found that one part on the north side was not known who should repair it, whereupon every one did go to such part as they were to repair, and one John Peppercorn, then occupier of Slowehouse, did lay his staff on the fence and said, "This must be made by my house".'

The Littlebury wardens, cited in 1571, complained that 'John Parker is inhabitant of Nether Hall in Birdhouse End, of old to repair the churchyard, viz. from the vicarage gate to Parkins' stile, thence to the pond and to the vicarage gate, at the cost of the lord'. The name of the lord of the manor is not disclosed, which is unfortunate as little is known of the manor of Nether Hall *alias* Burdeux *alias* Birdhouse.[1] At Sandon in 1580 Ralph Fryer was presented 'for not mending of the churchyard pale belonging to Knightbridge House'; also two other parishes, who were able to state that the defects had been made good since the visitation. The wardens of Steeple in 1592 expressed their opinion that 'most of the reparations belongeth to Sir Francis Willowbee' (lord of the manor of Steeple Hall). Those of Markshall in 1600, summoned because the churchyard was 'in decay', said, 'They know not who should repair it'; but the court apparently extracted some facts, and 'Mr. Tyll, farmer of the house and lands of Mr. Samford', was then cited; this was probably Thomas Till, a clothier of Coggeshall.

Occasionally the matter of repairing a churchyard stile came up, as at Virley in 1576; and in 1600 the wardens of Messing were assigned to repair the broken 'turnpike going into the churchyard' (a turnpike was a horizontal wooden cross, turning on a vertical pin, to keep out animals). In 1600 a Mr. Bussard of St. Peter, Colchester, had 'made a door out his house into the churchyard, where is none before'. He resisted the complaint, so the wardens had 'to show how this door is noisome to the churchyard'. Their contention, that the 'annoyance to the churchyard is because Bussard keepeth an alehouse', caused the judge to compromise by forbidding him to use the offending door 'for any victualling'.

In a few places the churchyard boundary was evidently repaired by means of a rate: a fact that is learned from the presentments in two parishes of individuals who refused to pay. William Welles of St. Botolph,

[1] Morant, *History of Essex*, ii, 595; *Essex Place-Names*, 531.

Colchester, in 1590 was thus assessed at 2s. Strangely enough, he was accused of 'reserving three gravestones to himself, which he will not deliver to the parish again'.

The present-day problem of keeping churchyards from being overgrown seldom finds any mention in our period, apart from a few being presented as 'undecent'. Controlled grazing was apparently the means. But casual invasion of churchyards by livestock was a common occurrence. This is deduced from no less than twenty-eight presentments of farmers and husbandmen, the majority because of their hogs being allowed access.

At both East and West Mersea 'the churchyard pale is greatly rooted up by the hogs shamefully'; at East Tilbury, 'swine root up the graves'. Sometimes the trouble was due to the wardens' negligence. Those of Great Totham in 1597 had 'built a hogscote in the churchyard where hogs are served'. At All Saints, Colchester, in 1588 they 'suffered the churchyard to lie open and hogs to root up graves'. In 1564 the Walthamstow officers explained somewhat lamely that 'the hedges and the pales be not so close but that some places be wider than other, whereby the hogs may go in'; and they were ordered to remedy the defects. A Walthamstow parishioner was later summoned for 'suffering his hogs, not being yoked, to come into the churchyard'. Another defendant denied having put his hogs in the churchyard, 'only his kine', and he promised to reform. Four Ingatestone men were ordered 'to fence the places where the hogs come in'; and a Feering man named Macharidge 'had a hog dead and suffered it to be in the churchyard and there stank, to the annoyance of the parishioners'. Richard Atkins, curate of Romford, had apparently let the grazing of his churchyard; in 1583 he was charged because it 'is rooted up with hogs; and for that he hath the profit of it he is to make up the fence'.

But swine were not the only unlawful intruders nor curates the only clerical misdoers. Philip White, the rector of Fobbing, 'put hogs, kine and horses into the churchyard', the wardens adding ominously, 'and many other things presented' (1580); and 'Mr. Knevett, the rector of Mile End, Colchester, hath his fence open and the hogs root up the churchyard, also he giveth his horse meat in the church porch', to which he replied that 'he was not privy to any such matter but through the default of William Hogg, his wife's brother' (1590). A resounding retort was voiced in court when John Laurence of Peldon was presented in 1600 because 'his sheep were in the churchyard and did defile it, so that it was noisome to the whole parish when they went to church'. The churchyard, he explained, 'did lie open so as a few sheep to the number of three or thereabouts were there, but there were a hundreth of other folks'.

The transgression of Richard Rodes of Dedham in 1596, prosecuted for 'annoying the churchyard with his cattle and giving them meat by the church porch, whereby they defile it', is matched by that of James

Luttman of Hadleigh in 1601 for 'keeping his cattle in the churchyard and lying in the church porch'.

While churchyard and church porch were all too convenient for secular uses, even the church could be used in an emergency. In 1579 John Goldringe, rector of Langdon Hills, who was to be charged ten years later with adultery, was confronted with a mundane problem – how to rescue his sheep. He solved it, but had to appear before the archdeacon to answer the charge that 'his servants by his consent or procurement did put his sheep into Langdon church' (now disused). He tried to justify his action:

> A little after Candlemas last his servants endeavouring to have his sheep saved from the covering of the great snow, which at that time so greatly did fall both by night and by day, and his servants being not able to bring them into any house and having a care to have them saved, having the key of the church door, near which church his sheep were then pastured, they then locked the same sheep into the church where they were two days first and last, being working days; and then by great labour and pains his servants when the fall of the snow was ended put them into another place and made clean the church again; which was done for great and extreme necessity sake and not in any contempt, all by his consent.

The archdeacon accepted this plea but enjoined the rector to perform penance on 'Allholland' (All Hallows') Day: 'Immediately after the gospel ended, he shall openly confess his fault, confessing himself heartily sorry therefor, and then and there with the consent of the churchwardens he shall distribute amongst the poor 6s. 8d.'.

It is tempting, before the next case of sheep trespass, to quote from an early Colchester archdeaconry book. In 1543 the Tollesbury wardens presented that 'certain men in the town do keep cossets, which continually do frequent the churchyard and sit in the porch by night, to the noyance of all the parish'. This delightful and rare word for lambs has not been found in the *Oxford Dictionary* before 1579. Desecration of God's Acre was in fact far from being confined to our period or to Essex. In a later century, for instance, the churchwardens of Hitchin in Hertfordshire even 'took a toll per score of sheep depastured there';[1] and wardens' accounts in other counties yield similar examples.

An indictment of 1594 mentioned in the previous volume referred to forty ewes being milked in the marsh pastures of Woodham Ferrers; ewes' milk was made into the 'cheeses of extraordinary bigness', as related by Camden and Norden.[2] In the neighbouring parish of North Fambridge Alexander Pye was presented in 1602 for 'keeping of a cow in the churchyard and milking of sheep in the church porch' and had to confess his guilt before the minister and wardens. The churchyard at Wix proved useful, too, in 1594 when it was 'annexed by William Vesye gentleman in scattering straw through it and serving his cattle there in winter time'. Three years later 'Goodman Banckes, churchwarden of Much Wenden, affirmed that Mr. Marsh, vicar there, did thresh corn in the church porch

[1] R. L. Hine, *History of Hitchin* (1927), i, 237. [2] *E.L.: Disorder*, 122.

and laid chaff in the church solar'. He admitted that 'he had five faggots there and chaff in the bell house', all of which the judge advised him to remove.

To an adjoining occupier, the churchyard could serve as a private convenience. So a Prittlewell man thought in 1595, until he was summoned for 'annoying the churchyard with a sink' (either a cesspool or a drain, the result being much the same). It was used as a dumping ground by a parishioner of St. Runwald, Colchester, in 1595, thus 'annoying the church wall with much dirt and buggish cast up against the same, whereof a common passage is made into the churchyard to the annoyance of the whole parish of Trinity'; one of the wardens apparently coined 'buggish', an aptly expressive word not otherwise recorded.

The vicar of Great Wenden had secured cover for his own stuff, but the open churchyard could also be a storeplace for timber. Several men were censured for making use of spaces outside St. Runwald's, All Saints', and Trinity churches at Colchester. In 1587–88 complaints were made about other men, including William Maynard, who sold shoes in St. Runwald's porch, and Anthony Crobrooke of St. Botolph, who 'let the church porch to William Maynard'. Five years afterwards two curriers named Evered and Culpach 'dried their leather upon the church and the church wall' of St. Nicholas' and Andrew Steward and another man made sails inside St. Leonard's church. Hugh Mills of Stock also found the church belfry a handy place in which to store his cattle fodder in 1591; and William Phillips laid a load of broom in St. Peter's church, Maldon, in 1599.

There was ample precedent, both clergy and laity probably thought, for using the church for storage and trade. Had not Christ driven the moneylenders from the Temple, and did not the booksellers, whose shops were in St. Paul's Churchyard, use the cathedral vaults for their stocks?

If such misuse of churches was far from uncommon, it is not surprising to learn that homeless people followed suit when in dire need. In 1600 William Wallis and his wife of Stanford Rivers were cited because 'they have made their habitation in the south porch of the parish church, and therewithal he doth not otherwise provide, but hath suffered his wife to travail in childbirth therein and to continue there a whole month'. The scribe's addition, 'He said he could', reads like the mumbling reply in court of a distressed father. Throughout the centuries, too, destitute folk have tried to gain shelter in churches as well as church porches. An instance is seen in 1598, when Edmund Garlyng of Little Birch 'dwelleth in the church and we cannot get him out'; somewhat incongruously the scribe's note this time was, 'To pay fee'. About the same date Little Birch church was being reported as having no services in it – evidence perhaps that it had already become ruinous and was being abandoned.

By immemorial use there were in most parishes footpaths providing short cuts to the church, and many of these 'churchways' are still walked. A few gave rise to disputes. In 1599 John Yeoman of Kelvedon, accused of stopping up such a path, asserted that it had not been used for the past five or six years; John Akerson, a fuller, maintained, however, that it had been in use for forty years. So the judge demanded proof by witnesses at the next court; but the record is silent. Another case occurred in the same year in the next parish of Feering, the wardens of which reported Robert Deathe for 'ploughing the church or bier path there'. Also in 1599 the hundredal jury for Chelmsford presented to Quarter Sessions that Christopher Goff, vicar of Great Waltham, had 'nailed up the usual gate on the south side of the churchyard, so that it is noisome for the parishioners and especially for the old folks and children to come to their church' – a homely phrase conjuring up scenes of their flocking to the church of one of the most extensive parishes in the county: those in the extreme north could attend Black Chapel, as already stated. In the previous year the vicar had been indicted as a common barrator (quarreller). In 1589, the jurors of Chelmsford hundred presented that 'at Ingatestone at the fair there was buying and selling of merchandise in the churchyard, viz. by one Thomas Ware of Hatfield Peverel, petty chapman', who was duly indicted; but the verdict is not given.

Parsonages

The Church court books have scores of entries about dilapidated parsonages (including lay rectory houses) and vicarages, most of which were probably of late medieval date,[1] though there were some new buildings. Most of the Essex glebe terriers, compiled in 1610 or 1637 and summarized by Newcourt[2], mention the houses and outbuildings briefly, but more than twenty rectories are described in detail. Of these, Ashdon and West Hanningfield are the only parsonages mentioned below (see Appendix). The latter was a building of average size, and probably the 'new-built study' and some of the outhouses date from shortly after the rectory was stated to be ruinous. The visitation of the archdeaconry of Essex in 1565, as shown, produced reports of their disrepair in seventeen parishes. The earlier act books of the same archdeacon and of the Bishop of London's Commissary for 1561–62 mention only two. Thomas Aylett, farmer of Leaden Roothing rectory, presented because 'the mansion (i.e. dwelling) houses are out of reparations', said that some were repaired and he undertook that 'the rest shall be repaired betwixt this and Michaelmas come twelvemonth'; and Thomas Davyes, an otherwise unknown rector of Ashdon, was ordered to repair his own parsonage.

[1] Cf. P. Heath, *English Parish Clergy* (1969), 139.
[2] Newcourt, *op. cit.*, vol. ii; the parsonages of Copford and High Ongar had dovecotes, those of Stanford Rivers and Epping were moated, and Witham vicarage had as many as 21 rooms.

As with churches, we shall refer only to those buildings in very defective condition. West Hanningfield and Danbury rectories and Mundon vicarage were all 'ruinous' (1566); 'Chignal SS. Mary and James' parsonage was 'almost down' (1572); Broomfield 'vicarage houses be in great decay and ready to fall down, and some be down already' (1575); 'the curate's house of Romford and the curate's house of Havering are in great decay' (1576), John Legate, rector of the mother church of Hornchurch, having been named as responsible; 'the buildings and timber of Great Holland rectory are most lamentably spoiled and the timber burned to an utter spoil' (1585); Little Oakley parsonage was 'likely to fall' (1583), but Hugh Branham, the rector, while admitting this, said that, 'when he entered, it was very ruinous, and yet withstanding he had in three years built a barn of new and is ready to bestow £10 upon the rest as he is able'. Mr. (Thomas) Farrer, rector of St. James, Colchester, evidently resented presentment and asserted that 'his parsonage house is better in reparations than it was this sixteen years' (1596). Cited in 1578 because 'he letteth his parsonage house', Lewis Madocke, rector of Fryerning, disagreed, 'saving that he suffereth a poor kinsman of his wife's to dwell in the same without any rent, for poverty's sake'.

A few rectories were of course not clerics' residences, but were owned by the lay rectors who received the great tithes, though sometimes occupied by their 'farmers', or lessees. Presentments were put in against the farmer of Sutton because 'the rectory is ruinous' (1566); Mr. (Gabriel) Pointes of North Ockendon because 'the parsonage houses want reparations' (1591); against 'William Bradbury, gentleman', of Wicken Bonhunt (1594), as 'our parsonage housing is burnt, and to be repaired by him'; and against 'Mr. (Richard) Champnes, farmer of the rectory of Stanford-le-Hope' (1598), in respect of 'the ruin and decay of our parsonage houses, as namely, dwelling house, barn, stable and storehouse for corn, and cart-house, all which were consumed by misfortune of the fire and not yet re-edified'. Of the last, the terrier gives 'a mansion-house, a kitchen, new-built, a barn and a stable',[1] and the *Inventory* states that the barn 'was built early 17th century'.[2] All three defendants were patrons of the benefices.

The answer of William Banbrick, vicar of Tolleshunt Major (1588), 'touching the repairs of the vicarage', was that 'the chief of the decays is in the groundselling and he could not get any wood for groundselling and will repair so soon as he can'; but a year later, shortly before his resignation, he was again presented because it was then 'ready to fall down'. Structural details are also given in the charge against William Ponde of Langdon Hills, probably the lessee (1584): 'The barn lieth unthatched and undaubed in the east end, it lacketh a groundsel, and the north end lacketh underpinning, needling (inserting temporary beams during an underpinning operation), and daubing.'

[1] Newcourt, *op. cit.*, ii, 548. [2] *R.H.C.M. Essex*, iv, 150.

Rates

At the beginning of our period church expenses were paid for largely out of the profits received from ales. These were feasts at which much strong ale was drunk: at bride-ales, soul-ales (funerals), and church-ales. Some parishes had regular church-ales, usually about Whitsuntide; others organized these merry-makings on special occasions, to help to pay for re-casting the bells or even for rebuilding part of the church. A few references to bride-ales have already been noticed, but unfortunately the court books afford no echo of the bibulous fun of church-ales, to which parishioners had been exhorted to give malt for the big brewings. Church plays, also mentioned in an earlier chapter, were often associated with church-ales: players and minstrels, as well as cooks, figured in the expenses of the Great Dunmow May Feast in 1538.[1]

But these festive occasions led to drunkenness and disorderly conduct; and first the ales and then the semi-religious church plays were frowned upon by the puritans, especially in Elizabeth's later years. A few buildings survive to remind us of them. Church-houses, or church-taverns, near the church, were used for the brewings, storage of the utensils, and so forth. Romford still has its late fifteenth-century Church House, formerly the 'Cock and Bell' inn; Matching still boasts of its Marriage Feast House, built in the same century. But although Harrison inveighed against 'the superfluous numbers' of ales,[2] the Walden sessions of the Colchester archdeacon's court at which he presided in the 1570s disclose his dealing with no offenders on this score.

With the gradual suppression or decline of church-ales and the like, compulsory church rates became the normal means of raising money, though most parishes had the shilling fines for non-attendance at church and occasional legacies from the faithful 'for the reparations of the church' or more specifically towards the rebuilding of the tower or casting of new bells. Details will be given in the next volume, which will deal with Elizabethan wills.

Liability for payment of rates has always been a source of business for lawyers, especially in later centuries, when poor rates rose to alarming heights. Even in Elizabethan times complications had already arisen, although church rates were the only levies until the tentative legislation for poor relief led to compulsory civil rates near the end of our period. The matter of rates for repairing churches or providing for bells or other church furnishings very seldom came before the spiritual courts in the early years. An exceptional note is found in 1561, but with no comment: 'Geoffrey Swayne of Rayleigh is bound in 100 marks for repairing the church and payment of all dues to the church'; in the absence of his will or other record, no explanation can be offered.

[1] *Trans. E.A.S.*, O.S., ii, 230. [2] Harrison, *op. cit.*, 36.

While 'rated by the whole parish' is very occasionally used by the churchwardens, it is only a general phrase, and 'rated by the headboroughs' or 'the chief men of our parish' is more accurate. In 1585, when the Walden wardens were cited because 'the steeple (i.e. tower) is decayed', the court instructed them 'to make a cessment and to cess the parishioners, calling to them the officers and chief commonalty of the same town to assist them and to give public notice thereof'. In 1602 the Coggeshall wardens replied, when summoned, that they had 'divers times required the parishioners there to make a rate and they have refused the same, and they (the wardens) are out of purse £30', which led the judge to commission them and seven parishoners to certify their remedying the default.

It must be emphasized that there were two kinds of church rates – for provision of communion wine and routine minor expenses, for which collections of an informal nature were probably made in the smaller parishes, and special rates for major repairs to the church fabric or for casting new bells or re-casting old ones. Some rate disputes have already been mentioned in the short account of cases about bells. In every church, too, there was a 'poor men's box', into which went the donations of the charitable and the fines of the transgressors levied in the archidiaconal courts.[1] Dovercourt poor's box (1589) is shown (plate 9).

Dilatoriness in paying church rates, or obstinate refusal, accounts for at least 200 presentments. The vast majority merely give the sum due, and only a few cases will therefore be mentioned. In 1590 Thomas Tailer of Horndon-on-the-Hill, accused of refusing to pay the rate towards the repair of Stanford-le-Hope church, said that he was willing to pay but declared that there was a legacy of 40s. yearly under the will of Sir Richard Champion (an extract from which he produced), viz. 20s. to the church repairs and 20s. to the poor, which the wardens had neglected to collect. He was dismissed, and three parishioners were ordered to answer the complaint. At the next session he went further in claiming that 'the church was repaired not many years since, the wardens had £12 in legacy by Mr. Champion's will in their hands, and the ratement doth not amount to the sum of £10'. They were enjoined to bring the rate list for the judge's inspection. In April 1591 the wardens of St. Peter, Maldon, were in trouble because their church was 'far out of reparations'. They pleaded guilty and were ordered 'forthwith to make a rate and to certify it with the names of such as will not contribute and to set their church in forwardness for the repairing thereof, so as it may be done before Michaelmas'. Mr. Bales of Witham, gentleman, presented for 'refusing to pay 3s. 4d. towards the reparations of the church', took umbrage. According to a marginal note, 'He offered to strike Salter the mandatory' (i.e. the apparitor who delivered his citation to attend)', saying that he cared for never a knave of

[1] About a dozen poor-boxes of *circa* 1480–1640 still remain in Essex churches; that of Steeple Bumpstead is illustrated in A. C. Edwards, *Essex Churches* (E.R.O., 1966).

the court'. (A Quarter Sessions record of 1616 refers to a 'late servant of Mr. Bale, one of the Grooms of Her Majesty's Privy Chamber'.)

The West Hanningfield wardens' statement, which has no exact parallel elsewhere, is a reminder that the old custom of making voluntary contributions as opposed to rates was not entirely forgotten and in this village had evidently been discussed at the public vestry meeting. 'The steeple is not repaired', they said, 'for that the parishioners cannot agree whether it is to be repaired by every man's devotion, by every man's ability, or by every man's land' (1596). It is possible, however, that one of the Ramsey wardens, who made no mention of a rate, also had the same means in mind when their church was out of repair (1594). He acknowledged that 'it hath been so of a long time and that he and his partner are unable (to repair) without the help of the rest of the parishioners of best ability, viz. Mr. James Goldingham, Mr. Herde, Edward Bridge and John Godfrey senior'.

Non-resident holders of land were a constant source of trouble to the churchwardens and often difficult to trace. Three 'out-dwellers', as occupiers not living in the parish were sometimes called, whose rates for the repair of Fobbing church were demanded in 1587, were Jasper Baker of Bowers Gifford, John Howe of Laindon, and Thomas Tailer of Horndon (again). Baker 'thinketh therefore that he is not bound to pay', and Howe 'says therefore he is not bound to pay'. The long-since ruined church of Virley is mentioned in 1603, when Arthur Lambe of Colchester refused to pay his 4s. Another determined opponent, cited in 1601, was Thomas Dryver of Studley Green in Danbury, who when rated for land he occupied in Rettendon 'utterly refused to pay, with contemptuous words, bidding them come by it as they can'. On being rated for repairing the church tower of Great Oakley in 1589, six Moze men and one Ramsey man in addition to seven parishioners refused. Next year 'Mr. Freebody of Rochford, farmer' (lessee) of a farm called Commes in Little Stambridge, was appointed to pay 16s. towards repairing the steeple of the latter parish, 'but the churchwardens cannot get it of him'; possibly his refusal lay in not being the occupier, as there was no liability on a lessee if he was not the sitting tenant. No less a person than the Archdeacon of Essex, 'Mr. George Withers, S.T.D., (rector) of Danbury', was named in 1601 by the wardens of Purleigh for refusing 'to pay to the church that he is rated at by the whole parish for 50 acres at 2s.'.

The most interesting presentment is one brought in 1600 by the Blackmore wardens against Thomas Witham of High Ongar, recalling Thomas Smith's suit in 1583. He disputed liability for the church rate because he occupied 'no other lands within the parish but only the lands belonging to the (former) Priory, which are charged with the reparation of the whole chancel and are of the glebe or endowment of the church as he believeth'.

Resident parishioners were of course by far the most numerous class of defaulters. Edmund Knappe, yeoman, for example, was cited in 1599 to pay, but it was alleged that he and Edmund Knappe, gentleman (his father?), were 'joint owners of the park of Wix and ought to pay'.

A small proportion of the defendants, irrespective of whether they were parishioners or non-resident occupiers, protested because in their opinion they were over-rated in relation to the acreage of their land or to the assessment of others. In 1588 Roger London of Tolleshunt Knights claimed that 'being taxed wrongfully to 9s. 5d. after the rate of ob.q. (i.e. ¾d.) the acre, he hath paid 3s. in part of so much ground as he hath after the same rate'; but in court he offered 3s. 9d. more in full payment. Two years later Robert Pollard of Tollesbury, who held 16 acres in Tolleshunt D'Arcy, would not give a mere 4d., asserting that he was rated 'very unequally and unproportionably, for that others in the parish of Tolleshunt D'Arcy having in their occupation 4 or 5 hundred acres are rated only at 12d.'. The wardens were cited to justify their assessment, but there is no subsequent entry. Thomas Freman of Radwinter, 'being reasonably rated' according to the wardens, retorted in 1594: 'The rate was not lawfully made and Goodman Smith of Radwinter Hall and Goodman Momford of Bendish Hall are not so much rated acre by acre as he is, and that he tendered himself to pay 12d. to the same effect, which is according to his ability.' So the court ordered the officers to answer; again there is no later reference.

The rich marshland pastures along the Thames estuary, despite their being liable to occasional inundation when the seawalls were breached, afford the only example of differential rating. In 1598 the East Ham wardens prosecuted William Gamage esquire for 'refusing to pay his full duty, being assessed at 1d. the acre of upland and 2d. the acre for marsh, which cometh in the whole to 4s. 1d.'; also 'Mr. Paul of London for 8d. assessed on 4 acres of marsh'.

A mysterious charge of 'detaining away the bill of rate' for the repairs of St. James's church, Colchester, was made in 1599 by George Harrison, late warden, against Limbert Crantem (Cranven?), a parishioner and 'one of the ratees', who, after most of the rates had been paid, 'by sinister means procured the same rate into his hands'. Although 'no such bill was delivered to him by the churchwardens', he admitted that 'he had such a scroll or bill lent him by Harrison', who refused to receive it back. More intelligible is the case in 1587 against the previous warden of Ashdon, who had 'gone out of the town (i.e. left the parish) and carried away with him the book of accounts and certain money which he gathered in the parish for the use of the church, as his fellow churchwarden sayeth'.

Chapels-of-ease had been established in early times for the inhabitants of Romford and Havering, both of which lay within the bounds of the extensive parish of Hornchurch. Mistress Joan Quarles, widow, of the parish of Hornchurch was presented in 1602 for 'not paying her assessment towards the church' (i.e. Hornchurch, the mother church), 'now ruinous.' Her former husband was James, lord of the manor of Stewards in Romford. Thwaites, her proctor, claimed that 'she occupieth no land within the division or quarter belonging to Hornchurch' (i.e. to the village itself). She was followed by Isaac Renowldes, John Hart and John Lorance, all of the same parish, for similar default. Of these the first, termed 'one of the churchwardens of the church or chapel of Romford', contended that 'the inhabitants of Nokehill, Portegoore alias Pirgo, Potters Herst, Harolds Wood, and Havering atte Bower from time immemorial had been accustomed to pay towards the repair of the said church (Romford) according to the lands possessed'. At the next session no less than fifteen Romford inhabitants were cited, for refusing to pay sums ranging from 4s. to 4d. 'rated to the reparations of their parish church (of Hornchurch) assessed by a vestry'. One said that he had paid it to the late churchwarden; three, they had paid to 'Hawke, a sideman who was appointed to gather the tax'; one, he was over-rated, and another, he was very poor and unable to pay (both were ordered to pay up). The rest failed to attend, but most of them soon capitulated; four recalcitrants were excommunicated, after which the case fades out – temporarily. In 1604–06, however, the matter arose again, and a major dispute ensued, with lengthy depositions being taken; but that is beyond our period.[1]

In 1587 the wardens of St. Giles, Colchester, presented Giles Arthur, who 'dwells with a Dutchman beyond the North Bridge and owes the rates to the minister'. Very occasionally poverty was put forward as the reason for default. In 1591 John Sadler of Langham was prosecuted 'for that he did not pay his ratement for the reparation of the church, which is 7s. 6d.', which of course was a high sum. Averring that he was 'a poor man and not able to pay, and not worth 20 marks (£13 6s. 8d.) in all the world', he was relieved of 4s. of that rate and completely so in the future. Five Fryerning men 'withheld rates' ranging from 12d. to 4d., 'saying they were poor, but,' they added naïvely, 'if they shall be hereafter of better wealth they will pay their dues'.

The raising of money for occasional or minor expenses other than for the fabric or bells is illustrated by a few cases. There is a solitary mention of a rate for buying a communion cup, already noticed. Now and again a parishioner was reported for not paying a rate for communion bread and wine. The presentment of John Wade of Wix for not contributing 3s. 4d. 'towards the bread and wine and mending of the bell knapple of Moze whilst he dwelt there' (1591) shows how a very small parish recouped itself. Rates for 'repairing the church stools' were refused by single individuals at Pontisbright (1596) and Inworth (1592). The Woodford wardens even made a rate to replace their stolen communion table cloth

[1] The case was written up in full by D. W. Gallifant (Emmison Prize essay, 1961, E.R.O., T/Z 13/59).

(1591); to a rate for 'the making of a surplice' for Tendring church William Skarfe and John Bateman objected to paying their 3s. 4d. and 3s. 8d. and were accordingly directed to do so (1582); and after the injunction had been issued for provision of parchment registers, Abraham Veysey of Wivenhoe failed to pay his share of the rate for that purpose (1598). It was not until the important Braintree church rate case was fought three and a half centuries afterwards that dissenters and others gained exemption from supporting the places of worship of the Established Church.

Appendix

Two Rectories in 1610

Both these parsonage houses were reported to be dilapidated in the 1560s (pp. 273–4). The description of West Hanningfield rectory is an unusually long one and gives a good idea of the interior and the numerous outbuildings.

> *West Hanningfield Rectory*
> One dwelling-house, tiled, having in it a hall with a loft over it for corn, a closet in the hall, two butteries with a loft over them for servants' lodging, an entry, a large parlour, with two lodging-chambers over it for servants, a study new-built, also a kitchen tiled with a corn-loft over it, a boulting-house with a cheese-loft over it, a brew-house newly set up with a fair corn-loft over it and a garret over that and a hen-house at the end of it, a hogscote boarded, a stable, a quern-house, two small cotes to fat fowl in, a cow-house newly-built with a cart-house at the end of it, another cart-house newly-built with a room over it to hold hay, one large hay-house with a cart-house at the end of it, another cart-house newly-built, a gate-house, wherein is a milk-house, with a loft over it for cheese and fish; the site of the house and yards, with two gardens, contains two roods; an orchard newly paled in containing three roods; and about 21 acres of glebe-land.[1]

Ashdon Rectory is dated *circa* 1600 in the *Inventory*; it contains some original panelling and an over-mantel with a richly-carved frieze.[2] The terrier does not mention its being newly-built, but it had been out of repair in 1561. This is the only ancient rectory among the parsonages referred to in this chapter which has survived from the Tudor period, albeit very late Elizabethan.

> *Ashdon Rectory*
> A parsonage-house and other houses of office, two barns, a stable, a hay-house, and a gate-house with rooms above and below, a dove-house, an orchard, a whiting-yard, and a pasture containing four acres, lying on the west side of the parsonage-house; (also about 80 acres of glebe).[3]

[1] Newcourt, *op. cit.*, ii, 309 [2] *R.C.H.M. Essex*, i, 7. [3] Newcourt, *op. cit.*, ii, 15.

9
Trial and Punishment

The earlier chapters have furnished many incidental illustrations of the procedure by which the spiritual courts dealt with defendants. It differed so widely from that of the secular courts, as related in the previous volume, that an account will now be given under its four main aspects of Penance, Purgation, Excommunication, and Contempt.

Penance

If the writer were asked to suggest stage scenes depicting facets of Elizabethan life that have no counterpart in our own day, he would certainly include a view of an archdeacon's court being held in a market-town church, with a small crowd of defendants, churchwardens, executors of wills, and others, waiting their turn to come forward. If the portrayal of such a session had to be limited to a single case, he would hesitate between two closely related procedures. It might be a prosecution for suspected sexual misbehaviour, with the accused 'proving' his or her innocence by purging and his witnesses filing up to testify that his oath was a true one; the compurgation possibly objected to by their puritan minister. Or it might reveal a perhaps even more bizarre scene in the guilty party's own church, while the large congregation, some prim-lipped with censure, others goggle-eyed with mirth, watched penance being performed with sham language, strange garb and awkward posture. Incredible as it may seem, either of these reconstructions of long-forgotten little dramas would be entirely typical of commonplace incidents all over Elizabethan England.[1]

The penitential act being virtually the court's only means of punishment except for enforced contributions to the poor's box and excommunication, some thousands underwent this humiliation in Essex alone. Roughly an equal number declared that they were not guilty and found or tried to find neighbours prepared to swear with them.

Church historians have usually stated that punishment by penance was given to those charged with immorality and involved the offender in having to stand in a white sheet, holding a white wand. The judge, however, had wide discretionary powers regarding the form or severity of penance. Some writers seem to have been unaware that it could be

[1] See *Ess. Rev.*, 1, 210–17 for some extracts from the Essex archidiaconal records concerning both penance and purgation for 1542–1639. Full transcripts of thirteen penitential confessions were given by Hubert Hall in 'Some Elizabethan Penances in the Diocese of Ely' (*Trans. Roy. Hist. Soc.*, 3rd ser., i, 263–77).

inflicted in a variety of ways, or that the sentence was not always confined to a single performance or awarded solely for sexual offences.

Penance was usually undertaken in public, thus serving a double purpose: the offender was penalised, and the witnesses had a deterrent lesson based on moral principles. It was generally performed in the party's or parties' parish church, on the next Sunday after the court sentence, and in morning or evening prayer between the first and the second lessons. Occasionally the judge specifically assigned it to take place on a festival Sunday (Easter or Christmas is found), on two fast Sundays, or on two successive ordinary sabbaths.

The penitential attire was a white sheet, and a white wand or rod was held. (In a solitary instance, a couple were commanded to bring sheets with them, but usually the wardens kept them in reserve.) 'A white sheet on his upper garment which is to cover his whole body', or 'a fair white sheet, in fulness of repentance' are normal phrases; once, a 'white bodice' instead of a sheet. A single exception to the loathed covering is found in 1600, when John Munt and Grace Hubberd of Thorrington, who had anticipated conjugal practice, got some mitigation in being allowed to 'acknowledge their fault at the time of solemnization of matrimony in their ordinary apparel'. The decree might state that the penitent should be 'bareheaded', 'barefooted', or 'face downward', or occasionally for a woman, 'with hair loose'. The delinquent had to stand 'openly in the church', or 'in the mid alley' (i.e. aisle, in this case the nave), at the choir door, in the porch, or had to perambulate the church. The five quotations which follow are all taken from the Bishop of London's Commissary's book for 1561–62, which has an unusually large number of penance and purgation entries set out in full.

An Otten Belchamp man's sentence was thus recorded:

> Upon Sunday next William Hylls shall be in the church porch by the second peal, having a white sheet about him and a white rod in his hand, and then at the beginning of the service to enter into the church, and all the whole time of service to kneel at the chancel door until the second lesson be read, then to go round about the church from 'yeale to yeale' (aisle to aisle) till he come to the chancel door, that done at such time as the parson or deputy there to go into the pulpit to read the first part of the homily of adultery, he to stand up before the pulpit and then to kneel in his foresaid place during the time of the whole service, and in like case the next Sunday following, and to certify at the next court.

The penance ordered for a Takeley man is worth quoting because his partner in adultery managed to produce five compurgatrices to purge her own sin:

> The offender shall put a sheet upon him and so go about the church and then to stand before the chancel door with his face towards the people from the beginning of the procession until it be ended, and there to remain until Mr. Vicar have made an exhortation unto the people concerning that matter or else to read the homily of adultery.

And to complete the farcical anomaly, he was directed also to perform penitence in the woman's church of Great Dunmow, where she must have been sitting in the congregation. The key to this apparent riddle lies in the fact that the courts had no alternative but to accept purgation if the defendant denied the charge, as will be explained in the next section.

The following extract illustrates how the formula had not yet become crystallized, nor was it indeed ever routine language in our period: the judges exercised both discretion and imagination in fitting the penance to the offence, as we shall see shortly. The frailties of the flesh brought a couple from the Hedinghams, both of whom received similar sentences:

> At such time as the ring all in (i.e. peal), he shall come into the church in his hose and doublet with a white sheet about him, and there right over the church door shall stand until such time till the first lesson be read there; that done he shall so arrayed go round about the church to his old place again, and there to remain until such time as the litany be read, when he shall come up and kneel before the chancel door with his face toward the people; that done at the time that the curate go up into the pulpit and read the homily of adultery he shall stand up with his face toward the people.

Christopher Cutler of Castle Hedingham and Margaret Marten of Sible Hedingham were the offenders, and each was ordered to perambulate in both churches on successive Sundays. But although she evidently went through it 'with hair loose', he arrogantly turned up at the next session and 'certified that he had not done penance and expressly refused', and was accordingly excommunicated. The proceedings had originated in their producing a bastard child, but both denied incontinence. While he was to purge with six neighbours, she claimed that she had been married at Tolleshunt Bushes (Knights) 'at Michaelmas was twelve month to Henry Marten by whom she brought forth this child, and Henry died a fortnight afore our Lady Day last in Lent'. She was told to bring certificates from the parish of her marriage and his death, and she had brought the double testimony of her innocence. Despite all this, the penance quoted above for both defendants had been decreed after they had been cited 'to hear the judge's will'. It looks as though the court was dissatisfied with the evidence produced.

The terms of a woman's sentence sometimes differed in so far as her confessional garb and head gear were concerned, especially if she was accused of bastardy. The order imposed on Dionisia (Denise) Snell of Farnham in 1562 is the sternest found in the act books. Failing to attend after citation, she had been excommunicated, but appeared at the next court, was absolved from the decree 'at her humble petition', and declared that 'Mr. Scroggs, sometime her master, was father of her child'. The court then decided on the seduced victim's retribution:

> She on Sunday next following shall barefoot and barelegged come into the parish church of Farnham in her petticoat with a white sheet about her, her hair loose, and a kercher upon her head, and there at the chancel door to remain standing with her face towards the people all the time of morning prayer until the end; that done to go about the church before the procession be read, and to come to the

> chancel door where she shall remain kneeling the whole time of the Litany until such time as the priest goeth into the pulpit and there to read the whole homily of adultery, whereat she shall come and stand before the pulpit, and then to depart.

But she was not destined to stand barefooted on the reed- or straw-covered or uncovered floor in an unheated church on a winter's day, nor to undergo such humiliation at once, for some parishioners to their credit spoke up for her. 'At the request of divers honest persons, for that she is but a green woman, and very sickly', the judge agreed to postpone her penance 'until such time as he shall be credibly informed that she be sufficient in health and able to do her penance'; to which order is added in another hand, 'and also of her good demeanour hereafter'. She was further enjoined, *sub pena juris*, 'to keep no more company with the said Scroggs', which doubtless she had no intention of doing. Poor wretch: a green woman meant that she was immature or simple-minded (p. 160). Nothing can be ascertained about Master Scroggs, who had taken advantage of her, nor was he cited, possibly because his abode lay in a different court's jurisdiction.

In the common charges against pregnant spinsters, the punishment was usually a combination of walking, kneeling and standing, as already described. But, in the sentence on a Stebbing woman who had confessed, naming the father 'and none but he', an extra clause was inserted that, after the reading of the homily against adultery, 'she shall desire the people to pray to God for her amendment'. Such a final act was often ordered for immoral offenders of both sexes, but she was given the extra mortification of having to repeat the whole penance in church on Whit Monday and Tuesday, which were holy-days with services.

Pompous and pontificating as these Elizabethan judges were, folk did not suffer the abnormal punishments given two generations earlier, such as that awarded by the Archdeacon of Buckingham's court to a quack doctor, who had to precede the procession every Sunday throughout Lent carrying a candle in his hand, to fast on bread and water every Wednesday and Friday for a year, and even to make a pilgrimage barefooted to the shrine at Walsingham, well over a hundred miles away.[1]

The court always called for the receipt of a certificate of performance as evidence that its sentence had been carried out. A few paper certificates, found loose in the act books, bear witness accordingly. Thomas Pargeter of Barking was excommunicated in 1580 because he had not certified properly, but appeared and produced his certificate of penance at Bridewell prison, on which he was dismissed on payment of 6s. 8d. fee. In 1590 John Gammes of Ardleigh exhibited the attestation document, viz. 'by letters from the minister and parishioners'; but whereas the certificate on inspection showed that he had not performed penance in a white sheet, the judge ordered that 'he shall receive the holy communion at the greatest

[1] *Trans. Royal Hist. Soc.*, 5th series, xxi, 72–3.

number of receiving of communicants and there in his usual apparel shall kneeling in audible voice penitently confess his fault, and to certify': clear proof that the court did not regard certificates as merely routine papers to be filed by the registrar. But one tells a different story:

> Bowers Gifford, 30 July anno 1600.
> I certify by these presents that Joan Mildesbe of the parish aforesaid did all the time of divine service and of the sermon stand in a white sheet, but would not confess her fault, although I persuaded her earnestly so to do.
> Per me GEORGE GLIDWELL, pastorem ibidem.

It is not surprising to find that another loose paper in one of the act books testifies to the Willingale Doe parishioners' dislike of that troublesome man, Richard Sampforde, one of the tribe whose violence was described in our previous volume.[1] The certificate of performing his penance was accompanied by a further certificate which ran:

> The bringer hereof Richard Sampforde hath put 6d. in to the poor men's box, which seemeth unto us a small penance for so great offence, for he hath not been at the church but once since Bartholomewtide and that was on Sunday last.

A testimonial from Coggeshall in 1595 reported ultimate penitence and harmony after chatter in church, conflict in churchyard and contempt in court. Henry Enewe (or Inewe) junior had been presented by the wardens. The charge ran: 'Talking in the sermon time, and being reproved by the minister and chief headboroughs in the churchyard he bade a turd for them and cared not for them; also for going out of the church in service time, and being admonished to tarry he answered that he had business to do and would not tarry. And William Clarke the churchwarden seeing him in his yard, Enewe called him and said he was a proved knave and a drunken knave and he would prove him so.' He admitted only the third part of the presentment. But penance being ordered, 'he said he would never do penance as long as he lived, although he were quartered'. At the next session, however, he alleged that 'he had acknowledged his fault before Mr. Newman, minister, the churchwardens, William Clarke and others, and Clarke and he were reconciled and made friends, as appears by letter of Mr. Newman'. He was discharged. His father had earlier sided with him, 'railing in the churchyard with William Clarke and calling him "Pert Jack knave"'. The Ennews were clothiers.

The ante-nuptial love-making of Silvester Dennis and Margery his wife in 1589 affords another of those rare references to the little chapel-of-ease in the parish of Great Waltham: they were to confess 'after public prayer in the chapel commonly called Black Chapel in the forenoon in their usual apparel'. (See plate 5.)

Having to stand publicly in the market-place of the nearest town was a common alternative to confessing in church, or more often an additional trouncing. In three cases belonging to 1578–81 guilty parties were thus sentenced, one in Colchester market 'with a basket at his back and a

[1] *E.L. Disorder*, 66–7, 187.

paper on his head' stating the nature of his offence; another in Maldon market 'in a white sheet with a pack saddle on his back for one hour'; and a third in Walden market 'from 10 till 12 o'clock with a white sheet about him in the ordinary place of penitents and ask forgiveness etc.'. At Chelmsford, the 'ordinary place' (a term used only in this Walden case) was the market-cross; at Colchester, 'the market at the Moot Hall door'; at Maldon, 'the bullring in the market'.

A Barking man and a West Ham woman charged with incontinence in 1565 were assigned penance in Romford market on a November day, 'stripped out of their clothes one hour and a half'; and an identical punishment was ordered at the same session for another couple. Their nakedness was covered by the penitential sheets, as a similar entry of the following year explains. A Horndon-on-the-Hill man, who 'nourisheth bawdery by keeping a harlot in his house' and had admitted his guilt, was enjoined to do his public penance in Brentwood market on Thursday for an hour, 'and there shall confess his fault penitently, having his coat off and his doublet and his hose, a sheet about him and a white rod in his hand, and in like manner he shall do on Sunday next in the parish church of Horndon in service time for one hour'.

A few sentences afford a little light on the areas of influence and probably the trade watersheds of several market towns. This is of some interest in the cases of Woodham Ferrers, Horndon and Aveley, as all three were never more than minor market towns and in decline by this period. Norden's maps of 1594 mark Horndon and Aveley as having markets, but the versions of his 'Description of Essex' give only Aveley and he could not name the weekday on which it was held. The extremely detailed survey of Woodham Ferrers, compiled in 1582, states that the Saturday market 'of late years hath not been used',[1] and a parishioner had been sent in 1572 all the way to Chelmsford market to perform his penance. In 1575 two Corringham offenders had to appear at Horndon market; also in 1571 a Mucking man and his maidservant on Saturday in the same market, 'when most people are there, to stand upon stools for the space of three hours'. In 1572 an immoral Cranham man and his maid were to do penance 'in the market place of Aveley'; but an Aveley woman seven years earlier had to perform it at Romford on Tuesday (Norden gives Wednesday as market-day) and at Barking on Saturday. While double humiliation was thus meted out only in some instances, one court order in 1563 shows how a Dagenham man was to be punished for incontinence by appearing publicly at Romford, Barking and Dagenham; the last had no market, so perhaps the church was intended.

Twelve other cases have been noted in which contrition was to be shown in both market or similar place and church. A few examples will suffice. A Great Burstead man who in 1566 condoned (*conciliavit*) his wife's

[1] *Trans. E.A.S.*, xxiv, 14.

alleged adultery had to suffer in his church and in Brentwood market, 'his fault written upon his back in text letters' (large or capital letters). In 1590 a Bradwell-juxta-Mare unmarried mother was directed 'on Saturday next to come into Maldon town where she shall be placed openly upon some scaffold about 11 o'clock and there stand until 1 o'clock in a white sheet and a white wand in her hand', followed by the usual penance in church on the next day. An adulterous pair of High Ongar were to confess in church and to stand for two hours in Brentwood market (Chipping Ongar, despite its prefix, meaning market, was not accorded one by Norden). The longest double sentence that has been noticed was registered against William Cock of Dedham in 1581:

> Upon Saturday next he shall in a white sheet about him, bareheaded and barefooted, about 11 o'clock in the forenoon, walk the length of the market place, holding a white rod in his hand and a paper on his head describing the cause, and then stand so apparelled at the Moot Hall door (Colchester) by the space of an hour, viz. till 12 of the clock, and then confess openly his fault of fornication with Alice Chase, and shall likewise apparelled stand in the middle alley of Dedham church the Sunday following by the time of all the morning prayer, and after that shall meekly kneeling on his knees confess his said fault of fornication, desiring God to forgive him.

Using his discretionary authority, the judge occasionally added a pecuniary fine to the bodily penance, or he might mitigate the severity of the oral confession in conjunction with a money payment. It seems fairly certain that in these cases he took into consideration the nature of the offence as well as the status and reputation of the offender. He was not permitted, however, to impose a fine by way of income for the court, and the money had to be used for pious or charitable purposes. The few examples of this method of punishment by the purse are narrated.

In 1566 Robert Stanton of West Ham[1] confessed to getting another man's servant pregnant. He was ordered to receive the Eucharist in a white sheet, doing penance, to give to 'the poor scholars in free alms what the judge should see fit', and to pay for the wench's maintenance (*alimonie*), presumably until after her delivery. She had to show her remorse in East Ham church and at Romford market on the following Monday. As there was no Elizabethan grammar school at West Ham, 'poor scholars' probably has the same meaning as in the punishment accorded to Nicholas Stephens of Maldon in 1572, who in addition to penance in church had to give 40s. to the poor of the town and 20s. to the poor scholars of either Oxford or Cambridge university. John Buck of Manuden, who had fathered his late servant's bastard, also had to pay 10s. 6d. to the wardens for the parish poor and 10s. 'to pious uses within the parish of Great Dunmow', presumably the girl's abode.

On four occasions it has been found that a copy of Foxe's *Book of*

[1] Cf. Robert Staunton of New Barns in West Ham, gentleman, whose house was broken into in 1567 (*E.L.: Disorder*, 129). He may have been the brother of Richard, also of West Ham, who made him the overseer of his will in 1565 and asked to be buried in the parish church (E.R.O., D/AER 9, f. 140 v).

Martyrs (the popular name for his *Actes and Monuments*) was bought by sexual offenders as part penance. George Thorogood of Hornchurch was ordered (see p. 39) at his own expense to buy a bible of the largest volume and Mr. Foxe's last book of monuments, the which book must be fastened with locks and chains upon desks within the church of Hornchurch at the directions of the vicar'. Three years afterwards Thomas Scott of Fairstead was punished for bastardy by standing in Chelmsford market bareheaded and in his church and by buying 'a Book of the Acts to be chained in the church'. A Cold Norton man who had been charged with immorality with his servant in 1583 had 'failed in his purgation, shall show that he is heartily sorry and promise to live more circumspectly hereafter, and shall give to the parishioners a Book of Martyrs and shall pay to the use of the poor scholars 20s.'. In the case against Thomas Stevens of Brentwood in 1592 the scribe entered, 'He shall according to his own offer give unto the church of South Weald with the chapel of Brentwood the Book of Martyrs to the public use of the whole parish, and further he do penance before Mr. Colepotes' (vicar). The last instance, linking martyr and martyrologist, was noticed in the section on Church Books.

A married couple presented for harbouring a pregnant girl were ordered to walk from the choir door 'to the place where the poor's box standeth, into which they shall put 2s.'.

Cases in which the delinquent was spared the ignominy of confessing before the whole congregation are relatively infrequent. Some illustrations of such semi-private penance will be afforded.

John Humfrey of Walden was commanded after evening prayer to confess before the (town) treasurer, the vicar, wardens, questmen, and 'four such others as the vicar shall think meet' (1579). William Sadler *alias* Sargiant of the same town had 'begotten with child his late servant' and had confessed (1586). 'He shall procure', the judge decreed, 'a Communion and receive the Communion in church before Mr. Dove the vicar, Mr. Treasurer, the churchwardens and half a dozen of some of the best of the parish communicants in his accustomable apparel, confessing his fault how that he ungodly behaved himself in committing such an evil act, promising amendment of life and not to do the like again. Also he shall pay towards the building up of the steeple of the parish church 20s' ('steeple' usually meant the tower at this period; the fine spire was in fact not added until 1831.) Robert Graves of Coggeshall 'submitted himself to correction' on an unspecified charge in the wardens' presentment (1577). The judge ordered him to confess next Sunday before the vicar and twenty-four 'principal parishioners'. The original reads 'xxiiij', and this otherwise exceptional figure must refer to the 'Four and Twenty', or select vestry, similar to the Braintree 'Four and Twenty', the now well-known oligarchy which ruled the town.[1]

[1] Emmison, *Early Essex Town Meetings* (1970).

Robert Woodhouse and Helen his wife of All Saints, Maldon, had anticipated matrimony (1592). The man submitted to correction, so 'at such convenient time as Mr. Palmer, the Official, shall think fit', they were to acknowledge their sin in church before him, the wardens, and Mr. John Morryse, Mr. Richard Bradway, Mr. Lowth, Christopher Lyving, Thomas Preston and Jonas Browning. A woman was directed (1576) 'to penitently confess and promise amendment before the vicar and twelve of the honest of the parish of Billericay in Billericay church after sermon', presumably after the congregation had left. (It is surprising that, for once, the church official forgot that Billericay was not a parish but a chapelry in the parish of Great Burstead.) Richard Macham of Leyton was before the court (1576) because he was 'a drunkard, a swearer and a slanderer; sometimes he is overseen with drink and by provocation he doth use unlawful oaths'. Having 'promised amendment', the judge decreed penance before 'the vicar or his curate, the churchwardens and six others of the chief of the parish' after morning prayer. The sentence on a Colchester slanderess ran (1577): 'Tomorrow after evening prayer she shall come into Mr. Upcher the minister his hall in St. Leonard's and there in his presence and that of five or six neighbours shall openly revoke the words by her spoken, desiring forgiveness.' A Great Chesterford man who had been presented (1580) for disorderly conduct towards his neighbours was allowed to admit his fault in front of the vicar, wardens and 'six or eight of the most substantial inhabitants'. In three further instances, all of bridal pregnancy, the couples' 'sorrow' had to be expressed only before the minister, wardens and questmen or sidesmen.

William Gyon of Coggeshall had not managed to produce the full number of compurgators (1581), but after an interval he appeared again in court stating that 'he had made competent penance to the satisfaction of the congregation in the presence of Roger Mercaunte, one of the churchwardens' (probably the Roger Markant, another clothier of Coggeshall, whose will was proved in 1602), and another parishioner, and he was discharged.

In these ways the social stigma of public, physical penance was to some extent alleviated, but it was applied only in a small minority of charges. Different kinds of penance were enjoined on the laity presented for other misdemeanours, and these tended to be appropriate to the offence.

Presented in 1561 as a common drunkard and pronounced excommunicate for not appearing in court, Barnard Bushe of Braintree later 'humbly submitted', and was absolved from excommunication, when the following decree was made: 'Upon Sunday next he shall stand at the chancel door, having before him all the time of service a table with a tankard or pitcher standing upon it with the bottom upward, and so desire the people to pray for him.' Five years later, two Maldon men were in court as common drunkards. One pleaded not guilty and had to purge with six witnesses.

The other got this sentence: 'On Sunday next after the gospel is read, he do go up to the chancel and bring with him an empty cup which he shall hold in his hand openly in the sight of the parishioners and there confess his fault and that he will amend the same.' Another man, reported in 1584 'for making people drunk', was ordered to 'come into church with a form and a quart pot set before him, and penitently confess'. Among the wearisome procession mostly of defaulters in sexual matters and church attendance, the judge must have been relieved to find a few whom he could punish differently. 'Being drunken in service time', Henry Collin of Moze had been directed in 1591 to purge with five parishioners, but produced none. His penance: 'To sit on his knees in the church porch with three empty pots before him till the second lesson with a white wand and then to come into the church to the minister and there to speak such words of penance after the minister as shall be delivered to him in writing.' Perhaps reluctantly suppressing a twinkle, the judge passed to the next case while Collin tried to hide his discomfort. A mixture of severity and sport was evinced by another judge when a Rayleigh man, convicted of misbehaviour in church, was obliged to distribute a barrel of beer to the poor; other apt penances, such as the 'horn hanging on her sleeves' method of punishing a woman who had ridiculed a cuckold in accordance with ancient custom, have been related in earlier chapters.

While every offender was expected to declare his grief, there are a few cases where the making of the formal sanctimonious declaration was not imposed. Gregory Pinchin of Sandon, having assaulted a parishioner in the churchyard, was merely ordered to 'say you are sorry', while in the usual penitential garb: more reasonable than the histrionic plea that one woman was ordered to make, in 'desiring God to forgive her and all the world'.

There remained a final alternative sanction – commutation of physical penance by a money payment only. Such compounding was extremely rare in the Elizabethan archidiaconal courts for two reasons: complete commutation was to be permitted solely by the bishop, and the sum involved, together with the preliminary cost of application for episcopal consent, militated against action by the ordinary suitor. Episcopal visitation articles almost invariably demanded to know whether chancellors, commissaries or archdeacons had discharged penance for money without the bishop's consent. Nevertheless, without such consent, three instances have been found. The first illustrates an occasion on which the court showed sympathy and common sense. In 1569 Roger Durant of Leyton had been commanded to do his penance in the usual garb both in Romford market and in church. But on the culprit's appeal, backed by the entreaty of some of his friends and neighbours, 'because he said he would kill himself', the judge directed him instead to pay 10s. each to three poor scholars of Cambridge and to contribute 10s. towards the repairs of his parish church. In 1570 George Slowman of Kelvedon, who stood excommunicate for not certifying his performance of penance, appeared and at his 'instant petition' the court commuted it into an immediate payment of 20s. to the scholars of Oxford and Cambridge and a further 20s. at the following Lammas Day. It is interesting to note that the judge was William Harrison, acting as surrogate for the archdeacon at his court held in Kelvedon church. The third case involved an irregular agreement with the churchwardens and availed nothing. Thomas Pollmer of East Ham in 1591 had unlawfully 'consented that Elizabeth Cox should not perform such order of penance as was enjoined her for her offence of incontinency committed with one William Jenckes'. Pollmer admitted that 'he was in some sort consenting and he paid 10s. unto the poor of Walthamstow for the redemption of the said punishment, and that she went away from his house without his leave and unknown to him and that he cannot learn where she is now became'. The court decreed penance on himself next Sunday, and warned him 'to use his best endeavour' to find and produce her to perform the order.

The West Ham wardens certainly had no hesitation four years later in bringing Richard Thornton to court for an unseemly incident in their church, when he 'did publicly encourage an adulteress, who was then doing penance, to go forward and to return again to her former folly the morrow after, as fresh as ever she did; who, being reproved by one of the sidemen for giving such lewd counsel and encouragement to sin, hath very uncharitably abused the said sideman with reproachful speeches'. Having been excommunicated, he later submitted to correction. One reprobate, at any rate, had even got some sympathy during her performance. But, despite the humiliating spectacle, did physical penance act as a deterrent? Probably not, to the thick-skinned used to seeing the farce; possibly, to some others.

Canon law forbade the Church courts to exact public penance from the clergy. Nevertheless the Essex records reveal several examples of such sentences, which were referred to under the Clergy; these were for fornication and drunkenness. A solitary instance of clerical penance being imposed after default in purgation is found in the case of Richard Archer, vicar of Little Wakering, who had been presented for 'divers disorders'. Not answering the charge, he had been suspended, but was restored on appearance and submission; failing to purge, the judge directed him 'to acknowledge his fault after receiving the Eucharist before the parishioners'.

Purgation

The mode of procedure under the canon law, known as purgation, or, more strictly, compurgation (Latin *compurgare*, to purify completely), is as strange and antiquated to the present-day reader as penance. If the defendant or suspect confessed, penance was enjoined, as we have related. But if he denied the charge, the judge directed purgation to be performed on an appointed day, first by his oath on the Gospels and then by the oaths of a prescribed number of his neighbours. In the more serious cases the court might demand as many as eight. They must be 'honest' (i.e. worthy), or of 'good fame and sober conversation' (i.e. life). In his own oath, the accused protested his innocence; that of his compurgators declared that they believed his swearing was true. If their joint action was fully satisfactory, the judge decreed that he was not guilty, the case was dismissed, and he was given a testimonial which restored him to 'good fame'. Should he fail to appear, or should the full number of compurgators not attend and verify, he was convicted and penance was ordered.

Having regard to the very large number of people who were presented for moral offences, only some of whom confessed, and the fact that the average number of compurgators demanded by the courts was five or six, it will be seen that a significant percentage of the population was thus involved directly or indirectly at some time in their lives.

Suspected immorality led to either the man or the woman or both being reported. In a fairly typical case, the male defendant brought as the witnesses to his oath three men of Thaxted and the female produced three women of Toppesfield and Stambourne. Their reputation was thus restored; but the judge ordered, 'They hereafter at no time keep company together but openly and in such places where no suspicion shall arise'. Sometimes 'such places' were specified as church and market.

The names of the compurgators were always given, hastily scribbled down by the registrar. Their status, like that of the accused party or parties, was generally humble, but in a few instances more substantial names are found. In an exceptional case, heard in the London house of the Archdeacon of Essex in the parish of St. Botolph, Billingsgate, in 1575, Thomas Ball of Maldon, gentleman, accused of incontinence with Eleanor Frauncis, brought William Twittie and Anthony Grenwaie, esquires, and David Simpson and Thomas Parker, gentlemen, who 'affirmed in their consciences that he was innocent', on which a testimonial was granted.

The number of those who were to give sworn testimony, expressed as usual in Latin, was '*quarta* (*quinta*, etc.) *manu*', or, more rarely in English, 'by fourth (fifth, etc.) hand'. '*Quarta manu*' denoted the accused and three supporters; '*quinta manu*', four neighbours (plate 15). A phrase very rarely used is, '*ad purgandum se quinta manu et se sexta*'. The figure normally ranges between three and eight, but there are exceptional numbers. In 1584 Thomas Baker of Kelvedon, presented as 'a common slanderer of his honest neighbours', brought as his compurgators Robert Besowthe and John Besowthe of Great Tey, Richard Barrett of Pontisbright, John Jollye of Fordham and John Warren of Wakes Colne, and (Robert) Monke, rector of Wakes Colne and minister of Pontisbright, John Willton, rector of Aldham, and Walter Richardson, vicar of Kelvedon; also, as 'supplementary' oath-takers, John Searles of Aldham, Thomas Berye, John Berye and John Baker of Fordham, Robert Kinge of Great Tey and Thomas Colfilde of Wakes Colne. The case was discharged and his good fame regained; immediately after which he was charged as an idolater, as already told.

Where both parties were accused of fornication or adultery and pleaded innocence, the judge might specify unequal numbers of parishioners bound to testify. As an example, in a double charge in 1567, the court assigned the woman to produce six and the man only four; but other instances are not numerous enough to justify our indicting the Church for discrimination between the sexes on this account.

A troublesome schoolmaster of Billericay, Marmaduke Middleton, who was at variance with Lord Rich in 1576 and was finally outlawed,[1] had been presented to the archdeacon's court a few months earlier. 'There goeth a rumour that he is not married to Alice that he calleth his wife, and that he is a great disturber of his neighbours.' Disputing the charge, he was assigned to find four to purge for him. One of them, John Norris, refused to swear on his behalf, purgation failed and penance was ordered, but the judge changed his mind and *ex gratia* gave him another chance to purge. This time he brought his four men, whom the judge refused to accept because the churchwardens had since reported him for suspected incontinence with Margery wife of James Parker. That Middleton also denied, so the court was again obliged to direct purgation – by six honest neighbours. Mistress Parker was also cited, but did not appear. Not surprisingly, Middleton having produced nobody to swear for him this time was once more consigned to the penitential white robe in Great Burstead church. Due to produce his certificate of performance at the next session, Thomas Middleton, perhaps his son, attended and explained that an inhibition had been issued transferring the case to the Court of Arches, whereon the judge, doubtless relieved, decreed that his own court's jurisdiction was superseded.

As an illustration of a minor and straightforward presentment, John Almond of Ardleigh pleaded not guilty to 'living suspiciously with Helen Sawye his maidservant' in 1590. Assigned to 'purge fourth hand of his neighbours', he produced three and the 'intimation' published by Mr. (Geoffrey) Alderton the vicar, and he was vindicated; but the court commanded him 'not to be in company with her except in market, church and other public places'.

Provided that the full contingent supported the accused party, it mattered little how strong the suspicion amounted to. Two sisters, both 'maids', were 'taken abed with one Quinton as the fame goeth'; the one

[1] *E.L.: Disorder*, 145.

cited produced six persons to testify to her innocence; and a 'bawd and harlot' of Brentwood brought four 'honest' neighbours who 'swore upon the Evangelists'. The pantomime of purging allowed even the prostitute to perjure herself and thus to exploit the law to the full. In such cases the Church courts were powerless in trying to get at the truth. In fact, a substantial minority, perhaps even one-half, of those cited for immorality proceeded to purgation.

There are, however, many examples of an objection being put forward after the defendant had protested his innocence. To ensure publicity, the court sent an 'intimation' to the minister of his parish, which was read out, inviting any convinced of the accused's guilt or of the dishonest character of his supporters to attend and make formal protest. In 1598, for example, Martin Lindsell of Terling was charged, failed to appear at first, was excommunicated, attended later, and was ordered to purge *sexta manu*; but Jane Skingle objected, alleging that one of the compurgators was his tenant and the rest were 'of small credit as she thinketh'; and as for Lindsell she said that he 'hath begotten her with child'. But he was given a discharge certificate. The absurdity of the procedure is seen in a similar case against a man who produced as required three to swear for him, at which Mary Graunte a harlot (*meretrix*) objected, affirming that he was the father of her bastard child. Yet again the judge ruled that he had sufficiently purged himself and granted the usual exculpatory testimonial. That inveterate criminal, Edmund Chevelie *alias* Lacie of Stock, whom we met in our first volume charged with unlawful disseisin, theft, and twice with poaching,[1] was before the archdeacon's court in 1579 for an offence, the nature of which has not been traced. He had to clear himself with six men of Stock and Buttsbury. He produced four from Stock and two from Bowers Gifford (perhaps a scribal error) and doubtless left the court grinning, to the disgust of the judge, who probably knew something of his reputation.

Likewise in 1585 Edward Nevell of Little Laver successfully introduced Richard Hamon of Moreton, John Palmer of Fyfield, Thomas Beard of Beauchamp Roothing and John Hoskins of Writtle, although Thomas Lynsey of Matching came and alleged that the offender 'was notorious and manifest or violently presumptive'. As a final instance of a layman's objection, a Boreham woman had to find six of her own sex, three of Boreham and three of Brentwood (doubless the male party's abode). She even managed to bring along four from each place. A Brentwood man protested. The result was no different from that in many other cases in which the scribe wrote, '*Nemo obiecit*' (nobody objected); and purgation was declared satisfactory.

Resistance to purgation was offered in vain by the puritan rector of Leigh, William Negus, with Thomas Peke, in 1587, because one of

[1] *E.L.: Disorder*, 128, 240, 246, 289.

Augustine Draper's compurgators, William Manfeld, had been accused of adultery. (Draper himself at the next session was in serious trouble with the judge personally for not acknowledging the immortality of the soul.) In 1579 Richard Wylkin of Lambourne, charged with bastardy, was commanded to clear himself by as many as ten witnesses. Seven turned up; John Reynolds, the curate, objected, and the defendant, who had denied the woman's accusing him with paternity, then refused to take the oath 'that he had not committed fornication with her in thought or deed'. The entry is unfinished. Nicholas Want of Fairstead in 1598 legally re-established his good character after a double objection by Henry Robinson, the rector. The accused was accompanied by Zachariah Allen, William Saunder, Thomas Smith and George Want. The rector declared that the fourth man was a 'natural son' of Nicholas and 'of evil name and fame, and is bound over for suspicion to the next Quarter Sessions' by Lord Rich; also that Allen did not dwell within 1½ miles of Fairstead church 'at the time of the assignation of the purgation'. George Want admitted the fact, but Allen claimed that he had lived in Little Leighs within the 1½ miles and now his abode was in Great Leighs. After technical argument the judge ruled in favour of the defendant.

Energetic canvassing of friends when the defendant knew that his innocence would be challenged must have been a main topic of talk in many villages. The courts were faced with some embarrassing denials of serious charges. We may take that of George Younge of Buttsbury, accused in 1590 of lechery with Margaret, wife of Thomas Gubberd of Stock. William Symons, curate of Buttsbury, opposed the man's purgation by six parishioners of Buttsbury, Mountnessing and Stock, as ordered. But Younge produced eleven men from these places. On the curate's side was the wife, who confessed to four acts of lewdness in the fields belonging to Sir John Petre; 'first, when Younge coming hither about the fall of calf, being the tithe gatherer of Buttsbury parish, did give to her 4d. to be naught with her'. After being told much by Gubberd, the curate apparently made up his mind to object to purgation, for the cuckolded husband had declared that 'Younge were better to give a hundred pounds than that Sir John Petre should know of his abuses', though he 'wished Younge would give him (Gubberd) 10s. for satisfaction, and all matters should be put up'. The judge carefully considered the matter, but seemingly found that he had no alternative but to 'pronounce that Younge had lawfully purged himself'.

A determined challenge was put forward to no purpose in a case that came from Walden in 1599. Philip Lewes had been gravely suspected of 'incontinent living' with George Richard's wife, and had to find four credible neighbours. She had to produce the same number of women. But her husband, 'not called, voluntarily said, "I will wipe the noses of you all and I did know what belonged to the matter so well as the best of you all, and Mr. Archdeacon was very importunate with me and my wife to agree"'. Clearly, he was not going to be dubbed a cuckold. For her compurgatrices Margaret Richard brought along Agnes Stallery, Elizabeth Gall and Elizabeth Boale, all of Walden, who begged to be admitted. But Elizabeth, wife of George Bower, also of Walden, objected, stating that one of the three women had been 'accused to have stolen corn from Mr. Ward of Walden, and that all three were *pauperes et corruptibiles* and such as do live of the common contribution and benevolence of the town'. And Agnes Stallery changed her mind and refused to take the oath. Yet, 'on Margaret Richard's petition, the judge of his grace assigned her to purge afresh with four neighbours, Bowers dissenting'; and the husband was forgiven for his interruption.

Purgation, however, was not always successful. In about a quarter of the cases it failed because the defendant could not find any neighbours willing to help, or an insufficient number came. Even if one was lacking, it went by default: one woman's purgation failed because one of the nine compurgatrices did not appear. In 1576 a male servant of Mr. Birchley of East Hanningfield had to find seven men to testify. They duly attended, but 'each and every of the compurgators refused to take the oath', so the man had to do his penance. In 1562 a woman was charged with misbehaviour with men, one of whom was also cited. He contested the matter, had to purge with seven pledges, but she 'at her petition was assigned to purge by eight honest women of High Easter and Great Bardfield concerning her honesty with all the men except Stokes', the other defendant. At the next session, whether because she objected to Stokes's purgation or not, all seven men – of Great Bardfield, Finchingfield, Bardfield Saling and Easter – refused to swear, and he was pronounced contumacious, whereon 'he appealed to the Bishop of London or his Vicar General'. It is a good illustration of the strong resistance put up in a small minority of cases.

A solitary example is found in 1579 of the judge ordering a layman, who had not produced any of the three requisite neighbours, to declare instead 'his being heartily sorry for giving offence of suspicion of incontinence'. The rector of Langford and the vicar of High Easter, having been commanded to purge, secured discharge without doing so (pp. 218, 220). A fourth isolated remission is seen in the case against John Allen junior of Ardleigh in 1599. Ordered to produce five men to swear with him, he alleged that 'he was first convented for the matter before Mr. Commissary; there was, neither is, any public fame of his incontinent living with Mr. Whetle's wife; since his first convention he never was in her company; and Mr. Commissary upon the hearing of the matter and his good name being proved by two honest witnesses, did discharge him of the said fame'. So the Colchester court also dismissed him.

Compurgation in the archdeacons' courts by suspect clerics is rarely seen.[1] A case in 1585 has therefore several interesting features. Harrison was no longer presiding at the courts held at Saffron Walden, and on this occasion it was held before Dr. William Bingham, the Official. John Luddington, the contentious vicar of Great Sampford with Hempstead, was accused of holding Romish views (in the often quoted report of 1584 he appeared as a non-preacher). The court enjoined him to purge with two clerks and two laymen that 'he is no defender of transubstantiation in the sacrament of the Lord's Supper'. But he produced Harrison, Richard Chaddesley (vicar of Hatfield Broad Oak), George Darlo (vicar of Ugley), and John Wilkinson (vicar of Stansted Mountfitchet), and he was duly purged and granted 'letters testimonial' to that effect. Harrison was no equivocator, and knew better than any what the oath implied, so that it may perhaps be assumed that he was acting with neighbourly tolerance. When 'Mr. (Edward) Bordman, rector of Fyfield', in addition to being prosecuted in 1576 for administering communion while being excommunicated, was presented as 'a common drunkard and disquieter of his neighbours', the judge assigned him to purge himself with six parishioners – three clerics and three laymen.

An abnormal case involved John Goldringe, rector of Langdon Hills, because of alleged perjury as well as public fame of adultery in 1589. The woman, also charged, was Isabel, wife of Robert Ashebie of the same parish. On their first appearance both denied any guilt. The rector was told to find 'four preachers or benefice holders in the deaneries of Barstable and Chafford'. At the next session held in Brentwood chapel on Friday, 6 July, he produced Robert Huettson of Pitsea, Stephen Ludington of Little Burstead, rectors, and John Powell, curate of Great Warley, preachers of the Word of God, also William Wassher of Upminster and Robert Boothe of Ramsden Bellhouse, rectors, and William Mapeltofte, curate of Langdon Hills, who were prepared to take their oaths that 'he is innocent from committing of adultery'. The usual call for any objection having been made, the husband stood up. The court then received from the wife a full confession of having lived incontinently with the rector, on which she was ordered public penance in his church. Amid some consternation, the judge adjourned the case to the next session to be held on the following day in Romford chapel: a criterion of the gravity of the affair, as adjourned cases, unless circumstances were exceptional, went to the next session for the same group of rural deaneries. Goldringe had already appeared, probably a few minutes earlier, to answer the accusation against him as rector of Cranham, seven miles away, for non-residence and failing to give to the poor and to provide monthly sermons; to which he answered that

[1] Clerical fornication or adultery should have involved purgation by six or twelve clerks respectively (P. Heath, *The English Parish Clergy on the Eve of the Reformation*, 1969, 115). As regards lay offenders, statistics from the York diocesan archives show that 'out of 284 cases, 154 successfully purged, 26 failed and 104 confessed' in the late sixteenth century (*ibid.*, 118).

the benefice 'was under the value' (for contribution to the poor) 'and he will be more diligent for the sermons'. Resuming the case next day, the court heard the amazing statement by Ashebie that his wife had at first denied adultery with Goldringe because Ashebie had been persuaded to enter into a bond with him 'not to trouble or molest Mr. Goldringe for any act or fact that he had committed with Isabel Ashebie and that he took them in bed together committing the abominable fact of adultery'. The wife confirmed that intercourse had taken place 'sundry times in his own house and lastly a little before Michaelmas and she asketh God forgiveness'. All the compurgators having attended again, 'every of them refused to take any oath with him, answering that they never heard neither of her confession nor of the bond until now, but they were made believe that she had denied the fact upon her oath'. The judge thereupon decreed that Goldringe had defaulted in purgation and was convicted as guilty. But because of his insufficient show of penitence he was to be punished by undergoing public penance in Langdon Hills church on *two* Sundays. Further, he was commanded to attend on the following Tuesday at Billericay chapel. To this order Goldringe 'dissented and protested'. His case was not entered in Tuesday's minutes. Isabel absented herself and was excommunicated, John Frith, rector of Hawkwell, to pronounce it; Ashebie and his wife, having also been ordered to certify their receiving the Eucharist but failing to appear, Frith was likewise told to excommunicate the husband. After the summer recess, Goldringe was due to certify his action as rector of Cranham in paying 6s. to the poor as well as preaching, but did not attend and was further excommunicated on that account, Frith being once more assigned. None of the three defendants' names occur again. There is confusion in the clergy list for Langdon Hills early in 1590 on his death, which suggests that his apparent flouting of the court's injunctions may have been due to his illness. Thus ends this unhappy episode. As a postscript, we may note that he had been presented by the hundredal jury to Quarter Sessions in 1585 as a drunkard and a quarreller.[1]

One of the few other instances in which purgation by a cleric is set out at some length is worth quoting. William Bangor, curate of Stanford Rivers, charged in 1599 with illicit intercourse, as described earlier under Clergy, was assigned to 'purge himself *quinta manu* of ministers'. He produced John Wood, vicar of Navestock, Robert Commin, rector of Doddinghurst, Thomas Nicollson, rector of Stapleford Tawney, and Lewis Hewes, rector of Kelvedon (Hatch). They formally sought to be admitted on Bangor's behalf, but James Clegg, apparitor, submitted an intimation with certificate from unnamed objectors to the compurgation. None, however, appeared, and they were duly pronounced contumacious. The defendant then took his oath on the Evangelists 'that he never had carnal knowledge of the body of Dorothy Barrett' and his supporters swore that

[1] *E.L.: Disorder*, 144; for his successor cf. Newcourt, ii, 359; *Trans. E.A.S.*, vi, 323.

they believed in their consciences that his oath was true. The judge thereon decreed that Bangor had canonically and lawfully purged himself and restored him to good fame. The fact that the proceedings were written out so fully – and the scribe just managed to squeeze the final lines in tiny scrawl at the foot of the page – shows how the court viewed the grave charge. But the county justices thought differently when the woman gave birth to a bastard, as we saw in the Clergy chapter.

As an alternative to purgation, an accused person on a few rare occasions was allowed to produce in court a written or oral testimonial on his behalf. Isaac Hewes of West Ham solemnly declared in 1591 that, 'only upon the malice and evil will of George Halliday, one of the sidemen, owed him, and knowing not how to be revenged, he caused the rest of his fellow churchwardens and sidemen unjustly to present him, they not knowing any cause of suspicion at all'. He showed 'a certificate under the hands of certain parishioners and neighbours and of Martin Brewster, one of the churchwardens', which the judge inspected and then warned Hewes not to consort with the woman in question; his good name, however, was virtually vindicated. Gabriel Evans of Grays Thurrock in the same year stated that he had 'failed to produce any compurgators, but if it please the Judge to accept his own oath for his innocency he is willing to take his oath', and three named men 'and others did signify to the Judge that he was presented wrongly upon the report of Agnes Howell' for suspected immorality. He secured his discharge. John Whitehand of Ashdon also insisted in 1596 that 'he was of good name and that there was no cause of suspicion, but only in his going to the house to demand his debt in the evening'. Ordered to exculpate himself, he brought at the next session William Faunce, curate there, and Gabriel Barker, churchwarden, who 'affirmed that in their opinions he is an honest man and not faulty in this accusation and that the report was spread upon evil will'. He was enjoined to give 5s. to the poor, but not to purge, so he, too, probably counted himself cleared.

Court fees incidental to purgation were heavy.[1] Attendances of the accused and compurgators normally involved further expense. In most cases the defendants probably bore the whole cost, and it is natural therefore that a few stated that they were too poor to pay for the others' fees, travelling expenses, and loss of time or wages. Lewis Billings of Barking, for example, pleaded in 1591 that he was 'a very poor man and not able to procure his neighbours to come to the court and bear their charges'. On another occasion William Byatt of Bradwell-juxta-Coggeshall alleged that 'he had compurgators ready, who could not come by reason of the wetness of this morning'. The woman in the case was 'a common

[1] No attempt has been made to study the question of fees, being an administrative aspect. The average total fees payable by most defendants was around £1 See E. R. C. Brinkworth, *Shakespeare and the Bawdy Court of Stratford*, 17–18, and *Ess. Rev.*, l, 214–15.

whore, who would have gotten loving powder to have made the said Byatt to have loved her'! He was ordered not to frequent her company. A Stanway man who was to be accompanied by five compurgators brought three, declaring that the others would have been his pledges but were 'hindered, dissuaded or threatened to the contrary by the worshipful Dr. Corbett, minister and preacher of Stanway, also that a sixth man, being requested, did promise but he also was threatened by Dr. Corbett'. The judge ordained that he must therefore perform public penance. John Taverner of Upminster, gentleman, had to purge 'eight hand' in 1584; but he did not appear, let alone any supporters. As a final instance, reverting to the Stokes case of 1562, the order to bring seven men was his second chance to purge, as the first order for five had resulted in his 'certifying that he had not brought his compurgators, for that it was so far off'.

The procedure which has been illustrated will have focused one of the main weaknesses of the spiritual courts – a weakness which brought them into disrepute with some of the laity. The two chief criticisms, only too patent, were the inherent risk of fraud by the defendant and his compurgators, sometimes amounting to perjury (see p. 58), and the high fees that had to be paid whether he was guiltless or not, though a few instances of the court waiving the fee for a pauper are found. Compurgation, by then a decrepit clown, was buried in 1660 (Act of 13 Charles II, c. 12).

Excommunication

Excommunication is chiefly remembered by Englishmen because of its sinister association with Tudor sovereigns, especially after the edict of Pope Pius V against Queen Elizabeth in 1570, and is also believed to have been rarely exercised by the Anglican Church. This is very far from being the case. Excommunication was in fact a not uncommon incident of Elizabethan life. In Essex alone, the act books for the two archdeaconries, covering about two-thirds of the county, show that at least 4,000 persons were interdicted in the period.

There were two degrees of excommunication – 'major' or 'minor'. The lesser, in the main, deprived the party from the use of the sacraments of communion and marriage, and attending divine service. It was generally issued against the contumacious, that is, those who refused to appear after several citations, though the sentence was sometimes given after a single default. The greater excommunication was awarded for proved assaults in church or churchyard, for getting married in a private house, and certain other irreligious acts which were more heinous in the eyes of the Church than in laymen's eyes. Those convicted were placed under severe legal and social disabilities. They were prohibited from conducting suits in the secular courts, from being buried in consecrated ground, and in theory they were excluded from all contact with the 'faithful'.

A considerable number of those awarded ordinary excommunication submitted fairly quickly and were then at once absolved from the sentence. An early illustration is seen in the Commissary's act book under 1561, when a drunkard sought absolution, which was given, together with the 'tankard' penance, as related earlier. Next year a case introduced the 'green woman', who likewise received immediate forgiveness.

It must be emphasized that a large proportion of the excommunication sentences were automatically given to all who did not appear at the half-yearly archidiaconal visitations or synods, when the clergy, church-wardens and sidesmen had to attend, the parish officers having to be sworn in to make their presentments; long lists of defaulters were written up on each occasion. Most were merely lazy, or were sick, but a few were the more obstinate dissenting clergy. Of other minor offenders, many executors and administrators failed to appear to prove wills, to produce inventories or accounts, or to pay legacies promptly, and were duly excommunicated to enforce attendance. But aggravated contumacy leading to excommunication resulted mainly from consistent refusal to attend church or to receive communion, and, ironically enough, it fell on both Catholic recusants and Puritan dissenters as well as on the irreligious malcontents.

Periodically, the court registrar felt the need to compile lists of the excommunicates. At least one officer of the Colchester archdeaconry regularly made out a fresh list after each session, including names from previous courts where absolution had not been granted. That for June 1594, for example, has 86 persons, including some wives, headed as usual, 'These stand excommunicate'. After several repeats, most of the hardy absentees' names are quietly left out: the spiritual sanctions of the court had been ignored with impunity. A more formal procedure was taken, at any rate, in the Essex archdeaconry, by the writing of a separate 'Excommunication Book'. It is the only surviving Elizabethan register of this sort, covers the period 1590 to 1602, contains nearly two hundred pages, and lists about a thousand names. Each list is preceded by a copy of the form of decree, with the date and place of the session. Most are signed, as proclaimed by William Tabor, the Archdeacon, or Robert Palmer, the Official, or by a minister, acting as surrogate. The latter was usually but not always the rector, vicar or even curate of the church in which the court was held, e.g. Anthony Brasier and his successor Nicholas Cliffe as rectors of Ingatestone, but at a session in Great Baddow church the memorandum was signed by Gilbert Annand, vicar of Boreham. A few lists contain up to eighty names, while others have only a few. The great majority were excommunicated merely for non-appearance; others for not seeing further process, i.e. not attending the session following first citation, or not certifying through the minister their having performed penance. A few of the later catalogues seem to be restricted mainly to recusants; one names only churchwardens who had failed to attend the synod. In all cases the excommunicates' parish is given. 'Absolved' is entered against a very small number of names, so that the register gives the present-day impression of its being a somewhat futile record. The evidence of this book and the Essex act books generally leads the writer to disagree with the view put forward half a century ago that 'he was a foolish layman who did not seek to extricate himself with all the speed possible'.[1] The conclusion drawn from the Essex archives certainly agrees with that of a more recent writer whose material was drawn from the Elizabethan act books of the consistory court of Gloucester.[2]

There was thus always a substantial hard core of obdurate offenders who remained under the decree of excommunication for long periods or nominally for life. Tracing the final outcome of many cases involving the sentence is very laborious and scarcely worth the effort of discovering the very few who sought restoration after several years' silent disobedience.

Its widespread use by the Church courts, unlike the secular courts, arose from their inability to impose imprisonment, a heavy fine or other severe punishment for grave offences, where the offender took no notice. Statistics from the Archdeacon of Taunton's act book for the single year 1623–4 show that, out of 488 persons cited for all offences, no less than 145 stood excommunicate.[3] On the other hand, similar figures for Yorkshire, Cheshire and Suffolk in 1590 and 1593 produce only 14 out of a total of 537.[4] A rough estimate of those for Essex works out at about half-way between the percentages in these two analyses.

Archdeacons were almost powerless to inflict on offenders any summary sentence other than excommunication – 'the rusty sword of the Church'.[5] But not wholly so. In exceptional cases they had the means, though far from effective, of bringing hardened excommunicates to book before the Court of High Commission, when some were fined and a few were incarcerated. The matter of pursuing such victims in detail, however, is outside the scope of this work. We may note, among the rare instances, the case against one well-known recusant, George Monoux of Walthamstow, in 1579. Failing to attend the court as well as his church, he was excommunicated. At the next session, 'Humphrey Monoux gentleman, son of Mr. George Monoux', appeared and stated that his father had been

[1] W. P. M. Kennedy, *Elizabethan Episcopal Administration* (1924), ccxxvi.

[2] F. D. Price, 'The Abuses of Excommunication and the Decline of Ecclesiastical Discipline under Queen Elizabeth' (*Eng. Hist. Rev.*, lvii, 108–15); he quotes figures to illustrate the 'growth of this disrespect for citations', e.g. in 1569–70 2 out of every 3 persons ignored the summons, and for individual sessions in 1574 102 out of 111 failed to appear.

[3] Som. Rec. Soc., xliii (1928), 10, 32.

[4] R. A. Marchant, *The Church under the Law* (1969), 219.

[5] Christopher Hill, *Society and Puritanism*, 354.

'convented before the Queen's Commissioners in Ecclesiastical Causes and at present is imprisoned in le Flete, and seeks absolution for his father'. He was duly pardoned, which meant of course only that the excommunication was rescinded.

The archidiaconal courts had an alternative and roundabout means of securing secular authority for the arrest of intractable excommunicates, but the machinery was seldom used. When thus goaded into action, the circumstances were somewhat similar to those in the long drawn-out proceedings of a case started in 1594. After giving an account of this protracted attempt to obtain the defendant's submission, we shall refer briefly to the last-resort method. Already mentioned in the first chapter, here are fuller details. Anthony Cornell sued Nicholas Wright for defamation because he had spread a report how Helen Keye, Cornell's late servant, said that Cornell 'did offer to give her 40s. a year to serve him by day and 40s. a year to lie with him on nights, and that if it were her fortune to marry from him he would give her bread and beer for so many as would come'. In other words, even if she left him to get married he would provide for all the guests at her wedding. The defendant, having failed to appear at three sessions, was excommunicated. At the following one, any doubt whether Helen Keye was subject to the court's jurisdiction was cleared, as she belonged to Walden. All parties were directed again and again to attend, but Wright defaulted after his first appearance. A few witnesses who had been cited came along, but there are no details of the depositions referred to. In December, at the request of Thwaites, Cornell's proctor, the judge decreed that the case be 'concluded' at the next session. Wright now decided to appear, and the court directed him to attend again to hear the sentence. This was duly read in the presence of Edward Rambold, curate of Walden, and Christopher Pakeman and John Clerke, perhaps the churchwardens. From a number of '&cs' indicating the omission of routine procedural phrases known to the registrar but not to the present-day reader, it seems that the sentence was to be published in Walden church. At the same time the judge settled the expenses of the case, as yet not recorded. After this long series of dull entries leading nowhere, the page is suddenly enlivened at the session held in March 1595. The registrar or his scribe scrawled in the margin:

> Pointing to Mr. Thwaites, 'Let him know what is set down, for I think you know', beckoning to the Judge not . . . words from Wright to the Judge. 'If I speak anything against myself, let those take hold of it that have cause.' Wright after the former words used these also in the church.

Clearly, the obstreperous defendant had had enough of the proctor's questioning and spoke his mind, while the scribe did his best to take down his exact words. But although such marginal jottings of contemptuous words in court are far from rare in the act books, on no other occasion did the clerk resort to ' . . . ' for words he did not hear or could not scribble down fast enough in the heat of the outburst. Next session the taxed expenses were recorded – at the heavy sum of £3 10s. The judge ordered these to be paid before Trinity Sunday and imposed a unique form of penance on Wright: 'At the next court to be holden in this place the 5th day of June coming, the said Nicholas Wright should in open court between the hours of 10 and 11 of the clock in the forenoon acknowledge and confess in humble and penitent manner that, whereas he hath slandered the said Anthony Cornell' (then changing temporarily into Latin), '*repetend: verba libellata et per testes probat:*' (meaning that the defamatory words were to be repeated), 'he is heartily sorry for the same and ask him forgiveness, and promise never afterwards to slander the said Cornell so again'. But, not surprisingly, Wright resumed his truancy. His name was 'called three times' without result. Yet once again at the next court day 'penalty of contumacy was reserved in not certifying performance of the sentence' – the usual phrase but nonsensical in the context of penance to be performed in the court. Two more sessions passed without any further progress – and the fees were still outstanding. At long last, in October 1595, after noting formally that Cornell had stood excommunicate for over forty days, the court took the ultimate step, authorising the registrar to 'write to the Queen's Majesty seeking the help of the Bishop of London etc. for the arrest of the said Wright', which was the curious formula employed in such cases.

The name of any person who in fact remained excommunicate for forty days after the sentence had been published in his parish church could thus be certified to the bishop, who could then, if he so decided, send a certificate commonly called a *Significavit* to the Court of Chancery, which in turn issued a writ *De excommunicato capiendo*, resulting in imprisonment! But neither the bishops nor the higher secular courts (Quarter Sessions and Assizes) adopted this procedure except rarely.[1] As Dr. Anglin has observed in his thesis, 'The lack of systematic and concerted policy towards these groups by the central authority saddled the archidiaconal court with large numbers of standing excommunicates who, to all intents and purposes, remained immune from the court's jurisdiction'. A few examples illustrate the inefficacy of handing them over to Satan.

Mr. (Thomas) Crowlye and his wife, Avice wife of John Fyshborne, and Edward Raye, Elizabeth wife of Thomas Orgar, and Elizabeth wife of John Milton (most, if not all, were recusants) were presented 'as wilful offenders and they have been excommunicated for half a year and do obstinately refuse to be absolved, whereupon we do greatly suspect that they be reconciled to the Romish religion' (1584). More briefly, as in most cases, we may refer to the prosecutions of Joan Shawe of Kelvedon for 'standing long excommunicate and seeketh not to be restored' (1589), or of John Frost, accused by the Great Sampford wardens because he

[1] Hale, *Precedents*, 172, citing an Archdeaconry of Essex case of 1579.

'standeth excommunicate and keepeth (i.e. lives) at Glemsford in Suffolk – his father is a clothier and a rich man'. As an instance of a penance decree for immorality being ignored, there is the wardens' presentment in 1591 of John Williamson of Colne Engaine 'for standing excommunicate of long time for his contempt in not satisfying the congregation for his offence in committing fornication as he was enjoined'; also of the woman. 'Standing excommunicate' was in itself a presentable offence.

Resort to higher authority was, however, not restricted solely to its initiation in the archidiaconal court, as is evidenced by an unusual private slander suit brought by Mary, wife of John Dew, against Elizabeth Sputtell, both of Great Wakering, in 1567. The plaintiff declared that her defamer had been duly excommunicated for more than forty days but 'continues contumacious and contemptuously violates the sanctions of the court', and she sought redress. As a result the judge determined that 'a letter be written to the Queen for the arrest' of the slanderess 'according to the custom and style of the court', which presumably implies reference to the Court of High Commission. As already seen, the 'letter to the Queen' was merely the set phrase for seeking aid for arrest. But in one of the few similar cases, when such action was to be taken in 1570 by 'writing to the Bishop', the excommunicate 'very humbly begged absolution from the sentence' through Thwaites, his proctor, and this was accorded.

Once and once only did the jurors in their hundredal presentments to Quarter Sessions name a perverse offender: in 1600 they reported Robert Fysher of Latchingdon, 'being of evil fame, for standing excommunicate and not seeking to be absolved'; but the result is not noted.

A few excommunicates insisted on their accustomed rights by attending divine service. A Great Oakley woman 'hath in contempt of the law, being excommunicated divers times, come privily to church and hath not been seen till service hath been ended'. Overtly, at Manuden in 1598, 'a disordered and contemptuous person who standeth excommunicate obstinately cometh into the church, to the great disturbance of the congregation'. Three years later at Chipping Ongar Edmund Wyland, 'being desired to depart, refused, so that the minister was constrained to desist from saying service'; and a similar incident occurred at Farnham in 1597. There were worse tumults at Elmstead and Stanford-le-Hope, as already recounted under Church Disturbances. On a single occasion the county justices received a hundredal presentment of this offence: John Willemson (*sic*, see above) in 1591 was 'a railer, for he standeth excommunicated, for he will go through the church in the despite of the parish, in at one door and out at the other, in the services'.

It is of course easy to condemn the authorities for relentlessly wielding this ancient weapon of coercion, because by and large it only earned discredit for the Church and undermined the laity's respect for the parochial clergy: the Tudor and Stuart periods were its heyday. As the law stood, the archidiaconal courts had no alternative but to pass sentence, despite their very limited opportunities to prosecute recalcitrants in the higher courts. It was their duty to try to secure conformity in all respects, whether moral or doctrinal, and it must not be assumed that the sentences were wholly ineffective. To many laymen the penalties and disabilities which went with excommunication were not to be disregarded, and sooner or later many sought reconciliation with the Church. The two main residual categories were the staunch Catholics and Puritans and the reprobates. But although the interdict in theory debarred the offender from social contacts, especially public gatherings (and in theory any friendly contact could himself be excommunicated), there is singularly little evidence of any general exclusion. Such social disapproval as was exhibited to prostitutes, gross drunkards, supposed witches, and those who were patently irreligious would have been shown whether they were excommunicates or not. The same almost negative testimony has been found by another writer, who remarks that 'presentments for consorting with excommunicated persons were very rare'.[1] Of some interest is a unique prosecution – so inhumane and unchristian as to border on persecution – of a Beauchamp Roothing man who refused in 1591 to ostracize his excommunicated parents. The charge lay against all three – Edward Collin and his wife and son Roger. 'Their son is daily in their house and in the company of his father and mother.' Roger's answer was polite to the judge but loyal to them: 'He doth but his duty to their company, and for his own part doth his best to persuade them to be reconciled', that is, to the Church.

A few instances are found of ministers who 'refused to denounce an excommunicate', as always enjoined, such as Brian Tuke, rector of Thorrington, in 1591, despite the decree against a woman being 'tendered to him by Christopher Cooke the apparitor'.

Clerical disobedience in not withholding the privileges of the Church from excommunicates accounts for ten cases; and on one occasion the Romford wardens allowed an excommunicated man to come to church. In 1561 the unnamed curate of Ingatestone failed to exclude John Bond, 'according to letters', i.e. the court mandate. 'For his default the judge ordered him (the curate) penance, viz. to stand and confess before the parishioners and to ask them to pray for him and to give 12d. to the poor.' Perhaps Bond was the innholder who was to be forcibly dispossessed by a mob in 1584.[2] William Serredge, the nonconforming rector of East Hanningfield, received excommunicates into his church in 1589. The judge explicitly ordained that, 'if he do know of any excommunicated persons, or understand of any to be in the church after admonition given, if they will not depart he is to desist whether he be reading of service, or in his sermon, *sub pena juris*'. In 1588 Mr. (William) Byrd, vicar of Great

[1] Marchant, *op. cit.*, 221. [2] *E.L.: Disorder*, 126.

Chishall, 'suffered' a woman to come to service although she had been 'sundry times denounced in his church as excommunicate'; Morgan Richards, rector of Little Sampford, in the same year buried an excommunicated man 'with a Christian burial'; in 1593 the vicar of Bradfield (John Richards) committed the same offence with a female corpse brought from just over the Suffolk border, as also did Mr. Turner, curate of Pontisbright, with Mistress Thurgood's corpse from London. Similarly, William Adams, vicar of Earls Colne, when an excommunicated couple 'did enterprize to solemnize matrimony together', united them. In 1588 Mr. Harris, (curate) of Manningtree, married John Smith, while actually 'having the excommunication in his hands; and being demanded by Cook (the apparitor) to deliver the excommunication unto him, would not, but said he was to deliver it himself'. Worse still, in the following year Mr. Cook, curate of Witham, shortly after publishing the sentence against two people, married them without licence on Ascension Day, within one of the prohibited periods. On one occasion the Romford wardens allowed an excommunicated man to come to church; and in 1589 Mr. (Thomas) Morris, (rector) of Layer Marney, was charged with not choosing a churchwarden and for suffering an excommunicate, who had been appointed to the office, to attend service.

In addition, as we have noted, there was always a sporadic sprinkling of puritan clerics who were excommunicated for violating ritual practice under the Settlement.

The author of the article on the Gloucester diocesan records emphasizes that 'the most prominent feature of this aspect of the decline of the ecclesiastical courts lies in their failure to employ the aid of the temporal power, as legally they might do', and he points out that 'with the progress of Elizabeth's reign the entries in the acts concerning issues of *significavit* become more and more rare'; due largely, he adds, to 'the ancient jealousy between the lay and the ecclesiastical jurisdictions'.[1]

Contempt of Court

In Elizabethan times the speech of the ordinary people was vigorously direct, as the many defamation cases reveal: in marked contrast to the circumlocution of the royal court circles. Essex folk have never been reticent in forcibly expressing their opinions of those in authority, and the archidiaconal records disclose how some defendants openly despised the Church courts. We learn this partly from formal charges of contempt of court and partly from the rude remarks bawled out by those who lost their tempers during interrogation or on conviction. Most of these illuminating comments and outbursts came from the Archdeaconry of Colchester,

[1] Price, *op. cit.*, 112–13.

whose officers were more inclined faithfully to chronicle such affronts than those of the other archdeaconry. They knew of course that nobody could pry into their books; they were not to guess that their archives would be examined centuries afterwards for their sociological interest. While the registrars may have thought that their marginal jottings would prove useful evidence against the declaimers if they reappeared on other charges, may we not also discern a sense of humour in their scribbling down the tumultuous taunts thrown at the judge and his myrmidons?

On being excommunicated in 1589 Robert Garrett of Wivenhoe was severely reproved for contempt in saying scornfully, 'Have me commended to my cousin Taylor and tell him that I will be no churchwarden'. (Thomas Taylor, bachelor of law, was the Archdeacon's Official and had held the session in the previous March.) Also in 1589 the same contumacious John Williamson of Colne Engaine, who had also been excommunicated for 'railing and brawling in the churchyard with the churchwardens and other honest men', apparently on hearing that he would be committed to prison, explained that 'the judge might as well cut his throat'. The same Colchester court officers were subjected to obscenities later in that year, when Joshua Newton of Aldham spoke his mind: 'It is a bad court. I care not a button for it. If I had not married yon f . . . g (*sic*!) woman who lived an arrant whore openly'; exclaiming, 'The judge did follow the cause against me with rough speech'; and to enforce his comment 'he clapped his hand divers times disorderly upon the book'. After entering an incontinence case in 1590, the scribe added, 'He behaved himself contemptuously in court with facing and brasing, and the judge willing him to depart he went away contemptuously'. ('Brasing', an apparently unrecorded verb, is obviously akin to 'brazen-faced'.) Anger, rather than derision, led to charges of contempt for abusive comments about the fees imposed by the officers. It was a frequent incident, and of course was by no means confined to the Essex courts. In 1579, for example, this was the reaction of Robert Pilgrim of Bradfield when cited for playing at cards in evening prayer time: 'In the presence of divers of his neighbours, he uttered these or the like speeches, "(Edward) Card our vicar by Cock's soul is an arrant knave thus to bring us to the spiritual (*sic*) to spend our money, who do nothing for him but laugh us to scorn. I care not for them all. I will lay our purses together and not stay in this court but remove it (i.e. the case) to London. Let us escape him."' Time after time, complaints about fees expressed the bitter grievance of those summoned to attend, often for the most trifling causes. John Heyward, a Ramsey warden, on being cited in 1588, declared, 'It was but a polling penny': a verb referring to extortion mentioned in the previous volume, in which we noticed a mounting tide of indignation against the Church court fees.[1]

[1] *E.L.: Disorder*, 91–2. Cf. Marchant, *op. cit.*, 15–31, 134–5, 190–5.

The identical term was used two years later by a woman. In the same year John Warren of Feering said in court, 'You keep your apparitors to go pricking up and down the country that they should cite for your own gains'; and in 1584 Robert Posford of East Mersea exclaimed, 'To be presented to this court is but a money matter'.

John Lea senior of Great Tey seven years later was even more determined. His statement ran, 'Mr. Chibborne (an Essex J.P.) did say that, if the judge would enjoin him to bring in his son, then he did more than he could do, and if he would not absolve him without money he should go away without his absolution and go to church notwithstanding; and afterwards said that he would stand excommunicate still, yet do what you can, and so departed not requiring the benefit of his absolution'. After a man had attended in 1593 to answer the Moze wardens for having 'railed' on them, the act book has: '*Nota*. He said that this court ought to be a Court of Conscience but it is a Court of Extortion.' A sarcastic bellringer's remark in 1598 is quoted under that subject. The pithy interruption of a cuckold, 'I will wipe the noses of you all', was just one incident in contested purgation proceedings in 1599 already related.

When the Burnham wardens in 1598 accused John Tilbrook of adultery with Joan, wife of Peter Castleford, they wrote: 'Having favour from your worship because of hope of amendment, he doth still continue his bad course of living; and being reproved by me Thomas Philpot he made answer, "It is but a money matter, I care not for the best nor the worst of them all. I will keep her company. What harm do you see by me?"' The wardens added, 'Tilbrook and his wife live unquietly because of this matter'. The man challenged their presentment, so he was given the chance of finding four neighbours to purge with him.

In 1600 Simon Dawson, one of the churchwardens of Mistley-with-Manningtree, 'said contemptuously, "What would you have me? Creep and crouch unto you?" And an hour after, departing, said to the judge *ironice*, "Shall I now depart in peace?"' The registrar's adverb helps us to visualize the incident.

Next year John Page, warden of Alresford, we read, 'spoke in anger to the judge, "I care not a pin for none of you all, and in faith I will not be churchwarden, do what you can; and I care not a fig for none of you all, and in faith I will be as good a subject as any you all"'. The court debarred him from the ministrations of the Church, but he afterwards made 'his humble submission, confessed his guilt, was absolved, and was sworn into the office of warden'.

In 1584 the registrar noted that Thomas Crabb of St. Botolph, Colchester, had 'spoken words of contempt of the judge and abused the court'; also that William Lurkin showed 'contempt in putting on his hat and saying that the judge did him wrong'; and next year two Rivenhall men, Thomas Hamelyng and Thomas Davyes, likewise 'sat in the church in judgement before the judge with their hats on their heads'. Essex rustics have always been noted for their intransigence.

Respect for authority was lacking, too, on the part of a cleric in 1588, when Peter Wentworth said, 'Do what you can, they should answer it in another place'. A rich pluralist, he was rector of both Great Bromley and Abberton, and vicar as well as lay rector of Gestingthorpe, also chaplain to Lord Darcy. His remark is written in the margin, but the offence that brought him before the judge is not given. At the previous session he had been directed to produce his ordination letters, which he did, showing Bishop Grindal's authority. Exactly a quarter of a century earlier, a very similar gibe came from the mouth of 'Mr. Walenger who has the rectory of Springfield'; when questioned by the judge who was his curate, he said that 'Mr. Cokerell is his curate whom the judge inhibited, upon which the same Wallenger said these words, "I know what you can do in your office. Do what you can. I am as good as you and I scorn to charge you with things", and other words in contempt.' There are no subsequent proceedings against him. George Cockerell was rector of the moiety of the benefice known as Springfield Richards from 1554 to 1572, having been presented by John Prowd; his successor's patron was William Barley. It looks as though Wallenger was the intervening patron. Was he the Thomas Wallinger who acquired in the same year (1563) the house called Priors in the adjacent parish of Broomfield?[1]

Impersonal complaints included the remarks of Stephen Marshall of Great Wenden in 1587, 'There is no justice to be had in the court'; and of Thomas Whithande of Walden a few months later, 'This court is a patch court', a term which seems to mean 'fools' court'.

But there was a much commoner and vulgar appellation for archidiaconal courts: the Bawdy Court – from the preponderance of immorality business. We have remarked that the term is found all over England, but was conspicuous contempt to use it. John Ponde of Walden was reported in 1569 'to have said that the court was a bawdy court', which he stoutly maintained by refusing to take the oath before the judge and was ordered to return in the afternoon, when he was discharged, presumably after making some sort of apology. In 1591, as previously related in a composite charge against Richard Fuller, he 'called the courts bawdy courts and courts appointed altogether for money'. When a man was accused by the wardens of Lawford in 1596 of allowing a loose woman to depart from his house, his retort was, that 'he had nothing to do with the Bawdy Court and bawdy matters'.

Turning to the other archdeaconry, the first incidents occurred in 1564–5. In Brentwood chapel a man was ordered public penance in Brentwood market 'for his blasphemy in swearing in the Court before a

[1] Newcourt, *op. cit.*, ii, 95, 539; Morant, *op. cit.*, ii, 77.

great multitude'; and in High Ongar church Robert Tornar of Chipping Ongar was charged with using these 'scandalous' (and rambling) words: 'He would use himself with such order of obedience as he shall where the said judge shall come will be glad to put off his cap and to be as good as he is, and threatening the judge, "If he were out of the place of justice he would talk more unseemly", and saying that he will tamper with him being bailiff in his office as the judge which is Archdeacon of Essex shall or can do with him.' Having spoken his mind, he probably apologized, as the scribe noted, 'For his contempt the court excuses him'. In 1571 an East Horndon man 'raileth against the judge, saying, "Do what the ecclesiastical judge can"'.

That obstreperous but unlicensed pedagogue, John Leche of Hornchurch, in 1584 tried to teach the court a little religious doctrine. Having been excommunicated for non-attendance, he appeared, was absolved, and launched into his defence in these words: 'He teacheth children and hath no licence but by word of mouth from Mr. Archdeacon. He is molested and called only but for money, and the Word of God doth allow no money for absolution, and the end is but for money; and the Church of God might well miss such officers and be well enough governed without them, meaning the judge and all other judges ecclesiastical and registers (registrars).' A further note runs, 'He affirmed that Mr. Archdeacon who sitting in judgement hath hardly dealt with him and hath accused him to be an anabaptist'. The Defamation chapter revealed that contempt out of court was perpetrated against the same John Walker, Archdeacon of Essex, in 1584. The defendant was alleged to have said, that 'he neither cared for Dr. Walker nor never a Walker in England'.

Contemptuous speeches, as already exemplified, were not the prerogative of laymen. William Asheton, rector of Wennington, also had no compunction in 1585, when directed to wear the surplice, about haranguing the court. 'He answered contemptuously that he would not wear it, affirming that drunkards and idle shepherds were maintained, and it was lamentable that the ministers of the Word should be called before the shepherd and his dog, for it was a shame for a judge to lie.' He was suspended from ingress to the church and administration of the sacraments 'for his contempt'. Three years later 'he affirmed that he was here the last court day, and that he that sat as judge' (Mr. Daniel, LL.D., the Official) 'the last day was more like an idol than a judge and therefore an unfit judge that can say nothing'. His letters of ordination being demanded, he declared that 'he had them not here, neither would he show them to any but to the Bishop, of whom he had them'. Evidently turning to the registrar, he came out with further invective: '"As for you", meaning Robert Lyne the Register, "you daub up adulteries and whoredoms for money".' Cited again for the next session, 'he expressly refused to take the oath, and on account of his manifest contempt the judge excommunicated him'.

He was deprived by the High Commission two years later because of his refusal to wear the surplice. A unique form of contempt was committed in 1590 by William Pinder, rector of Stock. When the Archdeacon (William Tabor) personally 'expostulated with him in Latin, Pinder would hold no converse with him in that tongue, and showed himself contumacious, contemptuous and loquacious'. The Archdeacon suspended him from all exercise of his ministry within the archdeaconry. Pinder then protested, saying that 'Mr. Archdeacon doth proceed of displeasure against him and somebody shall pay for it'. After the court had resumed in the afternoon, the rector apologized, and the Archdeacon withdrew his suspension. Pinder was one of the most cantankerous Essex clerics. Not only was he litigious, but he thought nothing of fighting a parishioner and even another cleric; but he was cuckolded.[1] His disputes with his flock have already been described; we shall meet him again as a defendant in the manor court, in the next volume.

It is perhaps to the courts' credit that few of the revilers seem to have been called to account. In fact, we should have underestimated their scorn, were it not for all these marginal scrawls. Mild penance in church was, however, awarded to Margaret Bulman of Great Wakering in 1580, for 'deriding the punishment that was assigned to her daughter, who was detected of evil life', so she was subjected to similar penance in company with her daughter; also in 1574 to 'Ely' Saunders of Woodham Ferrers, who had to confess 'for abusing the Archdeacon's court' and to pay 20d. to the parish poor.

The Elizabethan mind was thus extremely fertile in the use of forthright insolence inside the courts as well as oral obscenities outside. Let us quote a resounding remark made in Shakespeare's own church. It was spoken to the judge in 1596 and is taken, with permission, from a book on the proceedings of the Stratford Church Court recently published.[2] Cited as an absentee from the same church, the woman exclaimed, 'God's wounds, a plague a-God on you all – a fart of one's arse for you'. But which was worse – oral or anal contempt? Four years earlier Henry Cotten of Moze had been reported by the wardens for insolence to their predecessors as well as indirect contempt of court: 'Whereas he was before presented by the churchwardens for not coming to church, he coming by them very unreverently and contemptuously farted unto them and said, "Present that to the court".'

The apparitors were the courts' beadles or petty servants, whose chief duty was to deliver in person the citations, or summons, to defendants and witnesses, and generally to carry out the judges' orders. Sometimes termed summoners ('sumpnour' by Chaucer) or mandatories, they had

[1] *E.L.: Disorder*, 69–70, 144.
[2] E. R. C. Brinkworth, *Shakespeare and the Bawdy Court of Stratford* (Phillimore, 1972).

been from early times accused of extortion, and complaints by aggrieved laymen were commonplace. Their task was often an unpleasant one, and they were accordingly despised, disliked and derided, and, as with the Hearth Tax collectors of the next century, a few were assaulted. The abuse they received was probably much greater than the abuses they committed, for they were mostly humble officers obeying their superiors. If the defendant could not be found at home, it was the apparitor's task to serve the citation '*viis et modis*' (by whatever means possible), such as affixing it on the church door: we noticed in the Defamation chapter that one officer 'came into the mead to cite' a woman.

It mattered little whether the words were directed against the court or its servants until the defendant was present, when he might try to deny contempt. 'Where be the Jack-an-ape's articles?' had been demanded by Thomas Aylett of Fyfield (1584). Questioned personally by the Archdeacon, 'What he meant by those words, he answered that he meant it not to the defacing of Mr. Archdeacon's articles, but was spoken rashly, thinking no hurt in the same to Mr. Archdeacon (but he meant Witham the apparitor his articles)'. Dignity had been upheld, and Aylett was told to declare his sorrow before the minister and the wardens. A similar plea was put forward by churchwarden Thomas Goodey of Greenstead (near Ongar), who had refused to make, with Richard Marchall, his fellow, the annual presentment (1585). 'All the court is caterpillars in the market place', he was reported by Brooke the apparitor to have said; but in front of the judge Goodey claimed that Brooke was the insect in question.

The terse utterance of Robert Brewer of Paglesham was that 'he cared not for the somner nor the bawdy court' (1596). An age-old figure of speech was used by a Witham man when his sister was cited (1590): 'Shit on your process. Your court is a bawdy court. I care not for you nor your court neither.' The first word was used, with equal directness, by a Shenfield man to the summoner (1566) and by a Stanway man whose parents were served with process (1600): the apparitor was 'a knave and one that came to beshit his father and mother; and he offered to take up a cudgel out of another man's hand to beat the apparitor'. John Kendall of Earls Colne 'called Williamson the apparitor, "Varlet"', and was directed by the judge 'to show cause why he should not be punished for his rashness and contempt'.

The arrival of an apparitor was frequently treated with scorn. Goodacke Ferne, Cutlacke Ferne and William Nevell, all of Witham, were served with a citation for not receiving communion (1589). One of them 'did take the process out of the mandatory's hand and rent it in pieces'; another was charged with 'breaking the process and for violent dealing with the apparitor'; the third pulled the document from the officer's hand and tore it up.

Threatened or actual assault was a not uncommon occurrence. John

Owting and his wife of East Mersea 'called the apparitor knave, and she said he had gotten a knavish office and if she had had a pitchfork she would have thrust it in him' (1597). John Saunders of Weeley 'did call Pierpoint the officer of the court "Knave and rascal", and said that if he had not been gone he would have absolved him, meaning thereby that he would have strucken or beat him' (1587). The wife of John Pigbone of Tollesbury, presented for not receiving the Lord's Supper, would have 'beaten or hurt the apparitor with a bill when he came to cite her husband' (1588). 'Salter the mandatory' was similarly intimidated, as noticed earlier, by a Mr. Bales of Witham, a church rate defaulter (1600). When William and Anne Jermin were summoned for keeping ill rule in their house at Stanway, the alewife 'struck Pepper the mandatory with a pair of tongs', so he had to do penance in church (1590); and a suspected harlot of Manningtree 'struck the apparitor with a yard wand and had like to have broken his head, and broke the wand upon his crown defending his head' (1601).

In contrast, personal complaints of extortion by apparitors were few, but it is not easy to tell whether the apparitor was offered the bribe or took the initiative. Peter Philipps of Manningtree was charged because 'he, having no process, without cause did cite Thomas Stonarde of Kelvedon to appear in London and would have released him for 2s. 6d.' (1587). We learn from the Quarter Sessions records that he was one of the Bishop's apparitors and was at his tricks again four years later, when he extracted from a Moze man £3 17s. 4d. and a cheese worth 3s. into the bargain for his fee and a 40s. fine in the Prerogative Court of Canterbury for ploughing on St. Bartholomew's Day. The case was a bogus one, and he was sentenced to the pillory in open market.[1] John Thurland and his wife of Rayleigh, having been cited for pre-nuptial relations, the husband stated that 'he took order so far with Spittye that he paid him 6s. 8d. to discharge him and promised him 3s. 4d. more' (1597). Edward Eve of All Saints, Maldon, presented for incontinence, had to answer because 'he gave 10s. to Gilbert the apparitor to the end that he might not be called into this court' (1590); the penitential 'white sheet upon his upper garments' next Sunday was Eve's punishment. Richard Wright of Feering was alleged to have accosted 'Browne the apparitor when he came unto him to cite him' with the remark that 'he was a catchpole (petty official) and bribing knave' (1591).

[1] *E.L.: Disorder*, 92.

10

Licences

By the Royal Injunctions of 1559, repeated in the Canons of 1571, nobody was allowed to teach children, openly in a school or privately in a house, without a licence from the ordinary. Schoolmasters also had to take the oath of royal supremacy under the Act of 5 Eliz., c.1 (1563); and the Act of 23 Eliz., c.1 (1581), specifically imposed a penalty of £10 a month on any Catholic recusant employing a schoolmaster who failed to attend church and a year's imprisonment on the latter as well as deprivation from teaching. Restricted space allows only a sketchy account of the effect of these regulations.[1]

John Hobson of Terling was reported in 1590 not only as a gamester but also for refusing 'to bring his scholars to Mr. (James) Robinson his minister to be catechized'. He produced his licence, signed by a Mr. Lyon, at the next session and was discharged; but in the following year the wardens suspected him for incontinence. Six years afterwards the Billericay wardens presented Joseph Smith, 'our schoolmaster, for keeping a school, notwithstanding an approved (i.e. proved) adulterer', who stated that 'he had performed such order as Mr. Commissary did enjoin him' (presumably penance).

Two unlicensed schoolmasters at Romford, Nicholas Palsgrave and Thomas Rivers, were presented in 1569; 'Palgrave' (so spelt in his will, proved in 1574, in which he described himself as parish clerk) was also charged because 'he maketh a dunghill in the churchyard and suffereth it to be filed (defiled) with the children's ordure'. 'Mr. Presson of Stock schoolmaster had faced (defaced, damaged) the chancel in making a fire for his scholars' (1586). Also reported was George Deny of Fyfield, for 'keeping school in our church' (1599). More seriously, William Leaper of Burnham not only taught without licence but 'doth not deliver wholesome doctrine' (1586), and John Warren of Great Chishall was presented, 'being before inhibited by the court' (1595).

In 1595 'Mr. Thomas Wood schoolmaster of Coggeshall' stated that 'he had been licensed by Mr. Taylor, late Commissary', but added that he 'had put away his scholars and teacheth not'; 'Mr. Burghlye, schoolmaster of Coggeshall', likewise reported, was noted in the court book in 1590 as

[1] The fullest lists of licences granted to teachers, physicians and surgeons, and midwives, as well as to parish clerks, curates and preachers, are in *Canterbury Licences (General), 1568–1646* (ed. A. J. Willis, Phillimore, 1972).

having gone away; and Mr. Tye of Thorrington, schoolmaster, in 1598 denied having taught.

On several occasions the archdeacons' courts considered charges involving pedagogues who had acted as if ordained ministers. In 1574 John Marshall of Danbury at first 'refused utterly to make his appearance before his ordinary', but later confessed that 'he serveth the cure at Woodham Walter without letters of order' and was inhibited from teaching within the archdeaconry unless he procured a licence. John Knight, rector of Goldhanger, was censured in 1588 for 'suffering the schoolmaster, who is a mere layman, to preach at church'. On appearing, the vicar explained that, 'thinking him, Mr. Parker, to be a minister and a preacher, being as he hath sithence learned that he is not, did suffer him to preach'; and he added that Parker 'was commended to him by Mr. Drabye, the Bishop of Norwich'. Parker was in fact a schoolmaster of Peldon. A few months later he told the judge that 'whatsoever they do, he will not leave his calling without the Word of God'. On being asked if there were any proceedings in the court contrary to the Word of God he replied, 'Yea, that there is'. At the same session William Teye, rector of Peldon, was accused of 'receiving Mr. Parker to the Communion, knowing that he was then excommunicate'. In 1591 William Gilberte, vicar of Fingringhoe, was summoned for procuring and the wardens for permitting 'Mr. Benjamin Bonam, a schoolmaster and a mere lay man, to say divine service on the sabbath day'. Gilberte, who had been instituted only four months earlier, declared that the schoolmaster was 'a Master of Arts and a man of good reputation', but the wardens insisted that Bonam 'was not in fault, but Mr. Gilberte'. The case was dismissed. Three schoolmasters, William Mappletoft of Stock, Scofield of Great Bromley (both 1587), and Reignolds of Great Waltham (1598), were presented for saying service, but Scofield exhibited his licence from the Bishop of Norwich, dated four years earlier.

A more troublesome teacher was John Leech of Hornchurch, who was often before the archdeacon's court for puritan intransigence. He was accused in 1600 because 'neither he nor his scholars came orderly to his parish church', to which his reply was that he and they 'repair to Romford to hear the sermon there'. A somewhat different case had come before the Assize judges earlier in the year, when this schoolmaster was indicted for 'taking upon himself to interpret, expound and explain the sacred scriptures, though he had never been ordained or licensed by the bishop'.[1]

A reference to the Dutch colony at Colchester is found in 1600, when 'Peter Wayner Ramus, schoolmaster among the Flemings (*inter teutonicos*)

[1] There are many other entries about Leech in the act books (cf. Hale, *Precedents*, 191, etc.); he deserves a full study, using other sources, e.g. *Acts of Privy Council*, xix, 87–8. Is he identical with John Leech, curate of Northill, Bedfordshire, who 'satisfied the bishop with his study'? (A. T. Hart, *The Curate's Lot*, 52); he was married there in 1566 (Emmison (ed.), *Beds. Par. Reg.*, xiii (1936), 41).

at St. Peter, Colchester', was ordered 'to show by what authority he teaches'. He stated that he was 'a bachelor of arts and proceeded in the University of Cambridge'. He was then granted licence 'to teach boys in any language, Flemish, French, Roman or Greek'.

Charges of unlicensed (though very informal) teaching were made against a fishmonger named Hateck of Coggeshall, whose reply was that 'he did but write some few lines for examples to write for a friend's children' (1591), and against John Gosse of Ramsey, who explained that, 'at the request of certain neighbours, he did teach two or three of their children to read bonds and other instruments, not purposing hereafter to teach any way contrary to law' (1582). The offence of Matthew Barker of Messing was worded thus: 'He only learneth children abcye (ABC, the alphabet) and the primer and testament, being but a shoemaker and a cobbler doth take upon himself to instruct children to write and read, neither can (he) write true orthography, neither can he spell nor divide the syllables of words as a teacher ought' (1600). He had the satisfaction of hearing the judge 'find the presentment untrue', and the court licensed the man 'to the same effect' (*ad effectum predictum*). The entry continues, 'He said that Mary Diglett doth teach without a licence', whereon she was told 'hereafter to desist the teaching to write'. Had the woman been jealous of Barker and so falsely accused a rival? Having regard to many curates' imperative need to eke out their very low stipends with teaching and other work, it is to the credit of the Sutton wardens that they presented Margaret Shipden for 'teaching of a school, whereas our curate who is allowed by my Lord Bishop is willing and desirous to do the same for the more increasing of his living'.

Some light is also thrown on 'goodwives' and other women who taught without licence. Of the dozen presentments, six merely give their names and abodes, and two 'doth not teach any to read, but to sew'. The others are worth quoting. Juliana Brown of Coggeshall 'keepeth a school and taketh away the living of George Haven' (1587), who, five years later, when he was termed a surgeon, was found guilty of murdering a fellow townsman.[1] Sarah Unwin of Hadstock (1587) was 'a disorderly schoolmistress who teacheth her scholars disorderly and maketh them pronounce their words untruly, and those that told their catechism before she had them have now forgotten it'. The wife of Richard Dawes of Barking, whose husband explained that 'she teacheth some women and some men to read', was warned 'not to teach any man child above the age of 10 years until she be lawfully licensed' (1590). Finally, William Clarke's wife of South Weald, who 'teacheth a few children to read English', was given the alternatives of producing a licence or desisting (1591).

When John Turner, a Walthamstow pedagogue, was asked in 1565 'whether he would depart from the school, (so) that the patron might

[1] *E.L.: Disorder*, 152.

present another thereunto who should be a profound, learned man', he stoutly asserted, 'The school was given not to be united to any other living but only for a school master, and in that he would withstand all men and try law with them'.

These heterogeneous entries afford a somewhat prosaic account of the Church's dealings with schoolteachers. Of bare facts there is much more in the act books: scores of grants of licences are recorded, and almost as many charges against unlicensed schoolmasters.

In contrast to the great majority of these humble teachers, of whom so little can otherwise be ascertained (and very few of them left wills), a good deal is now known about Thomas Chitham of Boreham, presented in 1596 for teaching without licence. The full story of his part in the extraordinary Chelmsford ballad libel case, tried at the Assizes in 1602, was told in the previous volume.[1] The archidiaconal records show that he was again presented, doubtless as a result of his notoriety, in 1603, 'for that he is not licensed and for not resorting to his parish church and not receiving Communion at Easter last'. His defence was that 'he teacheth not *nisi licentiatus*, but he hath taught heretofore by B. Elmer's licence' (John Aylmer, Bishop of London).

There are no references in the court books to the former chantry schools or to grammar schools, and this is therefore not the place to refer to the effect of the Reformation and the suppression of chantry schools, except to remind readers of Dr. Joan Simon's pioneer reappraisal of A. F. Leach's standard work on the subject,[2] supported by Professors A. G. Dickens and W. K. Jordan and Dr. G. R. Elton.[3] The continuation of chantry schools as grammar schools in Essex, 'one suspects, reflects the educational zeal of the Mildmays, Sir William Petre, and Lord Rich, all of whom were fanatically loyal to the county'.[4]

The act books, however, furnish a good deal of information, not recorded elsewhere, about unlicensed teachers employed privately by persons of substance. The great majority were engaged by well-known Catholics. Recusancy being a subject only touched upon by the present writer, their children's tutors must also be left over for detailed study by specialist historians of Essex Catholics or schoolteachers. The presentment in 1576 of a man named Godsafe for not coming to church and for teaching boys without licence in the house of Mr. Pascall of Great Baddow is readily recognized as involving a recusant family and is typical of a score or so of its kind. A sprinkling of Anglican employers is also found, their tutors being directed to produce evidence of being licensed; but research is needed in some instances to determine whether the defendants were teaching in Catholic or Anglican households. Two indictments were

[1] *E.L.: Disorder*, 71–9. [2] A. F. Leach, *English Schools at the Reformation* (1896).
[3] Joan Simon, 'A. F. Leach: A Reply' (*Brit. Jnl. of Educl. Studies*, xii, no. 1, 1963).
[4] W. K. Jordan, *Edward VI: The Threshold of Power* (1970), 231, n. 1; for Chelmsford Grammar School, see my *Tudor Secretary: Sir William Petre at Court and Home* (2nd edn., 1970), 94–5.

preferred at Quarter Sessions, not against the teachers but against their Catholic employers. In 1589 Edward Arteslowe esquire (of Downham, who was the Earl of Oxford's physician) was thus charged with keeping an unnamed and unlicensed schoolmaster; and at the following Sessions the grand jury reported Mary wife of John Wright of Brook Street in South Weald (who lived at the Moat House) as an obstinate recusant and for keeping 'one Rodes a schoolmaster that teacheth her children privately, the which children do not come to church neither'. Education in Tudor and Stuart Essex would be a suitable subject for a postgraduate thesis and a valuable contribution to Essex history; it would necessitate study of a large number of sources, without which our present knowledge is regrettably imperfect.

The Church prohibited physicians and surgeons from practice unless they obtained a licence from the Bishop, the reasons for which are obvious. It seems doubtful whether the Bishop of London had deputed to the Archdeacons of Essex and Colchester any authority to grant licences to surgeons and physicians. In 1598 John Actor of Great Horkesley, surgeon, was cited, and he produced his licence to practise, which had been granted by the Commissary in the previous year. But in 1594 the act book records the grant of a licence, the fee being 4s., to Jeremiah Cochman of Coggeshall, surgeon.

Apart from these meagre entries, the little information afforded in the court books relates to unlicensed 'surgeons'. In 1580 George Wright, admitting that he was unlicensed, said that he 'doth exercise surgery for his neighbours'. In 1587 a man named Ellis had to answer a double presentment for practising without licence and for doubt whether he and his 'wife' were actually married; and Thomas Colte of Heydon had to answer for keeping them suspiciously in his house. It looks as though the Colchester archdeaconry officers had specially instructed the churchwardens in 1593 to report unlicensed persons, as no less than five were presented: Alexander Braddock of All Saints, William Hilles of St. Mary Magdalen, and a cobbler named Garrett, all in Colchester; also Alice, wife of William Giles of Wivenhoe, and Judith Chatterton of Coggeshall. In 1598 Owtrey Fayrfeild of Lexden was inhibited from practising 'unless he first produces letters granting him authority, and Margaret Wright, late of Little Bromley, now of Ramsey, was accused by the wardens of the former parish of 'taking upon her to cure sundry diseases and also for living apart from her husband, living at Ramsey', as well as for absence from church and communion. In 1602, David Stagram of Barking, who denied the charge of being unlicensed, was suppressed.

In the previous volume it was noticed that John Fyssher of Brentwood, surgeon, was acquitted on a murder charge in 1583.[1] Very few coroners'

[1] *E.L.: Disorder*, 152–3.

inquisitions are preserved in the Sessions rolls, but one of them, in 1587, describes in some detail the adverse verdict of the jury against the same Fyssher, again described as a common surgeon. He had 'taken upon himself to cure a broken leg', resulting from the falling of a beer barrel from a cart, and had 'warranted the right placing of the bones and the perfect health of the same leg'. Having taken his fee, he grossly neglected the patient, who died. A history of medicine in the sixteenth and seventeenth centuries, based on the many scattered references in diverse material relating to the county, would offer useful scope for academic research. It would be necessary to distinguish, where possible, between qualified physicians and surgeons and the humble barber-surgeons, a few of whom had unsavoury reputations as noticed in our account of Prostitution.

The courts also controlled the licensing of midwives, which included a sort of religio-medical oath, to enable them to baptize in case of emergency, each providing herself with witnesses where possible; and ministers were enjoined to instruct them in the form of words and the proper manner. Incidentally, bastardy examinations reveal how some midwives tried to exact from unwilling mothers during their birth-pangs the name of the putative father.

Midwives figure very seldom in the act books. In 1565 the wife of a man named Gee of West Ham was presented 'for taking upon her to be a midwife unlicensed, to maintain Alice Amans' whoredom by that act'. The scribe's laconic note reads, 'Is excommunicated'. Widow Bachelor of Romford, accused in 1584 of 'using the office of a midwife and not licensed', attended court but refused to take the oath of office.

One would have expected to find a number of reports of occasional, though illegal, midwifery aid being given by village 'goodies' or relatives, but the sole instance occurs in 1591, when Judith wife of John Raven of Kelvedon was brought by the wardens because she was 'not licensed nor authorized neither examined for a midwife by the Ordinary whether she be fit or not'. The parish may have had other things against her, but her reply was that 'for pity sake she hath done and executed the office of a midwife by reason of absence of an expert midwife': not a wholly convincing answer, for Kelevedon was a fair-sized village. At any rate, the judge 'warned her hereafter to deal faithfully in the function of a midwife'.

The incidence of immorality changes little from age to age: only the people's attitude. The Anglican Church strove to uphold its tenets and teachings against the mounting opposition or indifference of those cited before the 'Bawdy Court'. A cynical couplet, penned by the registrar on the fly-leaf of the Commissary's act book for 1561–2, doubtless expresses his own view of so much of the court buisness:

This I know and well can prove
That sorrowe is the end of love.

Index of Subjects

Index of Persons and Places

Counties. Places, other than those in Essex, are *grouped* under their respective counties. *Italicized parishes* are those for which there are *no* surviving Elizabethan Church Court records, or, for the Commissary of the Bishop of London's court, only the single act book for 1561–2. (See page ix and key to *map* inside back cover.)